Time Out

Vancouver

timeout.com/vancouver

Published by Time Out Guides Ltd, a wholly owned subsidiary of Time Out Group Ltd.
Time Out and the Time Out logo are trademarks of Time Out Group Ltd.

© Time Out Group Ltd 2008
Previous edition 2006.

10 9 8 7 6 5 4 3 2 1

This edition first published in Great Britain in 2008 by Ebury Publishing
A Random House Group Company
20 Vauxhall Bridge Road, London SW1V 2SA

Random House Australia Pty Limited 20 Alfred Street, Milsons Point, Sydney, New South Wales 2061, Australia
Random House New Zealand Limited 18 Poland Road, Glenfield, Auckland 10, New Zealand
Random House South Africa (Pty) Limited Isle of Houghton, Corner Boundary
Road & Carse O'Gowrie, Houghton 2198, South Africa

Random House UK Limited Reg. No. 954009

For further distribution details, see www.timeout.com

ISBN: 978-1-84670-055-2

A CIP catalogue record for this book is available from the British Library

Printed and bound by Firmengruppe APPL, aprinta druck, Wemding, Germany

The Random House Group Limited supports The Forest Stewardship Council (FSC), the leading international forest
certification organisation. All our titles that are printed on Greenpeace approved FSC certified paper carry the FSC
logo. Our paper procurement policy can be found at http://www.rbooks.co.uk/environment

Time Out Guides Limited
Universal House
251 Tottenham Court Road
London W1T 7AB
Tel + 44 (0)20 7813 3000
Fax + 44 (0)20 7813 6001
Email guides@timeout.com
www.timeout.com

Editorial
Editors Tom Charity, Fiona Morrow
Deputy Editors Ismay Atkins, John Shandy Watson, Yolanda Zappaterra
Listings Editor Michelle Rainer
Proofreader Cathy Limb
Indexer Ismay Atkins

Managing Director Peter Fiennes
Financial Director Gareth Garner
Editorial Director Ruth Jarvis
Deputy Series Editor Dominic Earle
Editorial Manager Holly Pick
Assistant Management Accountant Ija Krasnikova

Design
Art Director Scott Moore
Art Editor Pinelope Kourmouzoglou
Senior Designer Henry Elphick
Graphic Designer Gemma Doyle, Kei Ishimaru
Digital Imaging Simon Foster
Advertising Designer Jodi Sher

Picture Desk
Picture Editor Jael Marschner
Deputy Picture Editor Katie Morris
Picture Researcher Helen McFarland
Picture Desk Assistant Troy Bailey

Advertising
Commercial Director Mark Phillips
International Advertising Manager Kasimir Berger
International Sales Executive Charlie Sokol
Advertising Sales (Vancouver) West Coast Media
Advertising Assistant Kate Staddon

Marketing
Group Marketing Director Catherine Demajo
Marketing Manager Yvonne Poon
Sales & Marketing Director North America Lisa Levinson

Production
Group Production Director Mark Lamond
Production Manager Brendan McKeown
Production Controller Caroline Bradford
Production Coordinator Julie Pallot

Time Out Group
Chairman Tony Elliott
Financial Director Richard Waterlow
Group General Manager/Director Nichola Coulthard
Time Out Magazine Ltd MD Richard Waterlow
Time Out Communications Ltd MD David Pepper
Time Out International MD Cathy Runciman
Group Art Director John Oakey
Group IT Director Simon Chappell

Contributors

Introduction Tom Charity. **History** Michael Kluckner (*Going green* Charles Campbell; *The shipping news* Terence Tate). **Vancouver Today** Charles Campbell (*Games on!* Tom Charity). **Architecture** Lance Berelowitz. **West Coast Art** Craig Burnett (*Reid all about it* Fiona Morrow; *Tales of the city* Nancy Lanthier). **Where to Stay** Nancy Lanthier (*Howard's stay* Eve Gabereau). **Sightseeing Introduction** Tom Charity. **Downtown** Matthew Mallon (*Tickets to ride* Fiona Morrow; *Walk: Stepping out in Gastown* John Atkin; *Rain city* Nancy Lanthier). **Stanley Park** Charles Campbell. **The West Side** Tom Charity, Justin Smallbridge (*Grin and bare it* Camilla Pickard; *Flower power* Alison Appelbe). **East Vancouver** Nancy Lanthier, Fiona Morrow. **North Shore** Alison Appelbe (*High jinx* Tom Charity, Vanessa Richmond). **Restaurants & Cafés** Alexandra Gill, Fiona Morrow; additional reviews Lee Man (*The grapevine* Barbara Philip; *Between meals, Serving up sustainability* Fiona Morrow). **Bars** Nancy Lanthier, David Gayton (*Small beer* David Gayton). **Shops & Services** Lucy Hyslop, Rebecca Tay (*Where to shop, Gas injection* Rebecca Tay; *Granville Island* Fiona Morrow). **Festivals & Events** Fiona Morrow. **Children** Fiona Morrow. **Film** Tom Charity. **Galleries** Craig Burnett, Michael Harris (*Cat flight* Michael Harris). **Gay & Lesbian** Michael Harris, Meita Winkler. **Music & Nightlife** Nancy Lanthier; *Rock* Curtis Woloschuk (*Sweet harmony* Camilla Pickard). **Performing Arts** Tim Carlson; *Comedy, Dance* Michael Harris. **Sport & Fitness** Lucy Hyslop (*Free wheeling* Charles Campbell). **Getting Started** Tom Charity. **Excursions** Bowen Island Nancy Lanthier; *Steveston* Justin Oppelaar; *Richmond* Lee Man; *Fraser Valley* Chris McBeath (*China town* Lee Man). **Victoria & Vancouver Island** Fiona Morrow; *Southern Gulf Islands* Chris McBeath (*Walk: Echoes of the past* John Adams; *Spout and about* Tom Charity; *Spa partners* Chris McBeath). **The Okanagan** Alison Appelbe. **Whistler** Tom Charity, Julia McKinnell, Fiona Morrow (*On the tracks* Fiona Morrow; *Bro-Speak* Julia McKinnell). **Directory** Rebecca Tay.

Maps john@jsgraphics.co.uk, except the Downtown Transport map on page 256 courtesy of TransLink.

Photography by Alys Tomlinson, except pages 10, 17 2006 Alinari/ Topfoto; page 20 Getty Images; page 30 The Bridgeman Art Library; page 32 Trevor Mills, Vancouver Art Gallery; page 44 Bettmann/ Corbis; page 140 Leonard Imagery; page 170, 171 Ivan Hunter; page 209 Brian Sprout; page 216 Toshi Kawano; page 220 Ziptrek Ecotours Inc.

The following images were provided by the featured establishment/ artist: pages 179, 203, 205, 210.

The Editor would like to thank the Vancouver Art Gallery, Stephanie Laverdure and all contributors to the previous edition of *Time Out Vancouver*, whose work forms the basis for parts of this book.

Contents

Introduction

Coming in to land at Vancouver International Airport, it's already obvious why so many people have been seduced by Canada's third-largest city, although the reasons themselves have little to do with urban development, and everything to do with its immediate proximity to the sparkling Pacific Ocean, the beautiful Gulf Islands just a hop and a skip to the west, and the snow-capped Coast Mountains immediately to the north.

You might also glimpse the vast expanse of Stanley Park, the largest city park in North America, a short stroll from the West End; miles of easily accessible beaches; and a city skyline that's straining to challenge the big boys in stature and shiny self-belief. Norman Foster, Arthur Erickson and James Cheng all have buildings going up in time for 2010.

That's also when the Winter Olympics come to town, an occasion that has galvanised the booming British Columbia economy. For now, at least, there's a surplus of jobs, the governing provincial Liberal Party is rolling in cash, and local real-estate prices continue to go up and up and up.

Most of the Olympic sporting facilities are due to be open and running by early 2009 (some already are). There's little worry of an Athens-style scramble to the finish line here. The Games have also been the impetus for substantial improvements on the scenic Sea-to-Sky Highway, which connects Vancouver with its co-host Whistler, 100 kilometres (60 miles) to the north. The Canada Line, a new metro line that will connect the southern suburb of Richmond with the airport and the downtown core should be open by late 2009.

All this speaks of a city brimming with optimism and pride. Vancouver is regularly named as one of the world's most liveable cities, and most Vancouverites believe this to be true. It's a young, healthy, cosmopolitan place with a positive attitude towards diversity (there is a large and growing Asian community here) and a lot of lip service paid towards the environment (Vancouver was the birthplace of Greenpeace, and BC Premier Gordon Campbell has pledged carbon emission targets that outstrip California's).

Of course, this idyllic picture is not the whole truth by any means. For decades politicians have failed to address the problems of the Downtown Eastside, a derelict neighbourhood that is infamous for having the highest HIV infection rate in the western world. The widening social inequality endemic throughout North America is glaringly obvious here. Whether the Olympics can inspire real solutions for the homeless only time will tell, but a spate of gangland shootings in 2007 and 2008 reveals that drugs rings are deeply entrenched in the Lower Mainland, and conviction rates have been dismally low.

The airport itself is a symbol for Vancouver at its best and very worst. Its expansive, airy international lounges showcase displays of West Coast art, bubbling waterfall features, and even an aquarium wall. The ambience is serene and friendly. Yet this was also the site where, on 14 October 2007, 40-year-old Polish immigrant Robert Dziekanski died after being Tasered by Royal Canadian Mounted Police officers. He had been waiting ten hours in the customs area, apparently ignored by customs and security officers alike.

The one side of this split picture is no more true than the other. Vancouver is a beautiful 21st-century city with a lot going for it, as long as it stops buying into its own image and ignoring the problems on its own doorstep.

ABOUT TIME OUT CITY GUIDES

This is the second edition of *Time Out Vancouver*, one of an expanding series of more than 50 guides produced by the people behind the successful listings magazines in London, New York, Chicago, Sydney and many more cities around the world. Our guides are all written and updated by resident experts who have striven to provide you with all the most up-to-date information you'll need to explore Vancouver, whether you're a local or a first-time visitor.

THE LOWDOWN ON THE LISTINGS

Above all, we've tried to make this book as useful as possible. Addresses, telephone numbers, websites, transport information, opening times, admission prices and credit card details have all been included in the listings, as have details of other selected services and facilities. However, owners and managers can change their arrangements at any time. Before you go out of your way, we strongly advise you to call and check opening times and other particulars. While every effort has been made to

ensure the accuracy of information contained in this guide, the publishers cannot accept responsibility for any errors it may contain.

PRICES AND PAYMENT

Our listings detail which of these major credit cards – American Express (AmEx), Diners Club (DC), Discover (Disc), MasterCard (MC) and Visa (V) – are accepted by individual venues. Many businesses will also accept other cards.

The prices we've supplied should be treated as guidelines, not gospel. Fluctuating exchange rates and inflation can cause prices, particularly in shops and restaurants, to change rapidly. If prices vary wildly from those we've quoted, ask whether there's a good reason, then please email to let us know. We aim to give the best and most up-to-date advice, and we always want to know if you've been badly treated or overcharged.

THE LIE OF THE LAND

Surrounded by sea and bordered by mountains, Vancouver has not sprawled as much as other North American cities. Couple this with another unusual feature for the continent, an efficient public transport system, and you have a city that is easy to get around on foot, bicycle, boat or bus. For further orientation information, *see p56*.

To make both book and city easier to navigate, we've divided Vancouver into areas and assigned each one its own section in the Sightseeing part of the book. For consistency, these area designations have also been used in addresses throughout the guide.

For all addresses in the book, we've included a cross-street, details of the nearest public transport option(s) and a reference to the series of fully indexed colour maps at the back of this guide, which start on page 246. The locations of hotels (**❶**), restaurants (**❶**) and bars (**❶**) have all been pinpointed on these maps; the section also includes a transport map and a street index.

TELEPHONE NUMBERS

The area code for Vancouver and much of the Lower Mainland (including Whistler) is 604. You must dial this code no matter where you are calling from, including within the city itself. We've identified premium-rate and mobile numbers, which will incur extra calling costs.

The country code for Canada is 1. To dial numbers as given in this book from abroad, use your country's exit code (00 in the UK) or the + symbol (on many mobile phones), followed by the country code, followed by the number as listed. Callers from the US dial the number as they would for any long-distance call within the US. For more on phones, *see p236*.

ESSENTIAL INFORMATION

For all the practical information you might need for visiting the city, including customs and immigration information, disabled access, emergency telephone numbers, the lowdown on the local transport network and a list of useful websites, turn to the Directory at the back of this guide. It starts on page 226.

LET US KNOW WHAT YOU THINK

We hope you enjoy *Time Out Vancouver*, and we'd like to know what you think of it. We welcome tips for places that you consider we should include in future editions, and take notice of your criticism of our choices. You can email us at guides@timeout.com.

There is an online version of this guide, along with guides to more than 50 other international cities, at **www.timeout.com**.

Kitsilano Beach.

In Context

Woodcutters c.1900.

History

The city built on trees continues to grow and grow.

Location, location, location: what's true for real estate is doubly so for cities. From a 21st-century perspective, Vancouver is a great city because of its beautiful setting and easy access to pristine wilderness. To 19th-century settlers it was ideal for a different reason: its large, ice-free port with easy access to the ocean and the necessary raw materials to feed its sawmills and canneries. Add in the other requirements: not just a railway, but a railway terminus; enough land for the city to grow into; and a hinterland – the Fraser River delta – for dairying and vegetable-growing. And in Vancouver's case, perhaps an additional *raison d'être*: a international border only a few miles to the south. If there were no border, would there be major cities at both Seattle and Vancouver?

Location had also made the site of Vancouver significant to natives for 6,000 years before the arrival of European explorers and settlers. For the Stó:lo – the 'people of the river' – the important corridor was the Fraser River, along which were fishing grounds and gathering

places they used on their seasonal rounds. There were permanent settlements at Khwaykhway in today's Stanley Park, at Mahli near the mouth of the Fraser River and at Cheechilwhik on the North Vancouver shoreline. As with the other 'Pacific Northwest' nations, the Stó:lo were blessed with a natural bounty, most notably the western red cedar (*Thuja plicata*), which was easily crafted into ocean-going canoes, split into planks for the construction of sophisticated post-and-beam dwellings and carved into totem poles. Their hunters and gatherers also easily brought in a surplus of food for the community, allowing people of artistic talent to enrich the culture to an incredible extent.

European diseases devastated the Native communities before any Europeans arrived. Two-thirds of the Stó:lo died in the first great smallpox epidemic of 1782, which apparently had spread north through intertribal trading networks from Mexico City, where it had spread from the Spanish two years earlier.

Although subsequent epidemics also took their toll, it was the governmental policy of assimilation, including the banning of the potlatch ceremony, the building of individual family homes on reserves rather than the previous communal clan dwelling, and the introduction of residential schools, that almost wiped out native cultures. The recent renaissance of totem-pole carving and jewellery making has helped First Nations all along the coast to recover pride in their culture, while lengthy land claims negotiations continue with the provincial government. Supreme Court decisions confirmed that Aboriginal title was never extinguished in BC and the treaty process is leading First Nations towards a form of self-government in their traditional territories across the province.

The first Europeans to reach western Canada, in the 1790s, were explorers working for the Hudson's Bay Company (HBC) and its competitors. They began to trade with the natives, tapping into their long-established trading networks and using their trails.

By sea, the coastline had been 'discovered' in 1791 by the Spanish navigator José María Narváez. The following year, Royal Navy Captain George Vancouver, confirming and expanding on the information from James Cook's Pacific voyages of the 1780s, charted the future harbour and coincidentally met with another Spanish expedition off Point Grey.

The name Spanish Banks, for a beach near the University of BC, commemorates this meeting, and local and regional place names such as Langara, Valdez and Galiano recall Spanish attempts to expand their empire northward from their California outpost. Vancouver named Burrard Inlet after a British admiral and Point Grey after a fellow officer. A subsequent survey in 1859 noted the strategic potential of the peninsula at the first narrows and reserved it for military purposes. Like the Presidio base at San Francisco's Golden Gate, it later became parkland – Stanley Park, named for the governor general who is mainly remembered today as the namesake of a hockey trophy. A number of native names, in anglicised form, stayed on the landscape or were added to it: Siwash Rock in Stanley Park, for example. The Capilano River recalls a chief of the Squamish band, as does the now-trendy Kitsilano neighbourhood.

SETTING THE STAGE

The Hudson's Bay Company (HBC), which had been trading along the coast since the 1820s and had established Fort Vancouver (that is, Vancouver, Washington) at the mouth of the Columbia River, began to clash with American

migrants moving westward over the Oregon Trail. By the early 1840s, America's 'Manifest Destiny' was its dominant political issue. Militant American expansionists thought the USA should extend north as far as Russian Alaska, while the British believed the HBC had established a claim to Washington through its trading posts and farms. In the event, the 49th parallel, already accepted as the international boundary across the great central plain of

The Stó:lo were the area's first builders.

North America, was extended to the western shore. As the HBC had wisely established Fort Victoria in 1843, Vancouver Island remained British, and became a colony in 1849. On the mainland, Burrard Inlet was the nearest harbour north of the border.

A few years later, gold was discovered in California, triggering the first of the frantic rushes that moved a rabble of humanity westward. Prospectors then moved north, discovering gold and silver in the 1850s along the Fraser River. The British administration in Victoria moved quickly to establish a new colony on the mainland, naming it British Columbia. A city, imaginatively named New Westminster, was established on the Fraser River at the strategic point where it widens into a delta, thus ensuring control of river traffic attempting to get to the gold fields.

The gold rush had little immediate impact on the Vancouver area. However, disillusioned gold seekers soon returned to the coast. By the mid 1860s, there were sawmills operating on Burrard Inlet, one – Stamp's Mill – near the foot of modern Main Street. The loggers, like their compatriots in Oregon and Washington, had discovered the extraordinary stands of Douglas fir (*Pseudotsuga menziesii*), a tree second only to the California redwood in size, and were soon exporting timber from Burrard Inlet.

THE INVENTION OF VANCOUVER

Partly in response to the American Civil War and concerns that the violence might spread north of the border, the eastern British colonies confederated and became Canada. Before long, the government was negotiating to bring the isolated west-coast colony into the Canadian fold. The inducement was a railway that would connect the west coast with the settled east.

Meanwhile, late in the summer of 1867, while far-away Canada was celebrating its nationhood, a barkeeper named John Deighton came ashore just west of Stamp's Mill with, it is said, a barrel of whisky and another of nails, and invited the mill workers to help him build a saloon near a large native maple tree. Deighton was garrulous, bearing the nickname 'Gassy Jack'. Additional stores and saloons soon sprang up along the shore just west of the 'maple tree square'. Sleepy little Gastown, as it was commonly known, officially became Granville in 1870, when it was surveyed into a grid of six square blocks from Maple Tree Square at Carrall west to Cambie, and Water Street south to Hastings.

Little happened for a decade while far-off financiers and politicians haggled over the railway and its proposed route. Eventually, the Canadian Pacific Railway (CPR) decided

on the difficult southern route – mainly to ensure that perfidious Americans would not sneak spur lines into the province to ship away all the goods – with a terminus at Burrard Inlet. Suddenly, Gastown woke up to its new destiny.

CPR general manager William Van Horne visited his future terminal city in 1884, met with local businessmen and land speculators (losing heavily at poker with them) and was delighted with everything he saw. Except the name. According to legend, he reached back into his stock of historical lore and intoned, 'I name thee Vancouver.' After a little arm-twisting, everyone fell into line, and the new city was incorporated in April 1886.

'The city was truly born on the day the first through train from eastern Canada reached Vancouver.'

Land clearing crews – clearcutting as opposed to the selective logging typical of the 1860s and 1870s – pushed south and west during the exceptionally dry May of 1886. On June 13, a slash fire got out of hand and swept across the land, burning everything in its path, sparing only the sawmill and one Water Street hotel whose occupants soaked blankets and beat out the sparks. In retrospect a fine example of urban renewal, the fire forced Vancouverites to adopt safety codes and begin to rebuild their downtown buildings with more permanent materials. Before the ground cooled, buildings were rising again.

The following 23 May, the city was truly born, for on that day the first through train from eastern Canada reached Vancouver. The CPR had been busy, laying out grand streets in its new downtown centred on the corner of Granville Street and Georgia Street, building the Hotel Vancouver and an opera house there, and launching ships that would connect Vancouver with the Far East.

Transport brought first-class tourists – mainly English, travelling the world to see the Empire – and more colonists. Cargos of tinned salmon from canneries on the Fraser River went the other way. Flatcars left the city loaded with 'Vancouver toothpicks' – beams a metre square by 30 metres long (10.7 square feet by 98 feet) – the kind of timber that supported the floors of brick warehouses, including those on the site of the razed saloons and hotels of Gastown. One load of beams left Burrard Inlet in 1884 for Beijing's Imperial Palace.

Vancouver's port quickly became the hub of the western economy. A state-of-the-art electric inter-urban (tram) system connected the agricultural Fraser Valley with the city. By 1900 there were about 25,000 inhabitants, and boosters erected banners on the streets proclaiming (poetically if not accurately in terms of gender) that 'In 1910 Vancouver Then Will Have 100,000 Men!' They just made it.

THE EDWARDIAN BOOM

The first dozen years of the 20th century defined the city's basic urban form. In the downtown, landmark buildings – those that today define 'old Vancouver' – sprang up along the main commercial streets of Hastings and Granville. In the streetcar suburbs, middle-class families pursued the dream of a bungalow with a garden on a quiet street far from the city's factories. The wealthy abandoned their fine homes on so-called Blueblood Alley (today's West Hastings Street), first for new mansions above Sunset Beach in the West End, then for the curving streets of the CPR's Shaughnessy Heights.

Along the streetcar loop of Davie-Denman-Robson in the West End, shops lined the streets and apartments began to appear. New satellite cities in North and West Vancouver started ferry services for their commuters. In the summer, throngs of people went to English Bay in the West End or took the streetcar across False Creek to the new beach at Kitsilano.

Ethnically, the soggy Shangri-la was white and overwhelmingly British. Where it wasn't English it tended to be Scottish rather than Irish. (There's an old saying that England gave Canada its institutions and Scotland gave it its people.) It was church-going and predominantly Protestant but not church-building, at least compared with older Canadian cities such as Victoria and Toronto. Non-Anglo immigrant groups packed into the workers' community named Strathcona, just south of the Hastings sawmill and the port: a Jewish street here, an Italian one there. Natives still lived on reserves in Kitsilano and North Vancouver.

Going green

Located as it is on the verge of a vast pristine wilderness just waiting to be spoiled, Vancouver is a natural locus of environmental activism. Travel north from the city along British Columbia's mainland coast and you won't find another settlement of more than 15,000 people until you reach Alaska. The city's position was undoubtedly one of the keys to the emergence of Greenpeace in Vancouver in 1970 and '71.

'We had the biggest concentration of tree-huggers, radicalised students, garbage-dump stoppers, shit-disturbing unionists, freeway fighters, pot smokers and growers, ageing Trotskyites, condo killers, farmland savers, fish preservationists, animal rights activists, back-to-the-landers, vegetarians, nudists, Buddhists, and anti-spraying, anti-pollution marchers and picketers in the country, per capita, in the world,' wrote the late, great Bob Hunter (1941-2005), Greenpeace member 000 and the central genius in the organisation's early years.

There were also expatriate Americans – Vietnam-era draft dodgers and others looking for a kinder, gentler version of the United States. Dorothy and Irving Stowe brought the Quaker tradition of bearing witness to the anti-war and emerging 'ecology' movements in the early '70s. Their 'Don't Make a Wave Committee' opposed nuclear

testing on Alaska's Amchitka Island. In 1970, Marie Bohlen suggested sailing a protest boat to the island. That same year, after Irving Stowe concluded a meeting with the salutation 'peace', Bill Darnell fatefully replied, 'Make it a green peace.' In the fall of 1971, an old halibut trawler renamed the *Greenpeace* was sailing through the Gulf of Alaska's gales and into history.

A variety of ad hoc Greenpeace offices were soon established around the world on the strength of the media-savvy Vancouver activists. Anti-whaling and anti-sealing campaigns soon followed, and in 1979 Greenpeace International was formed, based in Amsterdam and headed by Vancouverite David McTaggart, who had been beaten by the French military while protesting against French nuclear testing in the South Pacific.

Today, Greenpeace is a £100-million (roughly $200-million) enterprise. Original member Paul Watson decries its ubiquitous door-to-door fundraisers as the Fuller Brush salesmen of the environmental movement. Yet, while some see Greenpeace as a neutered bureaucracy, the organisation can negotiate for environmental interests with the mere threat of a protest, and there is little question that its often controversial methods have been vindicated.

There were Asians, too: Chinese, Japanese and Indians. As the Union Pacific Railroad in the US had done in the 1860s, the CPR brought Chinese workers to BC to lay its tracks. When construction ended in 1885 they drifted to the coast, but few had enough money to return home. Vancouver's Chinatown adjoined the city's red-light district on low-lying, swampy land between the Hastings Street commercial district and False Creek. It was overwhelmingly male, as a head tax made it all but impossible to bring in wives or concubines. Formed into tongs (family societies), the Chinese built some substantial brick buildings along Pender Street, and tenements on the side streets and in narrow alleyways. Legally manufactured opium and illegal gambling occupied many of them (and the police), and fascinated the public.

'Japanese Canadians were stripped of their property and forced into internment camps in the BC interior.'

Unlike the Chinese, who had come to 'Gold Mountain' to make a fortune and then return home, the Japanese came as settlers and, because of Britain's military alliance with Japan, were not subject to head taxes. Highly organised and disciplined, and proud of their country's defeat of Russia in 1905, they attracted the enmity of the mainstream due to their success in fishing and market gardening, and began early in the 20th century to insist on the right to vote. Their community occupied the blocks of Powell Street east of Main.

In 1907, a hiccup in the economic boom caused disaffected whites to rampage through Chinatown, breaking windows, destroying businesses, and beating anyone who couldn't get out of the way. But when the mob tried to do the same to the Japanese, they were met with armed resistance and were forced to retreat.

The third Asian group were Indians, mainly Sikhs, although referred to as 'Hindoos' in those days, whose presence in Vancouver again reflected Britain's far-flung empire and alliances. Typically in the early years they worked in the sawmills along False Creek and lived in small houses nearby. For most Vancouverites, the Sikhs were out-of-sight, out-of-mind, but they were nevertheless disenfranchised in 1907. Things hadn't improved seven years later when the *Komagata Maru*, a chartered Japanese ship filled with Indian passengers, arrived in Vancouver harbour but, after a lengthy and ugly stand-off, it was refused landing.

WAR, DEPRESSION, WAR AGAIN

Vancouver lost a generation of its youth in World War I, while not benefiting as eastern cities did from munitions manufacturing and shipbuilding. Then, the roaring twenties merely squeaked along for several years, picking up as the city began to ship grain through the Panama Canal. The must-see landmark from that era is the art deco Marine Building at Burrard and Hastings.

But no sooner had prosperity returned than the Great Depression began. Drought on the prairies and industrial collapse in the east put thousands of men on the road, and the majority of them hopped freights west to the Terminal City. A makeshift relief system helped for a time, but once the heavy-handed federal government forced the unemployed into remote work camps, their militancy increased. A near-riot at Victory Square in 1935 began the On-to-Ottawa trek to demand work and wages. Three years later, the unemployed occupied the art gallery, the main post office (now Sinclair Centre) and the Hotel Georgia until police forced them out on 'Bloody Sunday'.

Depression-era bargains in Vancouver coincided with the rise of fascism in Europe, prompting the Guinness company to invest far from the potential fray. It bought the Marine Building in 1932, then several thousand acres of forest on West Vancouver's Hollyburn Mountain for an exclusive development called the British Properties. To connect their land with the city, the company completed the Lions Gate Bridge in 1938 with a roadway through Stanley Park. But its vision of a car-oriented future would have to wait.

In 1939, when World War II began, Vancouver was once again far from the action. But two and a half years later, after the Japanese attack on Pearl Harbor, the city mobilised. As in the USA, Japanese Canadians were stripped of their property and forced into internment camps in the BC interior, only returning to the coast after restrictions were lifted in 1949. A handful of wartime buildings, including a former seaplane hangar, survive today on the army base at Jericho. Two of these buildings have new roles as a youth hostel (*see p53*) and a theatre. The wartime shipbuilding operations on the North Shore and False Creek have disappeared.

MODERN TIMES

By the mid 1950s, with a rapidly growing population again, Vancouver was finally able to dream of itself as a modern city, with Los Angeles as a role model. In rapid succession, the ageing streetcar and inter-urban systems were dismantled, and the government began to plan for more cars. A new highway bridge

Electric trams were a visible sign of early Vancouver's booming economy. *See p14.*

crossed the harbour at the Second Narrows, a tunnel under the Fraser River opened up suburban lands to the south, and the public was captivated by the idea of a family home on a cul-de-sac in the Fraser Valley. The city's old residential areas were rezoned for apartments, and blocks of houses near downtown were demolished and paved over for parking. Shopping malls opened in West Vancouver, Burnaby and Richmond. Radical post-and-beam houses by young, cutting-edge architects like Ron Thom and Arthur Erickson began to dot the rugged slopes of West Vancouver, harbingers of a new West Coast lifestyle.

Hastings Street suffered the most. It lost thousands of daily visitors when the inter-urban line closed and the North Shore ferries were cancelled. The old warehouses on Gastown's narrow streets became obsolete as businesses migrated to the suburbs with their 18-wheelers. Plans were drafted for a waterfront freeway system, coming into downtown from the east and razing historic Gastown, Chinatown and Strathcona, all home to poor people with little political voice. Urban renewal – the demolition of old housing and its replacement by towers set in green space – completed the package.

But then Vancouver got lucky again. Its position way out on the edge of the plate, both geographically and politically far from the Ottawa power centre, made it slow to get the freeway and the urban renewal money that had already disfigured Toronto and Montreal. Meanwhile, it could observe what had been happening in the USA, especially in nearby Seattle. Accordingly, by the end of the 1960s when the government machinery was finally in place to transform downtown Vancouver, the times they had a-changed.

Like San Francisco's Haight-Ashbury, Kitsilano was a declining neighbourhood awaiting redevelopment – the perfect venue for communal living in cheap old houses. Fourth Avenue blossomed in 1967 and '68 with head shops and coffee houses. At the same time, young entrepreneurs were fixing up Gastown and opening art galleries and boutiques. The arch-conservative civic government, with its hippie-baiting mayor Tom Campbell, was a perfect target for the poets, folkies and American Vietnam war protestors who read and wrote for Dan McLeod's *The Georgia Straight* newspaper. Militant cyclists found common cause with antipoverty activists in the fight against urban renewal and the freeway. The Amchitka nuclear test galvanised Vancouver environmentalists into founding Greenpeace (*see p15* **Going green**).

The watershed came in 1972. Sustained protests persuaded the federal government to withdraw its support from the freeway plan. That summer, the 20-year-old conservative provincial government was defeated and replaced by a democratic socialist one. And in the autumn voters turfed out the civic governing party, replacing it with a group of liberals and academics with new ideas.

Modern Vancouver really began that year. The south side of the old False Creek industrial area was replaced with co-op and middle-income housing. The federal government turned its Granville Island property over to a trust that guided its transformation into an area of markets and galleries. In 1976, the city hosted the United Nations Habitat conference, concurrently holding a people's forum at Jericho Beach in the old seaplane hangars. And the downtown and harbour areas that had been spared the freeway juggernaut began to attract pedestrians, keeping the streets alive 24 hours a day. 'Vancouverism' – creating high-density neighbourhoods for people who live close to their work and play – has been a tremendous success. A heritage-preservation movement sprang up in the 1980s, helping the surviving historic neighbourhoods, ranging from rich Shaughnessy to poor Strathcona, to retain their character. Meanwhile, in Gastown, rocker Bryan Adams restored the old Oppenheimer Brothers warehouse as a recording studio.

'Expo '86 was the catalyst for splashy projects that still serve the city today.'

The world's fair, Expo '86, which reused the CPR's old rail yards on False Creek, completed the transition while celebrating the city's centennial. The 172-day Expo event

The shipping news

It isn't possible to explore downtown Vancouver without noticing a veritable flotilla of boats moored in the many inlets and marinas of the city: recreational sailing boats, commercial cruisers, supertankers laden with cargo, and so on. The city's maritime history has played – and continues to play – a pivotal role in its evolution.

The Port of Vancouver is the largest on the western seaboard of North America. Its deep-water, ice-free environment enables it to generate an economic output of $8.9 billion a year, including $1.5 billion in wages for its 62,000 employees. Trading with over 90 countries, particularly the emerging markets of the Pacific Rim, the port processes 70 million tonnes of cargo annually. It is also a key starting point for cruises to Alaska (*see p227*). Approximately one million passengers a year use the Port's cruise terminals and each sailing, of which there are 300 annually, generates a revenue of $1.5 million.

With its modern navigational aids, gamma ray scanning and a dedicated team of environmentalists, the Port of Vancouver is now one of the safest and cleanest in the world. These features were, however, sadly lacking back in March 1945, when the freighter *Greenhill Park* went up in flames and became the worst disaster in the history of the port. The blast killed eight dockers, injured 19 other workers and shattered hundreds of windows in downtown. The cause of the blast: a match, a barrel of contraband liquor and a cargo of sodium chlorate.

The modern port is a far cry from the late 1700s, when the waters off Vancouver were populated by nothing more demonstrative than the canoes and kayaks of the Salish Indians. Despite Captain James Cook landing at Nootka Sound in 1778, the Salish enjoyed another 14 years of peace and quiet before Captain George Vancouver entered Burrard Inlet in 1792, setting in motion successive waves of European exploration that culminated with the westward expansion of Canadian nationhood. Although the city was named after him, Captain Vancouver was more interested in locating the western end of the Northwest Passage than he was in lending his name to what would become one of the great cities of the world.

During World War II, Vancouver's shipyards built minesweepers, corvettes and cargo ships for service in the Atlantic Ocean. Around half of Canada's naval contribution to the Allied war effort came from Vancouver. A significant contribution was also made by the Royal Canadian Mounted Police vessel *St Roch*, built in North Vancouver in 1929, and currently residing in the A-frame annexe of the **Maritime Museum** in Vanier Park (*see p75*), though there is talk of returning it to North Vancouver in the next two years. Originally designed as a patrol vessel, its legendary World War II voyages across the put Vancouver on the map, attracting more than 22 million people (the population of Canada in 1986 was just over 26 million). With transportation as its theme, Expo was the catalyst for several splashy projects that still serve the city today, like SkyTrain, BC Place Stadium and the Plaza of Nations, which now hosts conventions and concerts on one side, and houses a casino and a radio station on the other. Following the addition of 2000's Millennium line and the Canada Line (set to be in operation by 2009), SkyTrain continues to expand, with the original Expo route serving as one of the last reminders of a name that was once on everything from drink cans to the tailfins of aircraft. The OMNIMAX and IMAX theatres are still there, but the buildings in which they are housed have undergone changes. Canada Place, having built additional cruise ship space, continues to act as the anchor of the upmarket Coal Harbour development

overlooking Stanley Park. Redeveloped into condos along with the adjoining Yaletown warehouse district, the False Creek area now houses about 40,000 people.

Between 1981 and 2001, the city's population expanded by a third (two million in the Greater Vancouver area, one quarter of them in the city). In the run-up to the handover of Hong Kong back to mainland China in 1997, Canada agreed to honour immigration applications from anyone holding a British or Commonwealth passport. The Canadian Consulate estimates about 30,000 Hong Kong citizens emigrated to Canada every year between 1991 and 1996, many choosing Vancouver (or neighbouring Richmond) because of the city's firmly rooted Chinese community, its historic trade ties with Hong Kong and the physical similarities between the two ports. In 1981, only 13.9 per cent of the Lower Mainland's population were of

Arctic made it the first ship to sail the Northwest Passage in both directions, an achievement that asserted Canada's sovereignty over its northern borders during the time of war. At a modest 31 metres (104 feet) in length, the *St Roch* really does not look capable of withstanding the rigours of the Arctic, and it embodies the spirit of those intrepid pioneers who tamed the vast expanses of Canada's endless rivers, lakes, bays and coastal waters.

All the world came to see Vancouver during **Expo 86**. *See p18.*

non-European origin. By 2001 that figure had soared to 37 per cent. Statistics Canada estimates that by 2017, half of the people living in Metro Vancouver will be of Asian descent. The influx of immigrants has fuelled a housing boom that continues to transform the city, and Vancouver now boasts the priciest real estate in the country.

The outer suburbs and towns in the Fraser Valley are, unfortunately, like elsewhere, a mix of congested roads, big box stores, strip malls and large, ugly houses. But Vancouver's downtown is young, hip and vibrant – almost inconceivably so compared with the quiet, laid-back provincialism of the post-war years. But only a Pollyanna could see the new Vancouver in completely rosy terms. As a seaport – aka drugport – Vancouver has always had its mean streets. But they began to get meaner in 1980, when the deinstitutionalisation of mental patients, and the exit of provincial and federal governments from public housing construction, coincided with the gentrification of the downtown and its neighbourhoods. As a result, Vancouver has homeless, drug, gang and property-related crime problems that are as 'world-class' as its cultural achievements. The impoverished Downtown Eastside is reported to have the highest HIV infection rate in the Western World, and life expectancy in this district

is on average a full ten years less than those in any of the surrounding neighbourhoods.

Efforts to address the drug problem were stepped up with Mayor Philip Owen's bold Four Pillars approach in 1999, which laid equal stress on treatment, prevention, harm reduction and enforcement. The most contentious – and pioneering – aspect of it has been Insite, North America's first supervised safe injection site, which opened in the fall of 2003. Here users can obtain needles and condoms, as well as information, counselling, first aid and referrals, all without judgement, in surroundings that look like they could be featured in an IKEA catalogue. While Insite has been judged a significant step in the right direction by independent researchers, it is under threat of closure from Prime Minister Stephen Harper's Conservative government.

The City of Vancouver, along with the BC provincial government are making moves to alleviate the plight of the homeless before the Winter Olympics take over the town in February 2010, but their actions have yet to match up with their rhetoric, and anti-poverty advocates fear the problem will be swept into the background. Meanwhile, very much in the foreground, developers are moving in, and the eastern borders of Gastown – some of the oldest streets in the city – are next in line for a 21st-century makeover.

Vancouver Today

City on the verge.

Vancouver is a lovely young city and one that harbours many myths: it's the newest city in the world; it's the most livable city in North America; it's a shining example of multiculturalism that works; savvy planners and political leaders have made it the model of sustainable development. Or, on the other hand: it's a no-fun city devoid of serious culture; its downtown is crammed with mediocre buildings; its economy is built on real-estate speculation; it's still a setting in search of a city.

Of course, all myths start with a kernel of truth, and every ambitious city obsesses over its image, but Vancouver's worry about whether the world really, really likes it distracts from the complicated and fascinating process of becoming a great city – an opportunity that few places in the world today are granted.

One of the most striking things about Vancouver is the pace of change. There are people living here whose parents were born before the city was founded in 1886. The city is not as young, say, as Las Vegas, but it's younger than photography. And so Vancouver goes about building and rebuilding itself with often inspired, sometimes naïve and occasionally reckless enthusiasm.

In downtown Vancouver this is exemplified by the development that followed Expo 86 on former rail yards and industrial land on the north shore of False Creek – probably the most explicit expression of 'Vancouverism'. These mixed-use podium-tower condominiums made former Vancouver planning director, Larry Beasley, an exportable commodity (he is now advising the crown prince of the United Arab Emirates on the development of Abu Dhabi).

Certainly the False Creek neighbourhood, along with the development of Coal Harbour on former rail yards near Stanley Park, is a fine example of effective urban redevelopment. It has put huge numbers of people within walking distance of their workplaces nad city amenities. It has also almost invisibly incorporated significant social housing and services. Along with the 1960s-era apartment towers in the West End, the redevelopment made downtown Vancouver a pedestrian-friendly urban core that is almost constantly active.

Too bad there are so few distinguished buildings among all the condo towers, though a recent modification to height regulations has encouraged the construction of half a dozen new skyscrapers. These are supposed to break up the city's skyline without blocking views of the North Shore mountains. The tallest, James Cheng's Shangri La, will stand 197 metres (646 feet) when it is completed in 2009. Renowned Vancouver architect Arthur Erickson has two twisted towers under construction; one of them, the Ritz Carlton, will dominate Coal Harbour at 167 metres (548 feet). Sir Norman Foster's Jameson House – a mere shrimp at 37 floors – should be completed by autumn 2009.

TERMINAL CITY

It's too bad Toronto's transit system still puts Vancouver's to shame. Again this has partly to do with the city's youth. Vancouver's modern rapid transit system is still being built out, and is only now recovering from the one big planning mistake the city shares with most North American centres – the destruction in the mid 20th century of a light rail network that once extended to the suburbs. In replacing it, Vancouver went with the capital-intensive commuter light rail known as SkyTrain, beginning with the elevated Expo Line built to Surrey from downtown just prior to the World's Fair. It was pushed by provincial and federal governments, which tend to favour spiffy infrastructure lending itself to a good ribbon-cutting. The cost, however, has left the city without the buses needed for people who are simply crossing town.

The latest transit indulgence is the 2010 Winter Olympics-driven $2 billion Canada Line to the Vancouver International Airport and the burgeoning, Asian-influenced suburb of Richmond. Vancouver will show the world what a big city it is, the thinking goes, even though much evidence suggests the line will be underused and further degrade bus services.

> **'Expo 86 helped overcome Vancouver's geographic isolation and residual provincialism.'**

THE WORLD'S FAIR

Culturally, Vancouver is also still busy building an infrastructure. It is a festival city, and most of the events – like the well-regarded Vancouver International Jazz Festival (*see p138*) – emerged during or after Expo 86. The World's Fair helped overcome the city's geographic isolation and residual provincialism by building connections between international

Games on!

Officially, the Winter Olympic Games begin on 12 February 2010 with a ceremony under the Teflon roof of BC Place Stadium (the first time the opening ceremony for a winter Olympics will be held inside and at sea level). But in the real world, the games begin long before the Games begin... indeed, Whistler (co-host for the event; *see p212*) was being touted as a potential Olympic venue in the 1960s before the resort had so much as a ski lift.

Vancouver won the backing of the Canadian Olympic Association in 1998. The IOC endorsed the city in July 2003, and mayor Sam Sullivan received the Olympic flag with a twirl of his wheelchair at Turin's closing ceremonies in 2006. A year earlier, the federal and provincial governments fired the starter pistol on the now traditional Olympic construction boom, allocating approximately $600 million to building or improving venues, with another $600 million earmarked for upgrading the twisty Sea-to-Sky highway that runs between Vancouver and Whistler, an enormous project that will supposedly halve the two-hour journey.

Then there's $2 billion for the Canada Line extension to Vancouver's SkyTrain, which will connect Richmond, the airport and Downtown. It's not officially an Olympic project, but this locally controversial scheme was rolled into the bid. The new Convention Center adjacent to Canada Place is likewise not an Olympic project, but it will house global broadcast networks during the games, assuming it's finally finished on time – the $800 million building is 40 per cent over budget.

With such enormous sums forthcoming for an event lasting for just 17 days (plus the ten-day Paralympics, which take place 12-21 March of the same year), it's inevitable that many activists and taxpayers have been vocal in condemning the Games. Vancouverites are only too aware that it took 30 years for the citizens of Montreal to pay off debts incurred in the 1976 Summer Games.

So far at least, pledges to make these the first 'environmentally sustainable' Olympics and eradicate the city's homeless problem for many ring hollow. On the other hand, the prospect of international media attention honing in on the impoverished Downtown Eastside is moving it up the political agenda. The flagship Vancouver Athletes' Village being built on reclaimed land in south-east False Creek is being touted as a model for sustainable development, promising a zero environmental footprint and a parcel of affordable social housing (albeit less than originally announced).

The construction boom has fired up the BC economy and helped inflate housing prices. Remarkably, most of the new facilities

artists and creating an appetite for sophisticated entertainment (one that is still being sated). Signature arts institutions in Toronto and Seattle may outshine Vancouver's – they're older, there is more corporate money and there are more people to draw on – but Vancouver has little to be ashamed of. The city is home to the creditable Vancouver Symphony Orchestra and Vancouver Opera (for both, *see p160*), a world-class Museum of Anthropology (*see p77*), and the increasingly important Vancouver Art Gallery (*see p60*), reflecting the rise of Vancouver's visual arts scene.

One of Vancouver's shortcomings is the absence of a great urban square where citizens can gather and celebrate. Partly, going some way back, this has to do with bad planning. When construction of the impossibly grand (and now demolished) Hotel Vancouver was beginning at the city's emerging epicentre at Georgia and Granville Streets, its owner, the Canadian Pacific Railway, offered the block to the north to the city for a public park.

City council, in its infinite wisdom, rejected the proposal on the grounds that CPR wanted the city to pay for a park to enhance its hotel. Now the city's key crossroads is occupied by an appalling mall, a department store and three hideous office towers – mostly cheap knock-offs of signature Toronto buildings. Nearby, the Arthur Erickson-designed courthouse complex south of the Vancouver Art Gallery never effectively fulfilled its ambition to be Vancouver's civic square.

The city also still suffers from the frontier Protestant town's distrust of large public gatherings. Sure, there's the Celebration of Light fireworks competitions (*see p139*), drawing huge crowds to English Bay, and in August the Pacific National Exhibition (*see p140*), which draws 100,000 people a day to Hastings Park on the East Side for amusement rides, sheep shearing and retro music. But the Hastings Park site is an awkwardly arranged collection of hockey rinks, concrete exhibition halls and a struggling racetrack, and few locals

are on schedule and should be in place a year before the Olympics, while the organising committee VANOC has repeatedly surpassed its own sponsorship targets. Speed skating events will take place inside a new rink in Richmond. In Whistler, a new Nordic Centre (to be used for cross-country skiing, ski jumping and biathlon) will complement the Whistler Mountain's Alpine Centre (for downhill skiing, slalom and Super G events). Neighbouring Blackcomb Mountain gets a Sliding Centre for bobsleigh, luge and the ominously named skeleton (in which one athlete occupies a prone, head-first position on a sled). Vancouver's Cypress Mountain has also been boosted so that it can host freestyle skiing and snowboarding events (*see also p178* **Powder play**).

Of course, there's something a little ironic about Vancouver – along with Victoria, the only city in Canada not to suffer from heavy snow – landing the ultimate prize. But the city doesn't lack for winter sports enthusiasts, and you can be sure that GM Place – home of the NHL's Vancouver Canucks – will be packed with 20,000 hockey fans paying up to $775 for the privilege to spectate. If that sounds a little steep, you could always egg on the cross-country skiers for just $25.

The first tickets for the games go on sale to Canadian residents in October 2008.

Non-Canadian residents are being referred to authorised sales agents for their respective National Olympic Committee.
For more information see www.vancouver 2010.com. **Dates** 12-29 Feb 2010.

think of it as a public gathering place at any other time of year. So instead Vancouverites tend to congregate along the gently beautified and wonderfully public waterfront.

VANSTERDAM

Vancouver is just now finding its way toward sensible big-city liquor laws. For Expo 86, the arbiters of public decency decided to allow the tourists to have a drink on Sundays – not that it was something the city might want for its own citizens. Even after Expo, people were not permitted to have a drink in a restaurant without ordering food. Standing with a drink, amplified music and even checkerboards were banned. Bars were required to close by 1am, and many stopped serving at 11pm. The rules have been loosened considerably, resulting in a proliferation of truly local watering holes, but these places still push the bounds of provincial and civic liquor regulation, and there's been some hue and cry about public drunkenness, especially along the central Granville Strip.

Despite a history of overregulation, Vancouver's restaurant scene has exploded in the last two decades. When Expo 86 took place, fine dining usually involved a big hotel, sidewalk cafés were in short supply, Latin American restaurants were of the faux Californian variety and Thai food didn't exist. Now there's a wealth of Thai, Vietnamese, South Indian, Szechuan, African and Latin restaurants, to complement the city's rich tradition of Cantonese and Punjabi restaurants. On a kilometre-long stretch of coffee-crazy Commercial Drive, there are restaurants representing more than two dozen countries.

Some prohibitions may have been relaxed, but others are being toughened. Vancouver considers itself a healthy place, so it follows that it's increasingly difficult to smoke in public. Some bars have separate smoking rooms, but they likely will be gone soon. It's ironic, then, that 'Vansterdam' is so tolerant of marijuana. A handful of pot cafés sell paraphernalia and allow smoking. While it is strictly illegal, you're quite likely to get a strong whiff of 'BC Bud' on the streets, and at least one 'compassion club' store openly sells marijuana for medical use. First-offence sentences even for significant pot-growing operations generally don't involve jail. The result is a huge hidden economy, with 'grow-ops' in residences throughout the city. But when the Da Kine Smoke & Beverage Shop opened in 2004 on Commercial Drive, selling pot to all comers, police dramatically shut it down. More recently, the Conservative federal government, partly possessed by the evangelical US war on drugs mentality, is trying to toughen marijuana sentencing and enforcement.

'While it is strictly illegal, you're quite likely to get a strong whiff of "BC Bud" on the streets.'

Vancouver's claim to liberal social values is more meaningfully found elsewhere. Its predominant ethnic communities – Indo-Canadians mainly from the Punjab, and Chinese from Hong Kong and the mainland's

Downtown Eastside.

Guangdong province – have their enclaves, but they are spread throughout the city. The West End's Denman and Davie Streets meanwhile are very comfortably gay. Vancouver also has a deserved reputation for being disability-friendly. That's partly because of locals like Rick Hansen, who powered his own wheelchair around the world, and Terry Fox, who embarked on a run across Canada on one leg in 1980 to raise funds for cancer research; halfway home his cancer returned and took his life. But the city's disability friendliness is mainly the result Vancouver's sheer newness. It's easy – or at least easier – to provide for the physically disabled when so much of the city was built in the last quarter-century, when the campaign for universal access emerged.

Another disabled community leader is the wheelchair-bound Vancouver Mayor Sam Sullivan, who broke his neck as a teenager skiing above Vancouver at Cypress Bowl. He sought engineers to create new technology for the disabled and as a result Sullivan and others can be found sailing small boats on English Bay using 'sip and puff' straw controls.

GREEN CITY?

Sullivan has been less successful as mayor, bringing equivocal leadership to causes he purports to champion, such as providing for the drug-addicted and destitute who populate Vancouver's troubled Downtown Eastside, and promoting his trademarked 'eco-density' initiative – really just a rebranding for eco-sensitive times of the compact, transit- and pedestrian-friendly planning the city has been pushing for years. Even BC Premier Gordon Campbell, a former Vancouver mayor whose politically conservative BC Liberal Party took power in 2001, is fashioning himself as a champion of the sustainability cause, meeting with Al Gore and California Governor Arnold Schwarzenegger, and proposing tough new environmental regulations. It's a bit of a switch for a premier who also wants offshore oil drilling, and who gutted mining and forestry regulations when he took office.

Suffice to say that contradictions abound in a province that gave birth to Greenpeace and trumpets its environmental awareness (*see p15* **Going green**), yet remains among the most profligate per-capita consumers of energy and water in the world.

Campbell, however, knows how to work a trend, and his government seems assured of re-election after the 2010 Olympics. Whether Mayor Sullivan will be re-elected in 2008, so that he can wave the Canadian flag at the 2010 Vancouver Winter Olympics (as he did at the 2006 Turin games' closing ceremonies), is an

open question, but Vancouver's fractured, in some ways backward, political system does have a tendency to favour the status quo.

Civic politics in Vancouver is a complicated business. Metro Vancouver, as the region is known, is comprised of representatives from 21 municipal governments, plus the University of BC's 'Electoral Area A' and, as of 2007, its first aboriginal government, the Tsawwassen Band. (The latter resulted from BC's first urban treaty, a landmark event in a province where, despite 150 years of colonial settlement, virtually no aboriginal rights treaties have been signed.) Most of Metro Vancouver's municipalities were created when they were main streets separated by forest and farmers' fields. Even Vancouver proper, which comprises about a quarter of Metro Vancouver's 2.2 million citizens, was once divided into several municipalities.

Development has knitted many of these together, but ocean inlets and the Fraser River delta's branches still divide the region, creating strong local suburban community identities. This amounts to another lucky Vancouver circumstance. The Canadian cities that have amalgamated have regretted it, and Metro Vancouver works well in serving communities.

DEVELOPMENT VERSUS PROTECTION

All the same, BC municipalities are weak creatures of the provincial government, which prevents them from taxing anything except property. It is generally the province that takes the lead on major urban infrastructure. One recent initiative is the Gateway Project, which will twin the major bridge to the southern suburbs and provide a secondary highway through those suburbs to a significant port facility in the community of Delta. This will help with goods movement, but critics argue it will only fuel a suburban population explosion. The suburbs of Surrey, Langley Township, Coquitlam and outlying Abbotsford are already projected to absorb 68 per cent of regional growth in the next 25 years, fuelling car culture and creating increased pressure to develop the province's precious Fraser delta farmland.

Although the current government has largely supported the Agricultural Land Reserve protection measure, which helped shape the region's often compact town centres, many doubt the depth of the development-friendly Liberals commitment to the policy.

POVERTY AND PROMISES

Many also doubt the BC Liberals' commitment to the poor. Upon taking office, the government reduced welfare rates, disqualified many young people from assistance and slashed the minimum wage for youth. Since then, homelessness in the Vancouver region has more than doubled. With unprecedented surplus revenue from the commodities boom, the BC Liberals can hardly help but spend a little money on the needy. All the same, they look set to break their promise to eliminate homelessness before the 2010 Olympics.

In fact, the problem could worsen. Despite progressive initiatives like the safe injection centre Insite (which the federal Conservatives may eliminate), and despite projects such as the redevelopment of a landmark department store site bordering the troubled Downtown Eastside, insufficient addiction treatment, care for the mentally ill and housing for the most needy are aggravating the worst open sore in a major Canadian city.

While events like the trial and conviction of Coquitlam pig farmer Robert Pickton for the murder of six of the area's street prostitutes have caused the city to recoil in horror (Pickton may yet stand trial on more counts; DNA from 30 missing women has been found on his farm), it is still proving very difficult to build the political consensus needed to meet the Downtown Eastside's deterioration head on.

MODEL MULTICULTURAL CITY?

Other social problems draw even less in the way of effective action. Vancouver presents itself as the exemplar of multicultural tolerance, and in most – if by no means all – regards North America's most Asian city is exactly that. However, the bungled $130-million investigation into the 1985 Air India bombing, in which 329 people were killed by BC-based Punjabi nationalists resulted in the acquittal in 2005 of key suspects. Like the police's initial inability to identify the murder of Downtown Eastside prostitutes as serial killings, the failure can be attributed substantially to the authorities' indifference to the plight of 'others'. Such problems continue, as exemplified by the murder since 1995 of more than 60 Indo-Canadian gang members. Almost all the murders remain unsolved.

There will be more challenges for politicians in the future. Amid the rhetoric about Vancouver becoming a world-class city, there's one clear indicator that it's arriving: world-class real-estate values. Residential prices have doubled in five years, and (so far) the frothy market has withstood the US downturn. Despite the city's planning successes, it risks becoming a two-tier city where urban housing is just too expensive for regular working folks.

The construction boom is so intense it creates the impression that real estate development is the region's only industry. Of course, there's the port, the largest on North America's West Coast

(*see p18* **The shipping news**) and the closest major port to Asia. Vancouver is also the third-largest film and TV production centre in North America, and companies like Electronic Arts have made it a major centre for video game production, and the area has historic mining and forestry industries. But the city lacks signature international companies like Seattle's Microsoft or Boeing, making it vulnerable in the event of a worldwide economic crash.

In the meantime, amid a few fictions of their own construction, Vancouverites have plenty to enjoy, and to gloat about. For those few who actually live the fabled Vancouver lifestyle, as opposed to just talking about it, it really is possible in springtime to go sailing on English Bay in the morning and ski at Cypress Bowl, half an hour from the city centre, in the afternoon. Pristine wilderness hikes abound at the end of North Shore bus routes.

On a perfect early summer day, hot but not too hot, cycling around the Stanley Park Seawall, or walking out on the endless sand flats exposed by low tide at Spanish Banks, or sitting on a Granville Island patio, with the snow still persisting on the Coast Mountains in the distance, Vancouver really does feel like one of the world's great cities. If it's all an illusion, it's a pretty good one.

Enjoying the view from the **Seawall**.

Concord Pacific Place. *See p29.*

Architecture

The future may be up, but there's plenty of heritage among the high-rises.

It is sometimes said that Vancouver's spectacular natural setting has allowed it to get away with mediocre architecture. While there is more than a germ of truth in this, Vancouver has its share of provocative, even sublime, architectural statements. As befits a city that was incorporated as recently as 1886, Vancouver showcases the eclectic and the new rather than possessing the architectural coherence of cities that have experienced centuries of development. And there is more than a whiff of the architecturally eccentric about the place as well.

Looking out over the glittering skyline of the downtown peninsula, it is hard to imagine that this was virgin rainforest less than 150 years ago. Not much remains of the first wave of urban settlement, when Vancouver was an isolated shipping outpost. Gastown's **Water Street** (*see also p62* **Walk**) offers the best glimpse into that largely vanished past, with its handsome brick warehouses and mercantile

stores, many of which have been restored as trendy shops and loft housing. The area is a designated Heritage District, and feels it.

If Gastown seems a bit too theme park-like, you can get a more authentic sense of the city's earliest residential architecture by venturing eastward into Strathcona, one of Vancouver's first neighbourhoods, with its narrow streets and largely intact wood-frame housing for workers. This edgy neighbourhood stands in contrast to the self-important architectural piles that the elite classes erected for themselves on the south side of False Creek in Shaughnessy Heights, Vancouver's first master-planned community. Here the genteel, curving boulevards hide some magnificent mansions, built in the early 1900s for the rich and famous and still today the city's premier residential neighbourhood.

Some of downtown Vancouver's more striking architectural statements, both historic and contemporary, include the following:

With its great copper roof, the **Fairmont Hotel Vancouver** (1928-39; *see p41*) at 900 West Georgia is Vancouver's rendition of the grand hotels that the Canadian National Railway commissioned across the country and which came to epitomise the tourist postcard view of Canada's transcontinental railway. From the same period, the exuberant 1930 **Marine Building** at 355 Burrard Street (*see p59*) once dominated the harbour. With its stepped profile, terracotta decoration and marvellous lobby, it remains Vancouver's most expressive art deco building.

At the corner of Georgia and Hornby streets, there's no escaping the post-modern **Cathedral Place** (1990), a pseudo-Gothic amalgam complete with pre-cast gargoyles and nurses and a fake copper chateau-esque roof. In contrast to the tower's efforts at calling attention to itself is the cloistered courtyard at its north side, one of Vancouver's most elegant, contemplative public open spaces, and a hidden jewel in the city.

The former **BC Hydro Headquarters** tower at 970 Burrard Street and its little sibling **Dal Grauer Substation** next door (1955 and 1953, respectively) represent the best of classic modernism in the city. The lozenge-shaped tower is a stunning essay in steel, glass and coloured mosaic. Largely designed by Ron Thom, one of Vancouver's most iconoclastic modernist talents, the ensemble has lost some of its authenticity by being converted into a residential condominium (the Electra) in the 1990s, harbinger of a troubling trend that has continued to this day across Downtown.

Admire the **Crown Life Plaza** complex at 1500 West Georgia Street (1976-78). This crisply detailed curtain-walled tower and retail pavilion, obviously inspired by the late great British architect James Stirling, was one of the first projects designed by a then young Peter Cardew, himself a Brit who has since gone on to become one of Vancouver's most talented architects.

'The Athletes Village for the 2010 Winter Olympics is touted as a model of sustainable development.'

The yacht-like white fabric sails of **Canada Place** (1986; *see p59*), overlooking Burrard Inlet at the foot of Howe Street, are the closest thing Vancouver has to an iconic waterfront building in the vein of Sydney's Opera House. It is a legacy of the Expo 86 World's Fair, when it served as the Canada Pavilion.

More recent additions to the downtown skyline include several iconic towers by James Cheng, including the **Shangri-La** on West Georgia Street, which, upon the imminent completion of its 61 storeys, will become Vancouver's tallest building.

Arthur Erickson has left his mark on Vancouver, notably in the **Museum of Anthropology**.

Then there is Arthur Erickson. Vancouver's aging doyen of architecture has designed some iconic structures, including the magnificent **Museum of Anthropology** (*see p77*), a 20-minute drive from the city centre at UBC, and the classical **Simon Fraser University** campus acropolis atop Burnaby Mountain. But he has also been responsible for such questionable downtown urban constructs as the brutalist former **MacMillan Bloedel office tower** (1075 West Georgia Street) and – even more egregiously – the convoluted **Robson Square** complex (*see p58*), which failed to deliver the great public open space that downtown Vancouver still lacks. While flawed, Erickson's architectural legacy is unmatchable.

Vancouver's architectural eclecticism bubbles up all over the city. Compare, for example, the late Ross Lort's fairytale Cotswold cottages at 3979 West Broadway or 587 King Edward Avenue to the clean lines and abstract geometry of the same architect's **Barber House** at 3846 West 10th Avenue, one of the few intact examples of art moderne architecture remaining in Vancouver. The difference is schizophrenic. Contemplate the bizarre **Sam Kee Building** (1913; *see p65*) at 8 West Pender Street in Chinatown, at six feet wide the world's narrowest building. Or consider the California Craftsman-style bungalows on the 2900-block West 5th Avenue in Kitsilano, the wacky 2400 Motel out on Kingsway, the four-storey 'Dingbat' apartment buildings in the West End, and the ubiquitous if ironically named 'Vancouver Special' houses, with their shallow-sloped roofs, boxy proportions and utterly banal detailing, mass produced in the 1970s (such as the 6100-block of Elgin Street). And you can't miss the city's iconic spans: elegant **Lions Gate Bridge** (*see p81*) and flamboyant **Burrard Bridge**.

Burrard Bridge spans False Creek, which has been Vancouver's testing ground of urban planning since the 1970s. False Creek South, with its low-rise housing projects set in an enclave of discontinuous streets and park space, is a case study of 1970s planning ideology. Contrast this with False Creek North, the gleaming high-rise precinct – dubbed '**Concord Pacific Place**' – which has been developed on the former Expo 86 site by Hong Kong-based billionaire Li-Ka Shing as a high-density riposte. Finally, there's Southeast False Creek, east of Cambie Bridge, which will soon emerge as Vancouver's **Athletes Village** for the 2010 Winter Olympics (*see p22* **Games on!**). With its integration of building design, infrastructure, energy systems and public transit access, it posits a vision for the 21st-century city. A decade in the planning, this precinct is touted as a model of sustainable development.

Not all things architectural lie within the boundaries of the City of Vancouver itself. To get a better sense of Greater Vancouver's urban form, history and geography, take a ride out on the elevated SkyTrain transit line to Surrey, with a stop in downtown New Westminster. Here, walking down historic **Columbia Street** with its late 19th- and early 20th-century masonry buildings, one gets a strong sense of a grand but now faded past, when New Westminster was the first capital of British Columbia and a shopping destination for the entire region.

Getting back on the SkyTrain, you now cross one of the world's most impressive transit bridges, as the driverless automated train zooms high above the Fraser River on a suspended concrete ribbon. The views are spectacular, the experience breathtaking. On a clear day you can make out the volcanic profile of Mount Baker some 100 kilometres (60 miles) to the south-east. End your trip at Surrey Central Station, a nondescript suburban setting except for the **Central City Tower**, an expressionistic architectural statement and sophisticated, if still isolated, piece of urban design by Bing Thom, an Erickson protégé and one of Vancouver's most accomplished architects. Central City Tower offers a glimpse into Vancouver's architectural future, as the city urbanises into its surrounding low-density suburbs and begins to take on the trappings of a true metropolis commensurate with its spectacular setting.

The **Marine Building** is an art deco delight.

Comox Valley by **EJ Hughes**.
See p33.

See p33.

West Coast Art

From Emily Carr to Jeff Wall, BC's forested landscape has inspired artists aplenty.

'There was an anti-logging protest going on outside the art gallery…' Douglas Coupland, *Eleanor Rigby*.

Douglas fir, shore pine, sitka spruce, yew, amabilis fir, western hemlock, arbutus, red and yellow cedar – you could make the case that Vancouver's evolution owes a lot to its trees. In fact, if these trees didn't cover the west coast, there is a good chance that Vancouver wouldn't exist at all. They darken the mountains, lap up the never-ending rain, filter the air of pollutants and provide shelter, clothes, fuel and even the material for the north-west coast aboriginal peoples' vibrant cultural tradition. For the Kwakw'aka'wakw and the Salish, the forest equalled the sea for mystery and bounty, and yet it was a mundane thing too, a place of endless resources. And it is this paradox that persists today in local culture.

When the first Europeans arrived they found themselves surrounded by sky-scraping trees and impenetrable undergrowth, thick with sword ferns, huckleberries and salal. Timber was by far the biggest industry in town for a few generations, but has since been replaced by tourism: people coming to play among the trees they previously cut down. Everybody loves the trees – for some, they smell like money when logged; for others, they have the beauty of a Gothic cathedral and need to be treated with the same reverence. If a tree falls in a forest near Vancouver, everybody hears.

One of the earliest European artists to depict the forest was **GM de L'Aubiniere** who, along with her husband, was commissioned to paint 14 pictures to accompany an illuminated address for Queen Victoria in 1877. One such picture called, unsurprisingly, *Wood Scene*, shows a gentle, pastoral landscape, with a

Reid all about it

Born in Victoria in 1920 to a Haida mother and an American father, **Bill Reid** was oblivious to his native heritage until his teens. At 23, he visited Skidegate, his mother's home village in Haida Gwaii (the Queen Charlotte Islands) and discovered that his grandfather had been a carver and engraver. The seed of interest had been planted and some years later, while working as a radio announcer for the Canadian Broadcasting Corporation (CBC) in Toronto, Reid began taking extensive courses in jewellery making.

By the 1950s, Reid was living in Vancouver, still working for the CBC while creating jewellery at night. As he rekindled his relationship with the west coast, he found himself more and more drawn to the traditions of Haida art and began to merge his skills with the visual language of the First Nations' culture. In 1958, he was finally able to walk away from broadcasting: he took a job with the Museum of Anthropology (*see p77*),

recreating two Haida village houses and five totem poles. He was a full-time artist until his death 30 years later.

Reid's work can be seen all around Vancouver. His *Jade Canoe* graces the departures lounge at the airport, while *Killer Whale* is an imposing presence at the entrance to the Aquarium (*see p68*). Most impressive, though, is the work to be found at the Museum of Anthropology, from his early, exquisitely detailed gold boxes and jewellery, to his best known work, the monumental sculpture *The Raven and the First Men* (*pictured*).

Afflicted with Parkinson's disease, Reid was, towards the end of his life, unable to manage the fine detail his artworks required and relied on a number of assistants to achieve his vision.

In July 2007, the Bill Reid Foundation announced that the **Bill Reid Gallery of Northwest Coast Art** (*see p58*) would open downtown on Hornby Street in 2008.

*Scorned as Timber,
Beloved of the Sky*
by **Emily Carr**.

small pond and a few trees. It could be the suburbs of Paris. What kind of trees is she trying to paint? That might be a cedar at the water's edge, an alder over there, but really this could be anywhere. Yet there is also a feeling of claustrophobia, even mild threat. So perhaps she caught a whiff of the forest's essence in the density of trees and foliage, but for the most part this is an artist failing to see the newness of the landscape and the extraordinary, individual qualities of the trees. She looked into the forest and painted a self-portrait.

A generation later, **Emily Carr**, the founding mother of British Columbian art, fared a little better. She was, in fact, merely competent when it came to painting trees. Occasionally she gets it right, and the landscapes come with a whiff of tart cedar air, but most of the time we get thick slabs of undifferentiated green magma where we might expect the feathery fronds of a hem lock. It's all Carr – she replaces the cool, claustrophobic calm of the forest with the heavy broodiness that is a more accurate reflection of her mood than the forest itself. *Scorned as Timber, Beloved of the Sky* (1935; *pictured left*) is probably her most popular image, and it is easy to see why: the tree stands out, proud yet forlorn, amid a devastated forest. The sky radiates around it as if heaven felt its pain and loneliness. It announces so much of what has become synonymous with west coast culture: at once a romantic identification with the landscape and an image of land stripped to exploit its resources. But it is also a great painting, full of pathos and brilliant touches.

But Carr is equally, and justifiably, famous for her paintings of the totem poles and villages of Haida Gwaii and Kwakw'aka'wakw – or, as they were then called, the Kwakiutl. There is no better record of a culture in rapid decline and transition than, say, *Totem Poles, Kitseukla* (1912) or *Kwakiutl House* (1912). These are superb paintings, which blend anthropological research with the post-Impressionism that Carr discovered on her trip to France just two years earlier. With paintings like these, Carr established a tradition of art in Vancouver.

In 1926, **FH Varley** arrived from Sheffield, England, via Ontario, to take the position of Head of the Vancouver Art School (which then became Emily Carr College of Art and Design). He fell in love with the geography, producing paintings that carried on Carr's tradition. In 1932, he painted *Dhârâna*, a picture of his mistress on a wooden porch, her spine aligned with a thick post, transforming her into a kind of totem pole. A curtain of blue mountains fill the background and nearer, on the left, a cluster of faint totem poles tower with precarious

thinness. Varley incorrectly understood the title to mean a mental union with the landscape (it more accurately describes a state of meditation). But this is an important point in the history of west coast culture: his figure, his mistress, has been transformed into a piece of wood, a totem, and the painting enacts a total union between human soul and tree. Later that same year, he wrote a letter to a friend in Sheffield, describing the landscape and concluding, 'we have yet to understand its nature'.

'It conveys the ambivalence about trees inherent to the west coast: at once an object of desire, a resource and a potential danger.'

The lyrical landscape tradition inaugurated by Carr, Varley and others was taken up with great energy by the next generation: Toni Onley, Gordon Smith and – the best of the bunch – **Jack Shadbolt**, to name a few. These artists developed it through the middle of the 20th century and into the 1970s, and Shadbolt produced some of his best work well into the '80s. The tradition still persists today. But perhaps the west coast's true genius, a one-time student of Varley's, is **EJ Hughes**. He strips his palette of all the sodden, romantic muck of Carr. He's pragmatic, accurate, witty and direct, where she is gooey and solipsistic. Hughes picks out the different trees, the rocky beaches, the blue-black sea, the strange, perfectly formed blankets of clouds that are carved by the mountains of the Olympic range and Vancouver Island. Hughes paintings are notable for the way the sky, stones and trees are picked out in almost preternatural detail. He shows the coast as a working place, speckled by boats and ferries, humdrum activities against a backdrop as homely and pastoral as it is sublime. His style has something of the naivety of Henri Rousseau, yet in that clarity, the careful description of individual trees – you can distinguish a fir from a cedar in a Hughes painting – is a desire to see this landscape unencumbered by the conflicting emotions of avarice and empathy.

In the late 1960s and early 1970s, a new generation of artists emerged, a group that includes Jeff Wall, Ian Wallace, Ken Lum, Rodney Graham and – a little younger – Stan Douglas and Roy Arden. These artists built upon Vancouver's traditional relationship with the landscape mostly by resisting any romantic attachment to it. And **Ian Wallace**, perhaps Vancouver's most influential artist and teacher over the last few decades, was the catalyst in this regard. His work *Clayoquot Protest* (9 August 1993) is a group of nine panels that form a superb evocation of how the forest has created a culture of deep ambivalence. A group of people have gathered to protest the logging of an important first-growth forest. Wallace documented the groups of people with a series of photographs, then applied them to canvas with prints of wood grains. The patterns of the wood are both decorative and utilitarian, a perfect emblem of why there is such a battle over these trees: for the protestors, the trees are beautiful things that need to be protected; for the loggers, they represent a pay cheque.

Stan Douglas takes up similar ideas with *Nu.tka*. Shot in Nootka Sound, on the west coast of Vancouver Island, the piece shows two videos projected on top of each other, and the ghostly double picture is accompanied by voice-overs meant to evoke two early explorers of the region, Englishman James Colnett and Spaniard Jose Esteban Martinez. At the time, fur was the target (all those sea otters), but what we see is the landscape: forests and water. The two men squabble over the rights to the land, often becoming irrational and strident. **Rodney Graham**, who grew up partly in logging camps, represented Canada at the Venice Biennale in 1997, where he showed *Vexation Island*, a looped film about a buccaneer lost on a desert island who repeatedly awakes to shake a tree only to get knocked out by a falling coconut, ad infinitum. Though set on a Caribbean island, it conveys the ambivalence about trees inherent to the west coast: at once an object of desire, a resource and a potential danger.

Jeff Wall, certainly the best known of the bunch, comes to the local landscape a bit more obliquely. But one photograph seems to be partly a direct response to Carr's *Scorned as Timber, Beloved of the Sky*. *Pine on a Corner* also features a towering tree, this time a pine that is not native to the coast (it's a lodgepole pine, a few hundred kilometres away from its native land). With this picture, Wall questions the romantic attachment to the landscape that is so common among the painters in a so-called west coast tradition. The picture is at once more mundane and more penetratingly strange than Carr's. In another picture, *Park Drive*, a road zips through the centre of a Stanley Park forest, a strange alien presence in an otherwise primeval landscape. The forest has become everything the road is not: a great hindrance, a strange curtain that blinds the drivers from the outside world.

In all these cases, the landscape sits in the background like a mute, defenceless witness to human madness, and this idea is played out superbly in *The Inert Landscapes of Gyorgy Ferenc*, a short story by Nanaimo-born writer

Tamas Dobozy. The protagonist of the story describes the life of his father, a landscape painter celebrated in his native Hungary who brought his whole family to Canada to escape the Soviets. Upon arrival, however, he struggles with the new surroundings. 'My father was a landscape painter in a nation that would not be reproduced', the story opens, but it would not be reproduced only because his father considered the Canadian landscape a soulless, utilitarian place. The father was stuck in a romantic tradition, as described in the story by a fictional Hungarian critic: 'in his work… one senses the inextricability of geography and the soul'. Now, that's codswallop, and anyone who tells you different is probably trying to sell you a reproduction of an Emily Carr painting.

Ron Terada, a member of a younger generation of Vancouver artists, really tears into that idea with his piece *Entering the City of Vancouver*. The sculpture – or is it a picture? – addresses the landscape tradition of the city, from Emily Carr to Jeff Wall to Stan Douglas. A huge highway sign announces the geographical change, which is otherwise an invisible fiction: it's just a border. Terada replaces the oozing, romantic green of Carr with the utilitarian green of a highway sign. The sign itself is treelike – a single looming field of green propped up by wood. But there is no inextricable link between geography and soul here, just a big, utilitarian sign that marks an artificial border.

With Ron Terada's sign, we have come full circle from GM L'Aubiniere's *Wood Scene*. The former is a naïve attempt at a depiction of a landscape that outwits the artist, the second is a great big sign erected by the artist in an attempt to outwit the landscape. And yet the landscape, and the trees that it hosts, remain essential to the experience of Vancouver.

Malcom Lowry lived – rather grumpily and drunkenly – along the Burrard Inlet for many years, where he finished his greatest book, *Under the Volcano*. In his poem 'Happiness', he lists, along with the 'blue mountains', gulls and eagles, the 'trees with branches rooted in air' as a source of happiness. It's an image that brings to mind Carr's *Scorned as Timber* and Wall's *Pine on a Corner*, as well as tourist snapshots or west coast paintings. While Terada's sign is a brilliant parody of categorising art by region, it is, paradoxically, successful because it emerges from a tradition that has its beginnings in the omnipresence of trees.

Perhaps Varley is still right when he wrote, 'we have yet to understand its nature' about the west coast forest and landscape. But this will hasten things along. If you want to understand Vancouver's culture, by all means visit the Vancouver Art Gallery (*see p60*). Eat a cinnamon

Tales of the city

If London has Martin Amis and New York has Don DeLillo, then **Douglas Coupland** is Vancouver's very own brilliant and sardonic literary guide.

Coupland is, of course, best known for his debut novel *Generation X*, a witty glossary of pre-millennial disaffection. For coining such terms as 'McJob' and 'knee-jerk irony' he was designated 'the voice of a generation' by a grateful media. The 1991 book, pegged as the new *Catcher in the Rye*, would be the first of many – 18 so far – to affirm the North Vancouver writer's keen ability to catch the zeitgeist and document social trends.

Despite his disclaimers ('I speak for myself, not for a generation') Coupland litters his novels with brand names, up-to-the-second cultural references and, often, rich local detail. *Life after God* (1994) sifts the material effects of North American consumer society for a scrap of existential insight – and finds it deep in the forests of Vancouver Island. Set down the road in Seattle, his 1995 novel *Microserfs* – about the alienation of life on the information superhighway – was another demographic-defining novel, and one of the first reactions to the technology boom.

Girlfriend in a Coma (1998), a tender, end-of-the-world romance, begins with a typical Couplandesque setting: 'Karen and I deflowered each other atop Grouse Mountain among the cedars beside a ski slope.' *Hey Nostradamus!* (2003), about a Columbine-type massacre, is set in a fictional high school in North Vancouver.

Not surprising then that this observant multi-tasker – as renowned for his non fiction, artworks and other projects as for his fiction – would be commissioned to create a book dedicated to his home town.

Published in 2000, the picture book *City of Glass* 'is just the sort of whacked-out guide you wish was available for every great city in the world', claimed the *Globe and Mail*. In lieu of landmarks, Coupland shows what the city feels like to somebody who lives here. 'I spent my 20s scouring the globe thinking

there had to be a better city out there,' he writes, 'until it dawned on me that Vancouver is the best one going.'

From BC Ferries to YVR, dim sum to real estate, Coupland's lexicon of the city is uniquely personal and full of insight. 'If you're a Vancouverite, you find the city's lack of historical luggage liberating – it dazzles with a sense of limitless possibility,' he writes. 'We're at our best when experimenting with new ideas, and at our worst when we ape the conventions of elsewhere. Vancouver is, literally, one of the world's youngest cities. Some day we'll be old and creaky, but not now – right now is for being young.'

Two years later, Coupland would be welcomed as the tour guide for the country in the *Souvenir of Canada*, an art installation and two-volume book (and eventually a film) – all in loving tribute to stubbie beer bottles and bilingual cereal boxes.

Coupland's original plan was to be an artist, not a writer. He graduated from Vancouver's Emily Carr Institute of Art and Design in 1984, then studied in Italy, Japan and Hawaii before working as a designer at a Tokyo magazine. He returned to Vancouver in 1987 and was given a show of his sculptures at Vancouver Art Gallery. Since then, his paintings, collages and multi-media work have shown throughout Canada and the world. In 2004, he created and starred in the play *September 10*, and the following year saw the production of his screenplay *Everything's Gone Green*.

Nevertheless, he's still a prolific writer, and *jPod*, 'a sequel, of sorts' to *Microserfs*, was published in 2006. He loves writing, he says, so that's what he does: 'Since 1991 we've been through massive cultural, social, technological changes, and the only thing that protects me or you or anyone, the only thing that can protect you in all this is figuring out what it is that you like to do, and then sticking with it. Because once you start to do what people expect you to do, or what your parents think you should do, or whoever in your life thinks you should do, you're sunk.'

bun and a turkey sausage, try some sockeye sashimi, shop in Chinatown, watch a hockey game, go for a swim at Kitsilano Beach, dance in the Commodore, have a gelato at sunset in English Bay, yes, do all that. But above all grab a book like *Plants of Coastal British Columbia* and go to Stanley Park. Crush some scaly red

cedar leaves in your hands, open your palms and inhale the fragrance, then caress the rough, fibrous bark of a Douglas fir. Don't make it a religious experience, but a practical one: learn the names of every tree you meet and get to know them. Let's face it – if they weren't here, you'd have gone to Disneyland.

Where to Stay

Features

Pan Pacific. *See p42*.

Pan Pacific. *See p42.*

Where to Stay

You'll find rooms with vroom thanks to Vancouver's Olympic overhaul.

As the city spruces up in preparation for the 2010 Winter Olympics, construction continues apace. The 60 storeys of the new Shangri-La building on the corner of West Georgia and Thurlow make it the tallest structure in the city, housing condos, shops and restaurants, with 15 floors reserved for Vancouver's top hotel. Another massive project is the Georgia Tower, transforming the stately, 1920s Hotel Georgia into 52 storeys of soaring glass in the Downtown centre. The 247-room luxury boutique hotel will open by 2010.

In response, the city's established facilities are smartening up: five years ago, most hotels acceded to the insistent beige – clean, minimal design whitewashed every interior. Then came high speed internet, followed by plasma TVs. Now everything's going green. Light fixtures feature low energy compact fluorescents; heating and air conditioning is controlled at a main switchboard so that they can be adjusted as soon as guests check out; room service boasts sustainable products and practices.

Most visitors to Vancouver will want to stay in the downtown core. How you narrow it down from there doesn't really matter; a 10-minute cab ride will get you from one side of town to the other. Though less obvious during the day, the city's neighbourhoods are clearly defined at night. The West End, though quiet and leafy, perks up later on, the cafés and restaurants on Denman Street buzzing with locals. Conversely, Robson Street, though busy with shoppers in the day and early evening, closes down come nightfall. Yaletown is the trendy place to hang at night, with Vancouver's most upscale bars and a clutch of its favourite restaurants, but has only one hotel, the stylish Opus. Nearby Granville Street is the entertainment district and is home to a seven-screen cinema, theatres and bars; it's also noisy and a bit seedy.

If you'd rather not stay in the hub, then the West Side is probably the best bet. Kitsilano's B&Bs offer easy access to the beach and there's no shortage of neighbourhood bars and great places to eat. For up-to-date information check with the Western Canada Bed & Breakfast Innkeepers Association (www.wcbbia.com). Unless you plan to spend most of your trip on the mountains, the North Shore is probably too far to be convenient.

RATES, GRADINGS AND SEASONS

For our purposes, hotels offering rooms under $100 are defined as budget; under $200 as moderate. When you get into the expensive and luxury categories, depending on the time of year and style of room you're after, the sky is the limit. The distinction between expensive and luxury is made on the range of services offered and the quality of the finishing touches.

Many hotels offer better rates through their websites and it's often possible to get a discount at the top hotels if their occupancy levels are

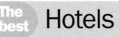 Hotels

For the view

The **Pan Pacific**: take in expansive mountain, harbour and city views while seaplanes buzz overhead – and on a clear day see all the way to the USA (*see p42*).

On a budget

The **Victorian Hotel**: One of the city's first guest houses still offers old-world charm and service, all in a lovingly restored setting that'll make you feel you're in a Victorian novel (*see p49*).

For mixing with movie stars

Sutton Place Hotel: follow in the softly cushioned footsteps of the likes of Elton John and Catherine Zeta-Jones in this AAA Five Diamond hotel (*see p42*).

For the beach

Mickey's Kits Beach Chalet: walk to Vancouver's liveliest beach in minutes or take a five-minute bus ride downtown from a hotel that goes the extra mile in catering to your needs (*see p51*).

For the lap of luxury

Wedgewood Hotel: an independent spirit permeates this small, opulent hotel, where top-notch service and personal touches make it stand out from the crowd (*see p42*).

❶ Green numbers given in this chapter correspond to the location of each hotel as marked on the street maps. See pp248-253.

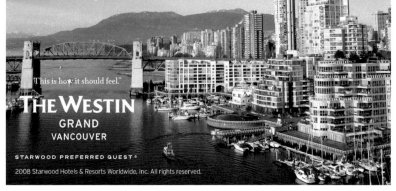

The classy lounge bar at the **Fairmont Hotel Vancouver**.

lower than expected. High season in Vancouver is May to October. Tourism Vancouver's site (www.tourismvancouver.com) has good information on the city's accommodation.

Downtown

Luxury

Fairmont Hotel Vancouver

900 W Georgia Street, at Burrard Street, V6C 2W6 (604 684 3131/toll free 1-800 257 7544/www. fairmont.com/hotelvancouver). All city-centre buses. **Rates** $219-$489 double. **Rooms** 556. **Credit** AmEx, DC, MC, V. **Map** p249 K3 ❶
Originally a Canadian National Railway hotel (recognisable by its stone exterior and oxidised copper roof), the Hotel Vancouver is a city landmark in the heart of downtown. It has changed a lot over the years and, as a result, the rooms vary greatly in size and shape. However, all have been refurbished recently with new plasma TVs and automated mini bars. Best to avoid the lower floors where some of the rooms have been converted from meeting spaces and can be vast and impersonal. For an extra $100 or so, the Fairmont Gold floors provide a private lounge with complimentary snacks, drinks all day and a hearty breakfast. Alternatively, Griffins restaurant serves its own copious buffet breakfast with an Asian option featuring eggs, smoked fish and steamed rice. In the open yet cosy lobby bar they serve free hors d'oeuvres every night from 5-7pm, followed by live jazz until 11pm – sometimes later. *Bar. Business centre. Concierge. Disabled-adapted rooms. Gym. Internet (high speed). Parking ($28/day). Pool (indoor). Restaurant. Room service (6.30am-1am). Spa. TV.*

Fairmont Waterfront

900 Canada Place Way, at Hornby Street, V6C 3L5 (604 691 1991/toll free 1-800 257 7544/www. fairmont.com/waterfront). All city-centre buses/ SkyTrain & SeaBus Waterfront. **Rates** $299-$499 double. **Credit** AmEx, DC, MC, V. **Map** p249 L2 ❷
The Fairmont Waterfront opened in 1991 and has since become an indelible part of the Vancouver skyline. The glass structure has accommodated everyone from the Queen to Bill Clinton. City or harbour views (or both, if you opt for a corner room) grace the immaculate, spacious and bright rooms, half of which have recently been restyled (with completion for the remainder pegged for 2009). The outdoor pool area is positively grand, as is the herb garden alongside it. There's also a fully equipped gym with eucalyptus steam baths in each changing room. *Bar. Business centre. Concierge. Disabled-adapted rooms. Gym. Internet (high speed). Parking ($30/night). Pool (outdoor). Restaurant. Room service (24hr). TV.*

Four Seasons Hotel

791 W Georgia Street, at Howe Street, V6C 2T4 (604 689 9333/toll free 1-800 819 5053/www.

Rates $250-$500 double. **Rooms** 372. **Credit** AmEx, DC, MC, V. **Map** p249 K3 ❸

Major renovations of the hotel's lobby and restaurants took place in 2007, including a multi-zone 200-seat eatery, offering an oyster bar, café/bakery and West Coast cuisine-inspired dining room. In the new lobby, carpet has been replaced by Italian marble floors and fantastic area rugs. All the rooms, meanwhile will undergo a complete restyling in 2008. Despite the overhaul, warm ambience is still key here. Its 372 rooms are quietly sophisticated, with complimentary breakfast, down duvets, and thick terry bathrobes. The health club, indoor-outdoor pool, whirlpool and sauna are minded by wellness concierges.

Bar. Business centre. Concierge. Disabled-adapted rooms. Gym. Internet (high speed). Parking ($26.75/night). Pool (indoor-outdoor). Restaurant. Room service (24hr). TV.

Hotel Le Soleil

567 Hornby Street, at W Pender Street, V6C 2E8 (604 632 3000/toll free 1-877 632 3030/www.lesoleil hotel.com). All city-centre buses. **Rates** $209-$225 double. **Rooms** 95. **Credit** AmEx, DC, MC, V. **Map** p249 K3 ❹

With furniture custom-designed in the 'Biedermeier' style, you might feel like you've walked into the 19th century. The beds are particularly luxurious, with feather pillows, down duvets, Egyptian combed cotton sheets and silk brocade bedspreads. And the bathrooms are a dream worthy of Cleopatra – extensively tiled in the finest marble. Not sure if Cleo would have appreciated the Aveda Body Care products, but today's guests sure do. The two penthouse suites are extraordinary, with high ceilings and huge plasma televisions.

Bar. Concierge. Disabled-adapted rooms. Internet (dataport, web TV). Parking ($22/night). Restaurant. Room service (6.30am-10pm). TV.

Pan Pacific

300-999 Canada Place, at Burrard Street, V6C 3B5 (604 662 8111/toll free 1-800 663 1515/ http://vancouver.panpacific.com). All city-centre buses/SkyTrain Waterfront. **Rates** $259-$610 double. **Rooms** 504. **Credit** AmEx, DC, MC, V. **Map** p249 L2 ❺

Located above the famous white sails of the Canada Place Convention Centre that have come to symbolise Vancouver, this rounded glass building has spectacular views of the North Shore mountains, Burrard Inlet, Stanley Park and the city all the way to the US border. The balcony suites are particularly impressive; you feel like you're on a cruise ship about to set sail for Alaska. The Pan Pacific has one of only two American Automobile Association (AAA) 5 Diamonds in the city, the Michelin stars of the hotel world. *Photo p38.*

Bar. Business centre. Concierge. Disabled-adapted rooms. Gym. Internet (high speed). Parking ($21/ 24hrs). Pool (outdoor). Restaurants (2). Room service (24hr). Spa. TV.

Sutton Place Hotel

845 Burrard Street, between Robson & Smithe Streets, V6Z 2K6 (604 682 5511/toll free 1-800 961 7555/www.vancouver.suttonplace. com). All city-centre buses. **Credit** AmEx, Disc, DC, MC, V. **Map** p249 K3 ❻

Since opening in 1986, the Sutton Place has established itself as the haven for visiting movie stars shooting in Hollywood North. This is an AAA Five Diamond hotel, with fine attention to detail and possibly the most attentive staff in the city. A recent $5million refurbishment means all the rooms are up-to-date, with new bedding, flatscreen TVs and DVD players, internet access and London's Gilchrist & Soames toiletries in the bathroom. A beautiful pool and jacuzzi with an outside terrace, a state of the art gym and the new, idyllic Vida Wellness Spa all make for a very luxurious stay.

Bar. Business centre. Concierge. Disabled-adapted rooms. Gym. Internet (high speed, wireless coming soon). Parking ($26/night). Pool (indoor). Restaurant. Room service (24hr). Spa. TV.

Wedgewood Hotel

845 Hornby Street, at Robson Street, V6Z 1V1 (604 689 7777/toll free 1-800 663 0666/www. wedgewoodhotel.com). All city-centre buses. **Rates** $225-$900 double. **Rooms** 83. **Credit** AmEx, DC, MC, V. **Map** p249 K3 ❼

This friendly, independent hotel is quite small with just 83 rooms and always has the most beautiful fresh-cut flowers on display. The rooms are ornate and spacious; some with fireplaces. The award-wining restaurant and bar Bacchus (*see p91*) is a favourite even with locals. Check out their intoxicating martini list or the traditional afternoon tea.

Bar. Business centre. Concierge. Disabled-adapted rooms. Gym. Internet (dataport, high speed wireless). Parking ($21.50/night). Restaurant. Room service (24hr). Spa. TV.

Expensive

Metropolitan Hotel Vancouver

645 Howe Street, between W Georgia & Dunsmuir Streets, V6C 2Y9 (604 687 1122/toll free 1-800 667 2300/www.metropolitan.com). All city-centre buses. **Rates** $195-$459 double. **Rooms** 197. **Credit** AmEx, DC, MC, V. **Map** p249 K3 ❽

Rooms feature Italian linen and duvets on oversized beds and great big soaker tubs – so if you're looking for more bed than space, this is a good place to stay. It has a skylighted lap pool too, and one of the city's most highly regarded restaurants: Diva at the Met (*see p95*). They're serious about their feng shui here, so if you want your bed to align with your Yan Nian or Tien Yi directions it's an ideal temporary domicile. And just to ensure the gods of luck stay on your side, rub the Chinese lion's head in the lobby on your way out to guarantee a lovely day.

Bar. Business centre. Concierge. Disabled-adapted rooms. Gym. Internet (high speed). Parking ($28/night). Pool (indoor). Restaurant. Room service (24hr). TV.

Sheraton Vancouver Wall Centre

*1088 Burrard Street, at Helmcken Street, V6Z 2R9
(604 331 1000/toll free 1-800 663 9255/www.
sheratonwallcentre.com). Bus 2, 22.* **Rates** $189-$399
double. **Rooms** 730. **Credit** AmEx, DC, Disc, MC, V.
Map p248 J4 ❾

Made up of two tall glass skyscrapers, the Wall
Centre dominates the Vancouver cityscape. Light
tubes at the pinnacle of each tower are 11m (36ft)
high and lit by a single 250 watt metal halide bulb
– a technology developed and patented at the
University of British Columbia but now used around
the world. With floor to ceiling windows, rooms on
any of the 40-plus floors offer almost uninterrupted
views of the ocean and mountains. The grand courtyard features waterfalls and a Roman-style, hand-
laid stone driveway. Rooms can be small but each
has a well-stocked refreshment centre.
*Bars (2). Business centre. Concierge. Disabled-
adapted rooms. Gym. Internet (high speed). Parking
($26/night). Pool (indoor). Restaurants (2). Room
service (24hr). Spa. TV.*

Terminal City Tower Hotel

*837 Hastings Street at Howe Street, V6C 1B6
(604 681 4121/toll free 1-888 253 8777/www.
tctowerhotel.com). Bus 2, 22.* **Rates** $159-$399
double. **Rooms** 60. **Credit** AmEx, DC, MC, V.
Map p249 L2 ❿

Sometimes you want to arrive in a city and be a part
of the club. Stay here and enjoy the privileges of
Vancouver's foremost private member's club, the
Terminal City Club, with its state of the art fitness
studio and swimming pool, historic billiards room,
library, restaurants and bar. A closely held secret of
its devoted regular guests, this 60-room boutique
hotel offers plush rooms with breakfast bar
(microwave oven and compact fridge) and suites
with full kitchen and ensuite dining for four.
*Bars (2). Business centre. Concierge. Disabled-
adapted rooms. Gym. Internet (high speed). Parking
($22.80/night). Pool (indoor). Restaurant. Room
service (6am-10pm). Spa. TV.*

Westin Grand

*433 Robson Street, at Homer Street, V6B 6L9
(604 602 1999/toll free 1-888 680 9393/www.westin
grandvancouver.com). Bus 15.* **Rates** $199-$279
double. **Rooms** 207. **Credit** AmEx, DC, Disc, MC, V.
Map p248 L4 ⓫

Located on the edge of Downtown and Yaletown,
this fully serviced boutique apartment hotel is chic,
central and reasonably priced. All the suites have
Westin's signature 'Heavenly Beds', as well as deep
soaker tubs in the spacious and grand bathrooms.
An efficient office space can be created with the
room's functional desk, two-line phone, and high
speed wireless internet access. It may be a high-
end chain in a pretty impressive building, but there
isn't much soul here.
*Bar. Business centre. Concierge. Disabled-adapted
rooms. Gym. Internet (dataport, high speed). Parking
($21/night). Pool (outdoor). Restaurant. Room service
(24hr). Spa. TV.*

Moderate

Century Plaza Hotel & Spa

*1015 Burrard Street, at Nelson Street, V6Z 1Y5
(604 687 0575/toll free 1-800 663 1818/www.
century-plaza.com). Bus 2, 22.* **Rates** $89-$209
double. **Rooms** 236. **Credit** AmEx, DC, MC, V.
Map p248 J3 ⓬

Although the Century Plaza has one of the best
spas and hair salons in the city, it is not a luxury
hotel. It is, however, a great place to stay downtown and relatively new decor is light and modern.
Regular studios and suites have large kitchenettes,
while the corporate suites look like a CEO's tower
office. Beyond Restaurant and Lounge is the hotel's
newest addition, a gorgeous space that serves allur-
ing contemporary cuisine. Check the website for
deals where a spa treatment or night out is thrown
in for less than the room-only rate. A comedic
bonus for guests: Yuk Yuk's comedy club (*see
p171*) is on the ground floor.
*Bars (2). Concierge (high-season only). Disabled-
adapted rooms. Internet (dataport on request,
high speed wireless). Parking ($12.75/day).
Pool (indoor). Restaurant. Room service (6.30am-
10pm). Spa. TV.*

Days Inn Vancouver Downtown

*921 W Pender Street, at Hornby Street, V6C 1M2
(604 681 4335/toll free 1-877 681 4335/www.
daysinnvancouver.com). All city-centre buses.*
Rates $109-$239 double. **Rooms** 85. **Credit**
AmEx, DC, MC, V. **Map** p249 K2 ⓭

With its European-meets-West Coast room design,
this chain hotel does have some personality – albeit
a tad on the busy bright side. Both rooms and one-
bedroom suites are mostly suitable for two people
but some can accommodate four. A complimentary
shuttle service (7am-7pm) services the cruise ship
terminals and Pacific Central (if you're catching a
train or bus out of town). Both the Chelsea
Restaurant and Lounge and Smiley O'Neal's are
good for sports enthusiasts, as the many TVs ensure
you won't miss what's going on.
*Bars (2). Internet (high speed). Parking ($16.95/day).
Restaurant. Room service (11am-10.30pm). TV.*

Howard Johnson

*1176 Granville Street, at Davie Street, V6Z 1L8
(604 688 8701/toll free 1-888 654 6336/www.hojo
vancouver.com). Bus 4, 6, 7, 10, 16, 17, 50.* **Rates**
$79-$279 double. **Rooms** 110. **Credit** AmEx, DC,
Disc, MC, V. **Map** p248 J4 ⓮

How things have changed. Howard Johnson used to
have a reputation as a family-friendly chain with
very little charm, but where you could always count
on a good ole Canadian pancake breakfast. But this
Ho-Jo is stylish and central. With 110 rooms over
five floors, you have the choice of rooms from twin,
double or queen right up to one-bedroom suites
with sofabeds. The prices are beyond reasonable
too, especially given the location. It's true Granville
Street can be noisy, but the hotel is just beyond the

Howard's stay

In 1972, Vancouver was abuzz with news that the elusive billionaire Howard Hughes was coming to town. He checked in to the Western International (now the Westin Bayshore; *see p45*) and stayed for six months – less a day.

His people called to reserve a number of rooms and, when told that the hotel was full, responded that Hughes would buy the place – just as he had done with the Desert Inn in Las Vegas in 1966. The top four floors were quickly made available for him and his entourage of Mormons, English boxer bodyguards and a personal chef. The lifts were shut off to these floors and surveillance cameras were installed.

From hang-gliders flying by to snap a photo, to cub reporters sneaking up the stairs attempting a scoop for the local paper, everyone was trying to get a glimpse of the reclusive Mr Hughes, who had not been photographed or seen in public for 15 years. But no one ever saw him – not that was reported anyway. It is rumoured that he went to an hockey game but that could be a myth.

Why Vancouver? Some say it was for his own security, others that he was involved with the CIA, or maybe for tax reasons, or to buy a local airline, or, well the list goes on. But a reliable source at the hotel insists it was for perhaps the most obvious of reasons: to see a woman: local actress/singer Yvonne de Carlo (Lily in TV's *The Munsters*).

When Hughes and his entourage left the hotel, staff found that plywood partitions had been erected, aluminium foil stuck on the windows and a huge mess left behind. The entire space (24 rooms) had to be completely refurbished. Today the Hughes Suite goes for up to $1,000 per night, depending on how many adjoining rooms you take.

Presumably because of de Carlo, Hughes's infamous visit wasn't his first, although it would prove to be his last. From Vancouver, he went to Nicaragua, then London, then Mexico for four years. He died during the flight back to Houston in April 1976.

Hughes had one further connection to British Columbia: his Spruce Goose plane (featured in the film *The Aviator*) was made of timber from the Queen Charlotte Islands.

concentration of bars and restaurants. Pancakes are still available at the Wing's Restaurant.
Bar. Concierge. Internet (wireless). Parking ($14/24hrs). Restaurant. Room service (7am-10pm). TV.

Rosedale on Robson

838 Hamilton Street, at Robson Street, V6B 6A2 (604 689 8033/toll free 1-800 661 8870/www. rosedaleonrobson.com). Bus 5. **Rates** $127-$225 suite. **Rooms** 203. **Credit** AmEx, DC, MC, V. **Map** p249 K4 ⑮

Offering one- and two-bedroom suites, the Rosedale is proudly independent. Top-floor rooms have been stylishly updated, and while other rooms don't quite impart anything beyond generic-hotel design, the Rosedale remains a very convenient, well-equipped, child-friendly place to stay, with a lovely indoor swimming pool that is big enough to do a few laps and a communal terrace that can be used year round. On the ground floor is Rosie's, a popular bar and grill.

Concierge. Disabled-adapted rooms. Gym. Internet (high speed). Parking ($11/day). Pool (indoor). Restaurant. Room service (7am-11pm). TV.

Budget

Bosman's Hotel

1060 Howe Street, between Nelson & Helmcken Streets, V6Z IP5 (604 682 3171/toll free 1-888 267 6267/www.bosmanshotel.com). Bus 4, 6, 7, 10, 16, 17, 50. **Rates** $79-$149 double. **Rooms** 100. **Credit** AmEx, DC, MC, V. **Map** p248 J4 ⑯

Bosman's is great value for its downtown location and lovely old heated outdoor swimming pool. You can overlook the slightly tacky decor in the lobby and rooms because they serve their purpose well and because the hotel is just so convenient. It's clean and the Grill on Ninth Avenue has inexpensive food.
Internet (pay terminal; high speed wireless in rooms). Parking (free). Pool (outdoor). Restaurant. TV.

Kingston Hotel Bed & Breakfast

757 Richards Street, between W Georgia & Robson Streets, V6B 3A6 (604 684 9024/toll free 1-888 713 3304/www.kingstonhotel vancouver.com). All city-centre buses. **Rates** $65-$155 double. **Rooms** 55. **Credit** AmEx, DC, MC, V. **Map** p249 K3 ⑰

Above the busy and well regarded Kingston Taphouse and Grille (*see p114*), the Kingston offers well-maintained single, double and twin bed rooms. Don't expect any extras, but you can count on a safe and central environment that is clean and a good price. Only 14 rooms have private bathrooms and TVs, the remaining 46 have sinks but you must share the shower and toilets located on each of the four floors. They play old movies in the communal lounge almost every evening and it is one of the few hotels that offers complimentary breakfast.

Internet (high speed wireless). Parking ($18/night). Sauna. TV (in some rooms).

YWCA

733 Beatty Street, at Robson Street, V6B 2M4 (604 895 5830/toll free 1-800 663 1424/www.ywcahotel. com). Bus 15. **Rates** $72-$137 single/double. **Rooms** 155. **Credit** AmEx, DC, MC, V. **Map** p249 L4 ⑱

Surprisingly immaculate and modern, the Y offers a good selection of rooms: ranging from a single bed with desk, to double doubles (two beds for four people), to quints (five single beds). Rates are very reasonable considering the area and the fact that part of the proceeds goes towards helping families, women and children in need. Unlike a hostel, here the rooms are not shared; it isn't a dormitory, so you only share with people you're travelling with. There's a fitness centre that includes a swimming pool, steam room, gym and aerobics studios.

Disabled-adapted rooms. Gym. Internet (pay terminal). Parking ($9/night). Pool (indoor). TV.

West End

Luxury

Loden Vancouver

1177 Melville Street, between Bute & Thurlow Streets, Coal Harbour, West End V6E 0A3 (604 669 5060/ toll free 1-877 632 3030/www.lodenvancouver.com). All city-centre buses. **Rates** $200-$250 double. **Rooms** 77. **Credit** AmEx, DC, MC, V. **Map** p249 K2 ⑲

After endless delays, the opening of this monument to modern design was imminent as this guide went to press. The talk of the town, the Loden's 77 deluxe rooms include six one-bedroom suites and a 1,600 square foot two-bedroom penthouse suite, with indoor and outdoor entertaining and dining areas. All rooms have heated bathroom floors, floor-to-ceiling operable windows and entertainment centre with 42in flatscreen TV. Chef Marc-André Choquette, formerly the number two at Lumiere, heads up the kitchen at signature restaurant, Voya.

Bar. Disabled-adapted rooms. Gym. Internet (dataport, web TV). Parking ($28/night). Restaurant. Room service (6.30am-10pm). Spa. TV.

Westin Bayshore

1601 Bayshore Drive, at Cardero Street, V6G 2V4 (604 682 3377/www.westin.com/bayshore). Bus 5, then 5min walk. **Rates** $229-$579 double. **Rooms** 510. **Credit** AmEx, DC, Disc, MC, V. **Map** p248 J2 ⑳

A classic Vancouver luxury hotel since 1930, the Bayshore had the first high-end hotel restaurant in town, Trader Vic's (now the more casual Seawall Bar and Grill). It feels like a holiday resort in the midst of the city, with its West Coast modernist architecture and heated outdoor pool looking out to sea. Howard Hughes (*see p44* **Howard's stay**), Prince Charles and Tina Turner have all stayed. The Bayshore now features the 'Heavenly Bed', made up of a bespoke pillow-top mattress, down duvet, crisp sheets and five plush pillows. They also have a free shuttle service, a hair salon, boat rentals and golfing packages.

Bar. Business centre. Concierge. Disabled-adapted rooms. Gym. Internet (dataport, or wireless on request). Parking ($23/night). Pools (1 indoor, 1 outdoor). Restaurant. Room service (24hr). TV.

Expensive

Listel Hotel

1300 Robson Street, at Jervis Street, V6E 1C5 (604 684 8461/toll free 1-800 663 5491/www.thelistel hotel.com). Bus 5. **Rates** $129-$600 double. **Rooms** 129. **Credit** AmEx, DC, Disc, MC, V. **Map** p248 J2 ㉑

Their relationship with one of the city's leading commercial galleries, Buschlen Mowatt (*see p151*), provides the Listel with an impressive collection of contemporary art in the lobby, and in all the rooms on the fourth and fifth floors. The hotel hosts a complimentary BC wine reception for guests every Tuesday and Thursday, between 5pm and 6pm. The lifts and hallways are a bit gloomy but O'Douls is a lively bar and restaurant with live jazz most nights. Aveda and local Deserving Thyme products are featured in the large bathrooms. *Photo p47.*

Bar. Concierge. Disabled-adapted rooms. Gym. Internet (wireless). Parking ($24/night). Restaurant. Room service (6.30am-11pm). TV.

Pacific Palisades Hotel

1277 Robson Street, between Bute & Jervis Streets, V6E 1C4 (604 688 0461/toll free 1-800 663 1815/ www.pacificpalisadeshotel.com). Bus 5. **Rates** $125-$390 suite. **Rooms** 233. **Credit** AmEx, DC, Disc, MC, V. **Map** p248 J2 ㉒

If you're hoping for a Hollywood encounter in Los Angeles' damper northern suburb, then the Pacific Palisades is the place to stay. It's popular with film and TV stars on location, as the hotel offers fully serviced luxury suites with long-term rental rates, as well as film and television production offices. Evening receptions with complimentary wine offer mingling opportunities. Bright and friendly, the hotel is big on environmentally friendly features). Pet-friendly amenities include a welcoming 'four paws program' and a designated animal corner

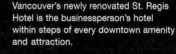

with, of course, a photographer available upon request. Check their website for specials, which can be half the rate card price.
Bar. Business centre. Concierge. Disabled-adapted rooms. Gym. Internet (high speed). Parking ($24/night; $12 if you drive a hybrid). Pool (indoor). Restaurant. Room service (7am-midnight). Spa. TV.

Moderate

Blue Horizon Hotel
1225 Robson Street, at Bute Street, V6E 1C3 (604 688 1411/toll free 1-800 663 1333/www.bluehorizon hotel.com). Bus 5. **Rates** $109-$299 double. **Rooms** 214. **Credit** AmEx, DC, MC, V. **Map** p248 J2 ㉓
Whirlpool, lap pool, sauna and treadmills – all at an affordable price and, what's more, in the centre of town. Awarded the Green Hotel award in recognition of its sustainability practices, Blue Horizon is a pleasingly conscientious place to stay. The spacious rooms have private balconies and the higher floors get the benefit of Vancouver's spectacular scenery. An outdoor café overlooks Robson Street in the summer, and there are two popular eateries open year round: Inlets Bistro (West Coast cuisine) and Shenanigan's sports bar and nightclub.
Bar. Gym. Internet (high speed). Parking ($14/day). Pool (indoor). Restaurants (2). TV.

Coast Plaza Hotel & Suites
1763 Comox Street, at Denman Street, V6G 1P6 (604 688 7711/toll free 1-800 716 6199/www.coast hotels.com). Bus 6. **Rates** $199-$799 suite. **Rooms** 269. **Credit** AmEx, DC, MC, V. **Map** p248 H2 ㉔
One of the most popular hotels in the city because of its good value and location – fitness centre and pool membership are included in the room rate and Delilah's, a restaurant famous for Martinis and elaborate menus, is practically next door. Pet-friendly

rooms, large suites, private balconies with big views – and even a 400-seat cinema for private hire.
Bar. Business centre. Concierge. Gym. Internet (high speed). Parking ($17/night). Pool (indoor). Restaurants (2). Room service (24hr). TV.

Empire Landmark Hotel
1400 Robson Street, at Broughton Street, V6G 1B9 (604 687 0511/toll free 1-800 830 6144/www. empirelandmarkhotel.com). Bus 5. **Rates** $89-$210 double. **Rooms** 357. **Credit** AmEx, DC, MC, V. **Map** p248 J2 ㉕
This hotel boasts the revolving bar and restaurant Cloud 9 at its apex on the 42nd floor. There's a bit of a convention centre feel but the rooms are spacious – if garish. In contrast, the fitness room is fantastic, complete with a whirlpool and cedar wood sauna. A stark yet functional lobby includes a car rental and sightseeing tour desk, a visitor information kiosk and a business centre conveniently located near the entrance. Discounts gives guests 5-40% off at a wide range of shops in the area.
Bar. Business centre. Disabled-adapted rooms. Gym. Internet (dataport). Parking ($10/night). Restaurants (2). TV.

Riviera Hotel
1431 Robson Street, between Broughton & Nicola Streets, V6G 1C1 (604 685 1301/toll free 1-888 699 5222/www.rivieraonrobson.com). Bus 5. **Rates** $78-$188 suite. **Rooms** 41. **Credit** AmEx, DC, Disc, MC, V. **Map** p248 J2 ㉖
The hallways of this moderately priced hotel feel like a slice of the south of France transplanted to the rather wetter environs of the West End of Vancouver. Although the rooms are basic, the separate bedrooms and fully equipped kitchenettes make this a perfect place for a family or a group. All the rooms feature a view, and higher floors have balconies.
Concierge. Parking (free). TV.

Listel Hotel. *See p45.*

Sunset Inn & Suites

1111 Burnaby Street, at Thurlow Street, V6E 1P4
(604 688 2474/toll free 1-800 786 1997/www.sunset
inn.com). Bus 6. **Rates** $109-$299 suite. **Rooms** 50.
Credit AmEx, DC, MC, V. **Map** p248 H4 ㉗
The Sunset Inn is a cheery place offering a choice
of newly renovated, studio, standard or large
rooms, to be rented by the night, week or month.
The country-home style rooms include fully
equipped kitchens, private balconies, and partial
views of the beaches or mountains. Front desk staff
are very friendly and helpful, and the website
includes a daily weather forecast and other useful
links for visitors to the city.
Gym. Internet (wireless). Parking (free). TV.

Sylvia Hotel

1154 Gilford Street, at Beach Avenue, V6G 2P6
(604 681 9321/www.sylviahotel.com). Bus 6. **Rates**
$95-$200 double. **Rooms** 120. **Credit** AmEx, DC,
MC, V. **Map** p248 G2 ㉘
You really can't get much closer to the beach or
Stanley Park than the Sylvia. Opened in 1913, this
hotel started out as an apartment block, but was
converted into a hotel in 1936 to help provide accommodation for merchant marine crews during the
Depression. In 1954, the hotel opened the first cocktail bar in Vancouver, one that remains a local
favourite today. Eight floors high, the Sylvia was
once the tallest building in western Canada and is
now listed and a city landmark, with Virginia vines
growing up the light brick exterior. The rooms range
from small singles to two-bed suites with kitchens.
Bar. Internet (high speed wireless) Parking ($10/night).
Restaurant. Room service (7am-11pm). TV.

Budget

Buchan Hotel

1906 Haro Street, at Gilford Street, V6G 1H7 (604
685 5354/toll free 1-800 668 6654/www.buchan
hotel.com). Bus 5. **Rates** $45-$135 double. **Rooms**
60. **Credit** AmEx, DC, MC, V. **Map** p248 H2 ㉙
Built in 1926, the Buchan is a small hotel with a big,
old house feel. It is ideally located for those wanting
easy access to Stanley Park and, though far from
luxurious, the price is right and the rooms are clean.
No breakfast, but free coffee is provided. Tucked
beneath is one of the city's best and most romantic
restaurants, Parkside *(see p100).*
Internet (high speed wireless). TV.

Bed & breakfasts

Barclay House

1351 Barclay Street, between Jervis & Broughton
Streets, V6E 1H6 (604 605 1351/www.barclay
house.com). Bus 5. **Rates** $155-$295 double. **Rooms**
6. **Credit** AmEx, DC, MC, V. **Map** p248 J3 ㉚
The winner of many best bed and breakfast awards
and accolades, Barclay House, with its vintage
chandeliers and crisp white linen, is the most sophisticated B&B you'll find in Vancouver. The restored
heritage building offers a gourmet three-course hot
breakfast, including organic coffee and speciality
teas. The spacious rooms boast en suite bathrooms
complete with either clawfoot tub or power shower
and gorgeous, luxuriously thick terry cloth robes.
Nice touches include a selection of newspapers,

'O Canada' House exhibits its lovely late-Victorian style inside and out.

magazines and DVDs, free evening sherry, Deserving Thyme products in the bathrooms, and cookies and bottled water delivered to your room every day.
Concierge. Internet (wireless). Parking (free). TV.

English Bay Inn
1968 Comox Street, between Gilford & Chilco Streets, V6G 1R4 (604 683 8002/toll free 1-866 683 8002/www.englishbayinn.com). Bus 6. **Rates** $139-$235 double. **Rooms** 6. **Credit** AmEx, DC, Disc, MC, V. **Map** p248 G2 ③
The Inn is a charming Tudor-style house that looks like its been transplanted from leafy Surrey to the even leafier West End. Should you wake up one morning and think you're on the wrong continent a glance outside at the surrounding, resolutely north American, residential high-rises will soon set your perceptions right. The main floor has a communal living room with chintzy sofas, antiques and a big fireplace, plus an adjacent dining room with Chippendale furniture. Of the four rooms and two suites, the Secluded Getaway is particularly nice.
Concierge. Internet (high speed wireless). Parking (free). TV.

'O Canada' House
1114 Barclay Street, at Thurlow Street, V6E 1H1 (604 688 0555/toll free 1-877 688 1114/www. ocanadahouse.com). Bus 5. **Rates** $135-$285 suite. **Rooms** 7. **Credit** DC, MC, V. **Map** p248 J3 ②
In a house built in 1897, this B&B maintains its late-Victorian style and feel. Its name comes from the Canadian National Anthem, O Canada, written by the original owner of the house, Mr Ewing Buchan. If it's available, try to book the cottage, with French doors that open on to a private terrace. Breakfast ranges from simple toast and coffee to waffles and maple syrup and eggs Benedict. The back garden and the front porch are tranquil places to rest between bouts of sightseeing – or to enjoy your nightly complimentary sherry. Note that children under 12 and pets are not allowed.
Concierge. Internet (wireless). Parking (free). TV.

Gastown

Budget

Victorian Hotel
514 Homer Street, at W Pender Street, V6B 2V6 (604 681 6369/toll free1-877 681 6369/www. victorianhotel.ca). All city-centre buses. **Rates** $60-$189 double. **Rooms** 39. **Credit** AmEx, DC, Disc, MC, V. **Map** p249 L3 ③
As soon as you step into the lobby of this lovely, European-style pension, you'll feel like you have discovered a special place. An old-world charm permeates everything at the Victorian Hotel, from the quietly polite staff at the wood-burning fireplace, to the floral wallpaper in your room (not to mention the claw foot soaker tub). Built in 1898 as one of the first guest houses in Vancouver, the Victorian Hotel's lovingly restored hardwood floors, intricate

Victorian Hotel.

moldings, high ceilings and exquisite bathrooms make an apt setting for beautiful period furniture.
Concierge. Internet (high speed). TV.

Yaletown

Luxury

Opus Hotel
322 Davie Street, between Hamilton & Mainland Streets, V6B 5Z6 (604 642 6787/toll free 1-866 642 6787/www.opushotel.com). Bus 15. **Rates** $199-$379 double. **Rooms** 96. **Credit** AmEx, DC, MC, V. **Map** p249 K5 ③
Voted one of the world's Top 100 Hotels by *Condé Nast Traveler* in 2005, Opus has a reputation for being hip and luxurious without attitude. Rooms feature five decor schemes, ranging from modern and minimalist to artful and eclectic – designed to appeal to particular personality types. The penthouse suite ($2,129/night) is nick-named the 'Diva Suite' since Jennifer Lopez, Gwen Stefani, Christina Aguilera, Cher and Shakira have all bedded under the African zebra bedspreads. We've heard reports that service is not always tip-top if you're not part of the jet set. *Photo p52.*
Bar. Business centre. Concierge. Disabled-adapted rooms. Gym. Internet (wireless and wired high speed). Mountain bike hire (free). Parking ($25/night). Restaurant. Room service (24hr). Spa. TV.

www.treesforcities.org

Trees for Cities
Charity registration number 1032154

Travelling creates so
many lasting memories.

Make your trip mean
something for years to
come - not just for you
but for the environment
and for people living in
deprived urban areas.

Anyone can offset their
flights, but when your
plant trees with Trees for
Cities, you'll help create
a green space for an
urban community that
really needs it.

Leave
Your
Mark

Create a green future for cities.

West Side

Expensive

Granville Island Hotel

*1253 Johnston Street, Granville Island, V6H 3R9
(604 683 7373/toll free 1-800 663 1840/www.
granvilleislandhotel.com). Bus 50, then 5min walk.*
Rates $150-$230 double. **Rooms** 85. **Credit** AmEx,
DC, Disc, MC, V. **Map** p248 J5 & p250 D4 ⑤

Far enough from the main public market area to
avoid the crowds but close enough to walk to in minutes, this hotel boasts a spectacular view looking
east out over False Creek, quite different from any
other establishment in a city well endowed with
spectacular outlooks. A low-rise, contemporary
West Coast building studded with windows, it features tasteful rooms, some overlooking the water
with classic wooden shutters, some with local style,
post-and-beam architecture, some even more elaborate, with marble floors and Persian rugs. Six suites
with floor to ceiling windows allow you to watch the
Aquabus ferries, kayaks and houseboats do their
thing on the water below. The Dockside bar and
restaurant can get quite busy on weekends.
*Bar. Concierge. Disabled-adapted rooms. Internet
(high speed). Parking ($12/night). Restaurant.
Room service (7am-10pm). TV.*

Bed & breakfasts

Alma Beach

*3756 W 2nd Avenue, between Alma & Highbury
Streets, V6R 1J9 (604-221-1950/toll free 1-866 221
1950/www.almabeachvancouver.com). Bus 2, 22.*
Rates $139-$169 double. **Rooms** 4. **Credit** DC,
MC, V. **Map** p251 B5 ㊱

Beautifully situated one block from Jericho Beach
and the Vancouver Yacht Club, this peaceful B&B
is a minute's walk from windsurfing, swimming and
beaching and a ten-minute drive to downtown. Each
generously sized room has a brass bed covered with
a luxurious silk duvet, a jacuzzi tub and heated towel
racks. Breakfast should be your dinner here; the affable owners love to cook and they'll prepare a
gourmet feast if it's your pleasure. Alma Beach also
features a self-contained, one-bedroom apartment
with private entrance and its own garden patio.
Internet (wireless). Parking (free). TV.

Hycroft

*1248 W 15th Avenue, between Birch & Alder Streets,
V6H 1R8 (604 307 2300/www.hycroft.com). Bus 10,
17.* **Rates** $110-$350 suite. **Rooms** 3. **Credit** AmEx,
DC, MC, V. **Map** p251 J8 ㊲

This high-end B&B is a fully restored 1929 house
on the edge of Shaughnessy and all its beautiful big
old houses – perfect for a walk or jog around. There's
a choice of a one- or two-bedroom suite, both with
kitchen and bathroom. Fireplaces and heated slate
flooring are nice features, plus there's a private
entrance for guests, so you don't feel like you're
walking in through someone else's living room.
Internet (high speed). Parking (free). TV.

Mickey's Kits Beach Chalet

*2142 W 1st Avenue, between Yew & Arbutus
Streets, V6K 1E8 (604 739 3342/toll free 1-888
739 3342/www.mickeysbandb.com). Bus 2, 22.*
Rates $95-$165 double. **Rooms** 3. **Credit** AmEx,
DC, MC, V. **Map** p251 F5 ㊳

Location, location, location. That's the key to
Mickey's. It's close to Vancouver's liveliest beach,
Kits, and only a five minute bus or cab ride to downtown. Three different rooms accommodate everyone
from a single traveller to a family or small group.

Granville Island Hotel.

Opus Hotel's style-conscious design extends from reception to the guest rooms. *See p49.*

The York Room has a kingsize bed (but could also be made up as two single beds), the south-facing Arbutus Room is perfect for sunlight (if it's not raining) and the Yew Room has a kingsize bed and pull-out sofa in a separate living area with a wood burning fireplace. Mickey's takes pride in catering to their guests' needs, especially dietary – just let them know when you make your booking.
Internet (wireless). Parking (free). TV.

North Shore

Moderate

Lonsdale Quay Hotel

123 Carrie Cates Court, at Rogers Avenue, Lonsdale Quay, V7M 3K7 (604 986 6111/www.lonsdale quayhotel.com). SeaBus Lonsdale Quay. **Rates** $149-$189 double. **Rooms** 70. **Credit** AmEx, DC, MC, V. **Map** p253 Z5 ⓷⓽
The Lonsdale Quay Hotel is part of the Lonsdale Quay market development, which is being built within close proximity to the North Shore mountains. Lovely big rooms or suites boast great city and harbour views and downtown is just a SeaBus ride away. The hotel is child-friendly and there are even two suites that come with kids' rooms – including a TV, VCR and single bunk bed with slide.
Bar. Disabled-adapted rooms. Gym. Internet (high speed). Parking ($7/night). Restaurant. Room service (7am-9pm). TV.

Budget

Horseshoe Bay Motel

6588 Royal Avenue, at Bruce Street, West Vancouver, V7W 2B6 (604 921 7454/toll free 1-877 717 3377). Bus 250, 257. **Rates** $89-$119 double. **Rooms** 23. **Credit** AmEx, DC, MC, V.
If you're setting off from Vancouver to the wide open spaces of BC, this is an option. From Horseshoe Bay you catch the ferry to Nanaimo, Bowen Island and the Sunshine Coast. It is also the last stopping place before Squamish on the road to Whistler. You can catch a glimpse of the water and ferry activity from the motel, but you might have to stand on tippy toes to do it. Rooms are fine but basic, with en suite bathrooms and TVs. The staff are a bit indifferent and the hotel doesn't offer any services, but if you're catching an early ferry or you get in late, it'll do. You can grab a coffee on the nearby pier or a full breakfast at the Boathouse Restaurant at the marina.
Internet (high speed wireless). TV.

Hostels

Hostelling International – Vancouver Central

1025 Granville Street, at Nelson Street, Downtown, V6Z 1L4 (604 685 5335/toll free 1-888 203 8333/www.hihostels.ca/vancouvercentral). Bus 4, 6, 7, 10, 16, 17, 50. **Rates** $28-$31 dorm; $66-$81

private room. **Rooms** 140 dorm beds; 38 private rooms. **Credit** DC, MC, V. **Map** p249 K4 ⓸⓪
The most central and newest of the three HIs, this is a fun place to stay, with comfy, quality beds, free linen and clean private bathrooms. No surprise it has won HI's Cool Atmosphere, Ideal for City Beat and Out of This World hostel awards. Like, totally.
Bar. Internet (pay terminal). Restaurant.

Hostelling International – Vancouver Downtown

1114 Burnaby Street, at Thurlow Street, West End, V6E 1P1 (604 684 4565/toll free 1-888 203 4302/www.hihostels.ca/vancouverdowntown). Bus 2, 6, 22. **Rates** $29-$34 dorm; $70-$88 private room. **Rooms** 180 dorm beds; 23 private rooms. **Credit** DC, MC, V. **Map** p248 H4 ⓸⓵
Despite the 'downtown' in its name, this HI is in the West End. Bike rentals and daily tours/activities around the city are offered. A family friendly place, it also caters well to the backpacker, with free daily breakfasts. Friendly, experienced staff will point you in the right direction for local grocery stores cultural fulfilment.
Internet (wireless & kiosk). Parking (free, limited).

Hostelling International – Vancouver Jericho Beach

1515 Discovery Street, West Side, V6R 4K5 (604 224 3208/toll free 1-888 203 4303/www.hihostels.ca/vancouverjerichobeach). Bus 4, then 5min walk. **Rates** $20-$27 dorm; $63-$71 private room. **Rooms** 200 dorm beds; 10 private rooms. **Credit** DC, MC, V.
Only open May-Sept, this HI is the most interesting in terms of architecture (ex barracks) and location (on the beach), although it is far from the centre of town (and any amenities). To compensate for the distance, they offer a free shuttle service to and from downtown. Shared and private rooms, a great licenced café, a big communal kitchen and loads of sporting equipment to use at the nearby beach makes for a flexible stay.
Internet (pay terminal). Parking ($5/24hrs).

SameSun Backpacker Lodge

1018 Granville Street, at Nelson Street, Downtown, V6Z 1L5 (604 682 8226/toll free 1-877 562 2783/www.samesun.com). Bus 4, 6, 7, 10, 16, 17, 50. **Rates** $25-$29.50 dorm; $70-$80 private room. **Rooms** 247 dorm beds; 9 private rooms. **Credit** DC, MC, V. **Map** p249 K4 ⓸⓶
As they aim to 'maximise your mingling' the SameSun is ideal for lone backpackers or travellers looking to meet young, like-minded people on shoestring budgets. It's raucous and noisy but also fun and very, very central. The Beaver bar provides good value food and drinks (and a DJ Saturday nights) and the desk sells cheap Vancouver Canucks hockey game tickets and Big Kahuna ski packages. The social director will tell you all about the best bars and clubs in town, and may even join you. Not one for those who value peace and quiet.
Bar. Internet (pay terminal; high speed wireless).

Sightseeing

Features

Maps

Grouse Mountain Skyride. *See p82.*

Introduction

Location, location, location.

If you had to pick a perfect spot to build a city, Vancouver wouldn't be a bad place to start. Look up and take in the snow-capped mountains. Walk 20 minutes from downtown and relax on a beach or in Stanley Park. Ski in the morning, sail in the afternoon, and eat exceptionally well as the sun sets over the Strait of Georgia.

A combination of happenstance, civic activism and clever urban planning, Vancouver's vibrant downtown – a thriving mix of office towers, shopping districts and high-density apartment developments that has brought a stream of residents into the city centre over the last decade – is now an international benchmark. 'The Vancouver Model', as it's called, is being replicated around the world, from nearby Portland, Oregon to far-off Dubai, whose sultan has built a full-scale replica of False Creek.

Downtown Vancouver is a large peninsula, bordered on three sides – north, west and south – by water, and capped by the vast green expanse of **Stanley Park**. To the east lie the more troubled but vibrant communities of East Vancouver. **Gastown**, the city's main tourist district, was historically the city centre but lost its importance as power moved west, to the business canyons of Howe Street and across the Cambie Street bridge to City Hall.

Gastown is currently undergoing a revival, as the planners and developers responsible for the Vancouver Model search out innovative ways to revive the area, still suffering from its proximity to Hastings and Main Streets (the notorious Downtown Eastside). Connecting the suits and ties of the central business district and the densely packed neighbourhood of the **West End** lies the glittering retail strip of Robson Street. Among Downtown's man-made highlights are the **Vancouver Public Library**, the **Vancouver Art Gallery** and the shiny new towers lining the waterfront at **Coal Harbour** and **Yaletown**.

Downtown includes the second largest **Chinatown** in North America, after San Francisco, and **East Vancouver** offers the lively Commercial Drive district and the hipster neighbourhood that stretches along Main Street. Over the Lions Gate and Second Narrows Bridges, the **North Shore** has the mountains, hiking and more great beaches.

High-tech **Science World** (*see p59*) appeals especially to children, as does the best way there...

The city's museums are mostly located on the **West Side**, in the Kitsilano/Point Grey area south-west from downtown across the Burrard Bridge; the **Museum of Anthropology** here is a must-see. This neighbourhood is celebrated for its long strip of sandy beaches (running all the way west to **Pacific Spirit Regional Park**) and for some spectacular parks and gardens. It's also on the West Side that you'll find **Granville Island**, with its maze of artist's studios, artisan stores and indoor market.

All across Vancouver you'll find good food, quirky shopping and varied (if not always distinguished) architecture. But most of the pleasures derive from its setting in the midst of a temperate rainforest, the vistas of mountains that appear at the end of busy downtown streets, the sparkling waters of English Bay, and the everyday epiphanies that come from the mix of city and nature so closely entwined.

Getting around

A small and compact city by North American standards, Vancouver is easy to negotiate on foot, at least until you venture to the North Shore. **TransLink** oversees an efficient public transport system; the bus service is as good as the sometimes congested roads allow, and the bus drivers tend to be remarkably sympathetic, offering travel advice and turning a blind eye if you don't have the exact change ($2.50 buys you 90 minutes' travel anywhere in zone 1).

Two **SkyTrain** lines serve commuters from sprawling East Vancouver and Surrey, and allow tourists a reliable means to access Science World, Commercial Drive or Canada's second-largest shopping mall, Metropolis at Metrotown. The Waterfront transport nexus close to the sails of Canada Place is also the terminal for the **SeaBus** to North Vancouver. A third SkyTrain route, the **Canada Line**, is due to begin running between Richmond, the airport and downtown Vancouver in 2009.

For details of tours – by coach, trolley car, horse-drawn carriage, boat and seaplane – *see p61* **Tickets to ride** and the Getting Around section of the Directory.

Mostly, though, visitors base themselves in Downtown and rarely stray far beyond Kitsilano Beach on the West Side, Chinatown to the east, VanDusen gardens to the south and Grouse Mountain to the north – all located within a 30-minute bus ride of Robson Square.

ORIENTATION

Streets run in gridlike blocks and street numbers climb 100 per block as you head south from Canada Place pier or west from Carrall Street (in downtown) or Ontario Street (the West Side). (East of Main Street, the street numbers climb again and take on the prefix East.) Note that suite or room numbers precede the building number in addresses. It sounds confusing but it seems to work. If you do lose your bearings, look for the mountains – always due north.

The best Sights

Beaches
Vancouver's a watery delight, with four beaches downtown, more on the North Shore and an ace strand on the West Side. *See p72* and *p85* **The shore thing**.

Granville Island
A bustling community hub on the water's edge, with a covered market, theatres and artist's studios. *See p71.*

Grouse Mountain
Take a cable car up the local slope for amazing views. Or pit your wits against the elements and try the Grouse Grind. *See p82* **High jinx**.

Stanley Park
No trip to Vancouver is complete without a visit to this expanse of cedar and fir trees, wrapped by the scenic Seawall. *See p66.*

board a tiny ferry from Granville Island. *See p71.*

Downtown

A city by the sea.

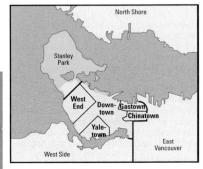

Map pp248-249

Downtown

Small is beautiful. The ocean placed a natural cap on Vancouver's urban sprawl. When the population started booming, builders found the only way to go was up – with the result that the downtown core of this 21st-century city remains eminently walkable. And that's definitely the best way to appreciate it.

When planning your sightseeing, you could easily organise it as a series of walks radiating out from the centre of town, usually considered to be the Vancouver Art Gallery. You don't have to stray far to cover the bases: shopping, great restaurants, beaches and nature are cheek-by-jowl and you can taste them all in a day – though you'll need longer to savour them.

The city's premier cultural institute, the **Vancouver Art Gallery** (VAG), stands at the very heart of downtown on Robson Square. The building started life as Vancouver's courthouse when the Francis Rattenbury-designed building opened in 1911. Arthur Erickson renovated the interior of the gallery in 1983 (he also designed the radical new Law Courts Building, which stands across the way at 800 Smithe Street) but big changes are planned this year to house the growing collection. The Gallery Café's patio (*see p90*) is a wonderful oasis for a glass of chilled white wine on a sunny summer day.

Nearby at 639 Hornby is the new home of the Bill Reid Foundation, the **Bill Reid Gallery of Northwest Coast Art** (*see p31* **Reid all about it**). It took five years for the foundation to find a suitable home to honor the life and works of the late Bill Reid, Vancouver's best-known First Nations artist. The gallery plans to exhibit a significant First Nations art collection, and also house the foundation's library of Coast Salish culture and art.

Two blocks east of Robson Square is Granville Street. One of the city's main arteries, the stretch running south from Robson to the Granville Bridge is known as the Entertainment District. Once home to many cinemas and theatres, few of which survive, it's now where you'll find the greatest cluster of clubs and bars.

A block north-west of Robson Square, the sandstone gothic revival **Christ Church Cathedral** (690 Burrard Street, 604 682 8441) is a mere stripling by European standards but, completed in 1895, it's the oldest surviving church in Vancouver. Be sure to check out the results of the 2004 $8.6 million restoration, which refurbished the 1895 Douglas fir floor and ceiling, once hidden behind white acoustic panels. For a different kind of cathedral, try the nearby HSBC building, at 885 W Georgia Street, long considered to be one of the city's finest examples of high-capitalist architecture (circa 1987), and home to the Pendulum Gallery, with its 27 metre (80 foot) aluminium pendulum.

From Hornby to Bute, Robson Street is the city's main see-and-be-seen promenade, an orgiastic display of high-end chain shopping and exclusive boutiques. Once fondly known as 'Robsonstrasse' for the preponderance of European merchants who lined its modest pavements, the area has vastly changed. Weekend evenings see bumper-to-bumper traffic as young men from the suburbs crawl along in tricked-out vehicles in a pre-clubbing ritual. From Bute to Denman, Robson's retail scene slowly peters out, but continue down the hill and you'll find yourself in the Asian student district, with its bars and restaurants.

North of Robson, **Coal Harbour** is Vancouver's newest downtown residential district, a shining spread of office towers and apartment blocks with stunning views and a charming seafront walk along Burrard Inlet. The Seawall starts at the foot of Burrard and continues into the West End and Stanley Park. Along the way are several fair-to-middling places to eat – Vancouver is still trying to solve the good food/good view conundrum. Of these, Lift Bar & Grill (*see p99*) is the most ambitious.

Jutting out into Burrard Inlet at the foot of Burrard and Howe Streets, **Canada Place** (999 Canada Place, 604 775 7200) is probably downtown's most photographed spot. A cruise ship terminal, IMAX movie theatre, convention centre, and restaurant and hotel complex, the sail-like structure is a legacy of the city's first large-scale international event, Expo 86 (*see p18*). Currently being built is a western extension to the convention centre which juts out over the waterfront. From the inside, its glass walls should provide a stunning outlook, but its most architecturally innovative touch is meant to be a 'living roof', less a roof garden than a roof park. It's due to open early in 2009.

While in the vicinity, take a moment to notice the beauty of the venerable **Marine Building**, at the corner of Burrard and W Hastings. Inspired by New York's Chrysler Building, the circa-1920 Marine was the tallest 'skyscraper' in the city until 1939. An art deco treasure, it is decorated with all manner of nautical motifs (sea snails, crabs, turtles, scallops, sea horses and so on) and the exterior is studded with flora and fauna in sea-green and gold.

Heading east brings you to **Waterfront Station** (601 W Cordova Street), the downtown transit hub. This handsome red-stone building between Granville and Seymour was built by the Canadian Pacific Railway in 1914 as the terminus of its transcontinental passenger trains. The beaux arts interiors were restored to their original glory in the late 1970s.

On your way to Gastown you may pass by the **Harbour Centre** (555 W Hastings Street, 604 689 7304), an undistinguished mall, capped by the Vancouver Lookout observation tower and the overpriced Top of Vancouver Revolving Restaurant (604 669 2220). The lookout tower offers panoramic views of the city accessed by an external glass lift. At 177 metres (581 feet) it's currently the tallest building in BC, but not for much longer; a revision in city planning rules has allowed up to half a dozen developers to up the ante.

The downtown area borders False Creek north of Yaletown. It's the one district given over to typical North American freeway-style development. Save for a family day out at **Science World** (1455 Quebec Street; *see p142*), tourists are unlikely to venture here, unless it's to take in a game at the sports nexus of the city: **General Motors Place** and its neighbour, BC Place. The 16,000-seater GM Place is the brash upstart of the two, built in 1995 as home to the vastly popular Vancouver Canucks hockey team, a '70s-era franchise that has never quite captured the Stanley Cup but still has the hearts of most citizens in a vice-like grasp. Music concerts are frequently hosted here (*see p161*). BC Place, a legacy/relic of Expo 86, is famous for its vast air-supported dome and white elephant status. A 60,000-seater, it's home to the BC Lions football team and will host the opening and closing ceremonies for the Winter Olympics, 2010. Stadium tours depart Gate H

Sightseeing

The sail-like roofs of **Canada Place** have become a Vancouver landmark.

every Friday, mid-June through September at 11am and 1pm, and at Gate A there's the **BC Sports Hall of Fame and Museum**.

Heading west up Robson Street from BC Place you'll find another of the city's more controversial buildings, the **Vancouver Public Library** (350 W Georgia Street, 604 331 3603). Debuting in 1995 at a cost of more than $100 million, the Moshe Safdie-designed structure's fans and many users are delighted by its handsome lines and ease of use. Detractors wonder why a modern building in Vancouver resembles Rome's Colosseum.

BC Sports Hall of Fame & Museum

Gate A, BC Place Stadium, 777 Pacific Boulevard South, at Expo Boulevard (604 687 5520/www. bcsportshalloffame.com). Bus 15/SkyTrain Stadium. **Open** 10am-5pm daily. **Admission** $10; $8 reductions; $25 family. **Credit** AmEx, DC, MC, V. **Map** p249 L4.

Unless you have a keen interest in BC sports heroes represented by shirts, trophies and faded photos, this modest exhibit inside BC Place stadium isn't likely to detain you. An interactive room with a ball pit and table hockey will amuse children for a while, and a couple of internal windows reveal the football field far below. A gallery dedicated to Canadian hero Terry Fox (who lost a leg to cancer but made it his mission to run coast to coast) is the highlight.

Vancouver Art Gallery

750 Hornby Street, at Robson Street (604 662 4700/www.vanartgallery.bc.ca). All city-centre buses. **Open** 10am-5.30pm Mon, Wed, Fri-Sun; 10am-9pm Tue, Thur. **Admission** $15; $6-$11 reductions; free under-4s. **Credit** AmEx, DC, MC, V. **Map** p249 K3.

The VAG is still best known for its extensive collection of works by the 1920s modernist Emily Carr (*see p33*), Canada's most celebrated female artist, who willed more than 150 paintings to the gallery in 1945. These post-impressionist portraits of western flora and First Nations subjects are arguably of more historical interest than artistic merit, but Carr was an impressive character in many ways. The third floor is also home to several important works by the Group of Seven. Under the leadership of director Kathleen Bartels there's been a more ambitious approach to bringing in important traveling exhibitions in recent years, as well as the acquisition of cutting edge modern work from the fertile local art scene.

Vancouver Lookout

555 W Hastings Street, at Seymour Street (604 689 0421/www.vancouverlookout.com). All city-centre buses/SkyTrain Waterfront. **Open** *15 Oct-29 Apr* 9am-9pm daily. *30 Apr-14 Oct* 8.30am-10.30pm daily. **Admission** $13; $6-$9 reductions; free under-4s. **Credit** AmEx, DC, MC, V. **Map** p249 L3.

In a city of great vistas, the Lookout tower offers a bird's-eye view. On a clear day you can see for miles, and this is the best vantage point to admire the older architecture and the docks of the Downtown Eastside, or get your bearings early in your stay, but it's a shame some of the signage hasn't kept pace with the city's rapid evolution. A meal at the revolving restaurant one floor up saves you the admission fee; the cost is mediocre food at high prices.

A great place to chill: the steps on Robson Square, in front of the **Vancouver Art Gallery**.

Tickets to ride

While Vancouver isn't really a big city, its attractions are well spread; an organised tour is a convenient way to get your bearings and visit some of the more outlying attractions.

For your basic 'hop-on, hop-off' tour, the **Vancouver Trolley Co** (toll free 1-888 451 5581, www.vancouvertrolley.com) provides a daily service with 23 stops covering the Downtown core, Stanley Park, Granville Island and the Vanier Park museums. You also get to travel in a reconditioned San Francisco tram (on wheels). Cost: $37; $19 children; free under-4s.

If you prefer not to rub shoulders with the hoi-polloi, **Wild BC Tours** (toll free 1-888 671 9523, www.wildbc.com) offer a variety of private tours for groups of two and upwards. Choose from a city tour, a trip to the North Shore and Grouse Mountain, or explore the city's gardens. Prices range from $66 to $239.

Stay ecologically sound with **North Van Green Tours** (604 290 0145, www.northvan greentours.com), whose vehicles run on vegetable oil. Pick-up is from Lonsdale Quay (take the SeaBus across) and the four-hour trip visits some of the harder to reach areas of the North Shore – Lynn Canyon Park, Seymour Mountain Forest and Deep Cove. Cost is $50 (with a discount if you are staying at a youth hostel) and you can

add on Grouse Mountain and the Capilano Suspension Bridge for an extra charge.

City By Cycle (toll free 1-888 599 6800, www.vancouver-tour.citybycycle.com) offers a half-day cycle tour of the Seawall with guide, bike, helmet and water taxi fare all included for $69. Other tours cover trails in Pacific Spirit Park and Seymour Reserve, with optional kayaking add-ons.

Foodies might fancy one of the various market tours (Granville Island, Chinatown, Commercial Drive) run by **Edible British Columbia** (604 662 3606, www.edible-britishcolumbia.com). A local chef will talk you through the various produce available and introduce you to the speciality vendors. Tickets start at $65.

From pick-ups Downtown, Sewell's **Marina Sea Safari** (604 921 3474, www.sewells marina.com) will put you in a water-proof jumpsuit and whisk you from Horseshoe Bay and into Howe Sound in a Zodiac boat for abundant views and wildlife, including a colony of Harbour seals. Tickets cost $67; $59 reductions; $37 5-12s.

And finally, if you're interested in the port as a working operation, **Ports Alive** (604 690 9920, www.portsalive.com) will get you up close and personal to oil tankers, cruise ships, areas of historical interest and, naturally, wildlife. Charters start at $350/hr.

The West End

One of North America's most densely populated neighbourhoods, the bustling **West End** is a major reason downtown is so liveable. Leafy, residential, and full of affordable rental units, it's home to the city's gay community, Asian students and service industry workers.

Away from the main roads it's easy to find quiet areas that reward a slow saunter past corner stores, streets patrolled by friendly tabby cats and children's playgrounds. The West End was first developed in the late 19th century by the Canadian Pacific Railway, which built grand residences for its officials in the area. At Barclay and Nelson, you'll find some vestiges of the old, genteel West End at Barclay Heritage Square, which preserves nine Victorian-era houses, including the **Roedde House Museum**, an 1893 family house in Queen Anne Revival style that offers guided tours (1415 Barclay Street, 604 684 7040, www.roeddehouse.org).

At the foot of Robson, turn south along Denman Street and proceed to Davie Street and English Bay, passing dozens of little shops and restaurants, cafés, gelato joints and the odd condom or gourmet dogfood store.

From English Bay you can join the Seawall, either heading west to Stanley Park, or east around False Creek, where it threads its way through residential developments and increasingly offers fine dining choices.

Parallel to Robson, Davie Street has a funkier, more residential feel. Heading east from Denman you'll pass by Gabriola, the old Rogers Mansion at Davie and Nicola, built entirely from Gabriola Island stone by the head of BC Sugar in 1900. It's now home to the Macaroni Grill restaurant (the indignity!). You're now on your way up the road to Davie Village (between Bute and Hornby), the home of Vancouver's gay community, featuring shops, restaurants and, of course, nightclubs. Highlights include **Little Sister's Book & Art Emporium** (see p123), a gay and lesbian

Sightseeing

Walk Stepping out in Gastown

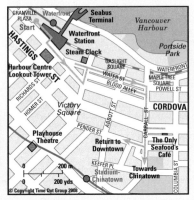

Start: Granville Street, at Cordova Street.
Finish: Carrall Street, at Hastings Street.

Begin on the plaza at the north end of Granville Street. From here there are great views across Burrard Inlet to the North Shore Mountains, the city of North Vancouver and Vancouver's working harbour (*see p18* **The shipping news**). Enter **Waterfront Station**, the CPR's former station, from the plaza (601 W Cordova Street) and descend the stairs into the concourse of the 1914 neoclassical building, where a set of oil paintings, installed in 1916, depicts scenes of the Rocky Mountains as seen from the train. Leave through the main entrance to Cordova Street and turn left. At the eastern end of the station is the 'Angel of Victory', a memorial for CPR employees who fell in the two world wars.

For most, Gastown's major attraction is **Water Street** with its decorative paving and old fashioned 'dragon head' lights, all part of a 1970s beautification project. **Cordova Street** is less known and grittier, but well worth checking out for the vintage clothes and collectibles found between Richards and Cambie Streets (*See p129* **Gas injection**).

It's hard to imagine this was once the city's premier shopping street, but the buildings do exhibit a faded elegance. Turn left on Cambie Street and continue to Water Street. Turn left and walk up to the crosswalk and cross; in front of you is the Greenshields building (345 Water Street), a Romanesque-style warehouse whose façade exhibits some excellent carved column capitals.

Turn right and continue along Water Street past the former Hudson's Bay Company liquor and fur warehouse (321 Water Street) to the **Steam Clock**, a unique – and modern (1970s) – piece that utilizes steam from the city's heating system to toot a Westminster Chime on its five steam whistles. The steam engine behind the glass is all for show though – the clockworks are driven by an electric motor tucked out of view.

Further along Water Street, nip into **Gaslight Square** (the entrance is next to Kites on Clouds at 131 Water Street) and head up the flight of stairs to get a close-up view of the working port. Back out on Water Street, carry on across Abbott Street to an array of new shops and restaurants. They jostle for trade with the **Old Spaghetti Factory** (53 Water Street). Occupying the ground floor of the former Malkin warehouse, it is one of the oldest businesses in Gastown – and has its own streetcar to sit in.

The large intersection at the end of the block is **Maple Tree Square**, the heart of the original town, overseen by a **statue of Gassy Jack** atop his whiskey barrel. Behind him on Carrall Street is the 1886 Alhambra Hotel, and the flat-iron building at the intersection of Powell and Alexander Streets is the Europe Hotel (43 Powell Street) from 1909.

As you walk up Carrall Street to Hastings you'll pass the entrance to **Blood Alley**, a name rich in possibilities but just plucked out of the air during renovations. Walk up the alley and look for **Salt Tasting Room** (45 Blood Alley; *see p116*) a hidden gem of a wine bar. On the corner of Carrall and Cordova is **Boneta** (*see p105*), one of the city's best new bars and restaurants.

This is the rough edge of town and as you get closer to Hastings Street you enter the Downtown Eastside. Things generally look worse than they are, but do be sure to tuck your camera out of sight.

At Hastings Street look for the neon sea horse of the **Only SeaFoods Café** (20 Hastings Street, 604 681 6546) which has been serving up great fish and chips, clam chowder and pepper stew since 1924. It's a great spot to stop and fuel up.

Afterwards, return to Carrall Street and continue into Chinatown or, to return to downtown, walk up Pender Street and pass through Chinatown's Millennium Gate.

bookstore famous for a long-running battle with Canada Customs and a real community centre, and the **PumpJack Pub** (*see p156*).

Yaletown

This former warehouse district east of Granville and south of Smithe had run into hard times by the early 1990s, a notorious site for prostitution and drug trafficking. Then the city planners got to work in the first wave of Vancouver's massively successful urban revitalisation movement, and **Yaletown** exploded.

The empty warehouses became the perfect spaces for high-tech companies and new media upstarts. Artists and would-be artists loved the retro-fitted lofts and the empty ground-floor spaces filled up with cutting-edge boutiques and ambitious, go-for-broke restaurateur dream projects. Today the area has weathered the dotcom bust and become a centre of fine dining and high-end shopping in the city, a model of success that's being copied by cities from Oregon to China. The expensive and rather trendy supermarket Urban Fare, at 177 Davie Street (*see p131*), has become a neighbourhood hub, but you'll find that the restaurants and stores are centred on Hamilton and Mainland streets. David Lam Park is a green focus for residents in the summer, and an appropriately modern contrast to the city's older and more staid recreational parks and gardens. Dress

well and shop – the retail emphasis is definitely on clothes, which befits Yaletown's traditional role as the city's garment district – then drop by George Ultralounge (1137 Hamilton Street; *see p116*) for a cocktail before doing the Vancouver thing and heading on to one of the area's restaurants as the evening's capper.

Gastown

Three blocks east of Canada Place, beyond the SeaBus terminal at Waterfront Station, the historic district of **Gastown** begins. The birthplace of frontier-era Vancouver, this area was once the very heart of the city. It burned to the ground in the fire of 1886, was rebuilt in the years immediately following, but fell on hard times during the middle of the last century. (For a guided tour of the district, *see p62* **Walk**).

Gastown is now going through yet another metamorphosis, as intelligently planned redevelopment turns it from an underwhelming tourist area with dubious restaurants into a living, working part of the city that has many delights for the discerning visitor – not least a much improved choice of restaurants.

Walk east along Water Street to observe the many finely restored circa-1890s buildings and warehouses, most now operating as retail and office spaces for funky design firms and the like. There's highly recommended innovative tapas-style Japanese food at Kitanoya Guu

An inukshuk frames the view of **English Bay** and the North Shore mountains. *See p61.*

With Otokomae, upstairs at 375 Water Street (604 685 8682). At Water and Cambie, the **Steam Clock** is an ingenious device that takes advantage of the old steam heating system that runs beneath Gastown's streets. Further down at Water and Abbott, you'll find the Dominion Hotel, a historic 1899 building that is in the process of being rehabilitated.

Off Water, on Cordova and nearby streets there are plenty of unique shops full of curios and designer clothes, but stray much further south-east than Cambie and Cordova and you will be in the drug-infested no-man's-land that separates Gastown from Chinatown. A couple of blocks further east the **Vancouver Police Centennial Museum** offers some revealing scraps of the city's history.

Vancouver Police Centennial Museum

240 E Cordova Street, at Main Street (604 665 3346/ www.vancouverpolicemuseum.ca). Bus 4, 7. **Open** 9am-5pm Mon-Sat. **Admission** $7; $5 reductions; free under-6s. **Credit** AmEx, DC, MC, V. **Map** p249 N3. The most noteworthy items in the museum, which is housed in the old Coroner's Court building, are the autopsy pictures of Errol Flynn, who died in Vancouver in 1959 in the arms of his 19-year-old assistant. There is also a collection of unusual weapons confiscated over the years and records of dastardly crimes committed by nefarious citizens. Despite (or because of) its prurient nature, it's kid-friendly, and the Police Historical Society runs a number of tours and family programmes, such as 'Forensic Science for Kids' (check the website for current activities). The shop offers 'Cop coffee' and

handcuff keychains. Not a large attraction, but guaranteed to fill a rainy afternoon.

Chinatown

Vancouver's **Chinatown**, the third largest in North America (after New York and San Francisco), is a busy marketplace crammed with restaurants, tea houses, grocers and souvenir shops. It's bounded by Pender, Union, Gore and Carrall Streets, with the historic core found along Pender and Keefer. Avoid Hastings Street, where Canada's worst skid row thrives.

Vancouver's Chinese haven't had it easy and you can still see traces of a dark past. In the 1880s, low-paid Chinese labourers settled in a ghetto in the Pender Street area. There were two race riots, and a hefty immigration tax made it near impossible to bring family over. Opium was the preferred vice; as many as eight opium factories operated in Vancouver in 1889. But by the turn of the century a merchant class had emerged, and various clans began to build impressive, southern China-style architecture. **The Chinese Cultural Centre** (50 E Pender Street, 604 658 8850, www.cccvan.com) offers a free brochure describing all of Chinatown's heritage buildings, including its oldest, the 1889 Wing Sang Building (51 E Pender Street).

Most visitors head straight for the world's narrowest commercial building, the **Sam Kee Company** and, across the street, **Dr Sun Yat-Sen Classical Chinese Garden**, a major Vancouver attraction. The first of its kind created outside China, the garden is a

Industrial awnings from the original warehouses are part of the charm of trendy **Yaletown**.

Rain city

You've heard it rains in Vancouver. Well, it's true. There are days when you can hardly see for the incessant deluge, as if the ocean itself has lifted up and stretched out a soaking arm over the city. In January 2004, a month's worth – 100 millimetres (four inches) – poured down in just 48 hours. Vancouver's longest downpour began on 6 January 1953 and ended 29 days later. On average, the city's annual rainfall is 1,117mm (44.3 inches) over 164 wet days.

But look on the wet side. Vancouver boasts some of the most spectacular public gardens in North America. The whole region brims with a lush, diverse horticulture and the damp air keeps Vancouver's annual pollution index low.

Just as heat inspires a way of life in southern locales, rain shapes the culture on the Pacific Northwest. Easterners are known to observe that Vancouver's temperate climate fosters a moderate people. Locals are neither wildly ambitious nor sluggishly laid-back, appreciative of the mildness that comes with rain instead of the deep snow and freezing temperatures of the rest of the country. Summer brings weeks of unbroken sunshine, but not the sweltering torpor that engulfs other North American cities.

And when it does rain, the trick is to get out there and enjoy it, just as Vancouverites do, donning high-tech, breathable, waterproof fabrics and splashing out. Our favourite rainy day excursion? At **Dr Sun Yat-Sen Classical Chinese Garden** (*see p65*), covered walkways and pavilions are rimmed with hand-made drip tiles. In a downpour, roof water flows from the drip tiles like a crystal bead curtain. Ming Dynasty scholars recommended listening to the symphony of water hitting the pebbled courtyard, smooth rocks and pond water.

It rains in other places, it's true. But the rain here shouldn't be avoided or endured. It must be embraced, relished even. If you are lucky, it won't be sunny the whole time that you're in Vancouver.

near-exact replica of a Ming-Dynasty scholar's retreat. The free Dr Sun Yat-Sen Park next door provides a hint of the garden's enchantment. At the end of the park, the **Chinese Cultural Centre Museum and Archives** (555 Columbia Street, 604 658 8880) displays the history of Chinese-Canadians in Vancouver.

After, walk up Keefer and slip into Ten Ren Tea & Ginseng Co (550 Main Street, 604 684 1566), an oasis of calm with free tastings. Then hit the streets to explore Chinatown's shops and, on Friday nights in summer, the **Chinatown Night Market** (*see p131*).

Since the 1980s, the suburb of Richmond has become a major base for Vancouver's quarter-million Chinese population, and consequently, the destination for the best Chinese cuisine in the region (*see p190* **China town**).

Dr Sun Yat-Sen Classical Chinese Garden

578 Carrall Street, at Keefer Street (604 662 3207/ www.vancouverchinesegarden.com). Bus 10, 16, 20. **Open** *15 June-31 Aug 9.30am-7pm daily. May-14 June, Sept 10am-6pm daily. Oct-Apr 10am-*
4.30pm daily. **Admission** $8.75; $7 reductions; free under-5s. **Credit** DC, MC, V. **Map** p249 M4.
Constructed in 1986 using traditional methods – no nails or power tools – this magnificent garden features rare rockery and architectural materials, horticulture similar to Chinese gardens and jade-green waterways. Exquisite courtyards and pavilions are connected by a maze of covered walkways and bridges. Both gaudy and serene, the retreat abounds with Buddhist, Confucian and Taoist symbolism. A guided tour sheds light on why pavilion rooftops arch to the sky and tiled walkways zig-zag.

Sam Kee Company

8 W Pender Street, at Carrall Street. Bus 10, 16, 20. **Map** p249 M3.
A private accounting business operates here but visitors can view it through large exterior windows. Chang Toy, who dominated Chinatown's early trade, originally owned a 9m (30ft) lot on this site, but most of it was appropriated in 1912 to widen Pender Street. Indignant that he wasn't paid for the remainder, Chang built a 1.8m (6ft) office, maintaining the original size below the street, as glass block windows embedded in the sidewalk show.

Stanley Park

A walk in the woods.

North Shore

Stanley Park

West End — Down-town — Gastown — Chinatown

Yale-town

West Side — East Vancouver

Map p69

Stanley Park has been called the soul of the city and the envy of the world. At 400 hectares (1,000 acres) it's slightly bigger than New York's Central Park, making it the largest urban park in North America. Yet its greatest virtue is that it's almost an island, wrapped with a Seawall that offers nine kilometres (five miles) of spectacular waterfront views. At its heart are natural landscapes that belie the fact that almost all of the trees are second growth.

Yes, Stanley Park was logged, beginning in the 1860s. But treacherous currents along its north shore stymied plans to turn much of the area over to other forms of industry. So in 1886 Vancouver's city council was able, as its first act, to call on the federal government to transfer the peninsula to the city as a public park. Of course, some city fathers may have been trying to enhance the value of their own adjoining real estate holdings. But whatever their reasons may have been, the park was created in September 1888 and dedicated the following year by Governor General Sir Frederick Arthur Stanley (of ice hockey's Stanley Cup fame).

But Stanley Park's history is not entirely one of beauty. In 1888, smallpox wiped out the Squamish village of Khawaykhway, at the site now known as Lumberman's Arch, and the buildings were razed. Squatters lived in the park until the 1920s and even today it is populated by homeless people, with one estimate putting the summer population at 200.

It's also been the site of grisly murders. In 2001, it saw the homophobic beating to death of a man near Second Beach, where gay men engage in 'trail hopping' in the woods at night.

In 1953, two long-dead children were found under a woman's fur coat, next to the axe used to kill them. The tragedy has become part of the city's lore. It's also central, along with the park's homeless population, to Timothy Taylor's acclaimed 2001 novel, *Stanley Park*.

The park itself bore the brunt of its own violence when winds of up to 119km/h tore into Prospect Point in the early hours of 15 December 2006. Some 45 hectares (110 acres) of forest were virtually levelled, and more than 10,000 trees were lost. The park was closed for the first time in over 40 years and it was 11 months before the Seawall could fully reopen. The restoration plan calls for 20,000 one-year-old trees to be planted to create a more resilient coastal forest made up of Douglas fir, western red cedar, hemlock, Sitka spruce, grand fir, big leaf maple and red alder.

Despite such devastating turbulence, for the most part the park remains an oasis of calm and beauty that Vancouverites and visitors are grateful for. The presence of the West End's dense apartments next to an expansive rainforest provides a stunning contrast. For those wondering what the contrast might have been like if the park had never been logged, the astonishing fact is that the old forest would have been taller than many of those blocks. To get an idea, take a look at the tree growing on the terrace atop the 17-storey, 60-metre (200-foot) Eugenia Place building at 1919 Beach Avenue, English Bay. That's the height of the original forest. Truly, this is an age of pygmies.

Stanley Park can be divided into three sections. The more developed eastern portion, from Pipeline Road to Coal Harbour, includes the Vancouver Aquarium, the totem poles, and a children's playground, waterpark, petting zoo and miniature railway. The central portion west of Pipeline Road and north of Second Beach is a largely undeveloped tract of forest and walking trails. A smaller triangle adjoining the West End and English Bay features a public pool, pitch-and-putt golf, lawn bowling, the Fish House restaurant and a picnic area.

For general information about the park, visit www.city.vancouver.bc.ca/parks/parks/stanley.

GETTING TO AND AROUND THE PARK

You can reach the park by public transport (bus 5, 6, 19, C21) or by the **Stanley Park Express Bus** (604 681 5115, www.stanley

park.com, May-Oct only), which picks up from Canada Place and downtown hotels, and drops off at the Tourist Information kiosk just inside the park. The $3 fare is waived if you pre-purchase a ticket to the aquarium (*see p68*).

The free **Stanley Park Shuttle** bus service is wheelchair friendly and runs every 12-15mins (10am-6.30pm daily, mid June-mid Sept only). There are 15 hop-on, hop-off stops around the park (including one at the first car park), making it an ideal way to explore without having to do it all on foot.

Stanley Park Horse-Drawn Tours (604 681 5115, www.stanleyparktours.com, $25, $15-$23.50 reductions) offers one hour rides around the park on a 20-seat wagon, with some photo opportunity stops and guided commentary.

For in-line skate rentals, *see p176*; for cycling options, *see p174* **Free wheeling**.

East from Coal Harbour

Most visitors to the park combine trees with ocean views by heading round the perimeter on the Seawall (or, for those confined to cars and buses, along Stanley Park Drive). Bicycles, joggers and skaters are directed anticlockwise around the park. Although the outer edge of the Seawall is reserved for pedestrians, most walkers choose to travel in the same direction as their wheeled brethren. The circuit (about ten kilometres or six miles) takes some 45 minutes on a bike, 90 minutes of slow jogging or a good couple of hours walking.

You can approach the park by bus (*see p66*) or on foot, along the Coal Harbour Seawall from the Seaplane Terminal. The latter, an easy one kilometre (half mile) stroll, affords beautiful views of the North Shore, and passes some attractive waterfront bars and restaurants.

As you enter the park, either from Coal Harbour or along West Georgia Street, keep an eye to the left: above Stanley Park Drive you'll see statues of Lord Stanley, Queen Victoria and Robbie Burns, and the first of a handful of children's playgrounds. Below the road is the 1911 Tudor-style Vancouver Rowing Club, which fostered a strong BC rowing tradition that persists to this day.

A few hundred metres on, there's a rudimentary information booth at the junction of Stanley Park Drive and a spur road that leads to **Vancouver Aquarium** (*see p68*). Stanley Park Horse-Drawn Tours begin just east of the booth, offering hour-long carriage rides from early March to the end of October.

The essential Britishness of the park's heritage continues as you proceed east along the Seawall, past the entrance to the Royal Vancouver Yacht Club and then Deadman's Island, a native graveyard that was annexed and named the HMCS *Discovery* by the Royal Canadian Navy in 1942. To the north, Brockton Oval still features cricket and rugby matches.

Views of the city and the port – the third-largest in North America – along this stretch are stunning. In the foreground, float planes drop to the water behind the fuel barges. At dusk, the city's glass towers reflect the setting sun. If you're in the park on a late summer's evening, listen for the Nine O'Clock Gun, installed in 1894 to help ships set their chronometers, and still fired nightly.

As you swing around the Seawall at its easternmost tip, Brockton Point, there's a modest 1915 lighthouse. However, the real attraction near here is a stand of totem poles. Mostly replicas, the eight totems include one made by Haida icon Bill Reid (*see p31* **Reid all about it**).

Stanley Park Horse-Drawn Tours: a low-carbon way to tour the park.

Further west is Lumberman's Arch, formed by an imposing first-growth tree that, after World War II, replaced an intriguing classical-style pavilion of raw logs built in 1912 to honour Prince Arthur, the Duke of Connaught, then Canada's Governor General. The grassy field adjoining the children's water park nearby has long been a popular picnic area. In fact, the field sits on a native 'midden' of discarded shells, a remarkable indication of its past use.

To the left is the spur road that leads up to the Aquarium and back towards Coal Harbour. This section of the park once included a modest display of animals, including a rather sad polar bear exhibit. That spectacle helped galvanise opposition to the zoo, which has been almost completely eliminated from the park. The Vancouver Aquarium, too, has its share of critics, and the last of its popular orcas was shipped off to Sea World San Diego in 2001. Tension persists over whether the remaining beluga whales provide a vital educational tool or a cruel example of imprisonment – a three-year-old born and bred in the aquarium died of causes unknown in summer 2005.

Just west of the aquarium is a monument honouring the Japanese-Canadian soldiers who served in World War I. An avenue of Kwanzen cherry trees, which bloom in March, leads to a column on a pedestal representing a lotus flower.

Beyond the monument is the **Children's Farmyard and Miniature Railway** (*see p144*). At Hallowe'en and Christmas the railway puts on specially created seasonal rides. Nearby, towards the park's entrance, is Malkin Bowl, built in 1933. The modest facility hosts community theatre productions in the summer, as well as the occasional concert. Try the newly refurbished Stanley's Park Bar & Grill (*see p101*) for a salmon burger and a beer in the old Stanley Park Pavilion.

Vancouver Aquarium

Stanley Park (604 659 3474/www.vanaqua.org). Bus 19, then 10min walk. **Open** *May-Sept* 9.30am-7pm daily. *Oct-Apr* 9.30am-5pm daily. **Admission** $19.95; $11.95-$14.95 reductions; free under-3s. **Credit** AmEx, DC, MC, V. **Map** p69.

Despite public qualms over the display of captive marine mammals no one seems to care much for the feelings of fish. The regular beluga show (three daily) is the most popular attraction here, though the space barely seems adequate. The belugas happily do a turn or two and wobble their fatty deposits for the crowds before giving them a good soaking. If you don't want to get wet, stand well back from the edge. The aquarium's (reasonable) concession stand is located here too, so it's possible to combine beluga and a coke. Other open air attractions include dolphins, a couple of ornery sea lions, seals, and the adorable sea otters, once almost as numerous as trees in this part of the world – but like the old growth forests, massively over-exploited by European traders. Inside, you'll find several astonishing exhibits. Tides and temperature make British Columbia's coast one of the richest marine environments in the world. If you're not prepared to go scuba diving, the aquarium is the best way to see it. The displays effectively recreate a wide range of underwater BC tableaux, featuring sharks, salmon, an octopus, jellyfish, and more spiny, colourful rockfish than you can name. There's also a tropical zone and a new interactive area that brings out the marine biologist in young and old alike.

The central park

Tour buses flock to the northern apex of the park, **Prospect Point**, a high bluff with great views of First Narrows, the Coast Mountains, and Lions Gate Bridge (*see p81*). Ironically, the views are much improved after this area suffered the worst of the storm damage. This northwest sector contained the remnants of the original forest, the park's biggest and oldest trees, so the devastation is particularly brutal. At time of writing many trails are closed.

Happily that doesn't apply to the Seawall. Traveling west from Prospect Point, you pass the site of the wreck of the SS *Beaver*, which gave its name to the lake in the centre of the

You *can* see the **totem poles** for the forest.

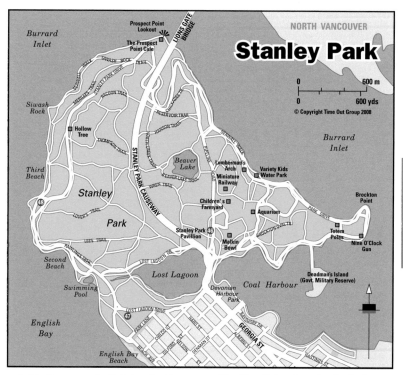

park. The *Beaver* was the first steamboat in the Pacific, in 1835, and came to its end near First Narrows in 1888. Its remnants are still visible during very low tides.

Alternatively, the shuttle bus takes Stanley Park Drive past the oft-photographed (dead but still standing) Hollow Tree, down to Ferguson Point, where the Sequoia Grill (*see p101*) offers fine sunset views. At the point where the road turns from Ferguson Point down to the relatively quiet Third Beach (which has its own modest concession stand), a cairn marks the grave of Pauline Johnson, who died in 1913. Johnson was a poet, the scion of an English mother and Mohawk father, and beloved by a Canadian and British public entranced by her exoticism. Lost Lagoon, into which she used to paddle in her canoe when it reached as far as English Bay, takes its name from one of her poems: 'O! Lure of Lost Lagoon'.

The Seawall offers a close look at a volcanic outcropping known as Siwash Rock. In *Legends of Vancouver*, Johnson recorded a story told to her by Squamish Chief Joe Capilano about its origins. As was the tradition, a young man was

washing himself clean by swimming in the sea while his wife was in labour. Four supernatural men, paddling a canoe, ordered him out of their path but he would not give way. In awe at his courage, the gods turned the young man to stone so that he might live forever as a symbol of his commitment to his family.

As you come further south, towards Second Beach, the forest is in much better shape; this is the best starting point for a walk in the woods.

English Bay

As you come round towards English Bay, you enter one of the Seawall's busiest stretches, as predominantly local visitors stream into the park from the West End. The Seawall passes the summer-only, outdoor Second Beach Pool (another concession stand offers the usual drinks, hot dogs, ices, and fish and chips). Second Beach itself is a narrow stretch of sand at high tide, and usually crowded in the summer, but with the *de rigueur* spectacular view. There's a pleasant playground here with a vintage fire engine to clamber on, and a large field for picnics and Frisbee. And if you're looking for First Beach, there isn't one, though English Bay and (further south) Sunset Beach Park could claim the title.

A stroll around Lost Lagoon is likely to involve close encounters with Canada geese, ducks, and possibly loons and grebes. You may also see bald eagles and even an osprey. Look for the colony of great blue herons nesting near the Park Board offices and the tennis courts near English Bay (*see below* **Wild at heart**). The Lost Lagoon Nature House (604 257 8544, www.stanleyparkecology.ca), located near the south-east corner of the lagoon, offers visitor information, interactive displays and a range of historical and nature walks – and an invitation to adopt a heron nest.

If you want a place to stop and replenish, dine at the Fish House on Stanley Park Drive (*see p101*). Overlooking the charming pitch and putt golf course, it is the park's best restaurant, with a pleasant deck and bar. From here it's just a ten-minute stroll to the West End (*see p61*) and the restaurants and shops of busy Denman Street.

To return to the park's Georgia Street entrance, you'll need to walk, cycle or drive past Lost Lagoon. If you're walking or riding this way, the obvious route is through the willows on the north shore, but there is also a rhododendron garden that stretches from the Lagoon to the pitch and putt. The lagoon has since been 'naturalised' but once every 20 years or so it gets cold enough to skate upon.

Wild at heart

Vancouver has a lot of animals, and we're not talking about drunken fans of the Vancouver Canucks. Most ubiquitous in Stanley Park are the eastern grey squirrels, which joined the noisy, native, brown Douglas squirrels around 1914 as a gift from New York's Central Park. Grey squirrels often come begging for nuts.

If you are keen to see a racoon, your odds are good at Prospect Point and along the north side of Lost Lagoon, where any number of well-meaning people violate park bylaws by feeding them. Racoons live throughout the city, plundering rubbish bins and eviscerating the odd housecat. You may also see a skunk. They're commonly seen at night in the West End, mainly because of the park, but can also be found, or smelled, throughout the city.

Deer and coyote both inhabit the park, but since they have become widespread through being unobtrusive you're unlikely to see one, though deer can sometimes be spotted swimming to the park from the North Shore.

Black bears have been pushed north by urban settlement, but when foraging is poor in the mountains they often make their way down into North and West Vancouver scavenging for rubbish. Although there's a chance you might glimpse one on a North Shore mountain hike, it's small. You're more likely to see one on the fringe of a dump, or from a chairlift in late spring or summer.

Cougars, occasionally a threat to people in isolated parts of the province, are also sometimes present on the North Shore. In the late 1980s, one confused animal somehow ended up in the Pacific Coliseum in Vancouver's Hastings Park.

Bald eagles offer far easier wildlife spotting opportunities. In the city, they're often seen being harassed by a small murder of crows. In December and January it's worth the hour's drive north towards Squamish to the Brackendale Eagle Reserve (*see p215*), where they congregate in thousands to feast on salmon that have spawned and died. Another birder's paradise, particularly from October to December, is the George C Reifel Migratory Bird Sanctuary (5191 Robertson Road, 604 946 6980, www.reifelbirdsanctuary.com) 30 minutes south of the city centre in Ladner.

One of Stanley Park's common spectacles is the great blue heron, a dozen of which roost in the trees near the Park Board office in the south-eastern corner of the park. They're big – a metre tall with a two-metre wingspan (three feet by six feet) – and can often be seen at close range making an ungainly landing along the shoreline. Further bird life can be spotted by looking out across the ocean, where you're guaranteed coal-black cormorants perched along the rocks.

Around Lost Lagoon, along with the mallards, wood ducks and non-native mute swans, is a small resident population of Canada Geese. In fact, their numbers got so out of control a decade ago, after they began over-wintering in the park, that they often stopped rush-hour traffic with their processional marches across Georgia Street and the Stanley Park Causeway.

And then there are the flocks of brazen, scavenging seagulls. If you're eating a hot dog anywhere in Stanley Park, watch your back, and guard your wiener.

The West Side

A vibrant public market, long sandy beaches, gardens and museums.

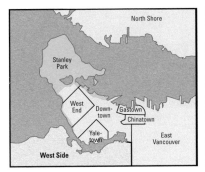

Maps p250 & p251

Visitors who base themselves in the West End are puzzled to look south across English Bay to what locals call 'the West Side'. (Even more confusingly, West Vancouver is a satellite on the North Shore). For many, the short journey across the Burrard or Granville bridges is a psychological block to further exploration – neither is particularly pedestrian friendly – although there are numerous buses, and the small passenger ferries (from the Aquatic Centre or David Lam Park to Granville Island and Vanier Park) make getting there simple and fun.

A pretty residential area that includes laid-back Kitsilano, affluent Point Grey and the elite Shaughnessy, the West Side makes the most of its long, sandy beaches and spectacular views. The obvious tourist attractions are Granville Island, shopping in the upscale South Granville strip, the beaches, a trio of museums in Vanier Park and the Museum of Anthropology at UBC. This area also includes some of the finest public gardens in North America, and some of the city's best fine dining.

Granville Island

One of the city's most popular destinations, **Granville Island** (www.granvilleisland.com) is home to a large public market, artist studios and shops. Coming from downtown, take one of the foot passenger ferries that run across False Creek to the island at the foot of Hornby Street, the Aquatic Centre, David Lam Park, or from Spyglass Place in Yaletown (www.theaquabus.com and www.granvilleislandferries.bc.ca). The number 50 bus comes from Gastown, then heads down Granville Street and stops on West 2nd Avenue, a stone's throw from the Island.

Granville Island isn't really an island, it's a peninsula, and False Creek isn't a stream, it's a long, narrow inlet extending from English Bay, the result of a lot of very deliberate engineering and digging. In 1915, crews started dredging 760,000 cubic metres of mud out of the marshy coastline to create Vancouver's harbour. They dumped most of that mud in one place, creating what was called Industrial Island when it opened in 1916. Its name was apt; tenants were businesses such as Vulcan Ironworks, Wallace Shipyards, coal companies, rope makers and sawmills. The island was a rail terminal and shipping nexus, and the buildings that housed many of those businesses are still here.

By the early 1970s industry was fading, and starting in 1973 the city worked to transform Granville Island into a mixed-use commercial and social centre, a renaissance completed in 1979 with the opening of the Granville Public Market. Emphasising local BC produce as well as speciality bakeries and craft stalls, the market is a treat for the senses at any time of year (*see p132* **Granville Island**). If the sight of such bounty makes you peckish, there are half a dozen places offering Indian, Chinese, hotdogs, crepes, pies and so forth, mostly clustered in the northwest corner, or you can stroll five minutes to Fisherman's Wharf for Vancouver's best chippie, **Go Fish** (*see p109*). The market opens at 9am, and gets busy quickly – in the summer or at weekends try to arrive before 10.30am to avoid the crowds.

Outside the market, Granville Island features a wide range of shops, from marine outfitters to tourist tat, but there are enough high quality boutiques, galleries and workshops to make it worth the wander – and no chain stores! There are several restaurants and bars, a couple of theatres that come to life in the evening, and the Kids Market to boggle little minds (this cluster of toy stores also has an arcade game area under the same corrugated roof). Nearby, there's a fun Water Park and playground (*see p143* **Water babies**), and the Model Trains Museum (1502 Duranleau Street, 604 683 1939, www.model trainmuseum.ca) should delight aficionados and young children with its impressive working diorama. Entry to the Model Ships Museum in the same building is included in your $7.50

Sightseeing

Eat, drink, shop, relax: whatever you do on **Granville Island**, enjoy the view. *See p71.*

admission. Less esoteric, perhaps, the Emily Carr Institute of Art & Design (1399 Johnston Street, 604 844 3800, www.eciad.ca) is one of the finest art schools in the country; its gallery and café are open to the public, as are many of the artist studios along Railspur Alley. The more active can rent a kayak to explore False Creek and English Bay from Ecomarine Ocean Kayak Centre (1668 Duranleau Street; *see p177*). Be aware that if you opt for whale-watching at one of the many outlets, it will involve a drive to Steveston (*see p189*) or further.

Granville Island is a good jumping-off point for further exploration. Walk south on Granville Street for home, antiques and clothes stores, and for a handful of the city's more upmarket art galleries. West takes you to Vanier Park and Kits beach (there's also a ferry stop at the Maritime Museum). Alternatively the Seawall hugs False Creek to the east, a pleasant walk through small, pretty Sutcliffe Park, Charleson Park (with a pond and waterfall), and on to Science World (*see p142*), about a mile in total; there are a couple of watering holes at Stamp's Landing, the halfway mark. During summer weekends – May to October – you can make the same journey on a restored turn-of-the-century streetcar, although operations are currently suspended due to construction work on the Canada Line and the Olympic Village. Check www.trams.bc.ca/dhr.html for updates. The False Creek ferries also connect Granville Island with Stamp's Landing, Science World and Yaletown – at $5 or less, this is one of the best sightseeing deals in the city.

Kitsilano

Running west from Burrard Street as far as Alma, and south from the Burrard Inlet to 16th Avenue, **Kitsilano** (or 'Kits') was named by the

Canadian Pacific Railway in 1904 for Chief Khahtsahlanough of the coastal Salish First Nations. It's doubtful they appreciated the honour – three years earlier they'd been displaced from their settlement at Sun'ahk, in the vicinity òf what is now Vanier Park.

Long popular as a destination for day-trippers, Kits Beach is still the neighbourhood's prime attraction. Although the coarse white sand isn't anything to write home about, the views are: you get the city skyline, Stanley Park and the Coast Mountains behind them, with sailboats and tankers in the middle distance. On a hot summer's day the foreground will have plenty of eye candy too: with its popular, free volleyball courts, Kits attracts a decidedly fit 'muscle beach' element, though not to anybody else's exclusion. By June the water is usually warm enough for swimming and it's reasonably clean, but local families tend to head to the spectacular saltwater outdoor swimming pool for a dip – at 137 metres (450 feet) it's Canada's longest pool (604 731 0011, open 19 May-3 Sept). Kits beach also offers free tennis and basketball courts (bring your own balls and rackets), a playground, and green parkland bordering the sand – as well as the neatly spaced logs which offer windbreaks and informal backrests on all Vancouver's beaches. Built in 2005, the Watermark on Kits Beach is a glass-fronted restaurant with the requisite stunning vistas compensating for hit-and-miss cuisine (*see p110*). Underneath, there's a cheaper concession stand selling fish and chips, sushi and coffee – the Vancouver staples. A five-minute walk up Yew Street to 4th Avenue produces many more drinking and dining options. To get to Kits Beach from downtown, catch a number 2 or 22 bus on Burrard and get off at Cornwall and Vine, or take the False Creek Ferry from the Aquatic Centre under the Burrard Bridge to the

Maritime Museum in Vanier Park, just around Kits Point. They run every half hour Mon-Fri and every 15 minutes on weekends, for $2.50 one-way (www.granvilleislandferries.bc.ca).

At low tide, you could practically walk all the way up the Burrard Inlet to the University of British Columbia, about eight kilometers (five miles) west, by way of the relatively wild Trafalgar Beach, followed by Jericho (which has a yacht club with kayaks and windboards for rent, and a café with beer, burgers and nachos; *see p175 and p180*), Locarno, Spanish Banks, Point Grey and Towers – each a little bit less manicured than the last – until you reach the infamous Wreck Beach, Vancouver's nudist enclave (*see p74* **Grin and bare it**), nestled discreetly beneath the Museum of Anthropology.

To the east of Kits beach, Vanier Park (named after popular Governor General Georges Vanier, it's pronounced 'Van-Yay') is relatively bare grassland stretching to the Burrard Bridge – save for the trees around Kits Point – but it's a great spot for kite-flying, and in the summer this is where you'll find the big tents that house the **Bard on the Beach** company (*see p138*), one of the highlights of the city's theatre season.

Appropriately enough, the white building that looks like a flying saucer is home to the **HR MacMillan Space Centre**, with plenty of rainy day family activities, including a planetarium. Apparently architect Gerald Hamilton intended the dome to evoke a coastal Salish hat. The Space Centre shares the building with the **Vancouver Museum**, although neither is so successful here that future tenancy is assured. The entrance, with its giant crab fountain, is on the south side. The **Gordon MacMillan Southam Observatory** (www.hrmacmillanspacecentre.com/observatory)

is tucked around the corner, and is open from sunset to midnight Friday and Saturday when the skies are clear – call 604 738 2855 to check. Admission is by donation.

Looking out over the waters of English Bay, the **Vancouver Maritime Museum** is also deemed to be underperforming, and may move over to the North Shore in the next few years. Inside the A-frame building you'll find the *St Roch*, an arctic patrol vessel with plenty of history of its own (*see p18* **The shipping news**). The dock to the right of the museum is the ferry stop. Don't miss the Mungo Martin totem pole on the south side of the museum, an exact replica of a pole presented to Queen Elizabeth II in 1958 (its twin is in Windsor Great Park). At 30 metres (100 feet) this imposing work was designed to mark British Columbia's centenary. It was carved from a single log of 600-year-old Red Cedar, and it weighs approximately 27,000 pounds. It's also a popular perch for bald eagles, a fairly common sight in these parts.

In the 1960s and early '70s Kits became a hippie hangout, Vancouver's very own Haight-Ashbury, but these days the neighbourhood's main thoroughfare, West 4th Avenue, is quite gentrified on its busiest stretch, between Cypress and Vine, with an influx of maternity and baby stores interspersed with sports and yoga boutiques and several notable restaurants. For a taste of Kits' former groovy glory, head to Sophie's Cosmic Café (*see p109*) at 4th and Arbutus Street, its walls bedecked in yard sale treasures. Brunch here is a local institution, with queues stretching down the street. Browse at Zulu Records (1972 W 4th Avenue; *see p135*) a genuine indie haunt and a good spot to pick up on local bands (the staff are

Sightseeing

Kitsilano Beach.

Grin and bare it

Wreck Beach, Canada's only and infamous nudist beach, affords a panoramic view of the ocean and distant San Juan islands, half a mile of sandy shore on which to bare your bunnies, a backdrop of coniferous forest, and the occasional eagle to remind you that you're at the edge of wilderness. It also features more dreadlocks than you can shake a stick at, a carnival atmosphere on weekends, and tuneful, partially clothed hawkers who sell everything from Chinese steamed rolls ('Get your hands on my nice hot buns!') to pot cookies made by Wreck's most famous regular, BC marijuana poster girl Watermelon. Half a million visitors make this pilgrimage every year, so don't expect privacy on a hot summer's day.

The beach is divided by tradition into three areas: at the bottom of the access stairs, turn right to reach the quieter family section, left toward the driftwood towers and the sound of bongo drums for party central (and your best access to comestible substances), all the way past the vendor stations to the far left to the gay area. Since 2003, Mary's Wave Massage has offered dollar-a-minute de-stressing by a tanned and friendly blonde in a hula skirt (every day except Wednesdays, Fridays, and rainy days). Stormin' Norman's Spirit Grill (in business since 1981) sells tasty dress-your-own veggie, beef, and wild game burgers for $6, and pricey handy supplies like rolling papers.

While the most spectacular views at Wreck may involve the clientele rather than the scenery, beach etiquette requires you not to gawk. Yes, everybody casts a discreet glance now and again, but don't ogle. Overt sexual activity is also unacceptable. (For more notes on etiquette, visit www.wreckbeach.org) Not everyone goes starkers: the word is clothing-optional, so dress for your own comfort.

GETTING TO WRECK BEACH

Located below the bluffs at the far west end of the University of British Columbia, Wreck Beach is separated from the campus by a steep but well-maintained stairway officially known as Trail 6. There's parking (cheap on weekends, pricey mid-week) beside the Place Vanier residences off Northwest Marine Drive; or take the convenient 99 bus to its terminus at University Bus Loop, follow University Boulevard downhill to Marine Drive, cross Marine Drive, and take the roadside trail to the right. A minute's walk will find you at the head of the stairway, where it's a good idea to buy water from the vendor whose sign announces 'Best Prices at Wreck Beach'.

An out-of-this-world attraction: the **HR MacMillan Space Centre** in Vanier Park.

often in bands themselves), or further west, sample 24-hour vegetarian fare at the popular Naam (*see p110*). Vancouver's coolest video rental store is another neighbourhood fixture: Videomatica (1855 W 4th Avenue, 604 734 0411, www.videomatica.bc.ca) stocks the sort of stuff Blockbuster wouldn't touch.

West Broadway (five blocks south) is the other main shopping street, though you're better off hopping on a bus between Granville and Macdonald Streets. The eight blocks from Macdonald Street to Alma are less ostentatious, evocative of the small town feel Vancouver had 20 years ago. It features a sprinkling of good second-hand bookstores, the cavernous Kidsbooks at 3083 W Broadway (*see p123*), independent shoe and clothing outlets, and numerous restaurants, including many unpretentious Greek tavernas and a couple of good Mediterranean delis (this is the city's Greek enclave). Back east a couple of blocks, three highly rated eateries – Lumière (no.2551; *see p109*), Feenie's (no.2563; *see p110*) and Mistral Bistro (no.2585; *see p109*) sit along one strip, making for a veritable gastronomic grand prix. You can also get an excellent beef pattie next door in Moderne Burger (*see p108*).

Kitsilano is only a ten-minute taxi ride from downtown across Burrard Bridge. Bus routes 2, 4, 7, 16, 17 and 22 run between Kitsilano and downtown, stopping along Cornwall, 4th or Broadway.

HR MacMillan Space Centre

1100 Chestnut Street, at Whyte Avenue, West Side (604 738 7827/www.hrmacmillan spacecentre.com). Bus 2, 22. **Open** 10am-5pm Tue-Sun. **Admission** $15; $7-$10.75 reductions; free under-5s. **Credit** AmEx, DC, MC, V. **Map** p251 G4.

Housed in the same building as the Vancouver Museum, the Space Centre is a small but well thought-out attraction that appeals most to school-age children. Much of this interactive exhibit employs computer screens, where budding astronauts can practice skills such as planning an interplanetary research mission. Hourly presentations in the lecture theatre on diverse science-related subjects move at a clip and are 'performed' by actors, and the Virtual Voyage full-motion simulator allows kids and adults alike to play Captain Kirk for a bumpy ten-minute star journey. Admission includes the audio-visual shows in the top floor planetarium (up to five daily on weekends). Evening laser shows featuring music by Radiohead, Led Zeppelin and (inevitably) Pink Floyd are extra ($10.75). Note: An Explore pass allows access to all three Vanier Park museums for $30 (adult), or $24 (youth and seniors).

Vancouver Maritime Museum

1905 Ogden Avenue, at Chestnut Street, West Side (604 257 8300/www.vancouvermaritimemuseum. com). Bus 2, 22. **Open** *June-Aug* 10am-5pm daily. *Sept-May* 10am-5pm Tue-Sat; noon-5pm Sun. **Admission** $10; $7.50 reductions; $25 family; free under-5s. **Credit** AmEx, DC, MC, V. **Map** p251 G4.

The main attraction here is the *St Roch*, the first vessel to have navigated the Northwest Passage in both directions (*see also p18* **The shipping news**). Regular guided tours follow a short video presentation relating the history and hardships of the journey and crew; the ship's Inuit guide slept in a tent on deck, with his large extended family and pack of huskies, the latter fed with walrus meat. There are a lot of model ships on display, some interesting photos detailing Vancouver's development as a port, and a good interactive discovery area for children. Outside, take a look at the *Ben Franklin* submersible – a craft found rotting in a scrapyard before being lovingly restored – and the collection of heritage boats at the nearby dock.

Flower power

Downtown may have Stanley Park on its doorstep, but the West Side boasts the highest concentration of spectacular public gardens in Canada, including the UBC Botanical Garden and Nitobe Memorial Garden (also at UBC; for both, *see p77*), and on the edge of rareified Shaughnessy at 37th and Oak Street, the **VanDusen Botanical Garden**, which is rated one of the best in the world. With its relatively mild winters and temperate climate, the Lower Mainland is fertile ground for a spectacular arrangement of plants. Although this former golf course hasn't the geological interest of Vancouver Island's Butchart Gardens, VanDusen's 55 acres are a horticultural delight; recreating an astonishing array of ecosystems from the Far East, Africa, South America, Europe and Australasia. The Rhododendron Walk and Sino-Himalayan Garden are standouts. But there are many gems – including gardens devoted (separately) to roses, herbs and heathers. And there's an Elizabethan hedge maze tucked away in the western corner. The features are set among hillocks, pocket lakes and winding paths, all with a northward view of the city and mountains. A dazzling Christmas Festival of Lights draws families through December. The site includes a large garden shop and the Shaughnessy Restaurant for smart dining (reservations are recommended: 604 261 0011).

VanDusen Botanical Garden

5251 Oak Street, at W 37th Avenue (604 878 9274/www.vandusengarden. org). Bus 17. **Open** 10am-sunset daily. **Admission** *Apr-Sep* $8.25; $4.25-$6 reductions; $19 family; free under-6s. *Oct-Mar* $6; $3-$4.50 reductions; $12.75 family; free under-6s. **Credit** AmEx, MC, V.

Vancouver Museum

1100 Chestnut Street, at Whyte Avenue, West Side (604 736 4431/www.vanmuseum.bc.ca). Bus 2, 22. **Open** 10am-5pm Mon-Wed, Fri-Sun; 10am-9pm Thur. Closed Mon from Oct to June. **Admission** $10; $6.50-$8 reductions; free under-5s. **Credit** AmEx, DC, MC, V. **Map** p251 G4.

Given that Vancouver doesn't have a great deal of history to call its own, you'll find only token gestures towards pre-history (ie before 1880) in this modest museum primarily aimed at families and schoolchildren; to explore the culture and heritage of the First Nations peoples you'll need to head to the Museum of Anthropology (*see p77*). The largely 20th-century collection of bric-a-brac is complimented by personal recollections, photographs and films. Children are encouraged to get the feel of period toys and clothes, while adults can listen to vintage radio shows. One corner shows how close the city came to running a freeway through Strathcona and across its northern waterfront, a plan scuppered by resident protests – worth remembering as you stroll along Coal Harbour today.

Pacific Spirit Park & UBC

Nearly twice the size of Stanley Park, the **Pacific Spirit Regional Park** consists of 763 hectares of forest and rocky foreshore, a greenbelt between Vancouver and the **University of British Columbia** (UBC), designated a nature reserve in 1988. It's an altogether wilder park than the urban Stanley Park, though it still features more than 50 kilometers (30 miles) of easy hiking trails, many of them accessible to cyclists and horseback riders as well as walkers and joggers. Most of these grounds were logged in the early years of the twentieth century, but the mixed deciduous and coniferous forest has asserted itself since to create a dark, hushed space that feels a world apart from the nearby city. Wildlife includes the Pacific Water Shrew and the Western Red-Backed Vole, and there's a significant Great Blue Heron population. Bus routes to UBC (bus 4, 9, 17, 44 & 99 B-Line) all pass through the park – alight near Blanca Street for the most convenient access. Amenities are bare-bones, but there is an orientation centre at 4915 W 16th Avenue. The 12,000-year-old bog (Camosun Bog) is on the eastern edge of the park at Camosun and W19th.

UBC itself holds little architectural interest, save for the Chan Centre for the Performing Arts (*see p161*), a cylindrical concert hall clad in zinc panels designed by Bing Thom Architects in 1997, and Arthur Erickson's superb **Museum of Anthropology** (*see p77*), the city's best museum.

UBC also boasts two outstanding gardens. The **UBC Botanical Garden** is a somewhat hidden (but sizeable) jewel at the intersection of SW Marine Drive and W16th Avenue. The garden sprawls over 110 wildly distinctive acres, with, at one extremity, an Asian garden with rare rhododendrons, and at another an alpine rockery growing rare vines and dwarf conifers. The site can be walked briskly in 90 minutes, and an extensive trail system includes the Walk in the Woods through an undisturbed second-growth forest.

A five-minute stroll from the Museum of Anthropology brings you to the smaller **Nitobe Memorial Garden**. An exquisite Japanese Garden named for scholar-statesman Dr Inazo Nitobe, this tranquil haven is an authentic expression of Japanese garden artistry and philosophy. Cherry trees bloom in spring, irises in summer (by the arched wooden bridge); in autumn, leaves create a spectacular effect. The site includes a traditional teahouse, with occasional openings for a formal tea ceremony.

Museum of Anthropology

6393 NW Marine Drive, at West Mall (604 822 5087/ www.moa.ubc.ca). Bus 4, 17, 44 then 10min walk. **Open** *Mid Oct-mid May* 11am-9pm Tue; 11am-5pm Wed-Sun. *Mid May-mid Oct* 10am-5pm daily (until 9pm Tue). **Admission** $9; $7 reductions; free under-6s. Pay-as-you-can 5-9pm Tue. **Credit** DC, MC, V.

Canada's largest teaching museum, and arguably Vancouver's only truly world-class cultural institution, the Museum of Anthropology began life in the 1920s in the basement of the UBC library. Designed by Arthur Erickson in 1976, the current building is an ingenious amalgam of concrete and glass, modeled to reflect the West Coast's traditional wooden post-and-beam structures. Look through the soaring glass walls of the Great Hall and you'll see some of them in the re-creation of two Haida longhouses in the museum's grounds. These windows allow the Great Hall's dazzling range of aboriginal sculptures, totem poles, feast dishes and masks to be admired in natural light. You are encouraged to touch some exhibits, notably Bill Reid's cedar bear and sea wolf.

Bill Reid (*see p31* **Reid all about it**) is considered the museum's most important artist, and his influence is strongly felt, but the museum also showcases carvings from First Nations communities of the Pacific Northwest. Even before you get inside you pass two imposing figures by Musqueam and Nuu-chah-nulth artists, and the magnificent 1976 wooden doors are by four Gitxsan woodworkers. Collections from Africa, Asia and Central America sometimes sit strangely with the local artifacts, but the museum's visible storage is another treasure trove, allowing the public to browse through 13,000 objects.

Nitobe Memorial Garden

1895 Lower Mall, off N W Marine Drive (604 822 6038/www.nitobe.org). Bus 4, 17, 44 then 10min walk. **Open** *Mid Mar-4 Nov* 10am-6pm daily. *5 Nov-mid Mar* 10am-3pm Mon-Fri. **Admission** *Mid Mar-4 Nov* $5; $3-$4 reductions; free under-18s; $10 joint entry with UBC Botanical Garden. *5 Nov-mid Mar* free. **Credit** DC, MC, V.

UBC Botanical Garden

6804 SW Marine Drive, at W 16th Avenue (604 822 9666/www.ubcbotanicalgarden.org). Bus 4, 17, 44 then 15min walk. **Open** *Mid Mar-4 Nov* 10am-6pm daily. *5 Nov-mid Mar* 10am-4pm daily. **Admission** *Mid Mar-4 Nov* $8; $3-$5 reductions; free under-18s; $10 joint entry with Nitobe Memorial Garden. *5 Nov-mid Mar* free. **Credit** DC, MC, V.

The fascinating **Museum of Anthropolgy**.

Queen Elizabeth Park

East of VanDusen Gardens, and across the road from the Nat Bailey Stadium (which hosts both baseball games and a popular mid-week farmer's market) sits **Queen Elizabeth Park**, the city's highest point at 167 metres (505 feet above sea level). A former stone quarry, the park now has an impressive arboretum and the much-loved Quarry Garden. Great views are to be had from the tables of Seasons in the Park restaurant (1 800 632 9422, www.vancouverdine. com/seasons) – if you can get in (it's a popular spot for weddings). Pitch-and-putt and tennis courts are available, and there are pathways throughout the park's 52 hectares (130 acres). At its pinnacle you'll come across the spacious geodesic dome that houses the **Bloedel Floral Conservatory**. Step from the cool park air into the climate-controlled conservatory to experience environments that run from tropical rainforest with trickling water to bone-dry desert with exotic palms. More than 100 birds – including Charlie the (charismatic) Cockatoo – fly free. Myriad blooms add to the colour.

Bloedel Floral Conservatory

Off Cambie Street and W 33rd Avenue (604 257 8570/www.city.vancouver.bc.ca/parks/parks/bloedel). Bus 15. **Open** *Apr-Sept* 9am-8pm Mon-Fri; 10am-9pm Sat, Sun. *Oct-Mar* 10am-5pm daily. **Admission** $4.50; $2.25-$3.40 reductions; free under-6s. **Credit** AmEx, DC, MC, V.

East Vancouver

Get off the tourist track for bargain hunting on the bohemian East Side.

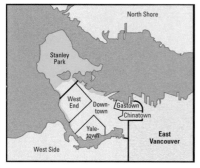

Map p252

In case you're wondering, Vancouver's cross-streets are designated east or west according to their relationship with Main Street. Main is one of the oldest thoroughfares in the city, dating from 1888, and initially connecting mill workers' homes in Mount Pleasant with the factories and city wharf on Burrard Inlet. While the West Side attracts wealthier citizens, **East Vancouver** has always been a diverse area where a succession of immigrants have lived before moving on to other parts of the city. Its mixed neighbourhoods – including Commercial Drive, Main Street to the Punjabi Market, and Strathcona on the edge of Downtown – are places to experience daily life on Canada's left coast. It's not about tourist attractions; this is where people shop, eat and hang out, paint their homes purple and show folk art on front lawns.

Strathcona

The city's oldest neighbourhood, **Strathcona** occupies a spit of land just east of Main Street and Chinatown. But age is no barrier to cool, as it's now the hippest parish in Vancouver. Stroll or cycle through the quiet, tree-lined streets and take in the plethora of arty 19th- and early 20th-century homes. There's not much else to do here other than snack at the homely Union Food Market (810 Union Street, 604 255 5025) or Benny's Market (598 Union Street, 604 254 2746), but you never know who you'll run into. During the autumn Culture Crawl (www.eastsideculturecrawl.com), artists open their studios to welcome a three-day procession of gawkers, and, in the spring,

Strathcona Artist at Home is a performance arts festival with a similar hospitable vibe. And to think Strathcona (bounded by Pender and Prior Streets, Campbell and Jackson Avenues), was up for demolition. Luckily, residents mobilised in opposition, but not before 15 blocks had already been razed. Those public housing projects surrounding the area? Brought to you by the city planners in the late 1950s.

Main Street

Once known as Antique Row, **Main Street** has adopted a newer, fresher character. Indeed, Main has made a comeback and it's now one of the most happening areas in the city, with coffee shops and bars aplenty.

The downside? It's all a bit stretched out and you might find yourself hiking many blocks to find what you're looking for. The street has three areas of interest: Broadway and Main's galleries, shops and cafés; the city's indie fashion district squeezed in from 19th to 21st Avenues; and Antique Row, running between 20th and 30th Avenues.

You can easily lose an hour sorting through the extensive and wonderfully eclectic vintage clothing collection at Burcu's Angels Funky Clothing Etc (2535 Main Street, 604 874 9773). A block just north of Broadway, at 8th Avenue, Lark (2315 Main Street, 604 879 5275) offers imaginative, locally made clothes, while across the street, Pulpfiction Books (2422 Main Street, 604 876 4311, www.pulpfictionbooks vancouver.com) is a cavernous affair, stuffed to the ceiling with used tomes. They regard their customers as 'well read, unconventional and bright' and stock their shelves accordingly.

Elaborate stained glass, chandeliers and antiques crowd the internationally renowned Architectural Antiques at Main and 8th (2403 Main Street, 604 872 3131), while an altogether younger turk, Dadabase (183 E Broadway; *see p127*) collides fashion, art and technology for a receptive, hip crowd. Two blocks east of Main, on 8th, Vancouver's first artist-run centre, **Western Front** (303 E 8th Avenue; *see p153*), features an art gallery, performance hall and multi-media studios.

There's plenty of variety in eats around this corner. On Broadway, Chutney Villa (147 E Broadway; *see p111*) offers spicy southern

Indian fare, while next door, Congee Noodle House (141 E Broadway, 604 879 8221) is a bustling, no frills Chinese joint with good roast meats and soothing, creamy congee. Slickity Jim's Chat & Chew (2513 Main Street, 604 873 6760) is a legendary all-day breakfast spot with wild paraphernalia on its red walls. For more refined environs try Soma Café (151 E 8th Avenue; *see p120*) for coffee and Wi-Fi, or its sophisticated small plates and a good wine list.

Further up Main, indulge in a fashion-as-art aesthetic in a number of clothing stores offering fresh local designs. Music lovers should check out Neptoon Records & CDs (3561 Main Street, 604 324 1229, www.neptoon.com), which houses several thousand vinyl LPs, from decades-old 78s to Arcade Fire. Antique Row begins just south of here. Many stores feature traditional antiques and 20th-century nostalgia, ranging from art deco accessories to 1950s and '60s kitschy retro items.

For some drinks, live music and food head to Cottage Bistro (4468 Main Street, 604 876 6138), Purple Crab (3916 Main Street, 604 484 2436, www.purplecrab.ca) or Montmartre Café (4362 Main Street, 604 879 8111).

Punjabi Market

It can take hours to explore this vibrant little version of India, a four-block area at Main Street and 49th Avenue, where exotic Indian groceries, Bollywood-loaded video stores, over-the-top jewellery shops and sari emporiums stuffed with dazzling embroidered silk cater to Vancouver's approximately 125,000 Indian immigrants. Hungry? Try the all-you-can-eat buffets offered for a mere $10 at both All India Restaurant and Sweets (6505 Main Street, 604 327 0891) and Himalaya Restaurant (6587 Main Street, 604 324 6514). The two eateries compete in presenting excellent curries, the most colours at a dessert counter and the cheesiest pop music videos. On the corner at New Delhi Paan Centre (209 E 51st Avenue, 604 327 0358), you can stock up on areca nut and betel.

Commercial Drive

Cafés, delis, unique shops and a cosmopolitan constituency make '**The Drive**' a diverse street experience. The faintly shabby, funky enclave was originally called 'Little Italy', but it's now Vancouver's most bohemian neighbourhood.

Still, a visitor may be more impressed with the variety of ethnic shops and restaurants that the 15-block street supports, including Jamaican, Ethiopian and Moroccan cafés, Thai fast food places, Spanish tapas bars, Portuguese coffee shops, sushi joints, organic and Chinese grocers, Italian tailors, French bakeries and the requisite hipster clothing shops. You can head out on a virtual tour of your own at www.thedrive.ca or visit

Punjabi Market.

www.clickthedrive.com for up-to-date listings. Easily accessed from the SkyTrain stop at Broadway and Commercial Drive, the area is the neighbourhood to head to if your visit coincides with any major sporting tournaments.

The action doesn't really get going until five blocks north of the SkyTrain, but you'll pass Café Deux Soleils first (2096 Commercial Drive; *see p120*), which serves fortifying breakfasts, afternoon pints, live music and slam poetry. There's something like a culinary Expo between 5th and 6th Avenues on Commercial Drive, each shop crammed with a different nationality of food. Bibliophile Bookshop (no.2010, 604 254 5520) and Audiopile (no.2016, 604 253 7453, www.audiopile.com) should appease book and record collectors, while foodies must slip into the First Ravioli Store (no.1900, 604 255 8844), an aromatic Italian deli with hand-rolled pastas and imported treats galore. Speaking of celestial experiences, Fratelli Bakery (no.1795, 604 255 8926) serves up angelic cream puffs.

Most people arrive at the Drive to stock up on giant cans of olive oil and organic groceries, and then to caffeinate. Coffee is a serious undertaking here. You'll pass JJ Bean, Prado Café (*see p112*), Calabria and the Continental Coffee before crossing 1st Avenue, then Roma, Joe's, Turks and at least a dozen others, each with their own faithful clients.

Gelato is another popular Commercial Drive indulgence; Dolce Amore (no.1590, 604 258 0006) and Gelato Time (no.1110, 604 251 4426) draw a steady stream of ice-cream fanatics.

Highlife Records & Music (1317 Commercial Drive, 604 251 6964), widely respected for its discerning collection of world and pop music, and the adjacent Magpie Magazine Gallery (no.1319, 604 253 6666), with the most diverse range of magazines in the city, are worthy perusals, as is Beckwoman's (no.1314, 604 254 8056), a hippies' paradise of crystals, moonstones and trinkets.

House-browsers should hike east on any of the streets north of 1st Avenue to view the large, colourful, early-20th century homes of Vancouver's first suburb. At Victoria Park (between Kitchener and Grant Streets), try to figure out who's winning at *bocce*, played daily by the elderly denizens of Little Italy. Back on the Drive, Grandview Park (at Charles Street) hosts mini-lawn sales, music jams and events, such as the Parade of the Lost Souls (Saturday before Hallowe'en, to 'honour the dead, wake the living and overcome our fears').

In the evenings, the Drive comes alive with nightly live entertainment in Lime (no.1130; *see p164*), Latin Quarter (no.1305, 604 251 1144), Libra Room (no.1608, 604 255 3787) and Café Deux Soleils (*see above*). Havana (no.1212; *see p120*), a popular Cuban restaurant, theatre and art gallery, and Waazubee Café (no.1622, 604 253 5299, www.waazubee.com) offer evening revelers more good vibes sans bands.

Beckwoman's captures the spirit of the Drive's countercultural vibe.

North Shore

Into the wild.

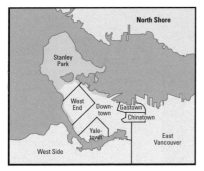

North Shore

Stanley
Park

West
End

Down-
town

Gastown

Chinatown

Yale-
town

East
Vancouver

West Side

Map p253

Vancouver's most desirable suburban districts, West and North Vancouver, sprawl along the Burrard Inlet foreshore between Deep Cove and Horseshoe Bay, and up the mountain slopes to just above the Upper Levels Highway. The **North Shore** is primarily residential, with a total population of 171,000 and development higher up the mountain continuing despite mudslides that have seen homes collapse. But there are parks and other spaces worth seeking out. In the winter, the ski resorts on Grouse, Seymour and Cypress become the city's playground; none of them is more than a 30-minute drive from downtown. In the summer, hikers square up to the challenge of the Grouse Grind (*see p82* **High jinx**) while tour buses gravitate to the Capilano Suspension Bridge. If you're under your own steam, there are many more trails to explore. You can kayak up Indian Arm, or mountain bike down some of the most demanding paths in the world. Access is via the Lions Gate Bridge (First Narrows) or Ironworkers' Memorial Bridge on Highway 1 (Second Narrows). Coast Mountain buses (604 953 3333, www.translink.bc.ca) pick up on Georgia Street in downtown for travel to North and West Vancouver.

A third entry point, particularly to North Van, is the passenger-only SeaBus, a catamaran ferry service from Vancouver's Waterfront Station to Lonsdale Quay. The crossing takes 12 minutes. From the quayside terminal, buses run to most North Shore destinations, including the major parks. All trips from Vancouver and around the North Shore cost $3.25, $2 for children and seniors ($2.25; $1.50 reductions

after 6.30pm and on weekends). Lonsdale Quay is a covered market selling food, clothes, toys and trinkets. There's a food court, or pop around the corner for good quality comfort food at Burgoo (3 Lonsdale Avenue, 604 904 0933, www.burgoo.ca). For dinner, try next door at Gusto Di Quattro (1 Lonsdale Avenue, 604 924 4444, www.quattrorestaurants.com) for reliable Italian fare in a convivial atmosphere. If it's shopping you're after, Park Royal (604 925 9576, www.shopparkroyal.com) near the Lions Gate Bridge has the dubious distinction of being the first mall in Canada, and offers all the usual suspects.

Lions Gate Bridge

Named for 'the Lions', two hump-like peaks above the North Shore, the Lions Gate Bridge was built over the First Narrows during the 'Dirty 30s'. It was the brainchild of local capitalist 'AJT' Taylor. Taylor persuaded the

Capilano Suspension Bridge. *See p83.*

High jinx

The North Shore Mountains are more than just a scenic backdrop across the Burrard Inlet. They're also responsible for Vancouver's generous annual precipitation (up to 3,000 millimetres, or 120 inches, on the North Shore), and they're an invaluable buffer against urban sprawl – not that developers haven't crawled up the lower slopes, only for some homes to be reclaimed in devastating mudslides. Most importantly for many Vancouverites, the mountains represent nature's most spectacular open-air gym: for hiking, skiing, skating, and snowshoeing.

Grouse Mountain (*see p84*) is easily accessible, a 25-minute drive over the Lions Gate Bridge from the city centre, or a short bus ride from Lonsdale Quay. There's a car park at the foot of the mountain, where you'll also find a Starbucks, the Guest Services office, and the **Skyride** (*pictured*), a giant gondola which departs every 15 minutes, 9am-10pm, seven days a week. The Skyride transports a maximum of 100 passengers to the top in less than ten minutes. The Alpine Station, located 1,100 metres (3,700 feet) above sea level, is a large stone complex that houses a ski and hiking store, tourist bits and bobs, and several dining options, ranging from fast food buffets to the **Observatory**, a fine dining establishment open 5-10pm (phone 604 980 9311 to reserve). Your Skyride ticket ($32.95 for adults) covers entrance to the Theatre in the Sky, an IMAX cinema which shows a couple of short BC travelogues on the half hour, and the wildlife refuge, a five-acre habitat that is home to a

pack of grey wolves (retired film stars who were born and raised in captivity) and orphan grizzly bears Grinder and Coola – the only grizzlies you'll meet in this neck of the woods (though it's possible you'll see black bears in the wild in spring and summer). Two resident peregrine falcons, Caliph and Emir, participate in flying demonstrations three times a day. From May to September, admission also includes a lumberjack show (at noon, 2.30pm and 4.30pm) and a guided eco walk (reservations advised). In winter, there are complimentary sleigh rides, and possible sightings of Santa and his reindeer. The pond becomes a skating rink – there is a small fee for skate rentals – and queues snake down the hill outside the ski and snowboard rental shop. Grouse can't compete with Whistler-Blackcomb for the length or breadth of its ski runs, but on a clear day the views over Vancouver are breathtaking. (The price of a lift pass includes the Skyride trip: currently $47 for an adult.) Floodlights allow night skiing on 13 runs until 10pm.

In the summer, a surprising number of visitors eschew the Skyride and pit themselves against the **Grouse Grind**, locally known as 'Mother Nature's Stairmaster'. Built largely of big wooden steps, the Grind gains about 850 metres (2,800 feet) in 2.9 kilometres (1.8 miles), with a gradient steeper than 50 degrees in parts. Signs caution that the 'extremely difficult and strenuous climb' is open May to October, but closes due to weather, erosion, 'or search and rescue'. Still confident? You can buy a Summit Seeker card (at Guest Services) for $20 and 'swipe in' to the timer at the bottom and the top. Inside the lodge, a computer spews out results. The average climber takes 1.5 hours. The computer will also let you know what you've achieved over the season – for example, 24 grinds equals Kilimanjaro, 54 equals Everest. Just don't expect to beat the record times, set in the annual Grouse Grind Mountain Run in September (26 minutes 19 seconds for men, 31 minutes 4 seconds for women). Check the website for current weather conditions and information regarding special paragliding and helicopter tours.

Guinness (beer) family that a bridge would foster development of an expanse of properties it owned in West Van. The Guinness syndicate coughed up $6 million.

A decade of planning, involving everybody who was anybody in Canada at the time, was bitter and fractious; the engineering immensely complicated. Yet thanks largely to Taylor, this sublime suspension bridge – three spans and a viaduct totalling 1,823 metres (5,980 feet) – opened in 1938. It was an immediate success, and fed the post-war growth of the North Shore.

In 1955 the province bought the bridge, neglected it, then talked of replacing it with a soulless tunnel. Heritage advocates, and all but the most commuting-obsessed residents of the North Shore, were outraged. Ultimately, the government took the cheaper route, and rebuilt. In 2002, over 56 nights during which the bridge was closed from 8pm to 6am, workers cut free the decks and replaced them with 54 20-metre long (66-foot) segments. The 112-ton sections were hoisted from barges and slipped into place.

Today, the Lions Gate Bridge is a beloved icon and National Heritage site – even if its three lanes (the centre one reversible) come to a crawl at rush hour. As for 'AJT' Taylor, such were the politics of the day that he watched the opening ceremonies from the sidelines. His story is said to be sealed in one of the stone lions that guard the bridge's southern entrance.

North Vancouver

The **Capilano River Regional Park**, off Capilano Road and Capilano Park Road in North Vancouver, illustrates the best of the original mountain habitat. In this deep, granite gorge, water tumbles down precipices and eddies around coves and pools. Traverse the wooden suspension bridge and a right turn will take you into a cluster of centuries-old Douglas firs. The largest is said to be 2.4 metres (eight feet) in diameter and 60 metres (200 feet) tall. Above the gorge you can see the 90-metre (295-foot) Cleveland Dam spillway. The salmon hatchery is open year round, but to see salmon jumping up the ladders, spawning season is November to December. There are 26 kilometres (16 miles) of easily accessible trails. This Metro Vancouver park is not to be confused with the privately run **Capilano Suspension Bridge** (*see below*), a popular tourist destination on a wilderness theme on Capilano Road.

Venturing over the suspension bridge at **Lynn Canyon Park** (off Lynn Valley Road and Peters Road) costs you nothing. Near the park entrance, the bridge over Lynn Creek (don't let 'creek' fool you – these streams become raging torrents) swings above a steep-sided canyon with a 27 metre (90 foot) waterfall. The 250 hectare (617 acre) district-run wilderness also has trails and an ecology centre suitable for kids (3663 Park Road, 604 981 3103, www.dnv.org/ecology). In summer an unofficial swimming hole is hugely popular.

A potentially demanding wilderness with 75 kilometres (47 miles) of trails, **Lynn Headwaters Regional Park** (604 224 5739, www.gvrd.ca/parks/lynnheadwaters.asp) is entered off Lynn Valley Road. Confine yourself to an amble around Rice Lake near the entrance, or download a map from the website and spend the day climbing the steep paths to Lynn Lake or several peaks. Beware of changeable weather and wandering black bears, a common visitor in these parts. If you do see a bear, keep your distance or back away slowly avoiding eye contact. Don't panic – there is zero chance this is a man-eating grizzly. The website lists current conditions and any trail closures.

The public is also permitted into the vast source of Greater Vancouver's drinking water, the **Lower Seymour Conservation Reserve** (604 990 0483, www.gvrd.bc.ca/water/lscr.htm). From June to September Metro Vancouver hosts free bus and walking tours exploring the ecology of the Seymour Watershed (604 432 6430 for reservations).

At the east end of North Van is the pretty village of **Deep Cove** on a long fjord known as Indian Arm. This is a base for canoeing, kayaking, motor-boating, fishing, mountain biking and hiking (www.deepcovebc.com). You'll also find ice-cream, coffee and sandwiches.

Capilano Suspension Bridge

3735 Capilano Road (604 985 7474/www.capbridge. com). SeaBus Lonsdale Quay, then bus 236. **Open** daily; phone or check website for hours. **Admission** $26.95; $8.30-$24.95 reductions; free under-6s. **Credit** AmEx, DC, MC, V. **Map** p253 X3.

Scottish engineer George Mackay extended a rope and plank bridge 137m (450ft) over the Capilano River in 1889 with the help of two men and a team of horses. Natives called it 'the laughing bridge' because of the noise it made in the wind. In 1903 the rope was replaced with steel cables, and the bridge soon became a tourist magnet. It's perfectly safe, but if you're scared of heights or don't enjoy the sensation of walking on jelly-legs 70m (230ft) above a raging torrent, bear in mind it doesn't take many people to make the bridge sway quite alarmingly. The admission price includes a pedestrian historical exhibit, totem poles, and the chance to chat with native carvers. On the other side of the bridge there is an interpretative centre, attractive trails and walkways. The highlight is the Treetops Adventure, an elevated platform that leads you through a series of trees 33m (100ft) above the forest floor. There's also a restaurant, café and souvenir shop. *Photo p81.*

Grouse Mountain

6400 Nancy Greene Way, North Vancouver (604 984 0661/snow report 604 986 6262/ www.grousemountain.com). Bus 232, 236, 247. **Open** *Skyride* 9am-10pm daily. *Office* 8am-8pm daily. *Grouse Grind* May-Oct dawn to dusk daily, weather permitting. **Admission** $32.95; $11.95-$30.95 reductions; free under-4s. **Credit** AmEx, DC, MC, V. **Map** p253 Z1.
For review, *see p82* **High jinx**.

West Vancouver

West Vancouver (or 'West Van', as it is commonly called) is a 20-minute bus ride from downtown to the mega-shopping complex of **Park Royal** at its entrance, and another 20 minutes out to **Horseshoe Bay**.

Originally settled by aboriginals, West Van's lovely contours caught the attention of a Welsh deserter from the British Navy in the 1870s. 'Navy Jack' then went on to earn a living ferrying Vancouverites across Burrard Inlet by rowboat for picnicking and camping, before a ferry-boat service began in the early 1900s. Immigrant Brits in particular took a fancy to this Cornwall-away-from-home, and built 'villages' along the waterfront with names like Caulfeild (after gentleman-scholar pioneer Francis William Caulfeild), West Bay, Dundarave and Ambleside.

In 1938, the Guinness family, recognising the potential of the view from the forested West Van hillside, built the Lions Gate Bridge over the First Narrows. Today the 1,500 hectares (3,700 acres) for which the family paid $80,000 would sell for millions. Indeed, there are not many homes on the West Van mountainside (still sometimes called 'the British properties') that would sell for under a million, and those on the waterfront are up in the stratosphere.

This privileged community is not known for its open arms. A few years ago a series of concrete plinths installed along Marine Drive to mark the entry points to secluded beaches mysteriously disappeared. The only hotel was demolished in 2005, although there's a motel in Horseshoe Bay (*see p53*) and a handful of B&Bs.

Long and narrow, with shops and houses built close to the shore, Ambleside has a European seaside town feel. You'll see fishermen on the pier, small, manicured gardens, and likely a harbour seal.

At the north-western extremity of West Vancouver snuggles **Horseshoe Bay**. Once a popular boating and picnicking destination, today it largely serves as the launching pad for BC Ferries trips to Howe Sound (particularly Bowen Island; *see p187*), the Sunshine Coast and Vancouver Island (*see p201*). If you have an hour to kill before your ferry leaves it's only a short stroll from the terminal to the village.

The loveliest part of the North Shore is the waterfront between Horseshoe Bay and Dundarave (*see p85* **The shore thing**). Despite over-use, 75-hectare (185-acre) **Lighthouse Park** remains a gorgeous reserve of old growth, with ten kilometres (six miles) of forest and shoreline trails. To its east lies the community of Caulfeild, with the well-loved St Francis-in-the-Wood church (4773 Piccadilly South Road, 604 922 3531, www.stfrancisinthewood.ca) and cottagey houses that recall West Vancouver in its British heyday. From below the church follow Pilot House Road along the foreshore called Caulfeild Park and see what all the fuss is about.

Treks & trails

Six peaks straddle the North Shore: Black, Strachan, Hollyburn, Grouse, Fromme and Seymour. Pioneer hikers have blazed trails up, across and over their steep-sided slopes. The Grouse Grind on **Grouse Mountain** (*see above*) boasts it's the most hiked trail in the world. Over 100,000 people stagger up every year.

Cypress Provincial Park (www.env.gov. bc.ca/bcparks), off the Upper Levels Highway in West Vancouver, embraces **Hollyburn**, **Black** and **Strachan**. Trails up Black and Strachan (1,220 and 1,450 metres – 4,000 and 4,750 feet – respectively), including moderately difficult Black Mountain Loop Trail, deliver great outlooks. **Hollyburn Mountain** (1,326 metres, 4,350 feet) remains a paradise of rustic log cabins and tiny lakes. The Howe Crest Sound Trail, for the fittest only, traverses to Porteau Provincial Park up Howe Sound.

Mount Seymour Provincial Park (1,455 metres, 4,774 feet), is accessed via the Mount Seymour Road off Mount Seymour Parkway (North Vancouver). From the parking lot, relatively easy trails go to Goldie, Mystery and Flower lakes and Dinky and Dog peaks. A longer, well-tramped route climbs to First and Second Pump peaks, from which (on a fine day) you can see to Vancouver Island. A full ten-hour (round-trip) hike continues on to Elsay Lake. Veteran hikers may consider the Baden-Powell Trail, running 48 kilometres (30 miles) across all six mountains, between Deep Cove and Horseshoe Bay (www.trailsbc.ca).

While much of the terrain has been logged, lush undergrowth remains; wild berries and flowers proliferate. Residents include deer, black bear, coyote, raven, jays, woodpeckers, grouse and owl. Caution: dress appropriately, tell someone where you're going, carry a good map, and stay on the trail. Every year hikers get lost and despite the efforts of volunteer rescue service North Shore Rescue (604 983 7441, www.northshorerescue.com), some perish.

The shore thing

West Van's beaches are an unpredictable blend of stone, sand, scattered logs and driftwood on a rocky foreshore. Most are poorly marked at best and the most remote are difficult to access. Neighbourhood signage can be unwelcoming. On the plus side, West Van has a superb Blue Bus system (604 985 7777, www.west vancouver.ca) that runs from downtown Vancouver along Marine Drive, and the driver will let you off at any of the following.

The first four are coves above which the rainforest meets country garden, and expensive houses cling to the hillside.

Whyte Bay, Whytecliff Park

At the extreme end of Marine Drive, west of Horseshoe Bay, Whytecliff Park sprawls over five hectares (12 acres) of bluff and forest. Whyte Bay beach looks out on big-rock Whyte Island, reachable at low tide. A drawback is that the beach is a training ground for scuba divers, so expect lots of rubber suits and oxygen tanks. There's a good takeout nearby.

Eagle Harbour

On Eagle Harbour Road, just before Fisherman's Cove, and a walkable distance from Marine Drive, lies Eagle Harbour and its small yacht club. This idyllic inlet is ideal for languorous swimming and the sandy beach is suitable for children. There are picnic tables and washrooms.

Sandy Cove

West Van's original 'secret hideaway', Sandy Cove is reachable by a short stairwell that begins on the north side of Marine Drive at Rose Crescent and runs under the road. Expect families on a hot day, teens at night.

Caulfeild Park Beach

This gorgeous beach on wide Caulfeild Bay is accessible by steps and woodsy paths from a small parking lot where Dogwood Road meets Pilot House Road, just west of Piccadilly South and Marine Drive. There's also a path from the latter junction.

Dundarave & Ambleside

The most public beaches, able to get Coney Island-ish in summer. Dundarave, at 25th Street, kicks up a good surf when the wind is up; there's a protected bay, pier, park and facilities. The Beach House restaurant (150 25th Street, at Bellevue Avenue, 604 922 1414) is upscale. Ambleside Beach, at 13th Street, is vast, with full amenities. Sandcastle building is big when conditions are right. Both beaches are close to eateries and shops.

Ambleside Beach.

Eat, Drink, Shop

Restaurants & Cafés

A medley of fresh seafood, Asian flavours and European panache.

Vancouver's restaurant scene is a constantly mutating affair: in 2007 alone, some 100 new rooms opened. Though the top restaurants offer remarkable value by European standards, some of the best eating in the city is a far more casual affair. The west coast trend is for small plates (somewhere between a starter and a main in size), often to be shared. Local produce is prized and showcased, often with a twist of fusion, reflecting the city's expanding Asian influence. That connection also brings Japanese *izakayas* (fun, bustling joints offering good food and sake), and dim sum and sushi in abundance. (If Chinese food is your passion, try and schedule a trip out to Richmond for the best you'll find in North America. *See p190* **China town**.)

Locals eat out a lot and with enthusiasm – the 4,000-odd restaurants may not all be filled to capacity every night, but it's surprising how many tables are turned.

Dress is generally casual and although shorts and sandals would be out of place in the smartest restaurants, nowhere requires a jacket or tie. Vancouverites like to eat early and many restaurants start dinner service around 5.30pm and close their kitchens at 10pm. Reservations are recommended, particularly at weekends. Tips are usually in the 15 to 20 per cent range.

THE CHAIN GANG

Though Vancouver may pride itself on its winning independent restaurants, the local chains are popular with younger crowds for their more Americanised fare and flat-screen TVs tuned into sports. **Earls**, **Joey's** and **Milestones** are the pack leaders, with the **White Spot** a much cheaper, more family-friendly business. **Vera's Burgers** is an example of fast food done well and has recently expanded to almost every neighbourhood.

The best Restaurants

For casual dining
Go Fish (*see p109*); Gyoza King (*see p96*); Phnom Penh (*see p106*).

For families
Café Crêpe (*see p90*); Little Nest (*see p112*); Rocky Mountain Flatbread Company (*see p108*).

For fine dining
Bacchus Restaurant & Piano Lounge (*see p91*); Bishop's (*see p110*); Ciopinno's Mediterranean Grill & Enoteca (*see p103*); Le Crocodile (*see p93*).

For sushi
Blue Water Café & Raw Bar (*see p103*); Okada Sushi (*see right*); Yoshi (*see p97*).

For style
Boneta (*see p105*); Chambar (*see p91*); Chow (*see p110*); Gastropod (*see p109*); Parkside (*see p100*); Vij's (*see p106*).

Downtown

Asian

Imperial Chinese Seafood Restaurant

355 Burrard Street, at W Hastings Street (604 688 8191/www.imperialrest.com). Bus 19, 22/SkyTrain Burrard. **Open** 11am-10.30pm Mon-Fri, 10.30am-10.30pm Sat, Sun. **Main courses** $19-$58. **Dim sum** $4-$5. **Credit** DC, MC, V. **Map** p249 K2 ❶
Although the stunning view from this glamorous art deco space is about to be lost to sprouting sky-scrapers, the dining experience will continue to entice customers. Local seafood features, with salmon in black bean sauce, sablefish (black cod) deep-fried with spicy salt, and live crab presented in a variety of ways. Service is elegant and unhurried at dinner, and fast and efficient for the excellent dim sum (*see p102* **Between meals**).

Okada Sushi

2nd Floor, 888 Nelson Street, at Hornby Street (604 899 3266/www.okadasushi.com). All city-centre buses. **Open** 11.30am-2pm, 5-10pm Mon-Fri; 5-10pm Sat. **Main courses** $12-$25. **Set meal** $40-$83. **Credit** AmEx, DC, MC, V. **Map** p248 J4 ❷
Okada is a calm, very traditional Japanese restaurant. The sushi and sashimi are excellent and comple-mented by robata, lobster and crab from the live

> ❶ Purple numbers given in this chapter correspond to the location of each restaurant and café as marked on the street maps. See pp248-253.

tanks, and a selection of *chazuke* (rice bowls mixed with green tea). You won't get any surprises, but what Okada does, it does well and, considering the maki rolls are (unlike in many places locally) more fish than rice, prices are competitive. The daily fresh sheet is only available at dinner and sells out fast.

Prima Taste

570 Robson Street, at Seymour Street (604 685 7881/www.primataste.com.sg). All city centre buses. **Open** 11.30-2.30, 5-10pm Mon-Thur; 11.30am-10pm Fri; noon-10pm Sat; noon-9pm Sun. **Main courses** $10-$15. **Credit** AmEx, DC, MC, V. **Map** p249 K3 ❸
A handy spot to grab a bowl of laksa or a plate of Hainanese chicken as it's located slap in the centre of downtown. Part of a Singaporean chain designed to showcase a line of packaged sauces, this branch is only the second in North America (although it is huge in Asia). In spite of Prima Taste's corporate origins, the food is surprisingly tasty and is served in pleasingly modern surroundings.

Chambar. *See p91.*

Wild Rice

*117 W Pender Street, at Abbott Street (604 642
2882/www.wildricevancouver.com). Bus 10, 16, 20.*
Open 11.30am-midnight Mon-Thur; 11.30-1am Fri;
5pm-1am Sat; 5pm-midnight Sun. **Main courses**
$14-$27. **Credit** DC, MC, V. **Map** p249 L3 ④
Strikingly lit minimalist decor, low-slung lounge
tables and artful presentation combine with experimental small plates – buffalo steamed buns, lamb
shank crispy wontons and Kung Po chicken with
spicy twice-cooked peanuts – to push Chinese food
beyond the same old, same old. The innovation
spreads to the cocktail list, which employs everything from cardamom to beets.

Cafés & diners

Café Crêpe

*874 Granville Street, at Smithe Street (604 806
0845). All cross-city buses.* **Open** 9am-midnight
Mon-Thur, Sun; 9am-2am Fri, Sat. **Main courses**
$4-$10. **Credit** DC, MC, V. **Map** p249 K3 ⑤
With its glossy red-wine walls, oversized art nouveau
poster art and throbbing techno music, this French
franchise is pure Parisian. The menu offers five types
of stuffed savoury crêpes that, with various add-ons,
make for a satisfying, light dinner. Baguettes are also
available, but aren't nearly as good as the crêpes,
which also come in about two dozen dessert varieties.
Gobble them down with cheap red wine or a kick-ass
espresso. It does an excellent breakfast deal too.
Other locations throughout the city.

Caffè Artigiano

*763 Hornby Street, between W Georgia & Robson
Streets (604 694 7737/www.caffeartigiano.com).
All city-centre buses.* **Open** 6.30am-9pm Mon-Sat;
7am-7pm Sun. **Credit** DC, MC, V. **Map** p249 K3 ⑥
Despite being sold off by the Piccolos – barista
brothers extraordinaire – in 2006, this local chain
continues to draw loyal customers addicted to its
excellent coffee. Panini and pastries are also served,
but the java's the thing.
Other locations throughout the city.

Elbow Room

*560 Davie Street, between Richards & Seymour
Streets (604 685 3628/www.theelbowroomcafe.com).
Bus 4, 5, 6, 7, 10, 16, 17.* **Open** 8am-4pm Mon-Fri;
8am-5pm Sat, Sun. **Main courses** $4-$15. **Credit**
AmEx, DC, MC, V. **Map** p248 J4 ⑦
Prepare to be offended. Owner Patrick Savoie, a flam-
ingly gay Québécois, specialises in (well-rehearsed)
verbal abuse that he and his staff hurl with every cup
of coffee. Celebrities appreciate the theatrics: framed
photos of Hollywood customers line the walls. A
bizarrely unique brunch spot that will collect a donation for AIDS charities if you fail to clean your plate.

Gallery Café

*750 Hornby Street, between Robson & W Georgia
Streets (604 688 2233/www.vanartgallery.bc.ca).
All city-centre buses.* **Open** 9am-6pm Mon, Wed,
Fri, Sat; 9am-9pm Tue, Thur; 10am-5.30pm Sun.
Main courses $8-$11. **Credit** AmEx, DC, MC, V.
Map p249 K3 ⑧

Bin 941. *See p95.*

Located inside the Vancouver Art Gallery (*see p60*), this upscale cafeteria boasts one of the prettiest terraces in the city. Slide your tray on to a wrought-iron table, surrounded by Romanesque stone columns and shaded by leafy greenery. Elegant lunch mains range from Thai noodles and wild mushroom pasta to Cobb salads and prosciutto panini.

Mink

863 W Hastings Street (on the park), at Hornby Street (604 633 2451/www.minkchocolates.com). Bus 10, 44/SkyTrain Waterfront. **Open** 8am-6pm Mon-Fri; 10am-6pm Sat, Sun. **Credit** DC, MC, V. **Map** p249 K2

Don't let the minimalist look fool you; Mink is all about decadence. Tucked away in the overlooked hinterland between Canada Place and Gastown, this is a steaming oasis of ethically sourced coffee and chocolate. Take your cocoa hot – milk, dark or mocha – try a good espresso with a truffle on the side, or go for broke with a chocolate and marshmallow fondue ($3-$8).

Sciué

110-800 Pender Street, at Howe Street (604 602 7263/www.sciue.ca). Bus 4, 7, 15. **Open** 6.30am-8pm Mon-Fri; 9am-6pm Sat. **Main courses** $8-$10. **Credit** DC, MC, V. **Map** p249 K3

Pronounced 'shooey', this Italian *pasticerria* and *enoteca* offers something for every appetite in a bustling, bright and casual spot perfect for taking the load off your feet. The *pane romano* (Italian flatbreads) ranges from the simple (margherita) to the

more sophisticated *gamberi* (marinated prawns), and are sold by weight. Panini come fully loaded, and there's always hearty pastas and risotto.

Templeton

1087 Granville Street, at Helmcken Street (604 685 4612/www.thetempleton.com). Bus 4, 6, 7, 10, 16, 17, 50. **Open** 9am-11pm Mon-Thur, Sun; 9am-1am Fri, Sat. **Main courses** $8-$16. **Credit** DC, MC, V. **Map** p248 J4

For comfort food with a health-conscious twist, head to the Templeton, an authentic '30s diner nestled among the nightclubs and sex shops on the seedy end of Granville Street. Burgers are made with organic beef, the prices are cheap, portions huge and service is friendly. *See also p102* **Between meals**.

European

Bacchus Restaurant & Piano Lounge

845 Hornby Street, between Robson & Smithe Streets (604 608 5319/www.wedgewoodhotel.com). All city-centre buses. **Open** 6.30am-11pm Mon-Fri; 7am-11pm Sat, Sun. **Main courses** $30-$42. **Credit** AmEx, DC, MC, V. **Map** p249 K3

Located in the Wedgewood Hotel (*see p42*), Bacchus is one of the city's choicest spots for power lunches. But when the sun goes down and the Murano-glass chandeliers are dimmed, this sumptuous room with its velvet banquettes, cosy booths, rich dark woods and Persian carpets is transformed into a romantic place for dinner. The executive chef Lee Parsons, who trained with Raymond Blanc, uses local seasonal ingredients in his lusty French cuisine – BC Salmon with roasted salsify, or braised oxtail and veal cheeks with parsnip puree and Bordelaise sauce. As you would expect in a restaurant of this calibre, the service is impeccable. *See also p102* **Between meals**.

Cassis Bistro

420 W Pender Street, at Homer Street (604 605 0420/www.cassisvancouver.com). Bus 10, 16, 20. **Open** noon-2.30pm, 5-10pm Mon-Fri; 5-10.30pm Sat. **Main courses** $6-$17. **Credit** DC, MC, V. **Map** p249 L3

Veer off the beaten path on to this grubby stretch of West Pender to find robust French country cooking in a stylish bohemian heritage building with soaring ceilings and polished wood floors. Bistro favourites include slow-simmered *daube de boeuf*, house-made sausages and bowls of bouillabaisse jazzed up with Pernod, fennel and orange peel. Portions are small, but so are the prices, with most mains ringing in under $12. A wine from the ho-hum list will likely set you back more than the meal.

Chambar

562 Beatty Street, between Dunsmuir & W Pender Streets (604 879 7119/www.chambar.com). Bus 10, 16, 20. **Open** 5.30-11pm daily. **Main courses** $20-$27. **Set meal** $55, $65. **Credit** AmEx, DC, MC, V. **Map** p249 L4

Eat, Drink, Shop

A sultry room of warm Moroccan tones and exposed brick walls, Chambar manages to please everyone from hip young things to romantic couples to groups out for a party. Chef-owner Nico Schuermans supplies a lip-smackingly sumptuous menu that includes the city's freshest moules-frites, small plates of beef carpaccio or fois gras terrine, and hearty mains such as braised lamb shanks with honey and dusted with cinnamon. If the extensive Belgian beer list isn't to your liking, try a Blue Fig cocktail – a martini with roasted figs and a side of blue cheese. *Photos p89.*

Le Crocodile

909 Burrard Street, at Smithe Street (604 669 4298/ www.lecrocodilerestaurant.com). Bus 2, 5, 22. **Open** 11.30am-2pm, 5.30-10pm Mon-Fri; 5.30-10.30pm Sat. **Main courses** *Lunch* $14-$28. *Dinner* $27-$42. **Credit** AmEx, DC, MC, V. **Map** p248 J3 ⑮

Since opening Le Crocodile in 1983, chef Michel Jacob has set the standards for French cuisine in Vancouver and trained many of the city's finest chefs (including Canada's most renowned, Rob Feenie). His signature menu items – classic onion tarts, garlic-sautéed frogs' legs, gin-and-tomato soup – hail from the Alsace region in France and are simply delicious. The rich, cream-laden sauces may not be fashionable in these health-conscious times, but you'll struggle not to lick the plate clean. This upscale bistro has – appropriately – formally dressed waiters, half-curtained windows, creamy yellow walls and excellent (though not at all stuffy) service.

Don Francesco Ristorante

860 Burrard Street, between Robson & Smithe Streets (604 685 7770/www.donfrancesco.ca). Bus 2, 5, 22. **Open** 11.30am-4pm, 5-11.30pm Mon-Fri; 5-11.30pm Sat, Sun. **Main courses** $30-$40. **Credit** AmEx, DC, MC, V. **Map** p249 K3 ⑯

Don Francesco's is a swanky celebrity hotspot, largely because of its location, across the street from the Sutton Place Hotel (*see p42*) and its many guests working in Hollywood North. The owner, a passionate opera singer (who performs on Saturday nights) caters to his fat-conscious clientele with numerous seafood options and wild game. For those not watching their diets, there are plenty of pastas too.

Il Giardino

1382 Hornby Street, at Pacific Boulevard (604 669 2422/www.umberto.com). Bus 2, 22. **Open** 11.30am-midnight Mon-Fri; 5.30pm-midnight Sat. **Main courses** $24-$48. **Credit** AmEx, DC, MC, V. **Map** p248 J4 ⑰

The owner is known simply as 'Umberto' – a one-name wonder who put Tuscan cooking on the map in Canada. At one time he had 17 restaurants, but currently presides over four (two in Vancouver, two in Whistler), plus a cookery school/hotel/vineyard south of Florence. His first venture on the West Coast, Il Giardino, in a venerable yellow house with a lovely garden patio, opened in 1973. Umberto's hearty grilled meats and simple pastas, still referred to as 'new' Italian continue to draw a well-heeled business crowd.

The bar's the thing at **So.Cial at Le Magasin** but the food is top-notch too. *See p105.*

Eat, Drink, Shop

The grapevine

The Vancouver wine-drinking scene is no slouch, with a local industry busily improving and expanding. BC wines don't yield enough for export, so it's well worth taking the time to try them here. The bulk of production is made in the Okanagan (*see p208* **It's a vine life**). Three big companies – Vincor, Andrew Peller and Mission Hill – make wine in commercially available quantities. The other 100-plus wineries produce tiny amounts; the quality can vary considerably, though.

Vancouver restaurants have long been supportive of the BC wine industry – and many of the Okanagan's boutique bottlings are only available when dining out. A good place to get your bearings is the Gastown wine bar **Salt Tasting Room** (*see p116; pictured*). Sommelier and general manager Kurtis Kolt also created the all-BC list at **Aurora Bistro** (*see p112*). At Salt, a constantly changing selection of wines includes only the very best from BC. Most are available as flights, so you can easily work your way through a few.

The Okanagan's unusual geography allows production of everything from sparkling, dry white and full-bodied red to ice wine. The region has yet to specialise in a particular wine style, however, and over 60 different grape varieties are planted in a vineyard area one 50th the size of Bordeaux. Some of the tastiest and most unique wines to look for are the Pinot Blancs, in which the peachy, floral taste reflects the area's strong orchard history. Luckily for consumers, Pinot Blanc lacks cachet so tends to be less expensive.

Consistent producers include Gray Monk, Blue Mountain, Lakebreeze Vineyards, Wild Goose and Mission Hill. Aromatic whites like Dirty Laundry Gewürztraminer and Tantalus Riesling are worth seeking out, especially to match with seafood. Successful pinks include the Joie Rosé and St Hubertus Rosé Gamay Noir. There are some ambitious reds made in the province, but don't be persuaded into paying the steep prices demanded by some producers. You won't necessarily get a better wine at $50 than you will at $25.

Pricier choices include Sandhill 'One', a Bordeaux-style blend made by two icons in the BC wine industry: grape-grower Richard Cleave and wine-maker Howard Soon. Old Vines Foch by Quail's Gate is made from a French/American hybrid called Maréchal Foch that was popular here before pure European varieties gained favour. And if wild sockeye salmon is your dish, you'll find a great match in CedarCreek Estate Select Pinot Noir.

● *Barbara Philip is Western Canada's first Master of Wine, and co-owner of Barbariain Wines (www.barbariainwine.com).*

Italian Kitchen

1037 Alberni Street, at Burrard Street (604 687 2858/www.theitaliankitchen.ca). Bus 5. **Open** 11.30am-3pm, 4.30pm-midnight Mon-Fri; 4.30pm-midnight Sat, Sun. **Main courses** $14-$30. **Credit** AmEx, DC, MC, V. **Map** p249 K3 ⓭

Opened in 2007 with a flash party and even flashier clientele, this upscale room is regularly bursting at the seams with the pretty people. An extensive menu helps the indecisive by offering sharing platters in different categories – antipasti, pasta, fish and meat – that also add to the perception that the place is less about the food than seeing and being seen. Lunch is less precious. Cocktails are suitably glamorous.

Seafood

C Restaurant

1600 Howe Street, at Beach Avenue (604 681 1164/ www.crestaurant.com). Bus 4, 7, 10, 16, 17, 50. **Open** 5-10pm daily. **Main courses** $33-$47. **Credit** AmEx, DC, MC, V. **Map** p248 H5 ⓮

Executive chef Rob Clark gets high marks from environmentalists for his sourcing of sustainable produce. The restaurant, however, turned ten years old in 2007 and is beginning to show its age – although if you're on the patio overlooking False Creek, you probably won't notice. Though laden with accolades and gushing reviews, C's reputation took a bit of knock after owner Harry Kambolis was quoted admitting the summer menu is dumbed down for tourists and that VIPs (including media) are served different dishes. It could be a pricey gamble if you don't resemble someone famous. *See also p108* **Serving up sustainability.**

Steaks

Gotham Steakhouse & Cocktail Bar

615 Seymour Street, at Dunsmuir Street (604 605 8282/www.gothamsteakhouse.com). All city-centre buses. **Open** 5-11pm daily. **Main courses** $27-$50. **Credit** AmEx, DC, MC, V. **Map** p249 K3 ⓴

Holy cow, Batman! The portions are almost as substantial as the prices, which hit $50 for Porterhouse. That's without any potato or veg, which must be ordered separately. Your bill subsidises the handsome room, appointed with high ceilings, dark wood and bold art-deco paintings. Eat on the lounge side, which has an unadvertised smaller menu with more reasonable prices. The owner recently opened the similarly spendy Shore Club (688 Dunsmuir Street, 604 899 4400) around the corner.

West Coast

Bin 941

941 Davie Street, between Hornby & Burrard Streets (604 683 1246/www.bin941.com). Bus 2, 6, 22. **Open** 5pm-1.30am Mon-Sat; 5-10.30pm Sun. **Tapas** $4-$16. **Credit** DC, MC, V. **Map** p248 J4 ㉑

The Bin has had numerous imitators, but this is the original – a funky hole in the wall, where the music throbs, the tables are tight and the flavours rock 'n' roll. Executive chef and owner Gord Martin, a former heavy-metal singer, catalysed Vancouver's craze for small plates (larger than traditional tapas). The prices have gone up in recent years, but it's still great value. Drinks are limited to a selective list of wine and beer. No reservations. *Photos pp90-91.*

Other locations Bin 942, 1521 W Broadway, at Granville Street, West Side (604 734 9421).

Diva at the Met

645 Howe Street, between Dunsmuir & W Georgia Streets (604 602 7788/www.metropolitan.com/diva). All city-centre buses. **Open** 6.30am-2.30pm, 5.30-10.30pm Mon-Fri; 7am-2.30pm, 5.30-10pm Sat, Sun. **Main courses** $24-$42. **Credit** AmEx, DC, MC, V. **Map** p249 K3 ㉒

One of the city's long-established dining rooms, Diva hit a bump in the critical consciousness in 2005 when, after ten years of business, it appeared to lose focus with Nike-style swooshes of pureed veg and overly sweet notes in savoury dishes. After a major overhaul of staffing, 2007 saw a return to form, with chef Dino Raenarts strongly favouring the finest Canadian produce, and preparing and presenting it in sophisticated fashion.

Nu

1661 Granville Street, north shore of False Creek (604 646 4668/www.whatisnu.com). Bus 4, 7, 10, 16, 17, 50. **Open** 11am-1am Mon-Fri; 10.30am-1am Sat; 10.30am-midnight Sun. **Main courses** $19-$39. **Credit** AmEx, DC, MC, V. **Map** p248 H5 ㉓

Gourmet finger foods are fun to eat: crispy fried oysters are skewered with plastic shots of Granville Island lager (pop it in your mouth and squeeze), and chicken wings are stuffed with goat's cheese. The custom-designed bar, featuring a pair of suspended booze racks that spin like roulette wheels, offers exciting cocktails and an exclusive wine list. The design theme is retro cruise ship, which is appropriate enough, since the circular restaurant is surrounded by a yacht club. Pull up a swivel stool and pretend you've sailed off on the Love Boat.

Rare

1355 Hornby Street, at Pacific Street (604 669 1256/www.rarevancouver.com). Bus 4, 7, 10, 16, 17, 50. **Open** 6pm-late daily. **Main courses** $26-$40. **Credit** AmEx, DC, MC, V. **Map** p248 J4 ㉔

The food at Rare, which specialises in local and unusual ingredients presented in unconventional ways, belies the rather sterile room. Menus are seasonal and constantly changing – recent highlights have included elk and sour cherry terrine, and toothsome root beer-braised veal cheeks. The chef's tasting menu (six courses for $65) will get you the best bang for your buck – going à la carte can work out surprisingly pricey.

Eat, Drink, Shop

Asian

Gyoza King

1508 Robson Street, at Nicola Street (604 669 8278). Bus 5. **Open** 5.30pm-1am Mon-Fri; 11.30am-3pm, 6pm-1am Sat; 11.30am-3.30pm, 6pm-midnight Sun. **Main courses** $10-$20. **Credit** AmEx, DC, MC, V. **Map** p248 J2 **㉕**

Sick of sushi? Then Gyoza King is more than worth a try. Dumplings are the speciality at this dark hovel that attracts young Japanese visitors looking for cheap eats and some of the city's best chefs relaxing after shift in their own restaurants. *Gyoza* dumplings are fatly stuffed with shrimp, pork and all sorts of vegetable combinations. The tapas-style menu also offers barbecued beef, deep-fried tofu, grilled fish, noodles, pork cutlets and any number of specials.

Hal Mae Jang Mo Jib

1719 Robson Street, at Bidwell Street (604 642 0712). Bus 5. **Open** 10am-2am Mon-Thur, Sun; 11am-5am Fri, Sat. **Main courses** $10-$25. **Credit** AmEx, DC, MC, V. **Map** p248 H2 **㉖**

There are so many Korean restaurants on this side of Robson, the area has been dubbed Little Korea. Ask any of the homesick ESL students and they'll lead you straight to this loud little hole in the wall where the prices are cheap and the dishes plentiful. Start with pork neckbone soup, then try *haemool pajun*, a huge seafood pancake topped with crispy fried noodles.

Kingyo

871 Denman Street, between Barclay & Haro Streets (604 608 1677). Bus 5. **Open** 5.30-11.30pm daily. **Main courses** $8-$25. **Credit** AmEx, DC, MC, V. **Map** p248 H2 **㉗**

Japanese *izakayas* (roughly translated as 'sit and drink spots') have been all the rage in Vancouver for some time. Small plates of casual Japanese food (more likely cooked, though sashimi is usually available) provide a solid foundation for the quantities of beer and sake enthusiastically ingested alongside. While Hapa and the many Guu branches were the local pack leaders, newcomer Kingyo arrived in 2007 and upped the ante with DIY stone grills and some nifty presentation. Noisy, boisterous and fun – so don't plan on a romantic tête-a-tête.

Kintaro Ramen

788 Denman Street, at Robson Street (604 682 7568). Bus 5. **Open** noon-11pm Tue-Sun. **Main courses** $7-$10. **No credit cards**. **Map** p248 H2 **㉘**

Looking for the perfect bowl of soup? Then look no further. Pork-based broths are the signature at Kintaro Ramen, except on Saturdays, when the chef also simmers up a seafood-based Forest Fire ramen with kelp instead of noodles. Ladled out in huge bowls, the soup is ordered according to grade (light, medium or rich), then layered with a dozen spices, spring onions, corn and thin slices of barbecue pork (you can choose from fatty or lean). Pull up a ringside seat at the steamy no-frills counter.

New Town Bakery & Restaurant. See p106.

Kirin Mandarin Restaurant

1166 Alberni Street, between Bute & Thurlow Streets (604 682 8833/www.kirinrestaurant.com). All city-centre buses. **Open** 11am-2.30pm, 5-10.30pm daily. **Main courses** $12-$18. **Dim sum** $4-$5. **Credit** AmEx, DC, MC, V. **Map** p248 J3 **㉙**

This is the original outpost of a highly regarded local restaurant group, where Cantonese refinement is given a gentle, warm spiciness. While large group banqueting is a speciality, à la carte is available, with an emphasis on fresh seafood dishes. The elegantly spacious room is popular with Chinese diners, though the service can be more efficient than friendly. Dim sum from a seasonally updated menu is an elegant affair (*see p102* **Between meals**).

Other locations 2nd Floor, City Square, 555 W 12th Avenue, at Cambie Street, West Side (604 879 8038); 2nd Floor, Three West Centre, 7900 Westminster Highway, Richmond (604 303 8833).

Legendary Noodle House

1074 Denman Street, at Comox Street (604 669 8551). Bus 5. **Open** noon-10pm Mon-Thur; 11am-10pm Fri-Sun. **Main courses** $5-$10. **Credit** DC, MC, V. **Map** p248 H2 **㉚**

After winning praise from no less than the *New York Times*, this family affair launched its third branch in 2007. The chewy noodles come fried or in soup, with various additions including freshly made dumplings. Cheap and cheerful, but quality can be variable.

Other locations 4191 Main Street, at E 26th Street, East Vancouver (604 879 8758); 1300-4540 No.3 Road, at Leslie Road, Richmond (604 207 9226).

Yoshi

689 Denman Street, at Alberni Street (604 738 8226/www.yoshijapaneserestaurant.com). Bus 5. **Open** noon-2pm, 5.30pm-10pm Mon-Fri; 5.30-10pm Sat, Sun. **Main courses** $10-$35. **Set meal** $53, $100. **Credit** AmEx, DC, MC, V. **Map** p248 H1 **㉛**

The view of Stanley Park and Coal Harbour is a perfect aid to digestion – not that savouring chef Yoshinobu Kobayashi's excellent food requires extra effort in that department. Exquisitely presented sushi, sashimi and robata are all wonderful, but the set meals are where the real action is. For a seasonal feast, try a traditional *kaiseki*, where strict progression of flavours and cooking techniques has been developed over centuries. Or sit at the bar and order 'omakase' (chef's choice) – it'll cost you, but nothing like as it would in Europe.

Zakkushi Charcoal Grill

823 Denman Street, between Robson & Haro Streets (604 685 1136). Bus 5. **Open** 5.30pm-midnight Mon, Sun; noon-2.30pm, 5.30-11.30pm Tue-Sat. **Main courses** $8-$18. **Credit** AmEx, DC, MC, V. **Map** p248 H2 **㉜**

A loud and boisterous *yakitori* diner where skewers of charcoal-grilled meats (*tsukune*) take centre stage, as does the grill, with its glowing red-hot coals. The stick foods, which cost less than two dollars each, range from conventional (chicken meatballs, chicken wings, pork, beef with ponzu, vegetable skewers) to courageous (chicken heart, chicken liver and beef tongue). Other small, cheap plates include bitter squash with eggs, barbecue rice balls in tea soup, chicken teriyaki bowls and noodles. The Japanese servers speak fluent English, but service can sometimes be slow.

Other locations 1833 W 4th Avenue, at Burrard Street, West Side (604 730 9844).

Cafés & diners

Delany's Coffee House

1105 Denman Street, between Comox & Pendrell Streets (604 662 3344). Bus 6. **Open** 6am-11pm Mon-Fri; 6.30am-11pm Sat, Sun. **Credit** DC, MC, V. **Map** p248 H2 **㉝**

The Belgian chocolate brownies are divine, the coffee comes from JJ Bean, the wooden tables are always crowded and the atmosphere is friendly – very friendly. Located in the heart of the gay village, this is a hot daytime pick-up spot. It's also handy for takeout coffee to drink while walking on the Seawall or looking out over English Bay.

Other locations 3099 Edgemont Boulevard, at Highland Boulevard, North Vancouver (604 985 3385); 2424 Marine Drive, at 24th Street, West Vancouver (604 921 4466).

Mondo Gelato

1094 Denman Street, at Comox Street (604 647 6638/www.mondogelato.com). Bus 6. **Open** 9am-11pm Mon-Thur, Sun; 9am-midnight Fri, Sat. **No credit cards. Map** p248 H2 **㉞**

Die-hard fans swear by Mondo Gelato, a local company that expanded to Beijing. Proximity to the beach and limitless free samples guarantee long queues in summer, but a mind-boggling array of fresh flavours make it worth the wait. Pistachio, biscotti, chocolate, mango and Nutella are all perennial favourites. Or, for something different, give the black sesame seed a try.

European

Café Luxy

1235 Davie Street, between Bute & Jervis Streets (604 669 5899/www.cafeluxy.com). Bus 6. **Open** 11am-11pm Mon-Fri; 9am-11pm Sat, Sun. **Main courses** $8-$17. **Credit** AmEx, DC, MC, V. **Map** p248 H3 ③⑤

A popular neighbourhood bistro with candlelight, wood panelling and mirror-lined walls, Café Luxy will satisfy any of your carb cravings with dozens of cheap and fresh pasta dishes – or choose from several daily specials. Portions are generous, and come with garlic bread and side salad. Decent breakfasts and lunch is a bargain.

Characters Taverna

1103 Davie Street, at Thurlow Street (604 685 9607/www.characterstaverna.com). Bus 6. **Open** 11.30-6am daily. **Main courses** $14-$19. **Credit** AmEx, DC, MC, V. **Map** p248 J3 ③⑥

The main thing to recommend this run-of-the-mill Greek restaurant is the fact that it offers full kitchen service until 6am. When you're stumbling out of

the clubs at 3am, a roast lamb dinner can be more enticing than a hot dog. At weekends, the place is packed with bar staff coming off shift.

CinCin

1154 Robson Street (upstairs), between Thurlow & Bute Streets (604 688 7338/www.cincin.net). Bus 5. **Open** 5pm-midnight daily. **Main courses** $24-$40. **Credit** AmEx, DC, MC, V. **Map** p248 J3 ③⑦

This popular Tuscan restaurant is a favoured haunt of Hollywood stars shooting locally – and very definitely on the tourist track, too. A spacious room and a pretty patio, plus a wide range of pastas, risottos, and meats or pizzas from the wood-fired grill and oven offer something for everyone – so long as you don't mind paying top dollar. The wine list is extensive, with hefty mark-ups. Pastas are reliable, mains erratic, and desserts overrated.

Saveur

850 Thurlow Street, between Robson & Smithe Streets (604 688 1633/www.saveurrestaurant.com). Bus 5. **Open** 11.30am-2pm, 6-10pm Mon-Fri; 6-10pm Sat. **Main courses** $24. **Set meal** $38. **Credit** AmEx, DC, MC, V. **Map** p248 J3 ③⑧

This underrated gem (formerly Piccolo Mondo) offers classic French cuisine, with a few nods to Italy, and not a whiff of pretension. Chef Stephane Meyer and his wife Nathalie learned their craft in several Michelin-starred restaurants in Europe, before eventually bringing their disciplined artistry and impeccable service with them to the New World. The regularly changing prix-fixe menu and a discerning wine list spell some of the best value

Vij's. See p106.

in town. And, for a change, the solo diner is not hidden away in corners like an unwanted guest but given pride of place at a large communal table in the middle of the room.

Latin American

Lolita's South of the Border Cantina

1326 Davie Street, at Jervis Street (604 696 9996/ www.lolitasrestaurant.com). Bus 6. **Open** 4.30pm-2am Mon-Fri; 3pm-2am Sat, Sun. **Main courses** $16-$22. **Credit** DC, MC, V. **Map** p248 H3 ③
Home-made corn tortillas, a friendly vibe, shaken margaritas, funky bamboo furnishings and late-night kitchen service make Lolita's a cosy neighbourhood cantina. The menu isn't strictly Mexican (paella, anyone?), but everything is made in-house and the prices are reasonable too. Go for the slow-roasted pulled beef taquitos or pan-seared halibut tacos; wash them down afterwards with a sweet and nippy Loco Limonada (gold tequila and mango liqueur with muddled chilli and mango lemonade).

Seafood

Cardero's

1583 Coal Harbour Quay, at Cardero Street (604 669 7666/www.vancouverdine.com/carderos). Bus 5 or 19, then 5min walk. **Open** 11.30am-11pm Mon-Sat; 11.30am-10pm Sun. **Main courses** $12-$29. **Credit** AmEx, DC, MC, V. **Map** p248 J2 ④

For a city by the sea, Vancouver's restaurants are curiously lacking in simply grilled fish. You can find it here at this casual nautical-themed dining room built on a pier in the marina, along with steaks, pizzas, burgers and Asian wok fries (be sure to try the crispy chilli-coriander squid). With its wonderful views of the inner harbour and mountains to accompany your meal, the (heated) patio is worth waiting for. Prices are right and service is friendly, especially in the fireside pub where staff indicate your table is ready by sending a flag up a line.

Joe Fortes Seafood & Chop House

777 Thurlow Street, at Robson Street (604 669 1940/www.joefortes.ca). Bus 5. **Open** 11am-11pm daily. **Main courses** $28-$49. **Credit** AmEx, DC, MC, V. **Map** p248 J3 ④
More than 20 years later, Joe Fortes' heated rooftop garden is still a favourite cocktail-hour destination for Vancouver's high-flying brokers. For something decadently different, tuck in to an icy seafood tower on a sunny Saturday afternoon. Surrounded by visiting rock stars, or at least glammed-up American Robson Street shoppers, you'll feel like you just landed in LA. The restaurant's signature cedar-planked salmon, crab legs and steaks are pricey, but portions are generous and the kitchen dependable.

Lift Bar & Grill

333 Menchions Mews, at Bayshore Drive (604 689 5438/www.liftbarandgrill.com). Bus 5, then 10min walk. **Open** 11.30am-10.30pm daily. **Main courses** $15-$39. **Credit** AmEx, DC, MC, V. **Map** p248 J1 ④

Floating on a concrete pad at the far edge of Coal Harbour, this sleek waterfront restaurant with vanishing glass walls offers a million-dollar view of the mountains. Make that $8 million, which is what Lift cost to build. If only the owners had invested in a kitchen large enough to accommodate the well-heeled crowds the room attracts. Without reservations, be prepared for a lengthy wait. Food service is none too swift either. The lunch menu is a simple enough affair if you fancy a smart stop to eat your burger or fish and chips after walking the Seawall. At dinner you might do best to stick to the simple pleasure of sipping drinks and nibbling sushi next to the fire pit on the upper deck.

West Coast

Delilah's

1789 Comox Street, at Denman Street (604 687 3424/www.delilahs.ca). Bus 5, 6. **Open** 5.30-10pm Tue-Thur, Sun; 5.30-11pm Fri, Sat. **Set meal** $31, $43. **Credit** AmEx, DC, MC, V. **Map** p248 H2
A West End institution for more than two decades, Delilah's boasts that it is the North American birthplace of the cocktail martini – whatever that means, they sure taste damn good. Fruit-infused vodkas reign alongside the drag queen entertainers who frequently pop in for a suitably glam cocktail. Hand-painted cherubs dancing on the ceiling and lush velvet banquettes lend high-camp glamour to the dining room. The menu leans on Mediterranean influences; desserts are decadent.

Parkside

1906 Haro Street, at Gilford Street (604 683 6912/ www.parksiderestaurant.ca). Bus 5. **Open** 6-11pm Mon-Thur, Sun; 6pm-midnight Fri, Sat. **Set meal** $55, $62. **Credit** DC, MC, V. **Map** p248 H2 ⓴
Tucked away on a leafy residential street near Stanley Park, Parkside combines the feel of a cosy neighbourhood haunt with the elegance of a classical European kitchen. It also boasts one of the city's nicest patios for summer dining. Chef/owner Andrey Durbach has developed a cult following with his robust menus, hand-picked wine list and heady selection of after-dinner cognac and *eau de vie*. Cuisine leans towards the rich and meaty, with strong French and Italian influences, but is balanced with zesty touches from local produce. Durbach's rapidly expanding empire also includes a small Italian bistro in Dunbar called La Buca and Pied-à-Terre (*see p109*).

Raincity Grill

1193 Denman Street, at Davie Street (604 685 7337/www.raincitygrill.com). Bus 5, 6. **Open** 11.30am-2pm, 5-10pm Mon-Fri; 10.30am-2pm, 5-10pm Sat, Sun. **Main courses** $26-$32. **Credit** AmEx, DC, MC, V. **Map** p248 G2 ⓴
Raincity Grill was an original pioneer of Pacific Northwest cuisine and remains one of the city's best. Harry Kambolis – the owner of C Restaurant and Nu (for both, *see p95*) – deserves high praise for a long-standing commitment to local small-lot farmers and sustainable fisheries, which supply the

Gastropod's minimalist decor complements its cutting-edge cuisine. *See p109.*

seasonal menus. Arrive between 5pm and 6pm for the early-bird three-course tasting menu, or linger as the sun sets over English Bay while trying to put a dint in the list of a hundred or so regional wines by the glass. In spring and summer, the take-out window offers sandwiches and salads for gourmet picnics. The only let-down is the service, which can be insufferably snooty.

Stanley Park

Cafés & diners

Stanley's Park Bar & Grill

610 Pipeline Road, opposite Malkin Bowl (604 602 3088/www.stanleysbar.ca). Bus 19, then 10min walk. **Open** *May, Sept* 11.30am-5pm daily. *June-Aug* 11am-10pm daily. Closed Oct-Apr. **Main courses** $12-$20. **Credit** AmEx, DC, MC, V. **Map** p69 ㊻

This quaint heritage building, which dates from around 1911, is located in the heart of Stanley Park, next to the rose gardens. Formerly a fairly sedate afternoon tea spot, it was given a makeover in 2007 to emerge as a grill offering a limited menu of burgers and fish and chips, as well as salads. There are seven beers on tap and a surprisingly decent wine list. It stays open longer on evenings when there's a gig in nearby Malkin Bowl.

Seafood

Fish House in Stanley Park

8901 Stanley Park Drive, at Lagoon Drive (604 681 7275/www.fishhousestanleypark.com). Bus 6, then 5min walk. **Open** 11.30am-10pm Mon-Sat; 11am-10pm Sun. **Main courses** $20-$30. **Credit** AmEx, DC, MC, V. **Map** p69 ㊼

Chef Karen Barnaby is a celebrity in the city and a real cool broad who tells it like it is. A stint at the Rivoli Restaurant in Toronto and a jaunt around Mexico, where she worked as a personal chef, gives her serious bohemian street cred. She is a fine chef, who has carved out a speciality with creative low-carb dishes and numerous books. The Fish House is a little frilly for an oyster bar, but it does serve an exceptional afternoon tea (*see p102* **Between meals**) and offers a better than usual kids' menu.

West Coast

Sequoia Grill at the Teahouse

Ferguson Point, Stanley Park Drive (604 669 3281/www.vancouverdine.com). Bus 19, then 5min walk. **Open** 11.30am-2.30pm, 5-9.45pm Mon-Fri; 11.30am-3pm, 5-9.45pm Sat; 10.30am-3pm, 5-9.45pm Sun. **Main courses** $18-$38. **Credit** AmEx, DC, MC, V. **Map** p69 ㊽

This ain't your grandma's teahouse any more, but she'll still love the panoramic view of English Bay. When Brent Davies (Cardero's, Seasons, Sandbar) took over this Stanley Park landmark in 2004, he threw out the doilies, landscaped the patio and turned this formerly fussy tourist trap into a modern West Coast bistro. The menu might bore if you've been to the group's other restaurants but on sultry summer nights, there's no better place to relax, sip a strawberry-basil martini and watch the sun go down over the Georgia Strait.

Yaletown

African

Nuba

1206 Seymour Street, at Davie Street (778 371 3266/www.nuba.ca). Bus 6, 50. **Open** 11.30am-10pm daily. **Main courses** $5-$10. **Credit** DC, MC, V. **Map** p248 J4 ㊾

Pita stuffed with crisp pillows of falafal makes a quick and easy lunch, but hang around for a table full of mezze and you won't be disappointed. Beef kebab is marinated in pomegranate, crispy cauliflower is tossed with lemon and sea salt, and it's the attention to such detail – along with the freshness – that elevates this no-frills eaterie to somewhere worth seeking out. Just between the Granville strip and upscale Yaletown, it's perfect for a pre- or post movie meal at the Vancity Theatre (*see p147*).

Other locations 322 W Hastings Street, at Hamilton Street, Downtown (604 688 1655).

Asian

Simply Thai

1211 Hamilton Street, at Davie Street (604 642 0123/www.simplythairestaurant.com). Bus 6, 15. **Open** 11.30am-3pm, 5-11pm Mon-Fri; 5-11pm Sat, Sun. **Main courses** $9-$26. **Credit** DC, MC, V. **Map** p249 K4 ㊿

Simply Thai is simply the best Thai restaurant in Vancouver. Mind you, there isn't a great deal of competition in this city. The chef and owner, Siriwan Rerksuttisiridach (call her Grace), apprenticed with Penpan Sittitrai, a celebrated fruit and vegetable sculptor who trains chefs for the Thai royal family. She goes back every year to take a refresher course. Arrive early for lunch and wrap your lips around some *cho muang*, purple flower-shaped dumplings stuffed with minced chicken, onions and secret spices. Grace only makes about five orders of these a day. These delights are accompanied by an outstanding wine list.

Cafés & diners

Cito Espresso

116 Davie Street, at Pacific Boulevard (604 633 2486/www.citoespresso.com). Bus 15. **Open** 6am-6pm Mon-Thur; 6am-7pm Fri, Sat; 7am-6pm Sun. **Main courses** $4-$9. **Credit** DC, MC, V. **Map** p249 K5 (51)

Between meals

Mind the gap with brunch, dim sum and afternoon tea.

BRUNCH

Vancouverites are big brunchers. So much so that lengthy queues at weekends are the norm; if you can book, do so. If it's a lengthy, multi-course, blow-out buffet affair you're after, possibly with champagne involved, the hotels are your best bet. The Sunday Market Brunch at the **Pan Pacific** (*see p42*) comes with live music and views for $49 a head (reductions for children, teens and seniors).

Less opulent brekkie can be had all around town, with excellent choices including the all-day options at the **Templeton** (*see p91*), where grease-free plates of free-range eggs and organic sausages are complemented by signature rosemary roasted potatoes. Head east, to **Crave** (*see p112*) on Main Street, and indulge in the best French toast, eggs Benedict and buttermilk pancakes in the city. It's licensed, too, so be sure to sample a Caesar, the local version of a Bloody Mary.

Tradition is everything to some, and explains the interminable queues outside **Sophie's Cosmic Café** (*see p109*) on weekends. A huge menu offers eggs done every which way (and more besides) served up with mounds of potatoes. The Tex-Mex options add spice, if not sophistication.

If it's a sideshow you're after, try the **Elbow Room** (*see p90; pictured*), where brunch is served with sass and the menu includes such gems as the Hilary Swank (Don't make me cry) omelette, or the Come-I-Wanna-Lay-Ya – poached eggs, ham, pineapple, banana, peaches and kiwi smothered in hollandaise.

DIM SUM

Just as authentic a local institution is dim sum. At **Kirin** (*see p97*), har gow (steamed shrimp dumplings) are the model of snappy freshness from an ever-changing seasonal carte. Try deep-fried local smelt dusted with a salt and peppercorn coating or spicy wontons in a bright piquant sauce. Finish with a bowl of deep-flavoured five-spice beef noodles.

Five full-time master chefs are employed to make only dim sum at **Imperial** (*see p88*). Small trays of dim sum are brought to your table. Delicately steamed rice rolls envelope salty sweet *char sui* (BBQ pork). Deep-fried crab claws (usually banquet fare) make a welcome appearance, and the fried rolls with bananas and shrimp reflect the odd Hong Kong penchant for mixing fruit and seafood.

But if, to you, dim sum proper means steam trolleys clattering around the tables, head to **Sun Sui Wah** (*see p111*) for *sui mai* (shrimp and pork dumplings) topped with Dungeness crab or congee with sweet geoduck clam. For adventure, try the succulent chicken feet in black bean sauce. Baked tapioca pudding and chilled mango pudding are top-notch desserts.

AFTERNOON TEA

There's really nothing quite so civilised as afternoon tea. Head to the fine surroundings of the **Sutton Place Hotel** (*see p42*) and choose between either English or Japanese tea service, plus the usual trimmings for $22.

The verdant surroundings of Stanley Park make for a beautiful backdrop for afternoon tea at the **Fish House** (*see p101*), perfectly situated for a well-earned pit stop after you've rounded the Seawall. Finger sarnies, scones and other treats can be yours for $24.

Weekends bring high tea at **Bacchus** (*see p91*), where temptation is proffered in the form of a glass of bubbly to wash down your éclairs ($29, $40 with champagne). The atmosphere is more gentlemen's club than hotel lobby: perfect for losing an afternoon and drifting seamlessly into the cocktail hour.

The beautiful people of Yaletown have a beautiful café where they can flirt or, even better, just admire themselves in the mirrored walls. This tall, airy room with designer furniture and lots of blond wood and blonder people is as inviting as the pastries behind the marble counter. The custom-blend coffee is deliberately cheaper than Starbucks across the street. Breakfast is happening.

European

Cioppino's Mediterranean Grill & Enoteca

1133 Hamilton Street, between Helmcken & Davie Streets (604 688 7466/www.cioppinosyaletown. com). Bus 15. **Open** 5-10.30pm Mon-Sat. **Main courses** $30-$48. **Credit** AmEx, DC, MC, V. **Map** p249 K4 ⓾

Cioppino's is the place where expense accounts go to die. Pino Posteraro's prices are on the steep side, but still comparable to other upscale Italian joints in the area and by far the best of the bunch. Indeed, the owner's deceptively simple pastas, pan-seared fish and hearty grilled meats make it one of the top fine-dining restaurants in the city and a favourite of visiting celebrities. Where else are they going to find 1959 Dom Perignon for $3,288 a pop? If your budget won't stretch, consider the Enoteca at lunch: a smart bowl of pasta or free-range roast chicken can be had for around $20.

Elixir Bar & Restaurant

350 Davie Street, between Pacific Boulevard & Homer Street (604 642 0557/www.elixir vancouver.com). Bus 15. **Open** 6.30am-2am Mon-Sat; 6.30am-midnight Sun. **Main courses** $23-$40. **Credit** AmEx, DC, MC, V. **Map** p249 K5 ⓾

This brassy brasserie – part bistro, part nightclub – pumps up the Moulin Rouge cabaret vibe with a dash of Baz Luhrmann's rococo kitsch. With a DJ spinning in the middle of the floor and gussied-up 'cougars' prowling the bar, dinner can be a frenzied experience. The bar menu is available until 12.30am on weekends, 11pm during the week. Service can be little slow.

Seafood

Blue Water Café & Raw Bar

1095 Hamilton Street, at Helmcken Street (604 688 8078/www.bluewatercafe.net). Bus 6, 15. **Open** 5pm-midnight daily. **Main courses** $32-$46. **Credit** AmEx, DC, MC, V. **Map** p249 K4 ⓾

Freshly shucked oysters, delicately flavoured sushi and simply prepared seafood in a swanky room. What's not to like about the Blue Water Café? Although main courses can be pricey, you'll receive decent value and an unforgettable tasting experience at the semi-circular raw bar. It's there that Yoshi Tabo works up his award-winning plates of sushi. The main bar offers 20 wines by the glass, a wide variety of chilled sakes and no fewer than

60 single-malt whiskies. Feeling extravagant? Then indulge yourself with a three-tiered tower of shellfish, sushi and a whole Dungeness crab.

Coast Restaurant

1257 Hamilton Street, between Drake & Davie Streets (604 685 5010/www.coastrestaurant.ca). Bus 15. **Open** 4.30pm-midnight daily. **Main courses** $23-$40. **Credit** AmEx, DC, MC, V. **Map** p249 K4 ⓾

The best way to enjoy this high-energy restaurant is to sit at the large communal table on the main floor, where the chef prepares the freshest catch of the day right in front of you. The room's clean contemporary design features lots of wood and light, and the menu has a huge variety of freshly grilled local fish, some with exotic flavours, including South Pacific John Dory and Cuban lobster tails. You won't be disappointed.

Steaks

Hamilton Street Grill

1009 Hamilton Street, at Nelson Street (604 331 1511). Bus 15. **Open** 11.30am-2.30pm, 5-10.30pm Mon-Fri; 5pm-midnight Sat, Sun. **Main courses** $16-$38. **Credit** AmEx, DC, MC, V. **Map** p249 K4 ⓾

This unassuming steakhouse is full of delicious surprises. Owner Neil Wyles is a passionate chef who sources his products from the city's best suppliers. The 16oz ribeye is a killer (in a good way), but be sure to leave room for the famously spectacular own-made gingerbread pudding.

Gastown

African

Le Marrakech Moroccan Bistro

52 Alexander Street, between Carrall & Columbia Streets (604 688 3714). Bus 4, 7, 50. **Open** 11.30am-midnight Mon-Fri; 5.30pm-1am Sat. **Main courses** $19-$25. **Credit** AmEx, DC, MC, V. **Map** p249 M3 ⓾

With its deep red walls, silk banquettes and a belly dancer performing on Friday and Saturday nights, Le Marrakech is a little bit of North Africa transplanted to Gastown. It opened in autumn 2007, and has just the sort of warmth the district needed. The seating may be slightly awkward (tables are a tad too low), but the tagines, laden with *smen* (clarified butter) and fragrant with toasted spices, are a heavenly retreat from a rainy Vancouver night. Try a mint tea mojito – mmm, now that's fusion.

Cafés & diners

Brioche Urban Baking & Catering

401 W Cordova Street, at Homer Street (604 682 4037/www.brioche.ca). Bus 4, 7. **Open** 7am-7pm Mon-Fri; 9am-6pm Sat, Sun. **Main courses** $7-$14. **Credit** DC, MC, V. **Map** p249 L3 ⓾

Eat, Drink, Shop

timeout.com

The hippest online guide to over 50
of the world's greatest cities

The pastries are divine – the display cases will stop sweet-tooths in their tracks – but there's so much more to enjoy here. Start with robust, white bean and pancetta soup and a hunk of freshly baked Calabrian bread. For light snacks, grab a thick slice of Sicilian pizza, garlicky Caesar salad or an Italian meatball sandwich. The pasta plates are massive and the desserts are made from scratch every morning. With dishes priced under $10 and a liquor licence to boot, Brioche bakes up one of the best deals in town.

Finch's

353 W Pender Street, at Homer Street (604 899 4040). Bus 4, 7. **Open** *9am-5pm Mon-Fri; 11am-4pm Sat.* **Main courses** *$5-$10.* **No credit cards.** **Map** p249 L3 ⑤⑨

Excellent filled baguettes, own-made soups, fresh salads, tasty breakfasts and an excellent cup of tea make this casual spot well worth a visit. Decked out like a funky old English tea room (but somehow hip rather than dusty), it's a great space to unwind, read the paper or people watch through the large windows. And you've got to love a place that serves perfect free-range boiled eggs. Lots of vegetarian options (brie with pear is a favourite) and mostly organic.

European

Incendio

103 Columbia Street, at Alexander Street (604 688 8694/www.incendio.ca). Bus 4, 7. **Open** *11.30am-3pm, 5-10pm Mon-Thur; 5-11pm Fri; 4.30-11pm Sat; 4.30-10pm Sun.* **Main courses** *$12-$26.* **Credit** AmEx, DC, MC, V. **Map** p249 M3 ⑥⓪

Good thin-crust pizza is hard to find in Vancouver but Incendio fills the void with the best skinny pizza pies in town, hand-flipped and baked in a brick oven. For something different, try the smoked-duck sausage or mango-basil butter sauce. It also makes pretty darn good pastas in this funky heritage-building room, where local artwork hangs on the exposed brick walls. Service is swift.
Other locations Incendio West, 2118 Burrard Street, at W 6th Avenue, West Side (604 736 2220).

Jules Bistro

216 Abbott Street, at Water Street (604 669 0033/ www.julesbistro.ca). Bus 4, 7, 50. **Open** *11.30am-2.30pm, 5.30-10pm Tue-Sat.* **Main courses** *$14-$26.* **Set meal** *$23.* **Credit** AmEx, DC, MC, V. **Map** p249 M3 ⑥①

This unpretentious bistro blew a breath of French air through the Vancouver dining scene when it opened in 2007. Its warm, bustling atmosphere, decent-sized patio and – more importantly – a three-course prix fixe of salad, steak/salmon frites and chocolate pud immediately drew crowds, and they've been lining up ever since. Stick to the set meal and you'll feel like you've eaten well for a bargain price. The à la carte can seem a little steep for uninspired renditions of classics. Service is authentically brusque. Reservations recommended.

Pubs

Steamworks Transcontinental

601 W Cordova Street, at Seymour Street (604 678 8000/www.steamworks.com/transcontinental). Bus 4, 5, 7, 20. **Open** *11.30am-10pm Mon-Fri; 5-10pm Sat.* **Main courses** *$10-$20.* **Credit** AmEx, DC, MC, V. **Map** p249 L3 ⑥②

A grandiose affair, the Transcontinental took over the former women's waiting room in the Canadian Pacific Railway Station, dropped millions of dollars on a stunning, nostalgic interior and opened in 2007 with an expensive menu that offered everything from fish and chips to lobster. A few months later, the restaurant was rebranded as a pub (it's owned by the Steamworks Brewery; *see p118* **Small beer**) with a cheaper and less ambitious menu. Still, it's a beautiful room and there are far worse places to hole up on a rainy afternoon, share some chicken wings or calamari, down a few beers and catch up on those postcards you've been meaning to write.

West Coast

Boneta

1 W Cordova Street, at Carrall Street (604 684 1844/www.boneta.ca). Bus 10, 16, 50. **Open** *5pm-midnight Tue-Thur, Sat; noon-3am Fri.* **Main courses** *$15-$20.* **Credit** AmEx, DC, MC, V. **Map** p249 M3 ⑥③

On an unprepossessing corner of the downtown Eastside awaits one of the warmest welcomes you'll find in the city. Owners Mark Brand, Neil Ingram and Andre McGillivary gutted the inside of this high-ceilinged room themselves, kipping on the floor at night, and their passion for their first enterprise is palpable. The bar is a gem. Fancy a cocktail? Try a Caesar, with bacon and quail egg – it's a meal in a glass – or a Devine (named for a famous local bartender), with its floating rose petal. Or get Ingram – sommelier par excellence – to talk you through his short, ever-changing wine list. Food, courtesy of ex-Lumière sous, Jeremie Bastien, is inventive, fresh and constantly evolving. But it's the atmosphere that makes this place rock: you'll never want to go home.

So.Cial at Le Magasin

332 Water Street, between Cambie & Richards Streets (604 669 4488/www.socialatlemagasin. com). Bus 4, 7, 50. **Open** *11am-11pm daily.* **Main courses** *$18-$27.* **Credit** AmEx, DC, MC, V. **Map** p249 L3 ⑥④

Sean Cousins is probably the most accomplished chef in Gastown, and this two-storey restaurant in a 1911 heritage building is one of the best-looking. Why, then, is it often sitting empty? Nothing to do with the excellent plates, including house-made charcuterie and phenomenal steaks – more likely the pretentious name and menu descriptions and a room bedecked for rich matrons, rather than the moneyed hipsters the area attracts. Efforts to soften its image include an afternoon happy hour in the downstairs oyster

Eat, Drink, Shop

bar ($1.25 a pop; 3-8pm Mon-Fri) and various drinks specials in the main bar. Not to be missed is the back-room butcher shop and deli, where huge, top-notch sandwiches are to be had for a snip: take yours into the bar for an accompanying drink. *Photos p93.*

Chinatown

Asian

Kam Gok Yuen

142 E Pender Street, between Main & Columbia Streets (604 683 3822). Bus 3, 8, 19. **Open** 10.30am-8.30pm daily. **Main courses** $5-$10. **No credit cards. Map** p249 M4 ⓫

A kitschy, cavernous room provides no-nonsense efficient service, though things get a touch chaotic when busy. The food is solid, comforting noodle-house fare and the barbecued repertoire, from duck to crispy-skin pork, is across-the-board excellent. Wontons are classically prepared – chunky with shrimp and bound with just the right amount of fatty pork to add flavour – and come in a tasty broth scented with dried flounder and sprinkled with yellow chives. Curried beef brisket with rice and peppered beef over rice noodles are also good bets.

New Town Bakery & Restaurant

158 E Pender Street, between Main & Columbia Streets (604 681 1828). Bus 3, 8, 19. **Open** 6.30am-8.30pm daily. **Main courses** $4-$8. **No credit cards. Map** p249 M4 ⓬

Complete with six stools at the counter and booths along one wall, New Town is, in spirit and decor, one of the very few true diners still thriving in trend-chasing Vancouver. Regulars come for familiar banter with the waitresses and rustic dim sum dispensed from stacks of giant steamers by the cashier's desk. Order a coconut cocktail bun with a cup of Hong Kong tea – brewed extra-strong and creamy with evaporated milk – or a meal-sized chicken deluxe big bun stuffed with chicken, ground pork, Spam and a salted duck egg yolk, then relax and feel the clock turn back to gentler times. *Photos pp96-97.*

Phnom Penh

244 E Georgia Street, between Main Street & Gore Avenue (604 682 5777). Bus 3, 8, 19. **Open** 10am-10pm daily. **Main courses** $6-$14. **Credit** AmEx, DC, MC, V. **Map** p249 N4 ⓭

Expect constant queues at lunch at the best Cambodian-Vietnamese restaurant in town, and without doubt the best meal you will find in Chinatown. Hot and sour soup with fish, prawns or chicken, is chunky with tomatoes, bean sprouts and pineapples. Refreshing Vietnamese chicken salad tosses impossibly crisp cabbage with mint, Thai basil, coriander and *nuoc cham.* Marinated butter beef is carpaccio seared on a hot plate splashed with lime juice, fish sauce and fried garlic. There's also fried oyster cake, stewed pork hot pot, garlic frogs' legs… Need we go on?

West Side

Asian

Tojo's

1133 W Broadway, between Alder & Spruce Streets (604 872 8050/www.tojos.com). Bus 9, 17, 99. **Open** 5-10pm Mon-Sat. **Main courses** $16-$29. **Credit** AmEx, DC, MC, V. **Map** p251 J7 ⓭

Though Hidekazu Tojo's position at the pinnacle of Vancouver Japanese dining is regularly reasserted in local awards, experiences can be mixed. Service is too often a problem – especially if you aren't planning to drop a significant sum on an *omakase* (chef's choice) menu – and the new, larger room lacks warmth or intimacy. There is no questioning the freshness of ingredients, or the chef's skill, though considering the quality available at Blue Water or Okada downtown, you might end the evening more satisfied elsewhere.

Vij's

1480 W 11th Avenue, at Granville Street (604 736 6664/www.vijs.ca). Bus 10. **Main courses** $22-$26. **Credit** AmEx, DC, MC, V. **Map** p251 H7 ⓭

Jamie Oliver described his dinner at Vij's as the most memorable on his trip to Canada. But don't take his word for it. Just ask the mobs that line up outside the doors every night why they keep coming back for wine-marinated lamb 'popsicles' in fenugreek cream curry, savoury jackfruit on corn-meal chapatti and other fusion dishes. Get there early and relax in the lounge with some of the complimentary nibbles and a glass of wine, beer or cider from the short but selective drinks list. And please don't go bitching about how they don't take reservations. *Photos pp98-99.*

Cafés & diners

49th Parallel Roasters

2152 W 4th Avenue, between Arbutus & Yew Streets (604 420 4901/www.49thparallelroasters.com). Bus 4, 7. **Open** 7.30am-7pm Mon-Sat; 8am-6pm Sun. **Credit** AmEx, DC, MC, V. **Map** p251 F6 ⓰

From the original owners of Caffé Artigiano comes this sleek coffee shop serving high-end, ethically sourced beans. Excellent espresso and cappuccino is served in cool blue china and there's an extensive menu of teas served by the pot. It goes without saying that the Thomas Haas pastries are worth every calorie.

Arbutus Coffee

2200 Arbutus Street, at W 6th Avenue (604 736 5644). Bus 4, 7. **Open** 6am-6pm Mon-Fri; 8am-6pm Sat, Sun. **Main courses** $6-$8. **No credit cards. Map** p251 F6 ⓱

This is a genuine neighbourhood coffee shop, beloved by its regulars for its heritage atmosphere (the building remains much as it was when it was a

The food is local and organic at **Chow**, the cocktails simply divine. *See p110*.

Serving up sustainability

The ocean's bounty is a serious presence on Vancouver plates: from sushi to cedar-planked salmon, fish is big business here. True to the city's environmentally astute history, local restaurateurs have become increasingly concerned about depleting fish stocks and the impact of farming methods on the industry.

Leader of the pack when it comes to sustainability is Robert Clark, executive chef of **C Restaurant** (see p95). He was the first (way back in 1999) to remove the threatened Chilean sea bass from his menu, replacing it with the local sablefish (also known as Alaskan black cod), before revamping the menu completely along sustainable lines. His most recent venture has been to source ethically farmed abalone.

In 2004, Robert Clark was instrumental in forming the Vancouver Aquarium's Ocean Wise programme, a resource established to provide current information to restaurateurs on which seafood is considered sustainable. Generally that means choosing the local halibut instead of cod in your fish and chips, eschewing tiger prawns and enjoying local BC spot prawns (in season), avoiding ahi (red) tuna in favour of the local (white) albacore, and ordering only wild salmon (sockeye, spring and white spring are favourites). It's really no hardship – the local fish is superb, and goes well with local wines (see p94).

Also big on promoting local and sustainable produce are **Go Fish** (see p108), **Chow** (see p110; pictured), **Bishop's** (see p110), **Fuel** (see p110) and **Raincity Grill** (see p100). To make life easier, you can look for the Ocean Wise stamp of approval on local menus or visit www.vanaqua.org/oceanwise for a list of participating restaurants.

---

grocery store in the 1920s). Everything is baked on site. Standouts include the deep-dish fruit pies and the German chocolate cake with sticky coconut topping; soups and panini are reliably tasty.

Moderne Burger
2507 W Broadway, at Larch Street (604 739 0005/ www.moderneburger.com). Bus 9, 17. **Open** noon-8.45pm Tue-Sat; noon-8pm Sun. **Main courses** $7-$10. **No credit cards. Map** p251 E6 ⓸
Newly expanded and refurbished after a fire, this turquoise diner draws crowds addicted to its top-notch burgers. The menu is short and to the point: choose from steak, turkey, wild salmon, veggie or lamb and customise from a succinct list of toppings. A burger platter, with hand-cut chips, makes for a serious meal. Old-fashioned shakes, malts, floats and flavoured colas add to the retro feel.

Pane From Heaven
1670 Cypress Street, at W 1st Avenue (604 736 5555). Bus 2, 22. **Open** 7am-6pm Mon-Sat. **Main courses** $6-$7. **Credit** DC, MC, V. **Map** p251 G5 ⓼

A useful spot for before or after visits the Vanier Park museums, just a block beyond Starbucks, and well worth crossing the road for. A cup of organic Fairtrade coffee with fondant-filled pain au chocolat goes down a treat. For lunch, try a toasted panini or own-made soup (don't pass up the Malaysian chicken). Service is friendly.

Rocky Mountain Flatbread Company
1876 W 1st Avenue, at Cypress Street (604 730 0321/www.rockymountainflatbread.ca). Bus 2, 22. **Open** 11.30am-9.30pm Mon-Wed, Sun; 11.30am-10pm Thur-Sat. **Main courses** $10-$22. **Credit** AmEx, DC, MC, V. **Map** p251 G5 ⓾
The thin-crust pizzas are worth their slightly elevated price tag here: everything is organic and real thought has gone into sourcing quality local ingredients; daily soups and pastas are also excellent. The room has a relaxed, friendly vibe and plenty of large tables support its family-friendly status. But be warned: if you want to avoid toddlers playing in the toy kitchen, or teenagers making their

own pies, opt for a later dinner. If you have children, you'll struggle to find such an amenable space with good and nutritious food. Desserts are worth saving room for. Take out available.

Sophie's Cosmic Café

2095 W 4th Avenue, at Arbutus Street (604 732 6810/www.sophiescosmiccafe.com). Bus 4, 7. **Open** 8am-9.30pm daily. **Main courses** $7-$14. **Credit** DC, MC, V. **Map** p251 F6 ⑦

Twenty years is a long time in restaurant terms, and Sophie's, which has been providing comfort food to the locals since 1988, certainly qualifies as a Kitsilano institution. The interior is crammed with '50s memorabilia and knick-knacks, making it a fun space to enjoy a burger or a slice of key lime pie. Weekend brunch is incredibly popular (*see p102* **Between meals**); if you're not in by 9am, expect to wait in line.

European

Bistrot Bistro

1961 W 4th Avenue, between Cypress & Maple Streets (604 732 0004/www.bistrotbistro.com). Bus 4, 7. **Open** 5-11pm Tue-Thur; 5pm-midnight Fri, Sat; 5-10pm Sun. **Main courses** $16-$19. **Credit** DC, MC, V. **Map** p251 F6 ⑦

A warm and unpretentious room presided over by the ever-affable owners Laurent and Valerie Devin. The lime green walls may be a tad lurid, but the country style French cuisine is anything but. Much of the food is perfect for sharing – meat or fish stews come to the table in cast iron casseroles to be ladled at leisure – and they make a mean braised brussels sprouts with lardons side. It's a cosy spot in winter, and the restaurant's wall of windows raise completely in summer, allowing a welcome breeze.

Gastropod

1938 W 4th Avenue, between Cypress & Maple Streets (604 730 5579/www.gastropod.ca). Bus 4, 7. **Open** noon-2.30pm, 5.30-10pm Wed-Sat. **Main courses** $16-$27. **Credit** AmEx, DC, MC, V. **Map** p251 F6 ⑦

Right next door to Fuel (*see p110*), and also hot on local, seasonal ingredients, Gastropod is a different beast altogether. Winner of *Vancouver Magazine*'s 2007 Best New Fine Dining award, this minimalist room is the closest Vancouver cuisine gets to the cutting edge. Chef Angus An is interested in molecular gastronomy and has an eye for an unusual concept. Standouts include the oysters with horseradish 'snow' and a delicious, witty salmon dish that wraps the fish in seaweed and deep fries it in a light tempura batter, served with wasabi sabayon. Service, though exceedingly polite, can be slow. *Photo p100.*

Lumière

2551 W Broadway, between Larch & Trafalgar Streets (604 739 8185/www.lumiere.ca). Bus 9, 17. **Open** 5.30pm-end of service (last dinner seating 9.30pm Tue-Sun). **Tasting menus** $85-$180. **Credit** AmEx, DC, MC, V. **Map** p251 E6 ⑦

A bitter feud between owners David and Manjy Sidoo and local celebrity chef Rob Feenie made headlines across Canada in 2007. New executive chef Dale Mackay (formerly sous chef in Gordon Ramsay's New York operation, The London) walked into a minefield and was left struggling to rebuild a restaurant that suffered badly from the publicity surrounding Feenie's departure. Canada's only freestanding Relais & Chateaux room, it is also one of the most expensive joints in Vancouver, with no option but pricey tasting menus. A less risky bet is the adjoining tasting bar, where you can sample high-end bar dishes – including the stunning squash and mascarpone ravioli – and partake of the restaurant's great wine cellar.

Mistral Bistro

2585 W Broadway, at Trafalgar Street (604 733 0046/www.mistralbistro.ca). **Open** 11.30am-2pm, 5.30-10pm Tue-Sat. **Main courses** $12-$32. **Credit** AmEx, DC, MC, V. **Map** p251 E6 ⑦

Perched on the opposite end of the block from Lumière (*see above*), Mistral opened in autumn 2005 and immediately seemed right at home in such prestigious company. Chef-owner Jean-Yves Benoit's CV includes a couple of three-Michelin-starred restaurants in Europe (El Bulli, L'Arpège) and his own award-winning L'Emotion in West Van. An unpretentious room belies the seriousness of the cooking here. Cassoulet, boudin noir, *daube de boeuf* – all executed to perfection and without a twist of fusion in sight. Flavours are true and deep, service is attentive and friendly.

Pied-à-Terre

3369 Cambie Street, between W 17th & W 18th Avenues (604 873 3131/www.pied-a-terre-bistro.ca). Bus 15. **Open** noon-10.30pm Mon-Thur; noon-midnight Fri; 5pm-midnight Sat; 5pm-10pm Sun. **Main courses** $17-$27. **Set meal** $20-$30. **Credit** DC, MC, V. **Map** p252 L8 ⑨

Bijou it may be, but that's the only thing about this modern French bistro from the owners of Parkside (*see p100*) that's small. Big, bold plates of coq au vin and boeuf bourguignon over pommes puree, or steak-frites and *salade paysanne* tantalise the tastebuds. The $20 *table d'hôte* lunch is a steal: you would be crazy to be on Cambie and not check this one out. Reservations recommended.

Seafood

Go Fish

1505 W 1st Avenue, at Creekside Drive (604 730 5040). Bus 50. **Open** 11.30am-6pm Tue-Fri; noon-6pm Sat, Sun. **Main courses** $8-$12. **Credit** DC, MC, V. **Map** p251 H5 ⑨

Tucked away on the Seawall between Granville Island and Vanier Park, this little shack serves up the best fish and chips in town. Owner Gord Martin (of Bin 941; *see p95*) buys fish fresh from the boats at the end of the jetty and, when the stock runs out,

Eat, Drink, Shop

he shuts up shop for the day. Choose from cod, salmon or halibut in a crispy, tempura-like batter with chips and Asian-inspired slaw, sandwiches (salmon, ahi tuna or oyster) or tacos. Daily specials include soups, grilled fish on greens and the always-delicious ceviche. The food is cooked to order and very popular, so expect to queue.

Vegetarian

The Naam

2724 W 4th Avenue, between Stephens & Macdonald Streets (604 738 7151/www.thenaam.com). Bus 2, 4, 7, 22. **Open** 24hrs daily. **Main courses** $5-$13. **Credit** AmEx, DC, MC, V. **Map** p251 D6 **62**

The Naam has been serving up its vegetarian staples since 1968, when West 4th was still known locally as Rainbow Road. More so than the neighbourhood, the Naam has retained its funky, hippie feel and remains a very popular spot, particularly in the evenings when there is live music, and at weekends. The food is mostly good, if rather worthy; service is notoriously erratic. Salads are great and the blueberry milkshake is too good to waste on the kids.

West Coast

Bishop's

2183 W 4th Avenue, at Yew Street (604 738 2025/www.bishopsonline.com). Bus 4, 7. **Open** 5.30-11pm Mon-Sat; 5.30-10pm Sun. **Main courses** $32-$38. **Credit** AmEx, DC, MC, V. **Map** p251 F6 **63**

It took a chef from Wales to introduce Vancouver to a modern regional style of cooking now known, and widely emulated, as Pacific Northwest. Nearly 20 years ago, John Bishop committed himself to using nothing but the freshest seasonal bounty of the region's oceans, rivers, fields and forests. The kitchen is now totally organic and run by the estimable Andrea Carlson. Bishop's continues to attract a loyal clientele of fashionable foodies, who come for the flavour and the restaurant's consummately charming but ever quirky host, who can sometimes be found trailing dirt to starched white linen tables to show off gargantuan beets and freshly foraged funghi.

Chow

3121 Granville Street, at W 15th Avenue (604 608 2469/www.chow-restaurant.com). Bus 10. **Open** 5-10.30pm daily **Main courses** $20-$40. **Credit** AmEx, DC, MC, V. **Map** p251 H7 **64**

With a supremely sexy bar serving up delectable cocktails in beautiful Spiegelau glassware, and a kitchen that not only sources its produce carefully, but creates magic with it, Chow is one of the best new restaurants on the scene. Focusing on local and organic (*see also p108* **Serving up sustainability**), the menu changes with the season – the sablefish and pork dishes are always good bets, soups are luscious, and desserts divine. A future lunch service is planned. *Photos p107.*

Feenie's

2563 W Broadway, between Trafalgar & Larch Streets (604 739 7115/www.feenies.com). Bus 9, 17. **Open** 11.30am-2.30pm, 5.30-11.30pm Mon-Fri; 10am-2pm, 5.30-11.30pm Sat, Sun. **Main courses** $14-$22. **Set meal** $35. **Credit** AmEx, DC, MC, V. **Map** p251 E6 **65**

Can't afford the 11-course chef's menu at Lumière (*see p109*)? Try its next-door sibling, created by former chef Rob Feenie as a place to dish up the food he likes to eat at home. The comfort food here is difficult to pass up: the shepherd's pie comes layered with duck confit, mushroom duxelle, corn and truffled mashed potatoes; the infamous Feenie's weenie is a custom-cured cheese smokie, which is smothered in sauerkraut, sautéed onions and lardons. Unfortunately, the servers are so insufferably hip – and don't they just know it.

Fuel

1944 W 4th Avenue, at Maple Street (604 288 2700/www.fuelrestaurant.ca). Bus 4, 7. **Open** noon-2.30, 5.30-10pm Mon-Thur, Sun; 5.30-10.30pm Fri, Sat. **Main courses** $27-$34. **Credit** AmEx, DC, MC, V. **Map** p251 G6 **66**

Chef Robert Belcham and sommelier Tom Doughty left C Restaurant to crank up the competition on West 4th. The regional, seasonal menu always reads great – sometimes better than it eats. Safe choices include trout when available and a stonking ribeye steak fried in butter (you can jog around the Seawall later). Lunch is a good deal and if you really want to see attention to detail, try a beautifully presented cheese plate. The room proper is a little anemic; sit at the kitchen bar and enjoy the show (that way, you can also keep an eye on which dishes are looking good).

Watermark on Kits Beach

1305 Arbutus Street, at Whyte Avenue, on Kitsilano Beach (604 738 5487/www.watermarkrestaurant.ca). Bus 2, 22. **Open** 11.30am-10pm Mon-Fri; 11am-10pm Sat, Sun. **Main courses** $15-$30. **Credit** AmEx, DC, MC, V. **Map** p251 F4 **67**

Vancouver's restaurateurs still haven't worked out how to combine a beach location with good food. This two-storey building is understatedly sleek and perfectly suited to the site. But behind the exterior the food can't compare to the architecture or the breathtaking view of English Bay. Though the kitchen has been through changes of personnel since it opened to poor reviews in 2005, the menu remains too pricey and mediocre. Still, the bar is an appealing spot for drinks, which are reasonably priced and include selections from some of British Columbia's best wineries. The all-weather balcony provides welcome blankets.

West

2881 Granville Street, at W 13th Avenue (604 738 8938/www.westrestaurant.com). Bus 10. **Open** 11.30am-11pm Mon-Fri; 5.30-11pm Sat, Sun. **Main courses** $35-$46. **Credit** AmEx, DC, MC, V. **Map** p251 H7 **68**

This swanky dining room is the showpiece in owner Jack Evrensel's collection of restaurants that include Blue Water Café, CinCin and Araxi in Whistler. But the kudos goes to former executive chef David Hawksworth, who left to prepare his own gaff – Hawksworth, in the Hotel Georgia redevelopment. Warren Geraghty, executive chef of London's L'Escargot took over the burners in February 2008.

East Vancouver

Asian

Chutney Villa

147 E Broadway, at Main Street (604 872 2228). Bus 3, 8, 19. **Open** 11.30am-3pm; 5-10pm Mon, Wed-Fri; 10am-10pm Sat; 10am-9pm Sun. **Main courses** $13-$20 **Credit** DC, MC, V. **Map** p252 M7 ㉟

There isn't much in Vancouver to offer visitors used to excellent Indian food at home, but this South Indian room – given the nod by the *New York Times* – is one of the best. Crisp dosas, well spiced, vibrant curries, house-made chutneys and good chai, as well as strong vegetarian/vegan dishes, make it well worth a visit if you're in the neighbourhood and tired of East Asian flavours. Much of the restaurant's charm comes from the warm welcome extended to all by bubbly owner Chindij Varardarajulu.

Hawker's Delight

147 E Broadway, at King Edward Avenue (604 709 8188). Bus 3. **Open** 11am-9pm Mon-Sat. **Main courses** $5-$7. **No credit cards**. **Map** p252 M9 ㉚

A no-frills, hole in the wall dishing up big bowls of curry Laksa and plates of Hainanese chicken rice or mee *goreng* (fried noodles) at bargain-basement prices. Everything is made on site from scratch: browse the photos lining the walls, and order at the counter. Tasty, filling and authentic – perfect for a quick pit stop, so long as you're not fussy about decor. Lots of vegetarian dishes available.

Sun Sui Wah

3888 Main Street, at E 23rd Avenue (604 872 8822/www.sunsuiwah.com). Bus 3. **Open** 10am-3pm, 5-10.30pm daily. **Main courses** $12-$18. **Dim sum** $3-$7. **Credit** AmEx, DC, MC, V. **Map** p252 M9 ㉛

This is the original Vancouver Chinese cuisine heavyweight and pioneer of using local seafood in Cantonese style preparations. A surprisingly good wine list meets the needs of a heavily seafood-focused menu bristling with flavour. Try the king crab in season, or whole fried fish. Service is polished and friendly in a large modern room that may be a little worn around the edges, but still buzzes with Chinese families and, on weekends, ladies announcing the specials on their dim sum carts. *See also p102* **Between meals**.

Eat, Drink, Shop

Head to **Crave** for a sophisticated, modern vibe – and great brunches. *See p112.*

Toshi Sushi

*181 E 16th Avenue, at Main Street (604 874 5173).
Bus 3.* **Open** 5-10pm Tue-Sun. **Main courses** $6-
$10. **Credit** DC, MC, V. **Map** p252 M8 ❷
Constant queues outside this 30-seat room means a
guarantee that the fish is fresh. Apart from that,
Toshi Saito's menu is fairly familiar territory, with
all the popular maki rolls (served foot long) and reliable fried items. Reasonable prices mean that waits
regularly hit the 60-minute mark.

Cafés & diners

Little Nest

*1716 Charles Street, at Commercial Drive (604 251
9994/www.littlenest.ca). Bus 20.* **Open** 9am-4pm
Tue-Fri; 9am-5pm Sat,Sun. **Main courses** $5-$9.
No credit cards.
It's not often someone opens a kid-friendly café that
actually cares about the food – so it's no wonder this
place is pumping at weekends. Scrambled eggs with
sunchokes, caramelised onions and bacon, puffy
French toast with bananas and syrup or good old
boiled egg and soldiers are just the beginning of a
constantly changing menu that takes care of all its
charges, big or small. Vietnamese coffee, rich with
condensed milk and served over ice is the perfect
buzz alongside excellent cakes (owner Mary
MacIntyre was once a pastry chef at Lumière; *see
p109*) while the kids decompress. The large, airy
room is furnished with indestructible tables, chairs
and copious high chairs, as well as a wealth of vintage Fisher Price toys. No one will sniff if your toddler runs around – and any tantrums will quickly
dissolve into the general din.

Prado Café

*1938 Commercial Drive, at E 4th Avenue (604
255 5537/www.pradocafe.com). Bus 20/SkyTrain
Broadway.* **Open** 6am-8pm daily. **Credit** DC,
MC, V. **Map** p252 Q6 ❸
Whitewashed walls, floors and minimal furnishings mark this café on the Drive as über-trendy.
The clean, spacious effect is further boosted by
huge floor-to-ceiling windows, perfect for surrepti-
tious people-watching over your Penguin Classic
edition of something Russian and serious. They
serve excellent and ethical coffee (sourced from
49th Parallel Roasters; *see p106*), alongside baked
goods that run the gamut from vegan to sinfully
delicious Nutella-stuffed muffins.

European

Federico's Supper Club

*1728 Commercial Drive, at E 1st Avenue (604 251
3473/www.federicossupperclub.com). Bus 20.* **Open**
5.30pm-midnight Wed-Sun. **Main courses** $18-$40.
Credit DC, MC, V. **Map** p252 Q6 ❹
The ensemble of velvet curtains, art deco flourishes,
children crawling under tables and the Fuoco
Family Band serenading the sweaty dancefloor with

equal measures of Italian schmaltz and Vegas-style
bombast will make you feel like you landed on the
set of *The Wedding Singer* with a couple of Tony
Soprano's mob thrown in. Dinner is served up New
Jersey-banquet style on long candlelit tables. The
hearty pastas and tender veal scaloppini are like
something mamma would make in the old country.

Latin American

Me & Julio

*2095 Commercial Drive, at E 5th Avenue (604
696 9997/www.meandjulio.ca). Bus 20/SkyTrain
Broadway.* **Open** 5pm-midnight daily. **Main courses**
$15-$20. **Credit** DC, MC, V. **Map** p252 Q6 ❺
Baby sibling of the popular West End latino eaterie
Lolita's (*see p99*), Me & Julio has a similar menu
and easy-breezy fiesta vibe. Ceviches and taquitos
are always good bets, as are cocktails – though you
can run into trouble if you go off list. A much bigger affair than Lolita's, Me & Julio nevertheless
crams too many tables in, making service awkward
and sometimes slow. After a few tequilas, though,
you're unlikely to care.

West Coast

Aurora Bistro

*2420 Main Street, between E 8th Avenue &
E Broadway (604 873 9944/www.aurorabistro.ca).
Bus 3, 8, 19.* **Open** 11am-3pm; 5.30-11pm Mon-Fri;
10am-2pm Sat, Sun. **Main courses** $23-$28. **Credit**
AmEx, DC, MC, V. **Map** p252 M6 ❻
Chef/owner Jeff Van Geest is one of the city's most
enthusiastic supporters of local produce. His menu
shows careful attention to sourcing and seasonality
– as well as a commitment to sustainable fish. Queen
Charlotte halibut, Vancouver Island organic pork
and Fraser Valley poultry are teamed with the likes
of sea asparagus, foraged mushrooms and pickled
beets. Sunday brunch, with truffled scrambled eggs
and house-made duck bacon is very popular. The
wine list is entirely BC (*see p94* **The grapevine**).

Crave

*3941 Main Street, at E 23rd Street (604 872 3663/
www.craveonmain.ca). Bus 3.* **Open** 11am-10pm
Tue-Fri; 9am-10pm Sat; 9am-9pm Sun. **Main
courses** $10-$24. **Credit** AmEx, DC, MC, V.
Map p252 M9 ❼
On a sunny day, the backyard patio of this small,
hip joint is a veritable oasis of calm from Main Street
traffic. Inside, dark wood and leather banquettes
give a sophisticated modern vibe – although space
is tight and tables may be too close for some tastes.
Food is winning: organic burger with blue cheese
and perfect fries; fall-apart lamb shank with sumptuous mascarpone mash. The brunch is one of the
best in the city (*see p102* **Between meals**). Clean,
unfussy plates that pack a tasty punch come courtesy of owner Wayne Martin, former executive chef
of the Four Seasons downtown. *Photos p111.*

Bars

Eat, drink and be merry.

Vancouver's strict liquor licensing policy doesn't allow for an abundance of drink-only establishments. Most licenses are allocated to restaurants – that is why you don't see Montreal- or European-like scenes of swiller lounging, or bars tucked into every third building. You might be hard pressed to find a 'just drinks' locale outside of a hotel lounge, but rest assured they do exist. Many of the places listed below are indeed officially 'restaurants'; but they do double-duty, offering both a comfortable space to share a drink and a full menu.

A series of neighbourhoods – mainstream Kitsilano; bohemian, multi-ethnic Commercial Drive; set-designed, antiseptic Yaletown – offer something for all tastes, be it the modest tippler in search of peace and quiet, a boisterous gang out for a night of ear-splitting music and drunken bliss, or blasé hipsters who'll only sip Negronis in the company of other blasé hipsters.

Sadly (or not, if hordes of bevvied-up 19-year-olds is your thing), most downtown bars are clustered around a brash, trashy six-block strip of **Granville Street**. Those willing to wander are rewarded with more diversity in venues and crowds. Renascent neighbourhoods – **Gastown**, **South Main** – also hold appeal for their dynamic nightlife.

A common Vancouver complaint is the paucity of seaside bars. But times are changing, and nowhere more so than in **Yaletown**, where martini bars and charming *boîtes* on the boardwalk flourish by the water's edge.

The best Bars

For romance
Bacchus. *See right.*

For wine
Salt Tasting Room. *See p116.*

For the view
Calling Public House. *See p115.*

For a game of pool
Soho Billiards. *See p116.*

For beer
Six Acres. *See p119.*

Downtown

Bacchus Restaurant & Piano Lounge
Wedgewood Hotel, 845 Hornby Street, at Robson Street (604 689 7777/www.wedgewoodhotel.com). All city-centre buses. **Open** 6.30am-midnight Mon-Wed; 6.30am-1am Thur, Fri; 7.30am-midnight Sun. **Credit** AmEx, DC, MC, V. **Map** p249 K3 ❶
Strange name, really. There are no toga-clad revellers and there is nothing particularly Bacchanalian about the silent nods asking for another round. The room exudes upscale warmth and crisp elegance, and the service sets the standard for the entire city.

Crush Champagne Lounge
1180 Granville Street, at Davie Street (604 684 0355/www.crushlounge.ca). Bus 4, 6, 7, 10, 16, 17, 50. **Open** 8.30pm-2am Wed; 10pm-2am Thur; 10pm-3am Fri, Sat. **Admission** $8-$25. **Credit** AmEx, DC, MC, V. **Map** p248 J4 ❷
Dimly lit, sleek and sophisticated, Crush Champagne Lounge is your open door to the rarefied world of the socially evolved – perfect for the day when you realise you're done with pounding music, drink-drenched dancefloors and sloppy pick-up lines but you still yearn to prowl. The DJ plays a clever mix of soul and acid jazz, people chill out on ottomans and sofas, and the bar proves that drinking champagne doesn't have to clear out your wallet. More incentive? Celebrities like Ben Affleck, Ashton Kutcher and Wesley Snipes have been known to quench their thirst here.

Gerard Lounge
Sutton Place Hotel, 845 Burrard Street, between Robson & Smithe Streets (604 682 5511/www. vancouver.suttonplace.com). Bus 2, 5, 22. **Open** 11am-1am Mon-Sat; 4.30pm-midnight Sun. **Admission** free. **Credit** AmEx, DC, MC, V. **Map** p249 K3 ❸
This is the cosy spot where the celebrity-obsessed wait in hope for a glimpse of Al Pacino or other visiting Hollywood stars shooting films in Tinseltown North. The piano tinkles in the background, bag-laden shoppers fresh from Robson Street's boutiques gulp cosmopolitans and chew their way through bowls of complimentary almonds, while bankers clang manhattans in a toast to a closed deal.

> ❶ Pink numbers given in this chapter correspond to the location of each bar as marked on the street maps. *See pp248-253.*

Eat, Drink, Shop

Ginger 62 Cocktail Den & Kitchen

1219 Granville Street, at Davie Street (604 688 5494/www.ginger62.com). Bus 4, 6, 7, 10, 16, 17, 50. **Open** 8pm-3am Fri, Sat. **Admission** free-$12. **Credit** DC, MC, V. **Map** p248 J4 ❹

The name is a homage to famous Gingers (Rogers, Fred Astaire's dancing partner, and Grant, actress Tina Louise from *Gilligan's Island*), while the bar attracts cool men in black and women in spaghetti straps (the savviest of whom arrive early to claim a sofa from which to hold court). The calm amber lighting here appears to make everyone beautiful. Inventive martinis, Asian fusion tapas and some of the city's sharpest DJs make for a memorable night.

Granville Room

957 Granville Street, at Nelson Street (604 633 0056/www.dhmbars.ca). All city-centre buses. **Open** 4pm-2am daily. **Admission** free. **Credit** AmEx, DC, MC, V. **Map** p249 K4 ❺

An institution in the entertainment district, this is the lounge where restaurant and bar industry folk choose to drink. Its gilded mirrors and chandeliers offer a sliver of elegance tucked between the flashy joints on the strip. An extensive cocktail list and dishes like beef carpaccio and ahi tuna spring rolls appease sophisticated palates.

Honey Lounge

Lotus Hotel, 455 Abbott Street, at W Pender Street (604 685 7777). Bus 10, 16, 20, N20, N35. **Open** noon-2am Wed, Thur; noon-3am Fri; 8pm-3am Sat. **Admission** phone for rates. **Credit** DC, MC, V. **Map** p249 M3 ❻

A beacon between Gastown and Yaletown, lurid Honey Lounge – think gold patina on the walls,

Marrakech-kitsch banquettes, aubergine tiled bar – welcomes all. They come in search of different grails: some to dance, some to preen, some to queen, but most to get their drinks in and their rocks off.

Kingston Taphouse & Grille

755 Richards Street, between W Georgia & Robson Streets (604 681 7011/www.kingstontaphouse.com). All city-centre buses. **Open** 11.30am-1am Mon-Sat; 9.30am-midnight Sun. **Admission** free. **Credit** AmEx, DC, MC, V. **Map** p249 K3 ❼

Six rooms on four floors means that there's something for everyone here: an intimate glass of wine by the stone fireplace, a game of pool downstairs in the WrecRoom, a big screen football game in the Taphouse Pub, or a flirty hang on the Oasis patio or the roof deck. A great place to start a serious night out, the crowd here is of the freshly educated, good-looking, meet-the-folks variety.

Lucy Mae Brown

Downstairs, 862 Richards Street, at Smithe Street (604 899 9199/www.lucymaebrown.ca). All city-centre buses. **Open** 5pm-2am daily. **Admission** free-$5. **Credit** AmEx, DC, MC, V. **Map** p249 K4 ❽

The restaurant's lounge bar, called the Opium Den in a nod to the neighbourhood's past, attracts ethereal women and Zara'd men. They come from 10pm onwards, lean against the bar, drink mojitos and feel as if they've arrived.

Morrissey Irish House

1227 Granville Street, at Davie Street (604 682 0909). Bus 4, 6, 7, 10, 16, 17, 50. **Open** 11am-2am Mon-Thur, Sun; 11am-3am Fri, Sat. **Admission** free. **Credit** AmEx, DC, MC, V. **Map** p248 J4 ❾

Lucy Mae Brown.

Morrissey Irish House represents the modern-day blueprint for a sleek, stylish Irish bar. There may be better-lit caverns in Vancouver, but here the dimness serves its purpose, allowing the visual warmth of the fireplace to create an appropriate atmosphere during the bleaker winter months.

900 West Lounge

Fairmont Hotel Vancouver, 900 W Georgia Street, between Burrard & Hornby Streets (604 684 3131/ www.fairmont.com/hotelvancouver). All city-centre buses. **Open** 11.30am-midnight Mon-Thur, Sun; 11.30am-1am Fri, Sat. **Admission** free. **Credit** AmEx, DC, MC, V. **Map** p249 K3 ⑩

The 900 wears its status as the city's poshest hotel bar with aristocratic insouciance. The attitude is shared by its clientele: bankers, you-only-live-once tourists and elegant singles, who are seemingly waiting for their shipping magnate to come in to port. The room is abuzz from cocktail hour (complimentary hors d'oeuvres between 5pm and 6pm) with the silky sounds of a jazz trio and the smell of money filling the air.

Republic

958 Granville Street, between Howe & Seymour Streets (604 669 3266/www.dhmbars.ca). All city-centre buses. **Open** 6pm-3am daily. **Admission** free-$15. **Credit** AmEx, DC, MC, V. **Map** p249 K4 ⑪

This gorgeous, warm and modern club has an upscale casualness, a place where cocktails are 'crafted', where people dance whether the dancefloor is populated or not, and where strangers smile at you, as though congratulating you for your good taste in being here. *Photos p117.*

Sip Resto Lounge

1117 Granville Street, between Helmcken & Davie Streets (604 687 7474/www.siplounge.com). All city-centre buses. **Open** 5pm-2am daily. **Admission** free. **Credit** AmEx, DC, MC, V. **Map** p248 J4 ⑫

Serving the pre-club mob upscale small plates and inventive tipples, this bar-restaurant deals in multiple environments packed into a small space: an open kitchen at the entrance, a glittering bar beyond and a darkened lounge at the rear. While the carefully styled food has garnered some acclaim, DJs are the key here (try Mayhem Monday or Steamy Saturday).

West End

Calling Public House

1780 Davie Street, at Denman Street (604 801 6681/www.dhmbars.ca). Bus 15. **Open** 11pm-2am daily. **Admission** free. **Credit** AmEx, DC, MC, V. **Map** p248 G2 ⑬

This beachfront bistro is almost too good to be true, with its unabashedly stylish room, inexpensive drinks, good-looking patrons and an amazing view of the sunset from the ringside patio off English Bay – even the staff have good energy. It's no surprise then to learn that this free house is an industry favourite – it's run by same folks who own Granville Room (*see p114*), Republic (*see above*), Bar None (*see below*), among other slick spots.

Yaletown

Afterglow Lounge

1079 Mainland Street, between Nelson & Helmcken Streets (604 602 0835/www.glowbalgrill.com). Bus 15. **Open** 5pm-midnight Mon-Wed, Sun; 5pm-1am Thur-Sat. **Admission** free. **Credit** AmEx, DC, MC, V. **Map** p249 K4 ⑭

Listed in *100 of the World's Best Bars*, this 50-seat lounge is located down the hall from the fancy Glowbal Grill & Satay Bar. Guys sport designer eyewear and cellphones, and girls flash lots of toned skin in this red-lit, high-brick-walled space. You'll want to linger languidly on the backless red divans, but the tony clique here would deem it improper.

Bar None

1222 Hamilton Street, at Davie Street (604 689 7000/www.dhmbars.ca). Bus 15. **Open** 9pm-3am Mon, Tue, Thur-Sat. **Admission** $5-$18. **Credit** AmEx, DC, MC, V. **Map** p249 K5 ⑮

The elegant, snaking post-and-beam room of Bar None, Yaletown's most enduring It-spot, was converted from a warehouse in 1992. Ever since then the place has been luring transfixed punters (as the queues testify). But persevere and you'll soon hear why its reputation as a turntabler's destination has not diminished in the nearly two decades since it opened its doors. Soul, funk and vinyl in Monday's 'Soul Stream' compete with Zak Santiago's Saturday Miami beats, as hipper-than-thou patrons bump along, trying not to spill their drinks.

Eat, Drink, Shop

George Ultralounge

1137 Hamilton Street, between Helmcken & Davie Streets, Yaletown (604 628 5555). Bus 15. **Open** 5pm-2am daily. **Admission** free. **Credit** AmEx, DC, MC, V. **Map** p249 K4 🔟

This is where the Pretty Young Things come to be seen in the city's best incarnation of a smart London bar. The room is dominated by a sculpted-glass sea anemone, aglow in the dim light. Southern hemisphere cocktails are the draw, reinvented with poise for advanced-course tipplers.

Opus Bar

350 Davie Street, at Hamilton Street (604 642 0557/www.opushotel.com). Bus 15. **Open** 5pm-1am Mon-Wed; 5pm-2am Thur-Sat; 5pm-midnight Sun. **Admission** free. **Credit** AmEx, DC, MC, V. **Map** p249 K5 🔟

The eponymous boutique hotel's smallish lounge – furnished in Philippe Starck/Louis XIV-garage sale style – attracts beautiful people with longer attention spans. They come in droves to sip cosmopolitans while pretending not to notice one another. Arrive early (or very late) to avoid the queue.

Soho Billiards

1283 Hamilton Street, at Drake Street (604 688 1180). Bus 15. **Open** noon-midnight daily. **Admission** free. **Credit** AmEx, DC, MC, V. **Map** p249 K5 🔟

Only eight years ago, Yaletown boasted four pool halls. Now Soho is the only one left. But it's the best, so that is some consolation for billiard buffs. This huge venue, painted deep red with exposed brick walls, manages to be both modern and cosy. A 50-seat front lounge offers a munchie menu for non-players, but mostly it's about the game and on weekends the hall's eight tables are invariably full. There's also foosball (table football).

Subeez

891 Homer Street, at Smithe Street (604 687 6107/ www.subeez.com). Bus 15. **Open** 10am-1pm Mon-Sat; 10am-midnight Sun. **Admission** free. **Credit** AmEx, DC, MC, V. **Map** p249 K4 🔟

Subeez is a welcoming and unpretentious venue that has become one of downtown's most reliable spots for a solid, predictable, loud night out. It appears to have been designed by someone infatuated with all things metal (and imposing art installations). The packed weekends are best; at other times the crowd is dwarfed by the vastness of the space.

Gastown

Alibi Room

157 Alexander Street, at Main Street (604 623 3383/ www.alibi.ca). Bus 3, 4, 7. **Open** 5pm-midnight Tue-Thur; 4.30pm-1am Fri; 10am-1am Sat; 10am-3pm Sun. **Admission** free. **Credit** DC, MC, V. **Map** p249 M3 🔟

While the glacial, pretentious service from aspiring actors can be annoying, the gorgeous room makes up for it with its narrow communal tables, vaulted ceilings and a slim bar. Hordes of local mediacrities, artists and film types call this their home from home. The weekends downstairs are lively for DJ scratches and, of course, much posing.

Cambie Pub

300 Cambie Street, at W Cordova Street (604 688 9158/www.thecambie.com). Bus 3, 4, 7. **Open** 11am-1am Mon-Thur, Sun; 11am-2am Fri, Sat. **Admission** free. **Credit** DC, MC, V. **Map** p249 L3 🔟

The room, down-at-heel and decorated as if by explosion, is one step up from squalor. So obviously it's immensely appealing to slumming university students. Grizzled bikers, sundry reprobates and off-duty longshoremen can all also be found downing their drinks here. Pool tables, a big patio, cheap food and cheaper beer further explain its allure.

Chill Winston

3 Alexander Street, at Carrall Street (604 288 9575/ www.chillwinston.ca). Bus 3, 4, 7. **Open** 11am-1am Mon-Sat; 11am-midnight Sun. **Admission** free. **Credit** DC, MC, V. **Map** p249 M3 🔟

The huge outside patio offers a top-notch view of Gastown and the inside is all gorgeous brick walls, hardwood floors and extravagantly draped windows. Clearly, the owners were striving for a comfortable neighbourhood bar vibe, but the place is more jumped-up than a casual catch-up joint. A miscellaneous gaggle of lined 'n' tanned nightlifers, young suburbanites and feisty tourists compete for each other's (and the waitstaff's) attention.

The Irish Heather

212 Carrall Street, at Water Street (604 688 9779/ www.irishheather.com). Bus 4, 7, 50. **Open** 11am-midnight Mon-Wed, Sun; 11am-1am Thur-Sat. **Credit** phone for details. **Map** p249 M3 🔟

One of the few businessmen prepared to brave Gastown before it became the haunt of Vancouver's newly minted hipsters, Sean Heather is now sitting pretty. The Irishman's empire has been growing steadily, most notably with the arrival of the Salt Tasting Bar (*see below*). But it all started with a pub. Not to be confused with the ubiquitous shamrock-coloured Irish theme bars, this was to be the real McCoy, with good draft Guinness and pub grub. Imagine, then, the dismay when in 2007, it was announced that the buildings in the block that housed Heather's was to be completely renovated. Rather than take compensation for an extended closure, Heather opted for a more radical solution and moved into new premises across the road. He then employed local impresarios Evoke, known for their sleek, trendy rooms, to come up with a design concept that would remain true to his cultural heritage, but still recognise that Ireland is part of the 21st century. As we went to press, the new venue was poised to open.

Salt Tasting Room

45 Blood Alley, between Carrall & Abbott Streets (604 633 1912/www.salttastingroom.com). Bus 4, 7, 50. **Open** noon-midnight daily. **Credit** AmEx, DC, MC, V. **Map** p249 M3 🔟

Republic. See p115.

Small beer

Some people argue that the pre-eminence of Vancouver microbreweries – in quality, if not in quantity – is the result of a collective thumbing of the nose at the dominant national breweries of the east: Labatt and Molson. Such Canadian 'brand' beers might trounce their American counterparts, but westerners merely see this as a case of being the tallest of the midgets. 'Make mine a Labatt Blue' is seldom heard on the left coast; rather, a mellifluous 'Two Granville Island Winter Lagers, thanks' rolls off the tongue more often. And so much the better...

The aforementioned **Granville Island Brewing** (1441 Cartwright Street, at Anderson Street, 604 687 2739, www.gib.ca, tours available) has been the standard bearer of quality and innovation since the release, in 1984, of the mythical – and still wildly popular – Island Lager, brewed in the traditional Bavarian style. An embarrassment of riches were to follow from the little brewery that could: Gastown Amber Ale, English Bay Pale Ale, Maple Cream Ale, Cypress Honey Lager – named not by a grad student in romantic poetry, but in honour of nearby city landmarks. Summer 2007 saw the release of Raspberry Wheat Ale, intended for 'sizzling, sunny days'. Slice of lemon optional.

Purists and proud locals drink nothing but GI, and the loyalty is much deserved. A six-pack of it, whether slung over the shoulder for a neighbour's barbecue, spirited down to the beach on a baking July afternoon, or paired with a hearty stew in December, is always the mark of the best in West Coast taste.

If only for the view of the snow-capped mountains across Burrard Inlet, the **Steamworks Brewing Company** watering hole (375 Water Street, at Richards Street, Gastown, 604 689 2739, www.steamworks. com; *pictured*) is destination enough. But inventive, unique beers – such as a charming, pale golden honey wheat ale – only improve the view. Seasonal specialities (espresso stout, raspberry ale, Scorpion Bitter) demand attention, and the after-work and weekend crowds only attest to their popularity. (Fun fact: the beers are brewed by steam heat, provided by the Vancouver Central Heat Company, the same company that supplies the steam for Gastown's landmark steam clock.)

The **Yaletown Brewing Company**'s pub (1111 Mainland Street, at Helmcken Street, Yaletown, 604 681 2739) makes its home in a vast, dilapidated warehouse. Its range of beers is ambitious, including a Yippee IPA,

a Downtown Brown, a smooth and malty Red Truck Ale and a Hill Special Wheat, named in honour of brewmaster Iain Hill. Afternoons on the vast shady patio are a delightful foil to the heat of the beach, and are best enjoyed with friends over a pitcher of a light, heathery lager. But all lemmings come down on Sunday evenings, for half-price thin-crust pizzas and a pint, in the gloaming of another weekend well spent.

At the **Dockside Restaurant & Brewing Company** (1253 Johnston Street, at Cartwright Street, 604 685 7070) on Granville Island, the eight in-house beers include a dark amber lager, a wheat Bavarian beer, the light fruity Jamaican Lager and Alder Bay Honey Lager, which is 'made with real BC honey'. A prettier locale to enjoy hearty beer-food pairings in the city is hard to find.

Across the pond, in North Vancouver, **Sailor Hägar's Brew Pub** (86 Semisch Avenue, at 1st Street, North Vancouver, 604 984 3087) concentrates on making some of the Lower Mainland's best beer, with quiet Scandanavian pride and purity of flavour. Offerings include a full-bodied Honey Pilsner to a more delicate, Belgium Whit Ale, to a brawny Grizzly Nut Brown Ale.

Though it has won numerous restaurant awards locally and nationally, Salt (tucked away down an alley in a less than salubrious neighbourhood) has no kitchen. What it does have is a great wine list (changed weekly) and a daily selection of ten cheeses and ten charcuterie offerings, paired with an interesting crop of condiments, such as local honeycomb and Marcona almonds. Sherries are also a speciality. Exposed brick, a long communal table and a zinc bar combine to give a stylish – if noisy – vibe, eagerly lapped up by hip locals looking for a more European-style tapas bar. Lunch is laid-back; evenings, the joint jumps. Go for pre- or post-dinner drinks and nibbles, or succumb to a big boozy night out.

Six Acres

203 Carrall Street, at Water Street (604 488 0110/ www.gastown.org/microsite/moons001). Bus 4, 7, 50. **Open** noon-midnight Tue-Thur; noon-1am Fri; 5pm-1am Sat. **Admission** free. **Credit** DC, MC, V. **Map** p249 M3 ❷⑤

An oasis in a sea of tourists and Blarney Stone jocks, this stylish brick-walled space pulses with its own sweet energy. The owners, four high-school friends bent on bringing something good to Vancouver provide great music surpassed only by a keen selection of import and micro-brew beers. There are 34 bottled beers alone.

West Side

Browns Social House

2296 W 4th Avenue, at Vine Street (604 733 2420/ www.brownsrestaurantbar.com). Bus 2, 4, 7, 22. **Open** 11am-1am Mon-Wed; 11am-2am Thur, Fri; 10am-2am Sat; 10am-1am Sun. **Admission** free. **Credit** AmEx, DC, MC, V. **Map** p251 F6 ❷⑥

If you prefer your Guinness with a side of TV and a high noise level, come to Browns – and expect to share the modern, dark panelled room with university boys, middle-aged couples in cowboy hats and large, boisterous parties. The place rates because of its solid beer menu – not a mainstream brew in the lot – and the yam fries. Gotta have the yam fries.

Chivana

2340 W 4th Avenue, at Vine Street (604 733 0330/ www.chivana.com). Bus 4, 7. **Open** 5pm-late daily. **Admission** free. **Credit** AmEx, DC, MC, V. **Map** p251 E6 ❷⑦

This second-floor hideaway, with its milk chocolate walls, fat brown couches and an enormous fireplace, gives off a stylish wreck room vibe. Take a seat at the 12-metre (40-foot) bar, or on the heated covered patio, order the daily drink special and contemplate whether Christian Slater had a good time hanging out here.

Hell's Kitchen

2041 W 4th Avenue, between Arbutus & Maple Streets (604 736 4355/www.hells-kitchen.ca). Bus 4, 7. **Open** 11.30am-1am Mon-Thur; 11.30am-2am Fri; 10am-2am Sat, Sun. **Admission** free. **Credit** AmEx, DC, MC, V. **Map** p251 F6 ❷❽

Home to trust-fund regulars and neighbourhood newbies, the east slope of lower Kitsilano owes much of its nightlife appeal to the Kitchen's boozy swagger. The colour scheme might best be described as postmodern abattoir, from the faux-inferno dark-brick walls to the curved, salacious bar and winsome staff. There's an impressive menu on offer too, though it's provided for a crowd that is more in search of sauce and, ultimately, each other.

East Vancouver

Brickhouse

730 Main Street, at Union Street (604 689 8645). Bus 3, 25. **Open** *8pm-12.30am Mon, Sun; 8pm-2am Tue-Sat.* **Admission** *free.* **Credit** DC, MC, V. **Map** p249 N4 **29**

This late-night tavern is one of the most favoured drinking holes in the city among artists and writers. It's a low-key, cosy bar with a pool table, a wall of books and laid-back clientele. After gallery openings, you can expect art talk here around the long tables late into the night.

Café Deux Soleils

2096 Commercial Drive, at E 5th Avenue (604 254 1195/www.cafedeuxsoleils.com). Bus 20/ SkyTrain Broadway. **Open** *8am-midnight Mon-Sat; 8am-5pm Sun.* **Admission** *free-$8.* **Credit** V. **Map** p252 Q6 **30**

The bric-a-brac design – including a painted plywood visage of a sun smiling down beatifically on the crowd – indicates the Two Suns' hippie stance. The place is crowded for its series of unplugged live acts, but the brunches, among the best on the Drive, are served *sans* music.

Cascade Room

2616 Main Street, between 10th & 11th Avenues (604 709 8650/www.thecascade.ca). Bus 3, 25. **Open** *5pm-midnight daily.* **Admission** *free.* **Credit** AmEx, DC, MC, V. **Map** p252 M7 **31**

Expectations were high when this Main Street newcomer opened for business late in 2007. The extensive cocktail list was designed by Nick Devine – a former Londoner with a cool grasp of mixology – and in the kitchen, chef Travis Williams had done more than decent work around town. The room stands up to the hype: effortlessly hip, with high tables and deep booths rounded out with music from the Clash to the Libertines. The laid-back vibe is taken a little too far, however: the cocktails are served in lumpen glassware, and the food can be unappetising and heavy.

Five Point

3124 Main Street, between E 15th & E 16th Avenues (604 876 5810). Bus 3. **Open** *11.30am-1am Mon-Fri; 10am-1am Sat; 10am-midnight Sun.* **Admission** *free.* **Credit** DC, MC, V. **Map** p252 N8 **32**

This stylish room in a refurbished heritage house draws scores of thirsty locals. The dim lighting suits the gaggles of single girls – and their would-be

lotharios, waiting at the bar. For those not prowling for partners, the patio is a fine place to spend an afternoon in the shade of the elms.

Havana

1212 Commercial Drive, between Charles & William Streets (604 253 9119/www.havana-art.com). Bus 20. **Open** *11am-11pm Mon-Thur; 11am-midnight Fri; 10am-midnight Sat; 10am-11pm Sun.* **Admission** *free.* **Credit** DC, MC, V.

Feeling depressed by another grey and rainy February day in Vancouver? Escape to Havana. Winter gloom is as foreign here as grey skies would be in Cuba. Brunches – taken either on its wide, noisy patio, or in the bustling, friendly dining room – are among the city's best secrets, but nighttime is best for dining at the bar: the music is loud, the mojitos conjure up sunnier climes and the heady *campesino* food can't be beaten.

Public Lounge Eatery

3289 Main Street, at 17th Avenue (604 873 5584/ www.publiclounge.ca). Bus 3. **Open** *4.30pm-1am Mon-Sat; 4.30pm-midnight Sun.* **Admission** *free.* **Credit** AmEx, DC, MC, V. **Map** p252 M8 **33**

Just a few blocks north of Main Street's indie fashion strip, this funky, youthful lounge offers a well-chosen, inexpensive drinks menu and well-executed nosh – drop your bags, relax and forget about your debt. In the evening, the cheap drinks draw a smart slacker crowd, who will inevitably diss the revolving controversial art on the chic, peeling walls.

Soma Café

151 E 8th Avenue, at Main Street (604 630 7502/ www.somavancouver.com). Bus 3. **Open** *9am-midnight daily.* **Admission** *free.* **Credit** AmEx, DC, MC, V. **Map** p252 M6 **34**

If it's a bona fide neighbourhood bar you're after, with a posse of emerging designers, artists and musicians, this is the house for you. A windowed wall highlights the bar, where patrons down superb local draft or BC wine. Music enthusiasts will appreciate the soundtrack with its emphasis on local bands, Animal Collective, Apostle of Hustle and the like. Free Wi-Fi and a past life as a legendary coffee joint keep the place populated all day.

Whip Restaurant Gallery

209 E 6th Avenue, at Main Street (604 874 4687/ www.thewhiprestaurant.com). Bus 3. **Open** *11.30am-midnight Mon-Thur; 11.30am-1am Fri; 10am-1am Sat; 10am-midnight Sun.* **Admission** *free.* **Credit** DC, MC, V. **Map** p252 M6 **35**

The South Main artsy set consciously avoid the yuppie narcissism of Yaletown – a stone's throw (or bathtub-toy ferry ride) away across False Creek – and instead opt to don their thoughtful eyewear and monochrome clothes to visit this bar-cum-art gallery. If you find the black bar and atrium a little austere, gravitate to the more relaxing atmosphere of the mezzanine. The Whip's an ideal place to settle back into the groove of a long DJ set while relaxing with friends at a giant communal table.

Shops & Services

Canadian chic.

Holt Renfrew.

Though Vancouverites' penchant for the outdoors might suggest a wardrobe entirely stocked with fleece and Gore-Tex, the city is not devoid of style. Certainly, the number of high-end brands (Tiffany & Co, Williams Sonoma) that have been setting up shop of late, suggests someone, somewhere has money to spend. Indeed, the 2007 opening bash for Holt Renfrew was the hottest ticket in town.

For a guide to Vancouver's shopping areas, *see p122* **Where to shop**.

PRICES AND TAX

Though the Canadian dollar has strengthened of late, prices remain attractive, especially to Brits. CDs in particular are a good buy, reputedly the cheapest in North America: you pay in dollars what you would in pounds. But books are expensive and, like everything else, taxed. Expect to add five per cent Goods and Services Tax (GST) plus the seven per cent Provincial Sales Tax (PST) to most marked prices.

One-stop shopping

Department stores

Holt Renfrew

737 Dunsmuir Street, at Granville Street, Downtown (604 681 3121/www.holtrenfrew.com). All city-centre buses/SkyTrain Granville. **Open** 10am-7pm Mon, Tue, Sat; 10am-9pm Wed-Fri; 11am-6pm Sun. **Credit** AmEx, DC, MC, V. **Map** p249 K3.

Canada's most luxurious department store chain manages to feel more intimate than ever, despite the opening of these swish, multi-million-dollar, 12,700sq m (137,000sq ft) premises in mid 2007. With ultra-friendly service and a top-notch Holts Salon & Spa keeping them happy, excited shoppers come in droves to scope out celebrity labels (such as Sienna Miller's Twenty8Twelve). Both men's and women's contemporary departments house 'denim walls', while semi-separate boutiques exist for the fashion bigwigs: Dolce & Gabbana, Prada, Marni, Hugo Boss, and more. The entrance atrium, with its cascade of Bocci lights, put the finishing touches to this unapologetic cathedral to consumerism.

Hudson's Bay Company

674 Granville Street, at W Georgia Street, Downtown (604 681 6211/www.hbc.com). All city-centre buses/SkyTrain Granville. **Open** 9.30am-7pm Mon, Tue; 9.30am-9pm Wed-Fri; 8am-7pm Sat; 11am-7pm Sun. **Credit** AmEx, DC, MC, V. **Map** p249 K3.

Canada's first, and most famous, department store began as a trading outpost for furriers in Eastern Canada. While there is still a fur department, most sales now take place in the ground-floor cosmetics and fragrance areas. It's worth venturing up to the Canadian by Design floor for a rare example of a mass Canadian retailer supporting its own. Hbc is also the official store for 2010 Winter Olympics merchandise.

Sears

701 Granville Street, at Robson Street, Downtown (604 685 7112/www.sears.ca). All city-centre buses. **Open** 9.30am-9pm Mon-Fri; 8am-8pm Sat; 11am-7pm Sun. **Credit** AmEx, DC, MC, V. **Map** p249 K3.

Where to shop

Gastown

In the process of gentrification, Gastown is where you'll find the city's hippest one-off stores (*see p129* **Gas injection**) tucked in between good old-fashioned tourist tat.

Granville Island

Art and artisans abound here. You'll find everything from designer pottery to organic charcuterie to boats for sale. *See p132.*

Kitsilano

West 4th Avenue between Burrard and Pine Streets is dominated by streetwear and sk8ter outlets. Further west, up to Yew, yogawear and highly priced baby stores are the main attraction.

Robson Street & around

Flagship stores of international brands line the city's premiere shopping street for the five blocks west of Granville Street. If you're after something higher-end than the likes of Zara and Gap, take a turn north on Burrard and walk a couple of blocks to Alberni. 'Affluent Alley', as this strip is dubbed, is where Hermès, Agent Provocateur, Tiffany & Co and the like reside. And don't forget to put the new upmarket Holt Renfrew store (*see p121*) on your itinerary.

South Granville

Defiantly upscale, Granville Street, from Broadway to 16th Avenue, offers designer fashions, housewares (think luxe US store Williams Sonoma) and North America's first Dyrberg/Kern concept shop. Walk down to 6th Avenue and you'll be in the market for contemporary art.

South Main

A few antique stores continue to ply their wares, but design-forward boutiques are busily taking over. A sprawling affair, **SoMa** (as it's known locally) is best attacked in chunks – between 19th and 23rd Avenues is best for local independent fashion.

Yaletown

Ultra-chic boutiques and top-of-the range design stores service Vancouver's yuppie neighbourhood. Cobbled streets, converted warehouses and plenty of trendy bars and restaurants along Mainland and Hamilton Streets add to the scene.

Mass-market, inexpensive US wares dominate, but this is a trusty stop for anyone seeking basics while abroad (socks and underwear come to mind). It also houses a large selection of small appliances, furniture, housewares and travel accessories, including branded (Nike, Roots and Samsonite) luggage.

Discount stores

Winners

798 Granville Street, at Robson Street, Downtown (604 683 1058/www.winners.ca). All city-centre buses. **Open** 9.30am-9pm Mon-Sat; 11am-6pm Sun. **Credit** AmEx, DC, MC, V. **Map** p249 K3.

Men's designer dress shirts, Benetton luggage and high-end cooking pots are sharply reduced at this downtown location of the Canadian discount chain (located on the second floor of the building). Scour the store for the random designer labels that show up from time to time. New stock arrives daily.

Malls

Metropolis at Metrotown Centre

4700 Kingsway, at McKay Avenue, Burnaby (604 438 4715/http://metropolis.shopping.ca). Bus 19/ SkyTrain Metrotown. **Open** 10am-9pm Mon-Fri; 9.30am-9pm Sat; 11am-6pm Sun. **Credit** varies.

Canada's second-largest mall has close to 500 stores, including international chains like Old Navy, Baby Gap and Town Shoes, as well as independent stores. With a direct SkyTrain link from Downtown, this is the easiest way to stock up on mainstream bargains to take back home.

Pacific Centre

Granville Street, between Robson & Pender Streets, Downtown (604 688 7235/www.pacificcentre.com). All city-centre buses/SkyTrain Granville. **Open** 10am-7pm Mon, Tue, Sat; 10am-9pm Wed-Fri; 11am-6pm Sun. **Credit** varies. **Map** p249 K3.

This downtown mall now comprises three city blocks and houses a variety of national and international stores at every price point, as well as a newly renovated food court. In addition to Holt Renfrew (*see p121*), there's Harry Rosen and Ermenegildo Zegna offering stylish, chic (read: pricey) menswear. Recent additions include BCBG (trendy women's clothing) and Canadian chain Browns Shoes, while spring 2008 promises at least seven new retailers set to occupy the old Holt Renfrew spot.

General

Book Warehouse

552 Seymour Street, at Dunsmuir Street, Downtown (604 683 5711/www.bookwarehouse.ca). All city-centre buses/SkyTrain Granville. **Open** 9.30am-9pm Mon-Fri; 10am-6pm Sat, Sun. **Credit** DC, MC, V. **Map** p249 L3.

An across-the-board 10% discount on new titles is one reason to head here, but the bargain bins hold hidden treasures too. Don't miss the local authors' section and the comprehensive Vancouver aisle. **Other locations** throughout the city.

Chapters
788 Robson Street, at Howe Street, Downtown (604 682 4066/www.chapters.indigo.ca). All city-centre buses. **Open** 9am-10pm daily. **Credit** AmEx, DC, MC, V. **Map** p249 K3.
Large chain store selling popular fiction, CDs and magazines, equipped with coffee bars and comfy chairs. **Other locations** 2505 Granville Street, at W Broadway, West Side (604 731 7822).

Mayfair News
1535 W Broadway, at Granville Street, West Side (604 738 8951). Bus 9, 10, 16, 17, 98. **Open** 8am-9pm Mon-Sat; 9am-9pm Sun. **Credit** DC, MC, V. **Map** p251 H6.
If you're looking to catch up on your favourite magazine, the latest political scandal from home or you're just addicted to glossy periodicals, this is your place. Besides the abundance of titles on scores of subjects and in several languages (26 Italian magazines alone), Mayfair offers more than 120 different dailies in at least ten languages.

Specialist

Barbara-Jo's Books to Cooks
1740 W 2nd Avenue, at Burrard Street, West Side (604 688 6755/www.bookstocooks.com). Bus 2, 22, 44. **Open** 9.30am-6pm Mon-Sat; 10am-5pm Sun. **Credit** AmEx, DC, MC, V. **Map** p251 G5.
The owner, Barbara-jo McIntosh, has over 25 years of experience in the food industry, as a bestselling cookbook author and, previously, as the owner of a local restaurant. Her thoughtfully selected stock includes cookbooks, wine periodicals and professional tomes from around the world, as well as rare finds and out-of-print editions. Don't miss the cooking classes and demonstrations in the test kitchen. **Other locations** 1666 Johnston Street, Granville Island (604 684 6788).

Golden Age Collectibles
852 Granville Street, between Robson & Smithe Streets, Downtown (604 683 2819). All city-centre buses. **Open** 10am-9pm Mon-Sat; 11am-6pm Sun. **Credit** AmEx, DC, MC, V. **Map** p249 K3.
Golden Age has one of the best selections of graphic novels and comic collections in the city. If you're searching for early issues of *Batman*, a 1970s *Star Wars* figure or a rare Magic: The Gathering card, this is the place to come.

Kidsbooks
3083 W Broadway, at Balaclava Street, West Side (604 738 5335/www.kidsbooks.ca). Bus 2, 9, 17, 22. **Open** 9.30am-6pm Mon-Thur, Sat; 9.30am-9pm Fri; 11pm-6pm Sun. **Credit** AmEx, DC, MC, V. **Map** p251 C6.

Canada's largest bookshop for children is a veritable treasure-trove of all things literary for under-16s, with frequent author visits and special events.

Little Sister's Book & Art Emporium
1238 Davie Street, between Bute & Jervis Streets, West End (604 669 1753/www.littlesistersbookstore. com). Bus 6. **Open** 10am-11pm daily. **Credit** AmEx, DC, MC, V. **Map** p248 H3.
You'll find the widest selection of gay and lesbian publications in town at Little Sister's. It also stocks used and new books, local and international magazines and newspapers, cards, gifts and T-shirts. There's a large sex toy/video area at the back.

Used & antiquarian

MacLeod's Books
455 W Pender Street, at Richards Street, Downtown (604 681 7654). All city-centre buses. **Open** 10am-6pm Mon-Sat; 11am-6pm Sun. **Credit** AmEx, DC, MC, V. **Map** p249 L3.
Specialising in Canadian history, MacLeod's stocks a wide selection of books on First Nations, BC and Vancouver history, including the often overlooked Canadian cowboy. No trashy reads, but a good variety of modern and classic novels at decent prices.

Tanglewood Books
1553 W Broadway, at Granville Street, West Side (604 736 8876). Bus 9, 17, 98, 99. **Open** 10am-8pm Mon-Wed; 10am-9pm Thur, Fri; 10am-6pm Sat; noon-6pm Sun. **Credit** DC, MC, V. **Map** p251 H6.
A fast turnover means you might find the latest bestseller in the window, but the dusty first edition of your favourite book might be in here too. Head further west down Broadway towards Alma for several more second-hand bookstores.

Children

Fashion

Belly & Beyond
4118 Main Street, at King Edward Avenue, East Vancouver (604 874 2298/www.bellybeyond.com). Bus 3. **Open** 10am-6pm Mon-Sat; noon-5pm Sun. **Credit** AmEx, DC, MC, V. **Map** p252 M9.
Quirky T-shirts for babies and young children, along with stretchy designer jeans and trousers and tops for yummy mummies and mums-to-be. It's also a good source of good-quality second-hand gear.

ModernKid
45 Water Street, between Abbott & Carrall Streets, Gastown (604 662 3181/www.modernkid.com). Bus 4, 7, 16, 20, 50/SkyTrain Waterfront. **Open** 10am-6pm Mon-Sat; noon-5pm Sun. **Credit** AmEx, DC, MC, V. **Map** p249 M3.
Modern and high-end fashions from quality brands, as well as a small selection of locally designed children's wear. Also find a vast selection of sleek, design-savvy, child-friendly furniture and decor items.

Eat, Drink, Shop

Toys & games

Kids Market (*see p142*), on Granville Island, is a dedicated kids' mall, with toys, books, food, play areas and more.

Hip Baby
2110 W 4th Avenue, at Arbutus Street, West Side (604 737 0603/www.hipbaby.com). Bus 4, 7. **Open** 10am-6pm Mon-Sat; 11am-5pm Sun. **Credit** AmEx, DC, MC, V. **Map** p251 F6.
This stretch of W 4th has a bevy of baby stores. In addition to Hip Baby's selection of care items, you'll find dolls and stuffed bears (including an asthma-friendly choice), and other toys for under-sixes.

Electronics & photography

General

Future Shop
796 Granville Street, at Robson Street, Downtown (604 683 2502/www.futureshop.ca). All city-centre buses. **Open** 10am-9pm Mon-Sat; 11am-6pm Sun. **Credit** AmEx, DC, MC, V. **Map** p249 K3.
Future Shop's CD selection is scant, but the DVDs are competitively priced. If you're a gadget-geek, you'll be in heaven.
Other locations 1740 W Broadway, at Pine Street, West Side (604 739 3000).

Leo's Camera Supply Ltd
1055 Granville Street, between Helmcken & Nelson Streets, Downtown (604 685 5331/www.leos camera.com). Bus 4, 6, 7, 10, 16, 17, 50. **Open** 9am-5pm Mon-Fri; 10am-4pm Sat. **Credit** DC, MC, V. **Map** p249 K4.
Professional shooters shop here too, but Leo's will also sort out all of your plebian photography needs.

London Drugs
710 Granville Street, at W Georgia Street, Downtown (604 448 4802/www.londondrugs.com). All city-centre buses. **Open** 8am-9pm Mon-Fri; 9am-9pm Sat; 10am-8pm Sun. **Credit** AmEx, DC, MC, V. **Map** p249 K3.
The quality of the one-hour developing service is high, and the computer department often has deals.
Other locations throughout the city.

Specialist

Cita
Office: 303-5360 Airport Road South, Richmond (604 671 4655/www.cita.info/rent@cita.info). **Open** phone for details. **Credit** AmEx, DC, MC, V.
Rent a mobile phone at a daily rate plus the price of the calls. Cita delivers the phone to your hotel or the airport for your arrival. Best to email in advance for the best coverage for your visit.

Mac Station
1014 Homer Street, at Nelson Street, Yaletown (604 806 6227/www.macstation.com). Bus 15, 17.

Open 10am-6pm Mon-Fri; 10am-5pm Sat; 11am-5pm Sun. **Credit** AmEx, DC, MC, V. **Map** p249 K4.
When your iBook implodes, head here, pronto. Prices are low compared to Europe.

Fashion

Athletic/yoga

American Apparel
872 Granville Street, between Robson & Smithe Streets, Downtown (604 685 5904/www.american apparel.net). All city-centre buses. **Open** 10am-9pm Mon-Sat; noon-8pm Sun. **Credit** AmEx, DC, MC, V. **Map** p249 K3.
Enormous parade of clothes from the hip LA athletic clothing experts. Expect to be helped by girls wearing gold lamé hot pants or similar.

Lululemon Athletica
2113 W 4th Avenue, at Arbutus Street, West Side (604 732 6111/www.lululemon.com). Bus 4, 7. **Open** 10am-6pm Mon-Thur, Sat, Sun; 10am-7pm Fri. **Credit** AmEx, DC, MC, V. **Map** p251 F6.
If there is one store that sums up the pioneering spirit, raging entrepreneurialism, health obsession, body perfectionism and anti-establishmentarianism of Vancouver, this is it. And the rest of the world is catching on too. The Lululemon 'athleisure' empire has now reached California, Asia and beyond, with its colourful, comfortable men's and womenswear. This, its first location, has spawned a number of competitors on W 4th Avenue, plus a sister store for sustainable wear, Oqoqo, at no.2123 (604 732 6188).
Other locations throughout the city.

Designer

Bacci's/Bacci's at Home
2788 Granville Street, at W 12th Avenue, West Side (604 733 4933/www.baccis.ca). Bus 10, 98. **Open** 9.30am-5.30pm Mon-Sat. **Credit** AmEx, DC, MC, V. **Map** p251 H7.
Side-by-side European designer clothing and posh housewares: what more could you want? Designer shoes and Kiehl's skincare, too? Well, you're in luck.

Basquiat
1189 Hamilton Street, at Davie Street, Yaletown (604 688 0828). Bus 15. **Open** 11am-6pm Mon- Sat; noon-5pm Sun. **Credit** AmEx, DC, MC, V. **Map** p249 K4.
Owned by the wife of a long-time National Hockey League star, North American and European labels found here are often Western Canada exclusives, meaning they're even more lustworthy than their name already makes them.

Betsey Johnson
1033 Alberni Street, between Burrard & Thurlow Streets, Downtown (604 488 0314/www.betsey johnson.com). Bus 2, 5, 22. **Open** 11am-7pm Mon-Sat; 11am-6pm Sun. **Credit** AmEx, DC, MC, V. **Map** p249 K3.

The wild and wacky New York designer brings her unique brand of flirty, feminine clothing here in one of her very few international shops.

Eugene Choo
3683 Main Street, at 21st Avenue, East Vancouver (604 873 8874/www.eugenechoo.com). Bus 3, 25. **Open** 11am-6pm Mon-Thur, Sat; 11am-7pm Fri; noon-5pm Sun. **Credit** AmEx, DC, MC, V. **Map** p252 M8.
An excellent, established source for up-and-coming local designers, as well as international brands such as APC, Converse, RVCA and Red Flag Designs, purveyor of stylish bags made from recycled sails.

Jonathan + Olivia
2570 Main Street, between E Broadway & E 10th Avenue, East Vancouver (604 637 6224/www. jonathanandolivia.com). Bus 3, 8, 19. **Open** 11am-7pm Mon-Fri; 11am-6pm Sat; noon-5pm Sun. **Credit** AmEx, DC, MC, V. **Map** p252 M7.
If you miss some of the lesser-known international brands available back home, make a point to visit this small but well-stocked boutique. Owner Jackie O'Brien carries cult men's and women's labels such as Opening Ceremony, Vena Cava, Vince, Oak NYC (the house label from the popular Brooklyn store) and Whyred from Sweden. Prices may be high, but we're talking high-class goods.

Komakino
8 Water Street, at Carrall Street, Gastown (604 618 1344/www.komakino.ca). Bus 4, 7, 8, 50/ SkyTrain Waterfront. **Open** noon-7pm Mon-Fri; 11am-7pm Sat; 1pm-6pm Sun. **Credit** AmEx, DC, MC, V. **Map** p249 M3.
Inspired by the Berlin guerrilla stores, this innovative menswear boutique keeps edgy and fresh by only staying in one location for a year or so (check the website to make sure they haven't moved their Vancouver location). Expect minimalist decor, maximum designer names. The owner is about to export his version back to Berlin too.

Leone
Sinclair Centre, 757 W Hastings Street, between Granville & Howe Streets, Downtown (604 683 1133/www.leone.ca). All city-centre buses/SkyTrain Waterfront. **Open** 10am-6pm Mon-Sat; noon-5pm Sun. **Credit** AmEx, DC, MC, V. **Map** p249 L3.
If it's Italian and designer, you'll find it here. But know you'll be competing with movie stylists on a label-hunt for discerning leading ladies. The gorgeous heritage building houses a little Italian café, and January's indoor sidewalk sale sees Dolce & Gabbana coats going for a song. Well, an aria anyway.

Mark James
2941 W Broadway, at Bayswater Street, West Side (604 734 2381/www.markjamesclothing.com). Bus 9, 17. **Open** 10am-6pm Mon-Thur, Sat; 10am-7pm Fri; noon-5pm Sun. **Credit** AmEx, V. **Map** p251 D6.
Suits from labels like Paul Smith and Armani, plus a jeans shop. Twice yearly clearance sales see sharp bargains for the sharply dressed man.

Discount

Alison
1628 W 4th Avenue, between Fir & Pine Streets, West Side (604 736 6262). Bus 4, 7. **Open** phone for details. **Credit** DC, MC, V. **Map** p251 G6.
Although it's frequently closed while the owner travels the world on buying trips, society ladies shop here for half-price designer skirt suits (DKNY and the like) and the kind of comfortable yet elegant label clothing that every mature woman wants but is damned if she can find. Buzz to get in.

General

Aritzia
1110 Robson Street, at Thurlow Street, Downtown (604 684 3251/www.aritzia.com). Bus 5. **Open** 10am-9pm Mon-Sat; 11am-8pm Sun. **Credit** AmEx, DC, MC, V. **Map** p248 J3.
Aritzia is the city's most service-conscious, trend-setting store for young women. It is a rite of passage for local girls to work here before becoming bankers, lawyers or journalists.

Atomic Model
1036 Mainland Street, between Nelson & Helmcken Streets, Yaletown (604 688 9989/www.atomicmodel. com). Bus 15, 17. **Open** 11am-7pm Mon-Wed; 11am-8pm Thur-Sat; noon-7pm Sun. **Credit** AmEx, DC, MC, V. **Map** p249 K4.
Yes, it is where models shop – for top LA and New York labels that are hot today, forgotten tomorrow. Don't forget your lap dog and massive sunglasses.

The Block
350 W Cordova Street, at Homer Street, Gastown (604 685 8885/www.theblock.ca). Bus 4, 7, 8, 50/ SkyTrain Waterfront. **Open** 11am-6pm Mon-Thur, Sat; 11am-7pm Fri; noon-5pm Sun. **Credit** AmEx, DC, MC, V. **Map** p249 L3.
An eclectic mix of fashion-forward designers – local and international – for men and women laid out in an easy-to-navigate sleek, contemporary space.

Brooklyn Clothing Co
418 Davie Street, at Homer Street, Yaletown (604 683 2929/www.brooklynclothing.com). Bus 15. **Open** 11am-9pm daily. **Credit** AmEx, DC, MC, V. **Map** p249 K4.
Tons of hot jeans and deconstructed sweats for the guy who is over Levi's but not at all interested in skinny black suits.

Hill's of Kerrisdale
2125 W 41st Avenue, at Arbutus Street, West Side (604 266 9177/www.hillsofkerrisdale.com). Bus 16, 41, 43. **Open** 9.30am-6pm Mon-Wed, Sat; 9.30am-9pm Thur, Fri; 11am-5pm Sun. **Credit** AmEx, DC, MC, V.
The younger Hill progeny have taken this clothing store, a family-owned institution that was once a dry-goods shop, to new levels of hip. One son grew the young women's department into one of the

country's top national chains (Aritzia; *see p126*), a daughter created a successful string of boutiques out of the jewellery counter (Blue Ruby; *see p128*), while another son created a cool outcrop of the young men's department (Ray Rickburn). But this is where it all began, and still happens today.

Spank

856 Granville Street, between Robson & Smithe Streets, Downtown (604 677 3202/www.spank clothing.ca). All city-centre buses. **Open** 10am-8pm Mon-Thur; 10am-9pm Fri, Sat; 11am-7pm Sun. **Credit** AmEx, DC, MC, V. **Map** p249 K3.
What started as a store on Commercial Drive now has locations in every major fashion corner of the city. Boasts excellent service, international and Canadian labels and mostly-modest prices.

Markets

Portobello West

Rocky Mountaineer Station, 1755 Cottrell Street, East Vancouver (www.portobellowest.com). Bus 3, 8, 19, 22/SkyTrain Main Street-Science World, then free shuttle (every 20mins) from corner of Station Street & Terminal Avenue. **Open** noon-6pm last Sun of mth. **Credit** DC, MC, V. **Map** p252 O6.
The original London market that inspired Portobello West was, in fact, Spitalfields rather than its namesake, but they preferred the latter's name. Distinctly Canadian in fashion, this European-style market is a great place to spot up-and-coming designers alongside art and creative crafts. Around 120 stallholders.

Punjabi Village

Fraser & Main Streets, above 46th Avenue. Bus 3, 8, 49.
Since pashmina shawls, beaded slippers and tunics, and Indian jewellery hit the mainstream, many of the best shops have closed to become internet businesses. But try Frontier Cloth House (6695 Main Street, 604 325 4424) and Rokko's Fabrics (6201 Fraser Street, 604 327 3033) for fashion finds and the newly opened Crossover-Bollywood Se (6468 Main Street, 604 321 6447), which is part-owned by action hero Sunil Shetty and carries glitzy East-West fusion clothing by numerous Bollywood movie designers. Food stalls here are also a treat (*see p131*).

Streetwear

AntiSocial

2425 Main Street, at Broadway, East Vancouver (604 708 5678/www.antisocialshop.com). Bus 3, 8, 19. **Open** 11am-6pm Mon-Sat; noon-5pm Sun. **Credit** DC, MC, V. **Map** p252 M7.
Set up like an art gallery (or a posh skate kid's dream bedroom, take your pick), AntiSocial is a shrine to West Coast skateboarding culture.

Dadabase

183 E Broadway, at Main Street, East Vancouver (604 709 9934/www.dadabase.ca). Bus 3, 8, 19.

Open 11am-7pm Mon-Sat; noon-5pm Sun. **Credit** AmEx, DC, MC, V. **Map** p252 M7.
Part art gallery, part techno hub, part fashion store specialising in reworked military clothing… it's all cool at this tiny shop. Hosts regular parties that spill on to the streets.

El Kartel

1025 Robson Street, at Burrard Street, Downtown (604 683 2171/www.elkartel.com). Bus 2, 5, 22. **Open** 11am-7pm Mon-Thur; 11am-8pm Fri-Sun. **Credit** AmEx, DC, MC, V. **Map** p249 K3.
The Latino gangsta fashion trend dubbed 'cholo chic' begins and ends here with cutting-edge labels for tough guys with skinny hips and fat wallets.

Headquarter

1232 Burrard Street, at Davie Street, Downtown (604 688 0406/www.headquarterstore.com). Bus 2, 6, 22. **Open** 11am-8pm Mon-Sat; noon-7pm Sun. **Credit** AmEx, DC, MC, V. **Map** p248 J4.
Weird Japanese collectable toys provide wacky eye candy amid the club gear and streetwear.

Used & vintage

Deluxe Junk Company

310 W Cordova Street, at Cambie Street, Gastown (604 685 4871/www.deluxejunk.com). Bus 4, 7, 8, 50. **Open** 10am-6pm Mon-Sat; noon-6pm Sun. **Credit** DC, MC, V. **Map** p249 L3.
Authentic Edwardian jackets have been spotted here amid contemporary and 1970s finds. Consignment pieces are marked down 10% every few weeks.

Komakino.

True Value Vintage

710 Robson Street, at Granville Street, Downtown (604 685 5403). All city-centre buses. **Open** 11am-8pm Mon-Thur, Sun; 11am-9pm Fri, Sat. **Credit** DC, MC, V. **Map** p249 K3.

TV stylists love that this store is so well organised and edited – there's no need to get your hands dirty. Londoners and New Yorkers leave agog at how untapped the Canadian vintage market still is.

Value Village

1820 E Hastings Street, at Victoria Drive, East Vancouver (604 254 4282/www.valuevillage.ca). Bus 10, 16. **Open** 9am-9pm Mon-Sat; 10am-6pm Sun. **Credit** AmEx, DC, MC, V.

A repository for second-hand goods from across BC, this large charity shop is where pickers start when filling their own vintage stores, so you might as well go straight to the source.

Other locations 6415 Victoria Drive, at E 49th Avenue, East Vancouver (604 327 4434).

Fashion accessories & services

Cleaning & repairs

Money's Drycleaning

585 Davie Street, at Seymour Street, Downtown (604 684 4241). Bus 4, 6, 7, 10, 17, 98. **Open** 6.30am-6pm Mon-Fri; 9am-4pm Sat. **Credit** DC, MC, V. **Map** p248 J4.

Be prepared for no-frills service, but nothing beats the easily accessible location and extended hours. Ask for eco-friendly options.

Quick Cobbler

430 W 2nd Avenue, between Cambie & Wylie Streets, West Side (604 682 6354/www.quickcobbler. com). Bus 15, 84. **Open** 9am-6pm Mon-Fri; 9am-5pm Sat. **Credit** DC, MC, V. **Map** p252 L6.

Quick and cobbler. Two words that ring like music in the ear when your heel has broken and you're on your way to the airport.

Stitch International

Pacific Centre, 777 Dunsmuir Street, at Howe Street, Downtown (604 689 2429). All city-centre buses. **Open** 10am-7pm Mon, Tue, Sat; 10am-9pm Wed-Fri; 10am-6pm Sun. **No credit cards.** **Map** p249 K3.

A walk-in spot with five locations where staff will fix a hanging hem while you wait.

Hats

Edie Hats

The Net Loft, 1666 Johnston Street, at Duranleau Street, Granville Island (604 683 4280/www. ediehats.com). Bus 50. **Open** 10am-7pm Mon-Fri; 9.30am-7pm Sat, Sun. **Credit** AmEx, DC, MC, V. **Map** p250 B2.

Although the signature Vancouver headgear must definitely be the knitted toque (spotted well into summer), you can buy all manner of fancy and casual toppers from this local milliner.

Jewellery

Birks

698 W Hastings Street, at Granville Street, Downtown (604 669 3333/www.birks.com). All city-centre buses. **Open** 10am-6pm Mon-Fri; 10am-5.30pm Sat; noon-5pm Sun. **Credit** AmEx, DC, MC, V. **Map** p249 L3.

Canada's answer to Tiffany & Co, this is where to stop for a chic christening gift or an engagement ring. Birks enlists global designers to contribute to its collections; however, some of the most covetable pieces are those you'll discover among the antique jewellery in the estate cases.

Other locations throughout the city.

Blue Ruby

1089 Robson Street, at Thurlow Street, Downtown (604 899 2583/www.blueruby.com). Bus 2, 5, 22. **Open** 10am-9pm Mon-Fri; 10am-10pm Sat; 10am-8pm Sun. Closes earlier in low season. **Credit** AmEx, DC, MC, V. **Map** p248 J3.

Jewellery is the ultimate travel souvenir: if it's interesting, everyone asks where you got it, and you get to say, 'Oh, this? I bought it in Vancouver.' Here's where to go to get that conversation started.

Other locations throughout the city.

Tiffany & Co

723 Burrard Street, at Alberni Street, Downtown (604 630 1300/www.tiffany.com). All city-centre buses. **Open** 10am-6pm Mon-Wed, Sat; 10am-8pm Thur, Fri; 11am-6pm Sun. **Credit** AmEx, DC, MC, V. **Map** p249 K3.

With its trademark art-deco-inspired stainless-steel gates and granite facade, Tiffany spent years waiting for just the right spot before opening its first Vancouver store in late 2006.

Lingerie & underwear

Scarlet

460 Granville Street, at W Pender, Downtown (604 605 1601). All city-centre buses. **Open** 11am-6.30pm Mon-Fri; noon-6.30pm Sat; noon-5pm Sun. **Credit** DC, MC, V. **Map** p249 L3.

Make someone turn, ahem, scarlet by donning something by Italian label La Perla – this boutique just happens to claim the city's widest selection. Service is phenomenal.

La Vie en Rose

1009 Robson Street, at Burrard Street, Downtown (604 684 5600/www.lavieenrose.com). Bus 5. **Open** 10am-9pm Mon-Sat; 11am-8pm Sun. **Credit** AmEx, DC, MC, V. **Map** p249 K3.

A more down-to-earth approach to sexy lingerie – lacy gear that's not just for that special occasion.

Gas injection

Five years ago, if all you really wanted was a cheesy T-shirt or postcard announcing you had visited Vancouver, Gastown was where you'd find it. In recent years, the once-seedy neighbourhood – named after 'Gassy' Jack Deighton, the British seaman who opened the first saloon here – has undergone a retail renaissance, with an array of pretty, independent boutiques now peddling a discerning mix of clothing and decor by local and international designers. Gastown is bounded by the Burrard Inlet, Chinatown, Cordova and Richards Streets, and most shops are located on West Cordova and Water Streets, with some on the smaller Carrall and Abbott Streets.

Head first to **John Fluevog** (65 Water Street, between Abbott & Carrall Streets, www.fluevog.com), a homegrown shoe retailer known for its often-quirky and colourful designs. The massive modern store – a tourist attraction in its own right – is a glassed-in space between two heritage buildings and was originally designed for Richard Kidd (the only place in the city to find washed deerhide pants hanging alongside vegan-friendly designs by Stella McCartney). Owner and designer Raif Adelberg moved his 'Rich Kidd' store further east in early 2008.

Skip across the street to **Inform Interiors** (50 Water Street, between Abbott & Carrall Streets, 604 682 3868, www.inform interiors.com), the airy two-storey home of big-ticket designer furniture and inventive living accessories. Buy (or covet) modern classics like the Charles Eames lounger, as well as contemporary pieces, including those by owner/designer Niels Bendtsen, whose Ribbon Chair is part of the permanent collection at New York's MoMA.

After refuelling at the award-winning **Salt Tasting Room** (*see p116*) in the reclaimed Blood Alley Square, head to **Hunt & Gather** (225 Carrall Street, at Blood Alley, 604 633 9559, www.huntandgather.ca; *pictured*), the perfect showcase for local designer Natalie Purschwitz's much-feted collections (which, incidentally, she sews right here). The chic decor (mosaic floor, curved display tables) receives worldwide honorable mentions for design in its own right.

Wander next to **Dutil** (303 W Cordova Street, at Cambie Street, 604 688 8892, www.dutildenim.com), the only men's and women's denim-only speciality store in

Vancouver. Don't underestimate Dutil on account of its teensy size: it stocks plenty of big-name brands and a wide selection of niche labels, including Smalltown, Rag & Bone and Cassette.

Round off your shopping at **One of a Few** (354 Water Street, at Richards Street, 604 605 0685, www.oneofafew.com) and its new, neighbour-cum-sister store (for footwear and menswear exclusively), **Two of a Few** (356 Water Street, at Richards Street, 604 605 0630, www.twoofafew.com). Favourite haunts of local hipsters and international fashionphiles, both boutiques carry an impressive range of designers and styles across all budgets.

Shoes

Dayton Boots

2250 E Hastings Street, at Nanaimo Street, East Vancouver (604 253 6671/www.daytonboots.com). Bus 10, 16, 135. **Open** 9am-5pm Mon-Fri; 10am-5pm Sat; noon-5pm Sun. **Credit** DC, MC, V.

Wondering where Johnny Depp got those black leather boots he's always wearing? Bingo. Loggers wore them first, then film crews, and eventually the stars themselves. Now people shop from all over the world via the website, but the original factory is still here on the gritty Downtown Eastside.

Gravity Pope

2205 W 4th Avenue, at Yew Street, West Side (604 731 7673/www.gravitypope.com). Bus 4, 7, 44, 84. **Open** 10am-9pm Mon-Fri; 10am-7pm Sat; 11am-6pm Sun. **Credit** AmEx, DC, MC, V. **Map** p251 F6.

With the most far-ranging selection in the city, Gravity Pope is the best stop for funky flats, bejewelled Birkenstocks, cowboy boots, leather clogs, espadrilles, or whatever else is causing a fuss this season. It recently opened a clothing outlet next door.

John Fluevog

837 Granville Street, between Robson & Smithe Streets, Downtown (604 688 2828/www.fluevog. com). All city-centre buses. **Open** 11am-7pm Mon-Wed; Sat; 11am-8pm Thur, Fri; noon-6pm Sun. **Credit** AmEx, DC, MC, V. **Map** p249 K3.

A local legend, Fluevog's been cobbling since the 1980s, when high-school girls wore his black pointy flats and street punks donned his 12-eyelet boots. From chunky to funky and back again, he's stayed true to his street-wise edge, which has earned him a global following, with stores in London and New York, as well as this, the original. A swanky new store is open in Gastown (*see p129* **Gas injection**). **Other locations** 65 Water Street, between Abbott & Carrall Streets, Gastown (604 688 6228).

Umeboshi

3638 Main Street, at 21st Avenue, East Vancouver (604 909 8225/www.umeboshishoes.com). Bus 3, 25. **Open** 11am-6pm Mon-Thur, Sat; 11am-7pm Fri; noon-5.30pm Sun. **Credit** DC, MC, V. **Map** p252 M8.

Its name means 'plum' in Japanese, and the shoe selection for men and women here is just that. Prices are reasonable, and established, loved brands such as Fly London, Coclico and Faryl Robyn are mainstays. Be sure to peruse the small selection of quality leather bags and wallets, and jewellery too.

Food & drink

Bakeries

Cupcakes

1116 Denman Street, between Pendrell & Comox Streets, West End (604 974 1300/www.cupcakes online.com). Bus 6. **Open** 10am-9pm Mon-Thur, Sun; 10am-10pm Fri, Sat. **Credit** DC, MC, V. **Map** p248 H2.

Forget doughnuts – cupcakes are the quintessential North American treat: brightly coloured, full of air and sugar, and yet somehow deeply satisfying. The store itself is so pink and cute, it begs you to buy a dozen and have yourself a tea party. Seating is limited so be prepared to take them to the beach. **Other locations** 2887 West Broadway, at Bayswater Street, West Side (604 974 1300); 3026 Edgemont Boulevard, at West Queens Road, North Vancouver (604 974 1300).

Drinks

BC Liquor Stores

1120 Alberni Street, at Thurlow Street, West End (604 660 4572/www.bcliquorstores.com). Bus 5. **Open** 9.30am-11pm Mon-Sat; 11am-6pm Sun. **Credit** AmEx, DC, MC, V. **Map** p249 K3.

When the government runs the liquor stores, it's no surprise they would be closed on Sunday and holidays – precisely when most people tend to want libations. These two speciality stores, however, have longer hours, large selections, and staff with some wine and spirits knowledge. **Other locations** 5555 Cambie Street, at W 39th Avenue, West Side (604 660 9463).

Marquis Wine Cellars

1034 Davie Street, between Burrard & Thurlow Streets, Downtown (604 684 0445/www.marquis-wines.com). Bus 2, 5, 22. **Open** 11am-9pm daily. **Credit** DC, MC, V. **Map** p248 J4.

In addition to a range of vintages, this longstanding private wine store also sells Reidel crystal and inexpensive pine crates for shipping gifts. Informal tastings take place on weekends.

Taylorwood Wines

1185 Mainland Street, at Davie Street, Yaletown (604 408 9463/www.taylorwoodwines.com). Bus 15. **Open** 10am-9pm Mon-Sat; noon-7pm Sun. **Credit** DC, MC, V. **Map** p249 K4.

Young professionals in Yaletown meet up at this BC wine specialist for complementary wine tasting happy hours on Thursday and Sunday afternoons. Cheers to that, we say.

General

Choices

1202 Richards Street, at Davie Street, Yaletown (604 633 2392/www.choicesmarket.com). Bus 6, 7, 10, 17, 50. **Open** 8am-11pm daily. **Credit** DC, MC, V. **Map** p249 K4.

A BC-owned store that prides itself on its extensive range of organic produce. **Other locations** throughout the city.

H-Mart

550 Robson Street (upstairs), at Granville Street, Downtown (604 609 4567/www.hmart.com). All city-centre buses. **Open** 9am-10pm daily. **Credit** DC, MC, V. **Map** p249 K3.

This Korean supermarket chain opened its second Canadian location in 2006. It specialises in imported Asian and Korean food and kitchen items, as well as a seemingly random selection of Western products. Bright and efficient, H-Mart offers quirky food items that are well worth a second look.

Marketplace IGA

909 Burrard Street, at Smithe Street, Downtown (604 605 0612/www.marketplaceiga.com). All city-centre buses. **Open** 7am-midnight daily. **Credit** AmEx, DC, MC, V. **Map** p249 K3.

Part of a chain, this is the most centrally located and reasonably priced downtown supermarket. It's no Tesco, however – two-for-one offers are rarely found. **Other locations** throughout the city.

Meinhardt Fine Foods

3002 Granville Street, at W 14th Avenue, West Side (604 732 4405/www.meinhardt.com). Bus 10, 98. **Open** 8am-9pm Mon-Sat; 9am-8pm Sun. **Credit** AmEx, DC, MC, V. **Map** p251 H7.

Like a French market with its flowers spilling on to the street, this upscale market offers gourmet brands and posh nosh, with a high-end deli to boot. The adjoining pâtisserie and lunch spot, Picnic, features a massive communal table.

T&T Supermarket

179 Keefer Place, at Abbott Street, Chinatown (604 899 8836/www.tnt-supermarket.com). Bus 10, 16/SkyTrain Stadium. **Open** 8.30am-9.30pm daily. **Credit** DC, MC, V. **Map** p249 M4.

On the edge of Chinatown sits this gleaming, teeming supermarket full of everything Asian. Try the black sesame soy drink, the salty but satisfying dried shrimp and seaweed crackers, or the delectable dried guava – all great hiking snacks. The hot takeaways aren't so good, but do sample the baked goods.

Urban Fare

177 Davie Street, at Pacific Boulevard, Yaletown (604 975 7550/www.urbanfare.com). Bus 15, C21, C23. **Open** 6am-midnight daily. **Credit** AmEx, DC, MC, V. **Map** p249 K5.

It's easy to lose track of time here while marvelling at how those with enormous incomes can dispose of them on mere groceries. That the baking section of this futuristic supermarket is negligible is but one indication that its clients don't cook. But why bother when there are fancy pre-packaged meals, $15 crackers, gourmet water and Poilâne bread flown in weekly from France at a legendary $100 a loaf? **Other locations** 305 Bute Street, at W Cordova Street, Downtown (604 669 5831).

Markets

Chinatown Night Market

Keefer Street, between Main & Columbia Streets, Chinatown (604 682 8998/www.vcma. shawbiz.ca). Bus 3/SkyTrain Main. **Open** 6.30-11pm Fri-Sun. Closed Oct-April. **No credit cards**. **Map** p249 N4.

Like a scene from *Blade Runner*, this frenetic street market is fun to wander for the smells, sights and neon signs that remind you Vancouver is indeed on the Pacific Rim. Go early and visit the very first Ming Wo Cookware (23 E Pender Street, 604 683 7268). Nearby, Chinese herbalists will prescribe all manner of inedible things for what's ailing you, while apothecaries and teashops abound.

East Vancouver Farmers Market

Trout Lake, 3350 Victoria Drive, at E 15th Avenue, East Vancouver (604 879 3276/www.eatlocal.org). Bus 20/SkyTrain Broadway, then 10min walk. **Open** 9am-2pm Sat. Closed Oct-Apr. **No credit cards**. **Map** p252 R8.

In the parking lot of a grassy public park that surrounds a small lake, this is the best of Vancouver's summer farmer's markets. What starts as mostly plants in May and June blooms into an Eden of heirloom produce, preserves, baked goods, chocolates and creations by guest chefs by the height of summer. With the bohemian East Vancouver location, you're as likely to see adults in line for the face painting and balloons as you are kids.

Punjabi Village

Fraser & Main Streets, above 46th Avenue. Bus 3, 8, 49.

A medley of spicy food and produce, and tons of Indian sweets amid the all-you-can-eat buffets and Punjabi clothes shops (*see p127*).

Riley Park Farmers Market

Nat Bailey Stadium, Ontario Street, at 30th Avenue, East Vancouver (604 879 3276/www.eatlocal.org). Bus 3, 15. **Open** 1-6.30pm Wed. Closed Nov-May. **No credit cards**. **Map** p252 M10.

If you miss the weekend farmers market at East Vancouver's Trout Lake (*see above*), fear not, as a small portion of the same farmers, artisans and purveyors set up at this baseball park in central Vancouver on Wednesday afternoons.

Specialist

Les Amis du Fromage

1752 W 2nd Avenue, at Burrard Street, West Side (604 732 4218/www.buycheese.com). Bus 2, 22, 44. **Open** 9am-6pm Mon-Wed, Sat; 9am-6.30pm Thur, Fri; 9am-5pm Sun. **Credit** AmEx, DC, MC, V. **Map** p251 G5.

The best place in town, bar none, to indulge your passion for all things cheese. Anywhere from 350 to 500 different varieties are stocked at any given time, and extremely knowledgeable staff will help you narrow down the choice from your favourite European offerings to an extensive selection of local products. Vancouver's own Lesley Stowe crackers and a high-end selection of preserves and other accompaniments are all available – perfect for an impromtu picnic. **Other locations** Park Royal Shopping Centre, 2002 Park Royal South, West Vancouver (604 925 4218).

Eat, Drink, Shop

Chocolate Arts

2037 W 4th Avenue, at Maple Street, West Side (604 739 0475/www.chocolatearts.com). Bus 4, 7. **Open** 10am-6pm Mon-Sat; noon-5pm Sun. **Credit** AmEx, DC, MC, V. **Map** p251 F6.

Sporting an ever-changing, elaborate chocolate sculpture in its window, this local purveyor of fine chocolates produces beautiful, inventive selections alongside seasonal treats and slabs of Valhrona. Chocolate Arts' signature First Nations solid medallions make great gifts.

Barking Babies

1188 Homer Street, at Davie Street, Yaletown (604 647 2275/www.barkingbabies.com). Bus 15. **Open** 10am-6pm Mon-Sat; 11am-5pm Sun. **Credit** DC, MC, V. **Map** p249 K4.

Stroll through Yaletown and you'll see decked-out pooches that likely shopped here: dresses and mini tuxes inspired by Penelope, Reese and Leo, Chanel-inspired carriers and collars with plenty of bling.

Granville Island

One of Vancouver's most popular tourist draws, Granville Island is also well used by locals. The centrepiece is the large **Public Market** with its huge selection of produce, local artisan specialities and a piazza that overlooks False Creek – perfect for a picnic with the pigeons. The market's culinary highlights include **Oyama Sausage Company** (604 327 7407, www.oyamasausage.ca), purveyors of fine charcuterie, much of it produced from their own naturally reared pigs. **Edible British Columbia** (www.edible-british columbia.com) is a one-stop shop for the best of what the province offers – try the cherries from Mission Hill soaked in Oculus wine, perfect gifts to take home. It also offers tours of the market and other foodie areas of the city (*see p61* **Tickets to ride**). **South China Seas Trading Company** (604 681 5402, www.southchinaseas.ca) stocks intriguing Asian wares and cookery books, and opposite, the **Granville Island Tea Company** (604 683 7491, www.granville tea.com) brews a mighty cuppa, offering a huge selection of black and green leaves, herbal infusions and own-ground chai.

Elsewhere on the island, independent shops and workshops abound and you can watch everything from glassblowing to boat building. Try the **Crafthouse** (1386 Cartwright Street, 604 687 7270, www.cabc.net) for a selection of work by BC artisans. Even if you're not in the market for a live lobster, it's fun to poke around the tanks at the **Lobster Man** (1807 Mast Tower Road, 604 687 4531, www.lobsterman.com), where staff in hip waders and wellies trade in sea urchins, snails, crab and oysters from the local waters.

Take a stroll along Railspur Alley and check out the crazy mechanised pieces of **IE Creative Artworks** (1399 Railspur Alley, 604 254 4374, www.iecreative.ca), try on a couple of Jessica de Haas's designer felt jackets at **Funk Shui** (1375 Railspur Alley, 604 684 5327), and taste the fruits of Masa Shiroki at **Artisan Sake Maker** (1339 Railspur Alley, 604 685 7253) before kicking back with a well-earned cup of organic Fairtrade coffee at the friendly (and Wi-Fi enabled) **Agro Café** (1363 Railspur Alley, 604 669 0724, www.agrocafe.org).

La Casa del Habano

402 Hornby Street, at W Hastings Street, Downtown (604 609 0511). Bus 2, 5, 22. **Open** 10am-7pm daily. **Credit** AmEx, DC, MC, V. **Map** p249 L2.

Selling exclusively Cuban cigars, this haven for the cigar smoker offers a luxurious smoking lounge, monthly seminars on choosing cigars to suit your mood, and advice on pairing them with wines and spirits. Cigars range from $3 up to $70, so anyone can indulge in a puff.

Hilary Miles Flowers

1854 W 1st Avenue, between Burrard & Cypress Streets, West Side (604 737 2782/www.hilarymiles. com). Bus 2, 22. **Open** 9am-5.30pm Mon-Fri; 10am-5pm Sat. **Credit** AmEx, DC, MC, V. **Map** p251 G5.

Even the tiniest little posy from the excellent Hilary Miles Flowers will be the height of glamour and sophistication – guaranteed.

Puff The Out of Sight Smoke Shop

712 Robson Street (upstairs), at Granville Street, Downtown (604 684 7833). **Open** 11am-7pm Mon-Sat; noon-6pm Sun. **Credit** DC, MC, V. **Map** p249 K3.

While stores selling marijuana come and go, this shop vending smoking paraphernalia, like pipes and bongs, lives on, dude.

Other locations 3255 Main Street, between 16th & 17th Avenues, East Vancouver (604 708 9804).

Rubber Rainbow Condom Co

953 Denman Street, between Barclay & Haro Streets, West End (604 683 3423). Bus 5. **Open** 11am-8pm daily. **Credit** DC, MC, V. **Map** p248 H2.

With the warm and friendly salespeople, buying a condom here is a happy, no-pressure experience. From basic to exotic, there is surely a shape and colour to tickle everyone's fancy, and for people easily irritated by latex it even carries wonderful lambskin versions (at $69.95 per dozen!).

Vancouver Art Gallery Shop

750 Hornby Street, between W Georgia & Robson Streets, Downtown (604 662 4706/www.vanart gallery.bc.ca). All city-centre buses. **Open** 10am-6pm Mon, Wed, Fri-Sun; 10am-9pm Tue, Thur. **Credit** AmEx, DC, MC, V. **Map** p249 K3.

The buyers here are always on to the hottest local jewellery designer or great art book. Start here for your best Vancouver souvenirs.

Womyns'Ware

896 Commercial Drive, at Venables Street, East Vancouver (604 254 2543/toll-free 1 888 996 9273/www.womynsware.com). Bus 20. **Open** 11am-6pm Mon-Wed, Sat; 11am-7pm Thur, Fri; 11am-5.30pm Sun. **Credit** DC, MC, V.

An informative, female-owned and -operated sex shop on Vancouver's east side. As the name suggests, it draws a mostly female clientele, although men are welcomed. Great selection of toys, strapons and leather accessories.

Health & beauty

Complementary medicine

Traditional Chinese Medicine Association of British Columbia

Office: 4857 Main Street, East Vancouver (604 602 7550/http.//tcmabc.org). **Open** phone for details.

From acupuncture to Tui Na Massage, this is the source for traditional Chinese complementary medicine practitioners in the city and environs.

Hairdressers & barbers

Axis

1111 W Georgia Street, at Bute Street, Downtown (604 685 0200). Bus 5. **Open** 10am-7pm Mon, Wed; 9am-8pm Tue; 9am-9pm Thur, Fri; 8am-6pm Sat; 11am-6pm Sun. **Credit** DC, MC, V. **Map** p249 K3.

It doubles as a hairdressing school and alumni have gone on to cut the locks of model Gisele Bundchen, and Leonardo DiCaprio in New York.

Other locations 757 W Hastings Street, at Howe Street, Downtown (604 608 0860).

Colourbox Hairdressing

305 W Cordova Street, at Cambie Street, Gastown (604 669 6354/www.thecolourboxhairsalon.com). Bus 3, 4, 7, 50. **Open** 9.30am-5.30pm Mon-Fri; 9am-5pm Sat. Eve appointments available. **Credit** DC, MC, V. **Map** p249 L3.

Colour is the speciality of this unpretentious, well-priced salon, but given its 20-plus-year history, stylists here are extremely adept at cutting too.

Opticians

Bruce Eyewear

219 Abbott Street, between Water & W Cordova Streets, Gastown (604 662 8300/www.bruceeye wear.com). Bus 4, 7, 8, 50/SkyTrain Waterfront. **Open** 10am-6pm Mon-Sat; noon-5pm Sun. **Credit** AmEx, DC, MC, V. **Map** p249 M3.

This design-forward Gastown shop is also a licensed optometrist, so you can actually see through those new Dior shades you just bought.

Eyes On Burrard

775 Burrard Street, at Robson Street, Downtown (604 688 9521/www.eyesonline.com). Bus 2, 5, 22. **Open** 10am-6pm Mon-Sat; noon-6pm Sun. **Credit** AmEx, DC, MC, V. **Map** p249 K3.

A massive designer selection and long-standing track record have kept this place on the map for years.

Other locations Eyes On Twelfth, 1493 W 12th Avenue, West Side (604 732 8812).

Pharmacies

Semperviva Lifestyle Store

2608 W Broadway, at Trafalgar Street, West Side (604 739 1958/www.semperviva.com). Bus 9, 17, 99.

Open 10am-7pm Mon-Fri; 9.30am-6pm Sat; 11am-7pm Sun. **Credit** AmEx, DC, MC, V. **Map** p251 E6.
Whether it's organic insect ointment you're after, or an emergency cold-sore cure, this is where to find it.

Shoppers Drug Mart
1125 Davie Street, at Thurlow Street, West End (604 669 2424/www.shoppersdrugmart.ca). Bus 6. **Open** 24hrs daily. **Credit** AmEx, DC, MC, V. **Map** p248 J3.
All the basics, all at decent prices, at all hours.
Other locations 2302 W 4th Avenue, at Vine Street, West Side (604 738 3138); 885 W Broadway, at Laurel Street, West Side (604 708 1135).

Shops

BeautyBar
2142 W 4th Avenue, between Arbutus & Yew Streets, West Side (604 733 9000/www.beautybar cosmetics.com). Bus 4, 7. **Open** 10am-7pm Mon-Sat; 11am-6pm Sun. **Credit** DC, MC, V. **Map** p251 F6.
Belly jelly for pregnant women, beard lube for macho men, and all kinds of fabulous make-up and skincare lines. A men's shaving station, a healthy herbal tonic bar and make-up lessons too.

Beautymark
1120 Hamilton Street, between Helmcken & Davie Streets, Yaletown (604 642 2294/www.beautymark.ca). Bus 15. **Open** 10am-7pm Mon-Sat; noon-5pm Sun. **Credit** AmEx, DC, MC, V. **Map** p249 K4.
If you've got an event, book here for an eyebrow shaping and make-up application, but be prepared to leave with a load of new cosmetics and jewellery that you just couldn't do without.

Spas & salons

Absolute Spa at the Century
1015 Burrard Street, between Comox & Nelson Streets, Downtown (604 684 2772/www.absolutespa. com). All city-centre buses. **Open** 8.30am-9pm daily. **Credit** AmEx, DC, MC, V. **Map** p248 J3.
If it's good enough for Elle and Gwyneth when they're in town, it ought to be good enough for you. This is the city's high-end but welcoming spa, where even diamond facials are on the menu.
Other locations Fairmont Hotel Vancouver, 900 W Georgia Street, at Burrard Street, Downtown (604 648 2909).

Miraj Hammam Spa
1495 West 6th Avenue, at Granville Street, West Side (604 733 5151/www.mirajhammam.com). Bus 10, 98. **Open** Women 11am-7pm Tue, Wed; noon-3pm Thur; noon-8pm Fri; 10am-6pm Sat. Men 4-8pm Thur; 2-6pm Sun. **Credit** AmEx, DC, MC, V. **Map** p251 H6.
A Middle Eastern oasis in the heart of the city: strip off, step into a steam hammam (or chamber) before an aesthetician exfoliates your body using black Moroccan soap. Dry off, then sip tea and relax in the Sultana Lounge. Bliss.

Skoah
1011 Hamilton Street, between Nelson & Helmcken Streets, Yaletown (604 642 0200/www.skoah.com). Bus 15. **Open** 10.30am-7.30pm Mon-Fri; 10am-7pm Sat, Sun. **Credit** AmEx, DC, MC, V. **Map** p249 K4.
Specialising in facials, this modern spa does away with whale music and fountains in favour of ambient techno and elite service. Men will feel equally at home as women in the clean, serene environment.

Vida Wellness Spa
Sutton Place Hotel, 845 Burrard Street, at Smithe Street, Downtown (604 682 8432/www.vida wellness.com). Bus 2, 22. **Open** 10am-8pm Mon, Sun; 9am-9pm Tue-Sat. **Credit** AmEx, DC, MC, V. **Map** p248 J3.
The owner funnelled profits from his lucrative dating website (www.lavalife.com) into this Ayurvedic spa, where ingredients are mixed to order depending on both the day and your dosha.
Other locations Sheraton Vancouver Wall Centre, 1088 Burrard Street, at Helmcken Street, Downtown (604 682 8432).

Tattoos & piercing

Sacred Heart
1685 Davie Street, at Bidwell Street, West End (604 669 4055/www.sacredhearttattoo.ca). Bus 6. **Open** noon-9pm Mon-Thur, Sun; noon-7pm Fri, Sat. **Credit** DC, MC, V. **Map** p248 H2.
Ask any Vancouverite sporting a well-drawn tattoo where they got it, and chances are it's from one of this parlour's outposts. View artists' portfolios online before making an appointment.
Other locations 725 Nelson Street, at Granville Street, Downtown (604 647 0826); 3734 W 10th Avenue, at Alma Street, West Side (604 224 1149).

West Coast Tattoo Parlour & Museum
620 Davie Street, between Granville & Seymour Streets, Downtown (604 681 2049/www.westcoast tattoo.com). All city-centre buses. **Open** noon-6pm Tue-Sat. **No credit cards. Map** p248 J4.
A tattoo is a surprisingly popular souvenir (maple leafs being the first choice). Get yours done here (alongside clients who fly in from around the world for intricate work) if you're ink-inclined and sober.

House & home

Antiques

Metropolitan Home
217 W Hastings Street, at Hamilton Street, Downtown (604 681 2313). Bus 10, 16, 20, 135. **Open** 10.30am-5.30pm Mon-Sat; noon-5pm Sun. **Credit** DC, MC, V. **Map** p249 L3.
Mid-century modern is the theme here; it's one of the few shops to have kept a retail presence, rather than catering exclusively to Vancouver's vintage-hungry film industry.

Shaughnessy Antique Gallery

3080 Granville Street, at W 16th Avenue, West Side (604 739 8413). Bus 10, 98. **Open** 10.30am-5pm Mon-Sat; noon-5pm Sun. **Credit** DC, MC, V. **Map** p251 H8.

Variety is the draw here, whether you're interested in 1960s stainless-steel desks or Victorian teacups.

General

The Cross

1198 Homer Street, at Davie Street, Yaletown (604 689 2900/www.thecrossdesign.com). Bus 15. **Open** 10am-6pm Mon-Sat; 11am-5pm Sun. **Credit** AmEx, DC, MC, V. **Map** p249 K4.

Cowhides, chandeliers and pretty accessories for fitting out your ski chalet, modern loft or heritage home, as well as gifts like *Tiffany's Table Manners for Teenagers*, plus beautiful cards and wrapping. Free shipping within North America.

Music & entertainment

CDs & records

Vancouver used to boast the cheapest new CD prices in North America, although it can't undercut cyberspace. For the best deals and discoveries check out second-hand stores such as **Charlie's Music City** (819 Granville Street, 604 688 2500) or vinyl specialists **Neptoon Records & CDs** (3561 Main Street, 604 324 1229). Those looking for more of a mom-and-pop experience should investigate **Red Cat Records** (4307 Main Street, 604 708 9422). Furthermore, the city offers many boutique shops for your more esoteric needs.

Beatstreet Records (439 W Hastings Street, 604 683 3344) will cater to your hip hop cravings, while **Scrape Records** (17 W Broadway, 604 877 1676) is devoted strictly to the hard stuff. In addition, the city supports a cavernous music store dedicated almost entirely to classical music: **Sikora's Classical Records** (432 W Hastings Street, 604 685 0625).

A&B Sound

556 Seymour Street, between Dunsmuir & W Pender Streets, Downtown (604 687 5837/www.absound.ca). All city-centre buses. **Open** 10am-6pm Mon-Thur, Sat; 10am-7pm Fri; 11am-5pm Sun. **Credit** AmEx, DC, MC, V. **Map** p249 L3.

This superstore features two floors of CDs, as well as DVDs and home electronics. Sadly, it's not the steal it once was, since the chain nearly went under.

Zulu Records

1974 W 4th Avenue, at Maple Street, West Side (604 738 3232/www.zulurecords.com). Bus 4, 7. **Open** 10.30am-7pm Mon-Wed; 10.30am-9pm Thur, Fri; 9.30am-6.30pm Sat; noon-6pm Sun. **Credit** AmEx, DC, MC, V. **Map** p251 F6.

One could easily lose an afternoon in Zulu's spacious confines. Separate areas are dedicated to new CDs and vinyl, while an upstairs loft is filled with an excellent selection of used CDs. Also on offer are an abundance of listening stations and a couple of vintage video games.

DVDs

HMV

788 Burrard Street, at Robson Street, Downtown (604 669 2289/www.hmv.ca). All city-centre buses. **Open** 10am-11pm Mon-Thur; 10am-midnight Fri, Sat; 10am-10pm Sun. **Credit** AmEx, DC, MC, V. **Map** p249 K3.

Get lost in time flipping through stacks of vinyl at **Zulu Records**.

With prime real estate at one of downtown's busiest corners (former home of Vancouver's only Virgin Megastore), HMV has the city's largest range of DVDs, often at sale prices.

Musical instruments

Tom Lee

929 Granville Street, at Smithe Street, Downtown (604 685 8471/www.tomlee.com). All city-centre buses. **Open** 10am-6pm Mon-Wed, Sat; 10am-8pm Thur, Fri; noon-5pm Sun. **Credit** AmEx, DC, MC, V. **Map** p249 K3.
The largest musical instrument retailer in Hong Kong also has a triple-level megastore in downtown Vancouver. Stop by for fantastic sales and helpful associates. Tom Lee also offers lessons and music study programmes.
Other locations throughout the city.

Sports & fitness

Comor

1980 Burrard Street, at 4th Avenue, West Side (604 899 2111/www.comorsports.com). Bus 5, 22, 44. **Open** 10am-6pm Mon-Wed, Sat; 10am-8pm Thur, Fri; 11am-5pm Sun. **Credit** AmEx, DC, MC, V. **Map** p251 G6.
From beachwear and eyewear, and skis to surfboards, this stocks the lot to achieve its slogan: Go Play Outside. Sister shop PacificBoarder is just around the corner at 1793 W 4th Avenue (604 734 7245, www.pacificboarder.com).

Mountain Equipment Co-op (MEC)

130 W Broadway, between Manitoba & Columbia Streets, West Side (604 872 7858/www.mec.ca). Bus 9, 99. **Open** *June-Aug* 10am-9pm Mon-Fri; 9am-6pm Sat; 11am-5pm Sun. *Sept-May* 10am-7pm Mon-Wed; 10am-9pm Thur, Fri; 9am-6pm Sat; 11am-5pm Sun. **Credit** DC, MC, V. **Map** p252 L7.
This giant store stocks virtually everything you require to be at one with the great outdoors, from camping and cycling gear to canoes and carbines. You need to be a member (it's $5 for a lifetime) but prices are a fraction of what you would pay in most other countries. Staff are knowledgeable and there's an invaluable noticeboard with used items for sale and people looking for trip companions.

Sigge's

2077 W 4th Avenue, at Arbutus Street, West Side (604 731 8818/1-877 731 8818/www.sigges.com). Bus 4, 7. **Open** call or check phone for details; closed May-Aug. **Credit** AmEx, DC, MC, V. **Map** p251 F6.
You'll find all the main cross-country paraphernalia and brands (Salomon, Fischer, Atomic, etc) in this family-owned and operated cross-country ski shop. The staff are great and also offer ski lessons and trips to Manning Park (one of the best spots for cross-country skiing; see p191). You will also find Telemark skis (dubbed 'ski ballet') and snowshoes here, which can be rented.

Tickets

Ticketmaster

Pacific Centre Lottery, Pacific Centre, 701 W Georgia Street, at Granville Street, Downtown (no tickets over phone; www.ticketmaster.ca). All city-centre buses. **Open** 7.30am-7pm Mon, Tue, Sat; 7.30am-9pm Wed-Fri; 10am-6pm Sun. **Credit** varies. **Map** p249 K3.
From rock bands to sports fixtures, if it's happening in the city then this is the place to get your tickets – either online or in person at these retail outlets.
Other locations Gate 10, GM Place, 800 Griffiths Way, between Expo Boulevard & Pacific Boulevard, Downtown; BC Place, 765 Pacific Boulevard, between Griffiths Way & Terry Fox Way, Downtown; SAK News, 115-925 W Georgia Street, at Hornby Street, Downtown.

Travellers' needs

Communications

FedEx Kinko's

779 W Pender Street, at Howe Street, Downtown (604 685 3338/www.kinkos.ca). All city-centre buses. **Open** 24hrs daily. **Credit** AmEx, DC, MC, V. **Map** p249 L3.
Should you decide to start publishing your own alternative 'zine or throw an underground party while you are here, line up with the others to format, print and copy your materials at 4am.
Other locations 1900 W Broadway, at Cypress Street, West Side (604 734 2679).

Luggage

Sears (*see p121*) is the best stop for luggage, stocking a great range, from smart, hard-backed suitcases to handbags (or purses, as they call them in Canada).

Shipping

The UPS Store

280 Nelson Street, at Mainland Street, Yaletown (604 608 6681/www.mbe-yaletown.com). Bus 15. **Open** 8.30am-6pm Mon-Fri; 10am-4pm Sat. **Credit** AmEx, DC, MC, V. **Map** p249 K4.
All the paper and packaging required to make shipping that chandelier home less of a hassle.
Other locations throughout the city.

Travel agents

Trek Escapes

1847 W 4th Avenue, between Cypress & Burrard Streets, West Side (604 734 1066/www.trekescapes. com). Bus 4, 7. **Open** 9am-5.30pm Mon-Fri; 10am-5pm Sat. **Credit** AmEx, DC, MC, V. **Map** p251 G6.
Got a last-minute hankering to head from here to Vietnam? The pros here will build your itinerary – economically and efficiently. International trips only.

Arts & Entertainment

Features

Contemporary Art Gallery. *See p151.*

Festivals & Events

Having a field day.

Many of Vancouver's established festivals are impressive international affairs, but locals are just as enthusiastic about celebrating their city's cultural diversity – and they do so at any given opportunity. Listed here are the city's major festivals and events, but it's always worth checking the local press, especially the *Georgia Straight*, to see what's going on when you arrive. Otherwise, check out www.tourism vancouver.com for the latest.

Spring

Vancouver Sun Run
Starting line: W Georgia Street, between Burrard & Thurlow Streets, Downtown (604 689 9441/www. sunrun.com). All city-centre buses/SkyTrain Burrard. **Map** p249 K3. **Date** Apr.
The most popular 10km (six-mile) run in Canada takes place on the third Sunday in April and includes a mini 2.5km (1.5 mile) route for under-12s and those not up to the full course. *See also p176.*

Vancouver Marathon
BC Place Stadium, 777 Pacific Boulevard, between Griffiths Way & Terry Fox Way, Downtown (604 872 2928/www.bmovanmarathon.ca). Bus 15, 240/SkyTrain Stadium. **Map** p249 L4. **Date** early May.
Fancy a whistlestop tour of Vancouver? The full 42km (26-mile) marathon usually starts at BC Place then heads off through False Creek and Gastown, round Stanley Park, over to Kitsilano and back again. *See also p176.*

International Children's Festival
Vanier Park, off Whyte Avenue, West Side (604 708 5655/www.childrensfestival.ca). Bus 2, 22. **Map** p248 G4. **Date** May.
The children's festival attracts circus acts, musicians and theatre companies from around the world. Each year, two days are Francophone. Popular with school groups, but families can buy tickets. Check website for ticket information.

Cloverdale Rodeo & Country Fair
6050A-176th Street, Surrey (604 576 9461/www. cloverdalerodeo.com). Bus 320 from SkyTrain Surrey Central. **Tickets** $8-$25. **Date** Victoria Day long weekend (third weekend in May).
An hour's drive from Downtown, this is the biggest rodeo west of the Calgary Stampede. The rodeo banned steer wrestling and calf roping after a calf broke a leg in the event in 2007 and had to be killed but remains subject to complaints from animal rights campaigners. The adjacent country fair has mechanical rides and the usual attractions.

Victoria Day Long Weekend
Date Mon on or before 24 May.
The de facto start of summer sees the city's outdoor swimming pools and water parks open.

Summer

Bard on the Beach Shakespeare Festival
Vanier Park, off Whyte Avenue, West Side (604 737 0625/www.bardonthebeach.org). Bus 2, 22. **Open** *Box office* 9am-5pm or showtime daily. **Tickets** $16-$31. **Credit** DC, MC, V. **Map** p248 G4. **Date** June-Sept.
Bard on the Beach used to be merely a popular success but these days it also commands respect. The festival programmes four shows in two tents (520 and 240 seats) in a beautiful park on English Bay, with the beach, water, city and mountains all as a backdrop, and sells at over 90% capacity throughout the four-month run. Arrive early to nab a good seat. On the bill for 2008: *Twelfth Night* and *King Lear* on the main stage, and *The Tempest* and *Titus Andronicus* in the smaller tent.

Dragon Boat Festival
Creekside Park, East Vancouver (604 688 2382/ www.adbf.com). Bus 3/SkyTrain Main Street-Science World. **Admission** free. **Date** June (summer solstice).
A weekend of seriously competitive racing in traditional Chinese dragon boats. More then 5,000 international competitors hit the city to take part in an ancient Chinese way of celebrating the summer solstice. It's not all about boats: the park throngs with children's entertainers, activity tents, live music and food stalls.

Vancouver International Jazz Festival
Various venues (604 872 5200/www.coastaljazz.ca). **Tickets** $10-$80. **Credit** AmEx, DC, MC, V. **Date** late June.
Some 40 venues around the city are involved in one of Vancouver's most impressive music festivals. 2007's diverse line-up featured Sonny Rollins, the Blind Boys of Alabama, Kid Koala and Bebel Gilberto. A number of restaurants host gigs and there are free outdoor events – the opening street party in Gastown is a favourite. Jazz aficionados planning to attend a number of performances can invest in a festival pass and make savings of up to 45% of the ticket price.

Arts & Entertainment

Canada Day
Canada Place, Downtown (604 775 8025/www. canadadayatcanadaplace.com). All city-centre buses. **Map** p249 L2. **Date** 1 July.
Those Vancouverites who own an island summerhouse make a mass exodus on Canada's birthday; most everyone else fires up the barbecue. Official celebrations take place in the Canada Place exhibition centre, which is filled with lumberjack shows, mechanical bucking broncos, bouncy castles and the like. Check local press for details of other events.

Dancing on the Edge
Various venues (604 689 0926/www.dancingonthe edge.org). **Date** early July.
Two weeks of contemporary dance from international and local companies, featuring work by both established and emerging choreographers.

Vancouver Folk Music Festival
Jericho Beach Park, West Side (604 602 9798/www. thefestival.bc.ca). Bus 4. **Tickets** see website for details. **Credit** DC, MC, V. **Map** p251 A5. **Date** July.
Marking its 31st year in 2008, the folk festival is the most direct route to Vancouver's hippie spirit. It even refuses sponsorship. The line-up tends to be eclectic but don't expect many big names. Even if you don't buy tickets to enter the open-air site, you should make the trip out to Jericho Beach, which, for the three days of the festival, turns into Woodstock-on-sea. Joss sticks, tie-dye and other hippie paraphernalia are all sold from makeshift stalls lining the edge of the beach, while families and stoners chill out on the sand listening to the music wafting over them.

Illuminares Lantern Procession
Trout Lake, at Victoria Drive & E 15th Avenue, East Vancouver (604 879 8611/www.publicdreams. org). Bus 20/SkyTrain Broadway. **Date** late July.
This free community project creates a magical sight on a summer's night, as hundreds of people gather to walk around Trout Lake carrying lit paper lanterns of all shapes, sizes and designs while music is piped through the trees. Don't attempt to drive here – the procession is in danger of becoming a victim of its own success. Lantern workshops take place earlier in the month.

Celebration of Light
English Bay, West End & West Side (www. celebration-of-light.com). All city-centre buses. **Date** late July-early Aug.
The biggest international fireworks competition in the world takes place over four nights spread across a fortnight at the height of summer, when Canada vies with three other countries for bragging rights and practically the whole city turns up to watch. Roads are chaotic so you're advised to walk to your nearest vantage point. English Bay, Kitsilano Beach and Vanier Park have good views, but be sure to find a spot early. Kick-off time is 10pm, when the whole bay becomes illuminated by spectacular pyrotechnics fired from a barge.

Popular culture: the **Bard on the Beach Shakespeare Festival**.

Arts & Entertainment

Powell Street Festival

Oppenheimer Park, E Cordova Street, between Dunlevy & Jackson Avenues, East Vancouver (604 739 9388/www.powellstreetfestival.com). Bus 4, 7. **Date** early Aug.

The free annual celebration of Japanese Canadian culture has everything from dance to martial arts to traditional tea services – with plenty of theatre, music and art of both local and international origin. Due to Olympic construction work the festival will relocate to Woodland Park on Woodland Drive (between Frances and Adanac Streets) for 2008 only.

Vancouver Pride Parade

Beach Avenue & Denman Street, West End (604 687 0955/www.vancouverpride.ca). Bus 5, 6. **Map** p248 G2. **Date** early Aug long weekend.

Pride is a major Vancouver event. In 2008, the Pride Society celebrates its 30th anniversary and is expecting up to 500,000 people to attend. Clubs and bars put on special events (see local press for details), and there are stalls, stages with live performances, tea dances and any number of beer gardens. The parade, which travels along Denman Street and Beach Avenue, boasts elaborate floats, drag queens done up to the nines and thousands of people in the mood for a party.

PNE (Pacific National Exhibition)

E Hastings Street & Renfrew Street, East Vancouver (604 253 2311/www.pne.bc.ca). Bus 4, 10, 16, 44, 135. **Tickets** phone for details. **Date** mid Aug-early Sept.

Dog shows, daredevil motorcyclists and duck races… the Pacific National Exhibition (the PNE, as everyone calls it) is a slightly hokey tradition in British Columbia geared towards all the family. Younger children especially love it, while truculent teenagers can let off steam at the next-door funfair, Playland (*see p144*). It can be reached by a (fairly long) direct bus ride from downtown but if you decide to drive, look out for local residents in the road waving cardboard signs – they want to rent you their parking spot for the day.

Festival Vancouver

Various venues (604 688 1152/www.festival vancouver.bc.ca). **Tickets** $24-$89 through Ticketmaster (*see p136*). **Date** first 2wks Aug.

Two weeks of all things orchestral, choral and operatic, as well as chamber music and even some jazz, Festival Vancouver is a relative newcomer on the scene. The focus is generally split between one composer and the music of a particular country, and includes both national and international performers.

The city's gay and lesbian community shows its colours at the **Vancouver Pride Parade**.

Vancouver Wooden Boat Festival

Granville Island, West Side (604 688 9622/www. vcn.bc.ca/vwbs/interest.htm). Bus 50. **Map** p248 H5. **Date** late Aug.
Wooden boat enthusiasts show off their vessels, children build and sail toy boats and live performers play sea shanties. Plus there's rowing, sailing and canoeing races in Alder Bay.

Autumn

Global ComedyFest

For listings, see p170. **Date** Sept.
Vancouver's esteemed comedy festival attracts the cream of local talent, as well as international stars.

Vancouver International Fringe Festival

Granville Island, West Side (604 257 0350/www. vancouverfringe.com). Bus 50. **Tickets** $6-$15. **Credit** AmEx, DC, MC, V. **Map** p248 H5. **Date** Sept.
The tourist mecca of Granville Island is about as far as you can get from 'fringe' Vancouver, but what this festival lost in grit it has made up for in audience numbers since moving from Commercial Drive some years back. The shows, programmed in island theatres, rehearsal spaces, tents and off-site works around the city, do strong business. The quality index would make for a line graph as jagged as the Coastal mountain range, but strong local performers, touring acts and showcase stars make for a fine festival. Advance tickets go on sale by mid August.

Vancouver International Film Festival

For listings, see p147 Vancity Theatre.
Date late Sept-mid Oct.
Vancouver's film fest is a friendly, largely celeb-free affair, championing diverse, often challenging fare. *See also p146* **The VIFF.**

Vancouver International Writers & Readers Festival

Granville Island (604 681 6330/www.writersfest. bc.ca). Bus 50. **Tickets** $12-$22. **Credit** DC, MC, V. **Date** mid Oct.
Literary giants share the stage with new writers in this hugely popular celebration of the written word. The week is made up of readings, poetry slams, workshops, the annual celebrity spelling bee and special events for children. Past guests have included Margaret Atwood, Julian Barnes, Alice Munro, Vikram Seth, JK Rowling and Peter Carey.

Vancouver Snow Show

BC Place, 765 Pacific Boulevard, between Griffiths Way & Terry Fox Way, Downtown (www.vancouver snowshow.com). SkyTrain Stadium. **Tickets** $10; $5-$8 concessions; $25 family; free under-6s. **Map** p249 L2. **Date** late Oct.
Everything you need to hit the slopes under one roof, plus much, much more in this annual weekend trade exhibition. From heavily discounted new gear to second-hand and a ski and board swap-shop, there are bargains aplenty to be found. Film screenings, acrobatic shows and other entertainment are provided. Tickets are valid for both days.

Winter

Festival of Lights

VanDusen Botanical Garden, 5251 Oak Street, at W 37th Avenue, West Side (604 878 9274/www. vandusengarden.org). Bus 17. **Admission** $10.25; $5-$7.50 concessions; $22 family. **Date** Dec.
The always spectacular gardens become simply magical in the run-up to Christmas when 20,000 fairy lights are draped through the trees.

Polar Bear Swim

English Bay Beach, West End (www.city.vancouver. bc.ca). Bus 5, 6. **Map** p248 G3. **Date** 2.30pm 1 Jan.
Just ten hardy souls braved the waters of English Bay on New Year's Day, 1920 – the first ever Polar Bear Swim in Vancouver. In 2006, some 1,550 people registered to take part, and a whole lot more found themselves overcome with the urge to strip off and take the plunge. If you're up for it, 2.30pm is when the charge takes place.

Annual Bald Eagle Count

Along Sea-to-Sky Highway, Squamish (604 898 3333/www.brackendaleartgallery.com). Contact Greyhound for buses (see p227). **Date** early Jan.
From December to February, thousands of bald eagles congregate to feast on dead or dying salmon in the Cheakamus Valley near Brackendale (about an hour's drive north of Vancouver; *see p215*). The highest concentration of birds is from mid December to mid January, with the annual count taking place the first Sunday in the new year. In 2007, the count was 1,757 eagles.

Chinese New Year

Various locations, Chinatown (www.vancouver chinatown.ca). Bus 3, 4, 7. **Date** Jan/Feb.
Held on the first Sunday of the Lunar New Year, these celebrations are understandably extensive given Vancouver's large Chinese population. The traditional parade in Chinatown is the big draw, but check local press for other events and don't forget to practise saying 'Gung hay fat choy' to wish people a prosperous New Year.

PuSh International Performing Arts Festival

Various venues, West Side (604 605 8284/www. pushfestival.ca). **Tickets** $15-$45. **Credit** DC, MC, V. **Date** late Jan-early Feb.
Entering its sixth season in 2008, the PuSh Festival is the best current expression of Vancouver's theatrical ambitions. A smartly curated set of hand-picked shows from Europe and across Canada mingle with new work by local hotshots, along with play readings, a cabaret and, on occasion, even a Kronos Quartet concert.

Arts & Entertainment

Children

Urban play par excellence.

Vancouver is great for kids. If it's sunny – and it is, sometimes – there are parks and beaches aplenty, plus two open-air swimming pools (*see p180*), while snow brings the best excuse to go play on the mountains. And the rest of the time? Well, there are enough first-class indoor attractions to keep the tykes amused.

Vancouver is also replete with day camps during school holidays – offering everything from skiing and snowboarding in the winter, to kayaking in the summer, with arts and drama classes year round. Summer camp listings can be found at www.bcparent.com.

Most restaurants welcome families, but some make more effort than others. For fuss-free dining, try **Rocky Mountain Flatbread Company** (*see p108*), with great organic pizza and a play area; the casual chains **White Spot** (with locations throughout the city) and **Café Crêpe** (*see p90*); and **Little Nest** (*see p112*), where toddlers get the run of the place.

BABYSITTING

Most of the big hotels will arrange babysitting for you, but if you need to organise it yourself, **Nannies On Call** (604 734 1776, www.nanniesoncall.com) has a good reputation.

Indoor attractions

Cliffhanger Vancouver

670 Industrial Avenue, East Vancouver (604 874 2400/www.cliffhangerclimbing.com). Bus 3, then 10mins walk. **Open** noon-11pm Mon-Thur; noon-9.30pm Fri-Sun. **Rates** $15-$17/day. **Credit** DC, MC, V. **Map** p252 O6.

With over 1,100 sq m (12,000 sq ft) of 12m (40ft) vertical surfaces, Cliffhanger is an ideal place for your budding Spider-man (or -woman) to begin their training in webslinging. Children from 5-17 can take part in scheduled programmes or drop-in sessions, and there are sessions for brave adults too.

IMAX Theatre

For listings, see p148.

From the spectacle of space to the mysteries of the ocean floor, this bigger-than-life movie experience is always a good choice on a rainy day. There are usually four or five different films to choose from.

Kids Market

1496 Cartwright Street, at Anderson Street, Granville Island (604 689 8447/www.kidsmarket.ca). Bus 50. **Open** 10am-6pm daily. **Credit** varies. **Map** p250 A4.

A two-level shopping mall with everything your child could desire, the Kids Market even has pint-sized doorways (don't worry, there are regular openings as well). Highlights include Knotty Toys, a store dedicated to old-fashioned wooden playthings that also stocks a mean Thomas the Tank Engine selection, and Kites and Puppets with its beautiful collection of both. Upstairs there are separate (paid for) play areas for toddlers and older kids, where they can tumble in ball pits, paint ceramics or get their video games fix. There's also a fast food eaterie, the Hairloft Princess Spa for little girls who adore all things glittery, and Everything Wet, a good place to stock up on swimsuits and raingear.

Roundhouse Community Arts & Recreation Centre

181 Roundhouse Mews, between Pacific Boulevard & Drake Street, Yaletown (604 713 1800/www.roundhouse.ca). Bus 17. **Open** 9am-10pm Mon-Fri; 9am-5pm Sat, Sun. **Admission** free. **Map** p249 K5.

On the site of the former Canadian Pacific Railway's switching yard, this community centre is home to the original Engine 374 that pulled the first passenger train into Vancouver in 1887. Train-obsessed small fry can clamber into its cabin and pretend to take it for a ride.

Science World

1455 Quebec Street, at Terminal Avenue, East Vancouver (604 443 7443/www.scienceworld.bc.ca). Bus 3/SkyTrain Main Street-Science World. **Open** 10am-5pm Mon-Fri; 10am-6pm Sat, Sun. **Admission** $16; $11-$13 reductions; free under-4s; $54 family. *With 1 Omnimax film* $21; $16-$18 reductions; free under-4s. **Credit** DC, MC, V. **Map** p249 M5.

Impossible to miss, the huge silver golf ball that is Science World is a significant part of the Vancouver skyline. It's also one of the best destinations on a rainy day for kids of all ages and easily accessible by SkyTrain from Downtown. Whether your child is into mind-bending puzzles, the natural world or more physical pursuits, you'll find a wealth of inter-active activities to keep them busy. Hourly fun and informative science shows blow things up and make loud bangs to keep youngsters' interest and there's a sectioned-off area for the under-sixes, complete with space for stroller parking. The wraparound Omnimax theatre (*see p148*) is spectacular. There's a White Spot on site that will satisfy the hungriest child's burger cravings and, if it's a nice day, you can make use of the picnic area and playground overlooking False Creek.

Vancouver Aquarium

For listings, see p68.

A real hub in Stanley Park, the aquarium is endlessly fascinating to young and old alike. Outdoors you can watch the regular dolphin, sea lion and beluga whale shows, not to mention fall in love with everyone's favourites, the adorable sea otters. Inside, the local BC tanks are as interesting as the humid tropical exhibits, with a camera-shy octopus, beautiful jellyfish and sea horses, and plenty of coldwater critters. There's a play area, a relatively new interactive area, and an underwater viewing room to watch the belugas. The outdoor café serves surprisingly good food – just be careful where you sit: the left side facing the whale enclosure is only for those who don't mind getting splashed. Very busy during summer.

Vancouver Aquatic Centre

1050 Beach Avenue, at Thurlow Street, West End (604 665 3424/www.city.vancouver.bc.ca/parks/rec/ pools). Bus 4, 7, 10, 16, 17, 50. **Open** phone for schedule. Closed Aug. **Rates** $4.85; $2.45-$3.65 reductions. **Credit** DC, MC, V. **Map** p248 H4.

A 50m (164ft) pool with shallows at either end, the aquatic centre is roomy enough to accommodate serious swimmers and silly splashers alike. There's nothing flashy, though various types of floats and inflatable rings are provided. A warmer beginners' pool offers respite and refuge for those with younger children (under-eights).

Vancouver Art Gallery SuperSunday

For listings, see p60 Vancouver Art Gallery.

Every third Sunday of the month, from noon until 5pm, the Vancouver Art Gallery opens its doors to school-age children eager to get hands-on about art. It makes for a great afternoon, filled with everything from screen printing and working with clay, to making mobiles and watching dance performances. Activities are alternated to tie in with the current exhibitions. It's very popular, especially on rainy days, but you're required to book in for popular activities on arrival, so queuing is not usually an issue. The gallery's café (*see p90*) is a nice spot to rejuvenate – particularly in summer when the patio overlooking Robson Street is open.

Vancouver Public Library

350 W Georgia Street, between Homer & Hamilton Streets, Downtown (604 331 3603/www.vpl.ca).
All city-centre buses. **Open** 10am-9pm Mon-Thur; 10am-6pm Fri, Sat; noon-5pm Sun. **Admission** free. **Map** p249 L4.

The central Library Square branch offers a well-stocked children's section downstairs, with multimedia computer stations, listening stations, internet access, story times, a toddler play area and a preschool learning centre (all free). A $25 visitor's card allows you to borrow items.

Water babies

When the heat begins to rise, Vancouver's water parks become a great way to cool those little bodies down. **Granville Island** is a watery paradise for kids with its fake fire hydrants, spray guns and large water slide. For dry pursuits, there's an adjacent sand-filled playground and plenty of shady trees for picnics. The water park is located on Cartwright Street, between the Information Centre and the False Creek Community Centre.

Located just past Lumberman's Arch, next to the Seawall, **Stanley Park**'s water playground includes a mini cave, as well as a walk-through dryer. There's scant grass for parents to sprawl on and the bike traffic can make journeys to the loos a bit treacherous, but there's a handy ice-cream stand and a takeaway serving hot dogs and fish and chips nearby.

Minimalism is the key in **Coal Harbour**, where the park at the end of Bute Street consists basically of water jets springing out of concrete. Despite its lack of apparent child-pleasing colour and gadgets, children love it; here it's all about simply getting drenched with no messing about. To add to its attractions (for parents at least), it's overlooked by the Mill Marine Bistro (1199 W Cordova Street, at Bute Street, 604 687 6455, www.millbistro.ca).

Arts & Entertainment

Outdoor attractions

Capilano Salmon Hatchery
4500 Capilano Park Road, off Capilano Road, North Shore (604 666 1790). Bus 236 from Lonsdale Quay SeaBus, then 10mins walk. **Open** *Nov-Mar* 8am-4pm daily. *Apr, Oct* 8am-4.45pm daily. *May, Sept* 8am-7pm daily. *June-Aug* 8am-8pm daily. **Admission** free.
This government-owned fish farm is designed to help stem the depletion of salmon stocks. The education centre allows you to learn about the life cycle of the salmon, view the fish in various stages of growth, and follow the process from the hatchery to the river and reintegration into the wild. October is the best time to see the salmon leap the fish ladders.

Capilano Suspension Bridge
For listings, see p83.
A pricey tourist attraction in the trees, this spectacular swinging bridge across a canyon also offers a treetops trail and other activities.

Children's Farmyard & Miniature Railway
Stanley Park, West End (604 257 8531/www.city. vancouver.bc.ca/parks/parks/stanley). Bus 19. **Open** varies. **Admission** *Railway or Farmyard* $5; $2.75-$3.75 reductions. *Bright Nights (Railway & Farmyard)* $7.50; $4.50 reductions. *Ghost Train (Railway & Farmyard)* $9; $5.50 reductions. **Credit** DC, MC, V. **Map** p69.
A popular double attraction inside Stanley Park where children can pet goats, sheep and pigs – as well as the odd reptile and llama – before taking a 15-minute train ride through the forest. The miniature engine is a replica of the one that pulled the first transcontinental passenger train into the city. In the run-up to Halloween, the railway operates at night, decked out as a ghost train, the surrounding forest decorated with a different ghoulish theme every year.

Lynn Canyon Park
For listings, see p83.
Another suspension bridge – this time free – in a park with plentiful trails and picnicking areas.

Maplewood Farm
405 Seymour River Place, off Old Dollarton Road, North Shore (604 929 5610/www.maplewoodfarm. bc.ca). Bus 210 to Phipps exchange, transfer to C15 shuttle. **Open** *Oct-Mar* 10am-4pm Tue-Sun. *Apr-Sept* 10am-4pm daily. **Admission** *Regular farm days* $4.75; $2.75 reductions. *Special events* $6; $5 reductions; $21 family. **Credit** DC, MC, V.
With some 200 farm animals, milking displays, pony rides and a large canopied area for stroking and feeding the rabbits, this North Shore attraction (once a working farm) is always popular. No refreshments beyond a couple of vending machines.

Nat Bailey Stadium
For listings, see p172.
This 6,500-seater open-air stadium is the home of the family-friendly Vancouver Canadians baseball team.

Playland
2901 E Hastings Street, at Renfrew Street, East Vancouver (604 252 3583/www.pne.ca). Bus 10, 16, 135. **Open** *Late Apr-Sept* phone for details. *Fright Nights* last 2wks Oct 6-11pm daily. **Admission** $31.75; $15.85 reductions. *Fright Nights* $20 Mon-Thur, Sun; $25 Fri, Sat. **Credit** DC, MC, V.
All the fun of the fair, with a roller-coaster, Ferris wheel and some 35 other gravity-defying rides. A bus ride out of town, Playland opens from late April until late September, combining with the PNE (*see p140*) in late August and reopening for a couple of weeks in October for the Halloween-themed Fright Nights. Admission includes unlimited rides; discounted tickets can be purchased at 7-11, Safeway and Shoppers Drug Mart stores.

Further afield

About an hour's drive from Downtown is the **Greater Vancouver Zoo** (5048 264th Street, Aldergrove, 604 856 6825, www.gvzoo. com), where a free 15-minute safari bus will take you inside the North American enclosure to view bear, bison, elk and wolves up close. Apart from the grazing animals, the bigger beasts are cramped for space – the hippo enclosure caused a scandal a couple of years back, though the problem has now been rectified. Not really worth making the trip unless you happen to be driving by anyway.

Fort Langley National Historic Site (23433 Mavis Avenue, Fort Langley, 604 513 4777, www.pc.gc.ca/lhn-nhs/bc/langley) makes for a good day out. Once one of the Hudson's Bay Company's original fur trading posts, it is now a government-run museum with costumed guides. The heritage village of Fort Langley is just two blocks away and the surrounding **Fraser Valley** offers plenty of trails (*see p191*).

Closer to town, **Burnaby Village Museum** (6501 Deer Lake Avenue, Burnaby, 604 293 6500, www.burnabyvillagemuseum.ca) also employs costumed guides to talk you through this replica early 20th-century village. Watch the blacksmith at work, discover the history of the local newspaper or catch a silent film, before heading into the ice-cream parlour.

Also in Burnaby is the **Variety Park Playground** (Central Park, at Boundary Road & Kingsway) designed to integrate able-bodied and disabled play. Adaptations are in place for both mobility and vision-impaired children.

Just before the BC Ferries terminal at Tsawwassen, **Splashdown Park** (4799 Nulelum Way, 604 943 2251, www.splashdownpark.ca) is open from June to September, and offers water slides of various heights, angles and speeds, plus a gentler area for small children, and volleyball courts and picnic areas.

Film

Making the scene.

The **Scotiabank Theatre** is a glitzy recent addition to the downtown scene. *See p148.*

Arts & Entertainment

San Francisco, Los Angeles, New York, Boston, London, Hong Kong, Seattle, Seattle, Seattle – Vancouver has played them all. For all its natural beauty, the city is repeatedly cast as a nondescript urban backdrop in the numerous Hollywood productions that come here to shoot on the cheap. In the late 1970s, the provincial government aggressively courted the American studios with tax breaks and industry services a decade or two before most of North America wised up. Today, the film industry ranks alongside timber and tourism as one of BC's biggest businesses, and Vancouver is the third largest production centre in North America. The 'Hollywood North' tag was coined as early as 1982, though Californians prefer a less flattering label: 'Brollywood'.

Lower union rates, provincial tax inducements and the exchange rate have all factored in this success, which is also why so many of the movies shot here in recent years have been so poor: *Are We Done Yet?*, *White Chicks*, *Alone in the Dark*, *The Fog*, *Little Man*, *Two for the Money* and *Scary Movie 4*, for starters. Fortunately for the industry, now

that the dollar advantage has gone, BC does have other attractions. *The X Files* filmed here for its first five seasons, before the rain got too much for star David Duchovny. When the series moved back to LA, it bequeathed a cadre of experienced local FX technicians that have serviced numerous Sci Fi Channel stalwarts such as *Stargate*, *Battlestar Galactica*, *Smallville* and *Flash Gordon*, as well as high-end special effects movies like the *X-Men* films, *I Robot*, *The Fantasic Four* and *Watchmen*.

Then there is the rich ecological diversity British Columbia can offer, within just a few hours of Los Angeles: the mountainous terrain showcased in *Shooter* (shot near Cache Creek), for instance; the pastoral farmlands of *An Unfinished Life* (Kamloops); the rocky isolation of *The Wicker Man* (Bowen Island); or the snowy wastes of *Eight Below* (Smithers). *First Blood*, with Sylvester Stallone, was filmed in and around Hope, which now offers a 'Rambo tour' to die-hard action fans.

Vancouver itself rarely merits a close-up, though you might spot a few give-away street signs in *Firewall* and *Things We Lost in the*

The VIFF

Canada's big three film festivals all jostle in the post-summer period: Toronto in early September, Montreal a week later and Vancouver's 16-day movie marathon spanning the end of the month and continuing through the first two weeks of October. The **Vancouver International Film Festival** is the least glamorous of the trio, but often the most enjoyable, with a relaxed, friendly atmosphere and a committed, adventurous crowd.

Festival director Alan Franey steers wide of Hollywood, reasoning that his job is to showcase eclectic international art cinema, political documentaries and independent films that would not otherwise reach this part of the world. Such a course has proved a hit with local audiences – so much so that the festival was encouraged to establish the Vancouver International Film Centre and **Vancity Theatre** (see *p147*) to present this kind of work year round. Reflecting the city's ethnic mix, VIFF has built up an especially strong international reputation for its East Asian section, Dragons & Tigers. Here you will quite possibly find the art-house stars of the future, even if the rest of the fest is strictly a celeb-free zone.

● *For further details about the festival, visit the website: www.viff.org.*

Fire (both ostensibly set in Seattle). Hollywood's condescending view of the city can be gauged from a caustic remark in the pilot of Aaron Sorkin's TV series *Studio 60* on the Sunset Strip: 'Why would we shoot in Vancouver? Vancouver doesn't even look like Vancouver.'

If you're looking for recognisable landmarks, your best bets are the 1986 Mel Gibson, Goldie Hawn thriller *Bird on a Wire* (which relocates the Harbour Centre Tower, Gastown and the BC Hydro Building to Detroit); the scenic Ted Danson, Isabella Rossellini romance *Cousins* (1989); *The NeverEnding Story*, which features a quick flight over the trainyard, with BC Place visible in the background; and especially 1994's *Intersection*, which has the rare distinction of actually being set in British Columbia (Richard Gere's architect works in Gastown and counts the UBC Museum of Anthropology among his designs). In terms of quality, the best of the bunch is undoubtedly Robert Altman's 1971 Western *McCabe and Mrs Miller*, set in a fictional Presbyterian Church but shot in West Vancouver and presenting a credible picture of the Pacific Northwest in the Gold Rush days. (Altman's less widely seen first feature, *That Cold Day in the Park*, was shot in Tatlow Park in Kitsilano and on Granville Street, in 1969.)

As for home-grown BC movies, again, the list is not particularly distinguished, although local filmmakers turn out more than two dozen features every year. The classics are *The Grey Fox* (1982); *My American Cousin* (1985) and *Kissed* (1997). Victoria-bred Atom Egoyan has generally filmed in Toronto, although his most successful movie, *The Sweet Hereafter* was shot in Merritt, northern British Columbia.

If you can, get hold of Paul Fox's breezy 2006 feature *Everything's Gone Green*, based on the first original screenplay by North Van novelist and artist Douglas Coupland. Coupland has often written about Vancouver in his books (*Life After God, Girlfriend in a Coma* and *Hey Nostradamus!*, for starters); he even wrote a typically gnomic A-Z of his hometown, *City of Glass*. A comedy about a twentysomething slacker who allows himself to be sucked into a lottery money laundering scheme, *Everything's Gone Green* could be 'City of Glass – the movie' for the way it foregrounds its location. Taking in such local touchstones as the booming real estate market, marijuana 'grow ops' and the movie industry itself, the film even begins with a bike ride around the Seawall. 'Vancouver is photographed as if it were New York in Woody Allen's *Manhattan*,' noted one admiring critic, putting his finger on this picture's unique charm.

Cinemas

Gone are the days when Granville Street held ten cinemas within five blocks. Today most locals watch movies at home or in suburban multiplexes, such as the relatively grand **SilverCity Riverport** (14211 Entertainment Way, Richmond, 604 277 5993, www.famous players.com), which also houses an IMAX screen and adjoins an entertainment complex. Nevertheless, the city can boast a little bit of everything, from the modern movie mecca that is the nine-screen **Scotiabank Theatre** to the septuagenarian fleapit, the **Hollywood**. Discerning types head for the **Fifth Avenue Cinemas** (actually on Burrard Street), **Pacific Cinémathèque** or the **Vancity Theatre**.

TICKETS AND INFORMATION
The local press carries daily cinema listings with disposable critical commentary. The *Vancouver Sun* and the *Georgia Straight* try to be comprehensive, but they seem uninterested in anything outside the mainstream. Check out

the websites for the Pacific Cinémathèque and the Vancity Theatre for information on art-house and repertory screenings. Online, www.cinemaclock.com provides a search engine for films and/or venues, with trailer links and user reviews, but you will have to phone or go to the exhibitors' websites to pre-book (recommended for weekend evening shows). Prices compare well with other major cities ($12 at the Scotiabank, cheaper elsewhere), and there are usually discounts for Tuesday screenings and matinées.

For more on the **Vancouver International Film Festival** (VIFF), *see p146* **The VIFF**.

Art house, repertory & second run

Denman Place Cinema

1737 Comox Street, at Denman Street, West End (604 683 2201). Bus 6. **Screens** 1. **Admission** $6; $4 reductions; $4 Tue. **No credit cards.** **Map** p248 H2.
Handily placed should that trip to Stanley Park be rained off, the Denman Place Cinema is a comfortable, single-screen movie theatre that occasionally mixes up new releases with a regular diet of discounted second-run features.

Hollywood Theatre

3123 W Broadway, at Balaclava Street, West Side (604 738 3211/www.hollywoodtheatre.ca). Bus 9, 17.

Screens 1. **Admission** *Double bills* $7; $5 reductions; $5 Mon. *Matinées* $6; $4 reductions. **No credit cards.** **Map** p251 C6.
Tucked away in Kitsilano, the Hollywood celebrates its 75th birthday in 2010. Remarkably, it has been owned and operated by the same family, the Farleighs, throughout that time. The programming is almost entirely Hollywood second runs, though the double features make it good value for money.

Pacific Cinémathèque

1131 Howe Street, between Helmcken & Davie Streets, Downtown (604 688 3456/www. cinematheque.bc.ca). Bus 4, 7, 10, 16, 17, 50, N9, N10, N17. **Screens** 1. **Admission** $9.50; $8 reductions. *Double bills* $11.50; $10 reductions. *Annual membership (compulsory)* $3. **No credit cards.** **Map** p248 J4.
The city's old stalwart rep theatre, the Cinémathèque attracts a loyal audience of die-hard film buffs with its month-long auteur retrospectives, seasons celebrating contemporary national cinemas and remastered prints of classic films. In vintage rep style you're made to suffer for your art, though a new projector has recently been installed and more comfy new seating is promised.

Vancity Theatre

Vancouver International Film Centre, 1181 Seymour Street, at Davie Street, Yaletown (604 685 0260/www.viff.org). Bus 4, 7, 10, 16, 17, 50, N9, N10, N17. **Screens** 1. **Admission** $9.50; $7.50 reductions. *Membership* $12 (incl cost of first film). **Credit** V. **Map** p248 J4.

Vancity Theatre.

A spin-off from the successful Vancouver International Film Festival (see p146 **The VIFF**), which operates it, the Vancity Theatre opened in early 2006. It delivers probably the most adventurous programming on the West Coast (think Pedro Costa, Arnaud Desplechin, Hou Hsiao-Hsien). The state of the art, 175-seat theatre puts comfort over commerce: double arm rests, spacious leg-room, excellent sightlines and a balcony. Vancouverites haven't really woken up to this gem yet, but cinephiles will think they've died and gone to heaven.

Mainstream & first run

Cinemark Tinseltown
Third floor, 88 W Pender Street, at Abbott Street, Chinatown (604 806 0799/www.cinemark.com). Bus 4, 7, N8/SkyTrain Stadium. **Screens** 9. Admission $10.75 Mon-Thur; $11.75 Fri-Sun; $8.75 reductions. *Matinées* $8.75. **Credit** AmEx, DC, MC, V. **Map** p249 M3.
Located on the third floor of an under-utilised mall on the western edge of Chinatown, within spitting distance of the Downtown Eastside, Tinseltown is an anonymous nine-screen multiplex that merits some praise for Cinemark's relatively adventurous programming. Mainstream fare is mixed up with a sprinkling of indie, subtitled and Canadian flicks.

Empire Granville 7
855 Granville Street, between Robson & Smithe Streets, Downtown (604 684 4000/www.empire theatres.com). All city-centre buses. **Screens** 7. Admission $7. **Credit** AmEx, DC, MC, V. **Map** p249 K3.
There were once ten cinemas within five blocks on Granville, but this is the last hold-out. Commonly known as 'the Granville 7', it could use a refurb, but it is conveniently located between Robson and Smithe and, unlike Scotiabank, it has THX sound.

Fifth Avenue Cinemas
2110 Burrard Street, at W 5th Avenue, West Side (604 734 7469/www.festivalcinemas.ca). Bus 4, 7. **Screens** 5. Admission $12; $7-$8 reductions; $7 Tue. *Matinées* $9 Mon-Fri; $10 Sat, Sun. **Credit** DC, MC, V. **Map** p251 G6.
Operated by Festival Cinemas, which also owns the Ridge and the Park (for both, *see below*), Fifth is a cosy five-screen venue specialising in left-field Hollywood, indie and art-house film. The theatre is actually located on Burrard Street, but that doesn't have the same cosmopolitan ring. There's even a cappuccino bar – though the Elysian Room around the corner (at 1778 5th Avenue) is a better spot for a leisurely movie fix.

Park Theatre
3440 Cambie Street, at W 18th Avenue, West Side (604 709 3456/www.festivalcinemas.ca). Bus 15. **Screens** 1. Admission $12; $7-$8 reductions; $7 Tue. *Matinées* $9 Mon-Fri; $10 Sat, Sun. **Credit** DC, MC, V. **Map** p252 L8.

Built in 1940 but fully refurbished in 2005, this local single-screen cinema continues with its commitment to art-house films of the middlebrow school.

Ridge Theatre
3131 Arbutus Street, at W 16th Avenue, West Side (604 738 6311/www.festivalcinemas.ca). Bus 16. **Screens** 1. Admission $12; $7-$8 reductions; $7 Tue. *Matinées* $9 Mon-Fri; $10 Sat, Sun. **Credit** DC, MC, V. **Map** p251 F8.
With the most iconic theatre awning in the city (complemented with a bowling pin from the alley next door), the Ridge is a characterful cinema a ten-minute taxi ride from Downtown. Opened in 1950, it retains most of its original features, including a balcony fitted with an sound-proofed glassed-in 'crying room' for infants. Programming is erratic, but expect to find 'soft' art-house titles here.

Scotiabank Theatre Vancouver
900 Burrard Street, at Smithe Street, Downtown (604 630 1407/www.cineplex.com). Bus 2, 22. **Screens** 9. Admission $12; $10 reductions. **Credit** AmEx, DC, MC, V. **Map** p248 J3.
A big, new, nine-screen multiplex, the Scotiabank opened in 2005 with a rave review from U2 (who had been invited in to see a sneak preview of *Kingdom of Heaven* here). Centrally located, the cinema appears to have been built around its first-floor food court, serving the usual odiferous junk food; an appropriate venue in which to consume mainstream Hollywood blockbusters. *Photo p145.*

IMAX

IMAX Theatre
201-999 Canada Place, between Howe & Burrard Streets, Downtown (604 682 4629/www.imax. com/vancouver). All cross-city buses/SkyTrain & Seabus Waterfront. **Screens** 1. Admission $12; $11 reductions. **Credit** AmEx, DC, MC, V. **Map** p249 L2.
The menu here tends to be mainly films related to the natural world, shown on the big big screen, sometimes in 3-D. Plus there's the occasional IMAX blow-ups of standard Hollywood blockbusters.

OMNIMAX Theatre
Science World, 1455 Quebec Street, at Terminal Avenue, Downtown (604 443 7443/www.science world.bc.ca). Bus 3, 8, 19, 22/SkyTrain Main Street-Science World/Aquabus. **Screens** 1. Admission $10. **Credit** DC, MC, V. **Map** p249 M5.
Even if you're jaded with IMAX screens, the all-enveloping sphere of the OMNIMAX is quite special, making excellent use of one of the city's biggest, most characteristic and most photographed landmarks, the golf ball-like protuberance that is the Science World dome (*see p142*). The screen itself is an extraordinary 27m (89ft) in diameter and five storeys high, while the resulting image is three times larger than 70mm and ten times larger than the standard 35mm print you normally see in theatres.

Galleries

Smart art.

Contemporary Art Gallery. *See p151.*

After an infancy characterised by 'pretty' landscape work by the likes of EJ Hughes and Emily Carr, Vancouver's art scene has spent the past half-century getting made over into a highly cerebral marketplace for new talent. So cerebral, in fact, that the locals often have no idea what's going on – for the latest scoop you'll want to do your research at the magazine rack, not a cocktail party. Vancouver artists, especially the famed conceptual photographers, are often more celebrated abroad than at home. (For a primer on West Coast art, *see pp30-35*.)

The phenomenon has its roots in the rigorous and conceptual work of Ian Wallace, the granddaddy of the city's contemporary art scene. Jeff Wall (*see also p34*) – Vancouver's prize artistic export, famous for his expensively produced, large-scale backlit photographs – was taught by Wallace in the late 1960s, and has in recent years staged solo exhibitions at New York's Museum of Modern Art and London's Tate Modern.

Vancouver's other creative kingpin, Douglas Coupland (*see p35* **Tales of the city**), started out as a student at the prestigious Emily Carr Institute for Art & Design. ECIAD, nestled near the market on Granville Island, is now a kind of holding pen for the year's crop of new artists, and its annual grad show is on every curator's calendar. Coupland continues to make visual art, and his work can be seen at **Monte Clark Gallery** (*see p153*), on South Granville. The **Granville Rise**, as merchants have labelled it, runs along Granville Street, between West 7th Avenue and West 15th. Refreshment won't be a problem, with two Starbucks on every block (we're only semi-kidding). The area's elite shops also provide ample retail distraction.

The city's rocketing real estate market has ensured that any gallery not moving high-priced items is relegated to odd little corners of the grid. You'll find artist-run spaces tucked into side streets and rubbing elbows with the seedier areas. Still, the hunt is worthwhile – especially if you're savvy enough to find artists before the international media build them into overpriced darlings.

Then again, not everyone is hunting for the photo-conceptual treasures the city has marketed to the world. Inuit stone sculptures and Northwest Coast wood carvings exist in an entirely different set of galleries, which

Cat flight

Art-dealing fat cats often hail the **Catriona Jeffries Gallery** (*see p153*) as the only commercial gallery worth visiting in Canada. Torontonians get tetchy over such claims and even Vancouverites, who generally abhor severe competition, can be overheard murmuring about the vice-like hold the gallery has on the marketplace. When Jeffries elected to ditch her location on the popular South Granville strip in 2006, it was a clear statement of confidence. 'The gallery is a destination in itself,' said Jeffries, 'we don't need window shoppers.'

This means that the city's most important commercial gallery now sits – in splendid isolation – on the eastern side of Vancouver, far from its mortal peers. Once you have managed to locate the converted warehouse – it's the building painted in a shade of grey about which photographer Roy Arden quipped, 'That grey says, "Do I know you?"' – you will

need to enter from the alley; note that there are only a few parking spots available.

Once inside, it's easy to see where the hyperbole comes from. The list of gallery artists reads like a 'Who's Who?' of the local scene: Brian Jungen, Ian Wallace and Kelly Wood all feature, to name but a few. A discussion with Jeffries or one of her gallery attendants is likely to be spectacularly well-informed (if sometimes intimidating). And visits from the world's most important art curators are common, including the folk representing the Tate Modern, the Sydney Biennale and the Munich Kunstverein.

When the flight from South Granville was still in the works and a rumour circulated that Jeffries was closing up shop entirely, the owner laughed off the notion: 'No, no, no,' she chuckled. 'That would be a catastrophe for Canadian culture.'

often dance on the line between gift shop and serious art dealer. The difference between tourist products and artwork is something that First Nations artists have been intimately acquainted with since colonial times. Question is: can you tell the difference?

Whatever your taste, you'll find Vancouver's galleries to be numerous and competitive, but

without ever aspiring to the pretension you find in New York's Chelsea. Maybe that's because the city's art giants – Jeff Wall, Rodney Graham, Stan Douglas – hardly ever exhibit here themselves. The city's art market, much like the city itself, isn't terribly concerned with established icons – Vancouver seems to be busy hunting for whatever comes next.

Downtown

Art Beatus

108-808 Nelson Street, at Howe Street (604 688 2633/www.artbeatus.com). Bus 2, 4, 6, 7, 10, 16, 17, 44, 50. **Open** 10am-6pm Mon-Fri; phone ahead to check. **Credit** AmEx, DC, MC, V. **Map** p249 K4.
Art Beatus exhibits some of the biggest names in contemporary Chinese art, along with a handful of other Asian artists. China's creative entrepreneurs have kept pace with their economic counterparts over the past few years, and two spaces in Hong Kong, as well as Vancouver's own large Chinese population, help Art Beatus to maintain strong links to the motherland.

Buschlen Mowatt Galleries

1445 W Georgia Street, between Broughton & Nicola Streets (604 682 1234/www.buschlenmowatt.com). Bus 5. **Open** 10am-6pm Mon-Sat; noon-5pm Sun. **Credit** AmEx, DC, MC, V. **Map** p248 J2.
One of the commercial engines of the city's art scene, Buschlen Mowatt has been plying a lucrative trade since 1979. The gallery flogs the kind of stuff that could happily fill a boardroom or a hotel lobby: big, colourful paintings and grand, imposing sculptures. The large, arresting sculptures it specialises in are now contentious fixtures in the city's public parks.

Contemporary Art Gallery

555 Nelson Street, between Seymour & Richards Streets (604 681 2700/www.contemporaryart gallery.ca). Bus 2, 4, 6, 7, 10, 16, 17, 44, 50. **Open** noon-6pm Wed-Sun. **Credit** AmEx, DC, MC, V. **Map** p249 K4.
Probably the leading not-for-profit gallery in the city, the Contemporary boasts ample space, a good budget and shrewd curators. Scott McFarland, Brian Jungen and other rising stars of the local scene have shown here. The exhibition schedule is matched by a series of talks and lectures, often by visiting artists and critics. The opening nights are among the best in Vancouver. *Photo p149.*

Gastown

Access Artist Run Centre

206 Carrall Street, at Water Street (604 689 2907/www.vaarc.ca). Bus 4, 7. **Open** noon-5pm Tue-Sat. **Credit** DC, MC, V. **Map** p249 M3.
The name says it all: this is a space for collaborative projects and artist-organised exhibitions. Many artists get their first show here.

Artspeak

233 Carrall Street, between Water & Cordova Streets (604 688 0051/www.artspeak.ca). Bus 4, 7. **Open** noon-5pm Tue-Sat. **Credit** DC, MC, V. **Map** p249 M4.
Just down the street from the Access Centre, you'll find Artspeak, another dynamic not-for-profit space. Expect to find work that is experimental, formally innovative and most likely politically engaged.

Centre A

2 W Hastings Street, at Carrall Street (604 683 8326/ www.centrea.org). Bus 10, 16, 20. **Open** 11am-6pm Tue-Sat. **Credit** AmEx, DC, MC, V. **Map** p249 M3.
A not-for-profit gallery dedicated to Asian art, Centre A is far edgier than the city's commercial equivalent, Art Beatus (*see above*). After moving into its expansive new space, Centre A became one of the most dynamic art spaces in Vancouver. Located between Chinatown and a decrepit stretch of Hastings Street, Centre A engages with both Asian heritage and raw urban realities. There is also an extensive library and monthly screenings are projected on the walls.

Helen Pitt Gallery

102-148 Alexander Street, between Main & Columbia Streets (604 681 6740/www.helenpitt gallery.org). Bus 4, 7. **Open** noon-5pm Tue-Sat. **No credit cards. Map** p249 N3.
Artist-run since 1975, the Helen Pitt Gallery is an important venue for non-commercial and experimental performances and exhibitions. Youngsters, recent graduates, artists whose work has yet to be gobbled up by the art business – you'll find them all exhibiting here, often collaboratively.

Inuit Gallery of Vancouver

206 Cambie Street, at Water Street (604 688 7323/ www.inuit.com). Bus 10, 16, 20, 44/SkyTrain Waterfront. **Open** 10am-6pm Mon-Sat; 11am-5pm Sun. **Credit** AmEx, DC, MC, V. **Map** p249 L3.
Located in Gastown since 1979, this is a good place to take a look at Canadian aboriginal art from the North-west Coast, as well as the arctic regions. Immense soapstone sculptures jostle for space with cedar masks and contemporary design pieces. Jewellery and prints are also available for purchase. Word has it that Damien Hirst shops here.

Marion Scott Gallery

308 Water Street, at Cambie Street (604 685 1934/ www.marionscottgallery.com). Bus 10, 16, 20/ SkyTrain Waterfront. **Open** 10am-6pm Mon-Fri; 10.30am-5.30pm Sat, Sun. **Credit** DC, MC, V. **Map** p249 L3.
Established in 1975, this is the best space in the city for Inuit art. Unlike most galleries that show native Canadian art – which can resemble production lines – Marion Scott Gallery holds carefully researched and presented exhibitions. Part of its programme is to focus on art 'less for ethnographic content and more for its aesthetic merit'. Always worth a look, the gallery is also starting to show work by non-aboriginal artists. *Photo p153.*

Spirit Wrestler Gallery

47 Water Street, between Abbott & Carrall Streets (604 669 8813/www.spiritwrestler.com). Bus 4, 7, 10, 16, 20. **Open** 10am-6pm Mon-Sat; noon-5pm Sun. **Credit** AmEx, DC, MC, V. **Map** p249 M3.
Spirit Wrestler Gallery takes in a range of work from aboriginal traditions, from Inuit to Maori and West Coast. However, the relatively small gallery makes the display a bit higgledy-piggledy, with the end

result that you sometimes have a Maori wood carving, all toothy-grinned and glaring, facing down an Inuit stone sculpture as if it were invading its turf. There's some interesting stuff nonetheless, with a selection not unlike the Inuit Gallery (*see p151*). Don't miss the jewellery and small objects downstairs.

West Side

Atelier Gallery

2421 Granville Street, at W 8th Avenue (604 732 3021/www.ateliergallery.ca). Bus 4, 7, 10, 16, 17, 50. **Open** 11am-5pm Mon-Sat; noon-5pm Sun. **Credit** DC, MC, V. **Map** p251 H6.

A well-established presence on Granville. It might sound cruel to say that the Atelier Gallery exhibits stuff that would like nice on your wall, but it's true, and it's not a bad reputation to have. Landscapes and drawings by local artists feature strongly, and a lot of it is worth a second look. Royal Art Lodge, the Winnipeg art collective, shows here, and its work is a madcap blend of whimsy and anguish.

Bau-Xi Gallery

3045 Granville Street, between W 14th & W 15th Avenues (604 733 7011/www.bau-xi.com). Bus 10. **Open** 10am-5.30pm Mon-Sat; noon-4pm Sun. **Credit** DC, MC, V. **Map** p251 H7.

One of the oldest galleries on Granville, Bau-Xi has been exhibiting local artists, mostly from the lyrical landscape tradition, since 1965. You'll find some terrific stuff – most likely competent, decorative and lovely – but it's unlikely to set your heart racing.

Bjornson Kajiwara Gallery

1727 W 3rd Avenue, between Pine & Burrard Streets (604 738 3500/www.bjornsonkajiwara.ca). Bus 4, 7, 44. **Open** 11am-6pm Tue-Fri; 11am-5pm Sat. **Credit** AmEx, DC, MC, V. **Map** p251 G6.

Just up the road from Tracey Lawrence Gallery (*see p153*), Bjornson Kajiwara is a relatively new space that shows a mix of youngish artists whose work, though fresh and contemporary, is not quite as avant-garde as their neighbour's. Craig Sibley's organic wooden sculptures alone make it worth a visit.

Charles H Scott Gallery

1399 Johnston Street, Granville Island (604 844 3809/information 604 844 3811/http://chscott. eciad.ca). Bus 50. **Open** noon-5pm Mon-Fri; 10am-5pm Sat, Sun. **Credit** DC, MC, V. **Map** p250 C3.

The gallery for the Emily Carr Institute of Art & Design shows work by international artists, as well as the respected annual graduation show. An academic and non-commercial agenda means that it can feature artists from far-flung parts of the world, whose work would otherwise be impossible to see. One of the best places in town for art books.

Diane Farris Gallery

1590 W 7th Avenue, at Fir Street (604 737 2629/ www.dianefarrisgallery.com). Bus 10, 16, 17. **Open** 10am-5.30pm Tue-Fri; 10am-5pm Sat. **Credit** DC, MC, V. **Map** p251 G6.

Diane Farris has been selling international and local artists just off Granville since 1984. The gallery's star artist, however, is unquestionably Dale Chihuly, the Washington State-based glass man whose gooey, biomorphic sculptures, in riots of intense colour, grace two of London's grandest foyers: the Victoria & Albert Museum, and Claridge's Hotel (in the tearoom). Conservative, mid-career local painters also show here.

Douglas Reynolds Gallery

2335 Granville Street, between W 7th & W 8th Avenues (604 731 9292/www.douglasreynolds gallery.com). Bus 10, 16, 17. **Open** 10am-6pm Mon-Sat; noon-5pm Sun. **Credit** AmEx, DC, MC, V. **Map** p251 H6.

Douglas Reynolds is the best place in the city to find top-notch Northwest Coast native art. If you want to see work by Robert Davidson, Bill Reid (*see p31* **Read all about it**) or other masters of the ovoid, you'll find that Douglas Reynolds offers the best selection outside UBC's Museum of Anthropology. Besides the masks and totems, the jewellery counter is a highlight, with exquisite work in silver and gold, some of it surprisingly affordable. The gallery also exhibits and sells rare historical carvings.

Douglas Udell Gallery

1558 W 6th Avenue, between Granville & Fir Streets (604 736 8900/www.douglasudellgallery.com). Bus 10, 16, 17. **Open** 10am-6pm Tue-Sat. **Credit** DC, MC, V. **Map** p251 H6.

Douglas Udell Gallery is a bit of a rattle bag: lots of established Canadian artists, along with a few from abroad, and a significant amount of secondary market, so you can pick up anything from a Picasso to a Dempsey Bob. American Caio Fonseca's abstracts and Tony Scherman's chunky encaustic paintings are both highlights.

Equinox Gallery

2321 Granville Street, between W 7th & W 8th Avenues (604 736 2405/www.equinoxgallery.com). Bus 10, 16, 17. **Open** 10am-5pm Tue-Sat. **Credit** DC, MC, V. **Map** p251 H6.

The elder statesman of Vancouver's gallery scene, Equinox has been dealing major international names and local favourites since the early 1970s. Lately, the vintage work of Fred Herzog – famed for photographing Vancouver's neon adolescence – has become a hot commodity.

Heffel Gallery

2247 Granville Street, at W 7th Avenue (604 732 6505/www.heffel.com). Bus 10, 16, 17. **Open** 10am-6pm Mon-Sat. **Credit** DC, MC, V. **Map** p251 H6.

More an auction house than a gallery, Heffel maintains an exhibition space and is probably the best place in the city to see the historical Canadian landscape: members of the Group of Seven, EJ Hughes and others are often shown. Tiko Kerr, a painter of wobbly local landscapes, can also be seen here. Check the website for temporary displays and the twice-yearly auctions.

The **Marion Scott Gallery** is renowned for the quality of its Inuit artworks. *See p151.*

Monte Clark Gallery

2339 Granville Street, between W 7th & W 8th Avenues (604 730 5000/www.monteclarkgallery. com). Bus 4, 7, 10, 16, 17. **Open** 10am-6pm Tue-Sat. **Credit** V. **Map** p251 H6.

You may have heard that Vancouver is a city that breeds conceptual photographers, documenters of the everyday and artists who like to point their lens at busted buildings or empty landscapes. Don't believe it? Come to Monte Clark Gallery. Here you'll find the likes of Roy Arden, Scott McFarland, Howard Ursuliak and other artists whose work bears superficial resemblance to that of Jeff Wall (*see p34*). This is the best space in Vancouver for photography, but you'll also find a selection of painters and other artists. Monte Clark also has a space in Toronto, and is one of the most respected galleries in Canada.

Tracey Lawrence Gallery

1531 W 4th Avenue, at Fir Street (604 730 2875/ www.traceylawrencegallery.com). Bus 4, 7, 10, 16, 17. **Open** 10am-5pm Tue-Sat. **Credit** AmEx, DC, MC, V. **Map** p251 G6.

If Monte Clark (*see above*) has taken up the Jeff Wall tradition, Rodney Graham's (*see p34*) presence can be felt at Tracey Lawrence. Tim Lee is probably its hottest artist right now, and others represented by the gallery include Shannon Oksanen, Kathy Slade and Jeremy Shaw. Photography, installation, video… you name it, they show it, as long as it's fresh, witty and preferably bringing a satirical edge.

East Vancouver

Catriona Jeffries Gallery

274 E 1st Avenue, between Lorne & Scotia Streets (604 736 1554/www.catrionajeffries.com). Bus 3/SkyTrain to Main Street Station. **Open** 11am-5pm Tue-Sat. **No credit cards.** **Map** p252 N6.

Catriona Jeffries is Vancouver's most important contemporary gallery and one of a handful in the city – some would say the only one – to boast an international reputation. Legendary father figure Ian Wallace shows here, as do a host of younger artists with growing worldwide presences: Brian Jungen, Ron Terada, Myfanwy Macleod, Damian Moppett and Geoffrey Farmer. If you want to find out what Vancouver's next generation of ambitious artists are up to, a trip here is essential. *See also p150* **Cat flight.**

Western Front Artist-Run Centre

303 E 8th Avenue, at Scotia Street (604 876 9343/ www.front.bc.ca). Bus 3. **Open** noon-5pm Tue-Sat. **Credit** DC, MC, V. **Map** p252 N6.

Vancouver's original artist-run centre has been an essential part of the cultural scene for a generation. Many of Vancouver's biggest names passed through these low-rent doors before becoming commercially successful. Along with exhibitions, media arts and performance (a Vancouver speciality), 'the Front', as it is affectionately called, also boasts an in-house magazine and runs a new music programme, so you can enjoy the soothing sounds of, say, the Nihilist Spasm Band, after enjoying some cutting-edge art.

Arts & Entertainment

Gay & Lesbian

The pride of the city.

Odyssey Night Club.
See p157.

When the pink bus shelters and garbage cans were installed along Davie Street, and rainbow banners were permanently fitted high above the sidewalks, many West End locals cheered (our very own neighbourhood!) and many others jeered (our very own ghetto!). It's undeniable, though, that the 'multicultural' West End, from Burrard Street to Denman, is dominated by gay men. That's beginning to change, though. As 2010 Olympic fever intensifies, more and more downtown peninsula has become a coveted residence for gays and straights alike.

Although a number of lesbians have made their way into the gaybourhood, the lesbian community generally makes its home instead on (vastly more affordable) Commercial Drive, where actual homes can be had, rather than small boxes in the sky. Meanwhile, the hipster queers – both male and female – are found at a mid-point between downtown and Commercial, on Main Street – along with some of the city's hottest boutiques and eateries.

When out and about, keep in mind that Vancouver's gay and lesbian population has an international reputation for being a little bit stand-offish. Unlike their queer peers in Toronto or San Francisco, Vancouverites are laissez-faire when it comes to making new contacts and you may find yourself playing flirty-eyes with someone for hours before you realise they aren't going to make a move.

The locals are, however, very forward in non-romantic avenues. The **West End Business Improvement Association** (411-1033 Davie Street, 604 696 0144, www.westendbia.com) is a key player in the West End's development and gay-owned businesses are prevalent. Even straight-owned companies are wise to the pink dollar: you'll spot rainbow stickers in windows all over the city.

Perhaps the city's most important gay business, though, is the marriage business. Since British Columbia became one of the first provinces to legalise gay marriage (in 2003), Vancouver has played host to countless American love birds looking for a place to get hitched. A marriage license from the **Vital Statistics Agency** (604 660 2937, www.vs.gov.bc.ca/marriage) can be obtained for $100.

Whether you are after information on gay marriage, bar suggestions, or just a silicone butt plug, **Little Sister's Book & Art Emporium** (1238 Davie Street; *see p123*) is your all-purpose shop – and yes, they do sell books as well. For a quarter century, Little Sister's has been the keystone of Vancouver's queer community. When the West End was seedier, back in the 1980s, prostitutes used to convene here and swap stories – but in more recent years the expansive store has been better known for the owners' tireless legal battles against censorship and seizures at the Canadian-American border.

For a slightly more glam shopping experience, head a little way east down Davie Street toward **Priape** (1148 Davie Street, 604 630 2330, www.priape.com), the Canadian gay chain outlet. Custom leather gear, porn, lube, and amyl-nitrate 'aromas' are all on offer.

August is the peak of gay tourist season, with the **Vancouver Pride Parade** (see *p140*) attracting upwards of 300,000 gawkers in early August, and the **Vancouver Queer Film Festival** (www.outonscreen.com) taking place later in the month.

INFORMATION AND LISTINGS

Xtra! West (www.xtra.ca) is Vancouver's only gay and lesbian newspaper, and has an exhaustive classified section, including club listings and other services. On the internet, www.gayvan.com is a valuable resource for tourists; www.superdyke.com is the leading site for women's listings.

Where to stay

You'd be hard-pressed to find a downtown hotel that isn't gay-friendly. The West End in particular offers hotels, hostels and B&Bs to suit everyone's fancy. You'll find several five-star hotels listed in the *Pink Pages* (www.pink pagesnet.com) that are all gay-friendly. If a queer environment is important, you're best off checking in at one of the lodgings listed below.

Nelson House B&B

977 Broughton Street, at Nelson Street, Downtown (604 684 9793/toll-free 866 684 9793/www. downtownbandb.com). Bus 5. **Rates** $88-$198. **Credit** DC, MC, V. **Map** p248 H3.
Nelson House is fronted by a fine garden and situated in the heart of the West End, only a few blocks from Stanley Park and the trendiest coffee houses on Denman Street. This three-storey character home has been gay-owned and operated since 1990, and is cosy, unpretentious and affordable. Theme bedrooms cover Hollywood, Bombay and lumberjacks.

A Place at Penny's B&B

810 Commercial Street, at Adanac Street, East Vancouver (604 254 2229/www.pennysplace vancouver.com). Bus 20 or SkyTrain to Commercial Drive, then bus 7. **Rates** $65-$175 double. **Credit** DC, MC, V.

A Place at Penny's, located on the Drive, has been offering discreet and professional female lodgings for over 30 years. It's so exclusive you have to call Penny directly – there is no front desk. Each apartment is decked out with antiques, Persian rugs and hardwood floors, spacious bedrooms and full kitchens. Mere blocks from parks, outdoor markets, cafés and Vancouver's thriving lesbian community.

West End Guest House

1362 Haro Street, at Broughton Street, Downtown (604 681 2889/toll-free 888 546 3327/www.westend guesthouse.com). Bus 5. **Rates** $95-$255 double. **Credit** AmEx, DC, MC, V. **Map** p248 J2.
A lovingly restored (pink!) heritage house in the gay ghetto. The walls are lined with photos of the city's early days and your inner diva will warm to the antique furnishings, parlour with fireplace and sun deck facing a well-tended garden. Full breakfasts, complimentary mountain bikes, fax and cable.

Restaurants & cafés

Worth a stop for sass and sarcasm is the **Elbow Room** (see *p90*), where in a bizarre form of performance art the waiters are required to scold you mercilessly. A number of pubs and bars also serve food (see *p156*).

Café Deux Soleils

2096 Commercial Drive, at E 5th Avenue, East Vancouver (604 254 1195/www.cafedeuxsoleils.com). Bus 20/SkyTrain Broadway. **Open** 8am-midnight Mon-Sat; 8am-5pm Sun. **Main courses** $5-$10. **Credit** V. **Map** p252 Q6.
The lesbian brunch spot on the Drive has a hippie vibe and a bi/lesbian/experimental crowd.

Davie Village Café & Bar

1141 Davie Street, between Bute & Thurlow Streets, West End (604 228 1429/www.davievillage.ca). Bus 6. **Open** 8am-11pm daily (closes later in summer). **Main courses** $4-$18. **Credit** AmEx, DC, MC, V. **Map** p248 J3.
On a sunny day, the DVC's back patio is a coveted oasis in the middle of the village, its high walls and potted plants shutting out urban life. A large breakfast menu and extensive martini list make visits worthwhile at any hour.

Delany's Coffee House

1105 Denman Street, between Comox & Pendrell Streets, West End (604 662 3344). Bus 6. **Open** 6am-11pm Mon-Fri; 6.30am-11pm Sat, Sun. **Credit** DC, MC, V. **Map** p248 H2.
A cruisy Denman Street café with cute baristas and cuter pooches out front. Ideal for people-watching.

Hamburger Mary's Diner

1202 Davie Street, at Bute Street, West End (604 681 1293/www.hamburgermarys.ca). Bus 6, N6. **Open** 8am-3am Mon-Thur; 8am-4am Fri, Sat; 8am-2am Sun. **Main courses** $7-$15. **Credit** AmEx, DC, MC, V. **Map** p248 H3.

Arts & Entertainment

Every strip needs a late-night hideout with a cranky jukebox. Don't go looking for health-conscious grub, though. You want the cheesy fries and you want one of the famous milkshakes. This is also a low-key weekend brunch spot.

The Majestic Restaurant & Lounge

1138 Davie Street, between Bute & Thurlow Streets, West End (604 669 2013/www.majesticvancouver. com). Bus 6. **Open** 11am-midnight daily. **Main courses** $6-$23. **Credit** AmEx, DC, MC, V.

This new, capacious resto-lounge has already carved out a niche in the West End foodie scene as the only Sunday Brunch with a drag queen. Friday nights are popular, too, hosted by the beloved drag star Symone.

Melriches Coffee House

1244 Davie Street, between Bute & Jervis Streets, West End (604 689 5282). Bus 6. **Open** 6am-11pm Mon-Sat; 7am-11pm Sun. **Credit** DC, MC, V.

The baristas often look like they're having a small house party behind the counter. Easily the best atmosphere in the village – slightly bohemian – with many local artists and writers calling it their office.

Bars & clubs

Drinking & relaxing

1181

1181 Davie Street, between Bute & Thurlow Streets, West End (604 687 3991/www.tightlounge.com). Bus 2, 6, 22, N6. **Open** 4pm-2am daily. **Credit** AmEx, DC, MC, V.

Gay Vancouver's hippest and most sophisticated joint is an oasis of New York cool, complete with cork-lined walls and low-lying couches. Make no mistake – the Abercrombie zombies assemble here in flocks. But gorgeous bartenders, intelligent DJs and über-chic design more than compensate for any attitude.

Fountainhead Pub

1025 Davie Street, between Burrard & Thurlow Streets, Downtown (604 687 2222/www.the fountainheadpub.com). Bus 2, 6, 22, N6. **Open** 11am-midnight Mon-Thur, Sun; 11am-1am Fri, Sat. **Credit** DC, MC, V. **Map** p248 J4.

A casual pub with hearty burgers and flirty waiters. Stake out a spot on the covered patio and monitor the line at Celebrities (*see below*). Or settle in for the night: it has electronic dart boards, pool tables and a wide selection of beer on tap. Popular for weekend brunch, it's also one of the only spots on Davie where you'll find gays and lesbians drinking alongside each other.

Oasis

1240 Thurlow Street, at Davie Street, West End (604 685 1724/www.theoasispub.com). Bus 2, 6, 22, N6. **Open** 5pm-midnight Mon-Thur; 3.30pm-1am Fri, Sat; 3.30pm-midnight Sun. **Credit** DC, MC, V. **Map** p248 J4.

Light and airy, this elegant piano bar with a baby grand has the widest selection of martinis anywhere in town. Go for the friendly waiting staff, excellent

food and heated patio, where the formal atmosphere inside gives way to a more sociable buzz. The entrance is just off Davie Street, up a flight of stairs.

Score On Davie

1262 Davie Street, between Bute & Jervis Streets, West End (604 632 1646). Bus 6. **Open** 11am-midnight Mon-Thur; 11am-2am Fri; 10am-2am Sat; 10am-midnight Sun. **Main courses** $7-$15. **Credit** AmEx, DC, MC, V.

Upbeat sports venue in the heart of the Davie village. All sporting events are screened on six flat-screen TVs, and there's a special interest in hockey and Ultimate Fighting Championships.

Cruising

Numbers

1042 Davie Street, between Burrard & Thurlow Streets, Downtown (604 685 4077/www.numbers.ca). Bus 2, 6, 22, N6. **Open** 9pm-2am Mon-Thur, Sun; 8pm-3am Fri, Sat. **Admission** free-$5. **No credit cards. Map** p248 J4.

This cruisy multi-level club is especially popular with the 30-and-up set and the unpretentious vibe allows for casual hook-ups or friendly chats. Numbers has pool tables, dartboards, video games and a small but often energetic dancefloor. Some of the sweetest bartenders in town dole out drinks specials and can be seen participating in the popular karaoke shows on Sundays and Wednesdays. An excellent place to meet Mr Right Now at the end of the night.

PumpJack Pub

1167 Davie Street, between Thurlow & Bute Streets, West End (604 685 3417/www.pumpjackpub.com). Bus 6, N6. **Open** 1pm-1am Mon-Thur, Sun; 1pm-2am Fri, Sat.* **Admission** free. **Credit** DC, MC, V. **Map** p248 J3.

For blue-collar types (and their admirers) the PumpJack is undoubtedly the top spot on the strip for cruising. Bowls of peanuts, community-minded management and cheap beer create a jovial, unpretentious atmosphere. It's also the neighbourhood pub for many local merchants, and the fulcrum for the leather and rubber scenes. Drop in Friday or Saturday nights and enjoy the scenery before clubbing.

Dancing

Celebrities

1022 Davie Street, between Burrard & Thurlow Streets, Downtown (604 681 6180/www.celebrities nightclub.com). Bus 2, 6, 22, N6. **Open** phone for details. **Admission** free-$10. **Credit** DC, MC, V. **Map** p248 J4.

The best mixed dance club in town, often featuring stellar DJs. Newly renovated, it has a large dancefloor, and state-of-the-art lighting and sound. Tuesday nights have been dubbed 'straight night', thanks to some insanely cheap drinks. Different crowds hit Celebrities on different nights, but the mainstay is a young, hip and well-heeled clientele.

All comers

Everyone from neophytes to hardcore BDSM players will find themselves indulged by Vancouver's busy kink scenes. Fetish events generally have strict dress codes, whether it's latex, rubber, leather or fur, so plan ahead – you're not getting in with street clothes (and be sure to carry photo ID at all times). The city's BDSM/fetish scene is, though, renowned for being friendly, sane and instructive. See www.vancouverleather.com for links to the scene's ever-changing events, but here are some stalwart regulars to get you started.

Sin City takes place at Club 23 (23 W Cordova Street, at Carrall Street, Gastown, www.gothic.bc.ca/sincity, admission $9-$12) on the second Saturday of every month. The biggest fetish party in Vancouver, this club offers three floors of entertaining action, an outside patio, large dancefloor and a well-equipped dungeon for BDSM play. Come see,

be seen, dance, play and have a blast. The Vancouver Dungeon Monitor Team (DM) supervises to ensure all BDSM play abides by house safety rules. Doors open at 9pm, but arrive at least a half-hour early – lines are long, and you might not get in until midnight or later. A strict dress code is enforced.

Rascal's BDSM/Fetish Play Party, at WISE Hall (1882 Adanac Street, at Victoria Drive, East Vancouver, www.rascals-club.com, admission $20 on the door) usually takes place on the third weekend of the month. Fetish wear is encouraged, and blue jeans, street clothes and athletic wear aren't allowed. Doors open at 8pm and the pan-sexual play continues till 1am, monitored by the Vancouver DM Team. Not everybody decides to engage in consensual play; you are welcome to be a voyeur provided that you do not disturb the action.

Lick

Lotus Hotel, 455 Abbott Street, at W Pender Street, Downtown (604 685 7777/www.lotussoundlounge. com). Bus 10, 16, 20, N20. **Open** 9pm-3am Fri, Sat. **Admission** $5-$12. **Credit** DC, MC, V. **Map** p249 M3.

Venture upstairs at Lick to meet, dance and play with Vancouver's hottest dykes at the city's only lesbian nightclub, featuring a roster of talented female DJs. Downstairs, you'll find the Lotus Sound Lounge (*see p165*), a fine venue for innovative sounds. The crowd at Lotus is either mixed or 'post-gay' – take your pick.

Odyssey Night Club

1251 Howe Street, between Davie & Drake Streets, Downtown (604 689 5256/www.theodysseynightclub. com). Bus 6. **Open** 9pm-3am daily. **Admission** free-$8. **Credit** DC, MC, V. **Map** p248 J4.

The Odyssey attracts all ages but is best known for its lithe youths bussed in from campus and their attendant chicken hawks. There is often a wait to get into the large outdoor patio equipped with its own bar, trailing grapevines and cobblestone flooring. Sunday nights feature standard but lovable drag shows and, every Saturday, the go-go boys go all the way. Discreet back door entry/exit. *Photo p154.*

Bathhouses

Fahrenheit 212

1048 Davie Street, between Burrard & Thurlow Streets, Downtown (604 689 9719/www.f212.com). Bus 2, 6, 22, N6. **Open** 24hrs daily. **Admission** Rooms $15-$30. *Annual membership* $10; phone for details. **Credit** DC, MC, V. **Map** p248 J4.

F212 is the mainstay for the sauna boys in town. It comes well equipped with three different room sizes, lockers, a snack bar, a fully stocked weight area, a 12-man jacuzzi enclosed in a steam room, and a second, hotter and more intimate steam room. Bonus: there's a porn room with leather couches and a fireplace. Men only.

Friction

123 W Pender Street, at Beatty Street, Downtown (604 684 0314/www.worldfriction.com). Bus 4, 7, 50/SkyTrain Stadium. **Open** 24hrs daily. **Admission** Rooms $10-$45. Lockers $5-$12. No credit cards. **Map** p249 L3.

Handsomely situated in a heritage building over towards Chinatown (nowhere near the gay village), Vancouver's newest bathhouse sprawls across 900sq m (10,000sq ft) of play space on two floors. The showers, steam room and video room are all stylish and well-done, giving the city's other steamers a run for their money. Men only.

M2M

1210 Granville Street, at Davie Street, Downtown (604 684 6011/www.m2mplayspace.com). Bus 4, 6, 7, 10, 16, 17, 50. **Open** 24hrs daily. **Admission** Rooms $12-$22. Drop-in charge $2. **Credit** DC, MC, V. **Map** p248 J4.

This one purports to be the city's hardcore bath-house – and it does seem to attract the leather and Levi's crowd. But don't be nervous – pretty much everyone seems to get along just fine. There's a play space decked out with public and private rooms, slings, lockers, group showers and a deluxe steam room. Weekdays, 11am to 3pm, try out the Dip & Dash – two hours for a fiver. Men only.

Arts & Entertainment

Music & Nightlife

Plenty of small venues – and no shortage of big sounds.

Rock & folk

With the Arcade Fire and Feist populating every second iPod on the planet, there can be no disputing that Canadian music has launched a major offensive on the zeitgeist. While Vancouver may not contribute as many foot soldiers to the surge as Toronto and Montreal, it certainly has its share of quality combatants.

Vancouver's **New Pornographers** are arguably responsible for popularising the term 'super group' in the indie rock lexicon. Headed by exemplary local songwriters Carl Newman and Dan Bejar, and featuring American chanteuse Neko Case, the band's infectious confections have charmed listeners worldwide for four straight albums. The Pornographers' pop inclinations find their ideal foil in the compellingly bleak retro-rock of **Black Mountain**. Chief Mountaineer Steve McBean has toiled for years in local bands and the recent international attention turned his way is a source of inspiration for many long-suffering local musicians.

At times, Vancouver seems intent on ensuring that all of its bands are relegated to 'struggling' status. In the past few years, an alarming rash of venue closures has struck the city. While a couple of new stages have appeared in sushi restaurants and karaoke bars, it's not uncommon for some of the city's better showcases of local talent to now occur in art galleries or warehouse spaces in marginalised neighbourhoods.

While such practices contribute to a certain insularity that plagues the music scene (you need to know the right people to know about the right shows), they're also indicative of local musicians' resourcefulness and sense of community. Once someone is 'in', they're practically omnipresent. It's common for any given Vancouver musician to have at least two projects on the go. This tendency even pertains to the city's heavyweights: the Pornographers' Bejar regularly marauds as the hyper-literate, highly lauded Destroyer. Meanwhile, Black Mountain's members also moonlight with the equally sombre Pink Mountaintops, Blood Meridian and Lightning Dust.

Such creative cross-pollination between bands regularly results in local acts that defy conventional classification. Ask what a certain band sounds like and you can expect a protracted analogy or a slew of hyphens (country-garage-rock, for example) as a response. That said, many of these same acts deliver immediate gratification onstage. You Say Party! We Say Die! and They Shoot Horses, Don't They? offer live performances as noteworthy as their punctuation. The likes of Ladyhawk, Bend Sinister and The Doers routinely leave stages sweat-stained, while the punishing Bison and Pride Tiger rattle audiences to the (hard)core.

Whereas some bands (Fake Shark – Real Zombie and The Tranzmitors) still start out in garages, art school educations flavour the more experimental Fond of Tigers and Secret Mommy Quintet. Anglophiles The Book of Lists and Elizabeth flaunt their UK influences, while The Be Good Tanyas, Octoberman, Carolyn Mark and Geoff Berner revisit the Canadian folk tradition. Vancouver doesn't spawn a wealth of hip hop or rap but Josh Martinez, Evil and Sweatshop Union are worthy of investigation.

Finally, Sealed With A Kiss, Live Nation and Timbre Productions are the premiere promoters in the city. Any of their names on a gig poster should be considered a mark of quality.

TICKETS AND INFORMATION

Free publications, such as the *Georgia Straight* and *The WestEnder* (both released every Thursday), offer listings and features concerning the local music scene and touring acts. You can also consult www.livemusic vancouver.com, which provides venue programmes and links to bands' websites. The 'Killer Daily' feature of webzine www. onlymagazine.ca will point you towards more unconventional offerings. Many club shows involving local acts don't sell advance tickets, instead charging a cover on the door.

For a relatively small city, Vancouver does a commendable job of luring top-flight talent. It's not uncommon for shows featuring either visiting performers or homegrown buzz bands to sell out well in advance. Tickets for most larger venues can be purchased through **Ticketmaster** (604 280 4444, www.ticket master.ca), which has several outlets in the city. Record stores such as Scratch, Zulu and Red Cat (for all, *see p135*) often carry tickets for many of the same shows. These shops also double as excellent sources for insider information as their staff are often either musicians or are closely tied to the music community.

Orpheum.
See p161.

Classical & opera

Vancouver may not be noted for its striking architecture but the city's classical music is heard in the best of it. The **Orpheum Theatre**, built in 1927, is the largest and most opulent theatre on the Pacific Coast. The Vancouver Symphony Orchestra can hardly play a wrong note in it – nearly everything sounds acceptable amid such exuberance. As well, there's the sleek, contemporary **Chan Centre** at UBC, which has earned an international reputation for its striking design and stellar acoustics.

Some fault the Vancouver Symphony Orchestra and Vancouver Opera for their populist programming. You'd do better seeking out Vancouver's specialised music societies and small- to mid-sized ensembles for the most adventurous programmes – and frequently the most luminous talents. Of particular note is the vibrant choral music scene (*see also p160* **Sweet harmony**), which counts heldentenor Ben Heppner as its most esteemed alumnus. Vancouver is also distinguished by an intimate but widely respected community of players and composers, who straddle the classical/jazz divide. The fusion of new music, classical influences from Europe and Asia, improv and free jazz gives the city's high-brow music scene a fresh and distinctively New World flavour.

To the dismay of local arts organisations, one of the city's most esteemed venues, the Vogue Theatre, closed in 2006 and its future remains uncertain. The city has, however, committed to building more concert venues in time for the Olympics in 2010; in the works are plans for an 1,800-seat concert hall, a 450-seat studio theatre and an outdoor performance plaza.

TICKETS AND INFORMATION

Tickets for major classical shows can be purchased through **Ticketmaster Artsline** (604 280 3311, www.ticketmaster.ca), which has several outlets throughout the city. Local newspapers (*see p233*) have concert listings, but for nearly comprehensive links and listings for classical performances in Vancouver, visit www.classicalvancouver.com.

Music societies

Early Music Vancouver

604 732 1610/www.earlymusic.bc.ca.
Early Music brings together high-profile visiting artists such as Sequentia and Musica Antiqua Köln, with local groups such as Pacific Baroque Orchestra

Sweet harmony

A plethora of worthy small- and mid-sized choral groups sets Vancouver's classical music community apart, and many of Canada's best choirs call Vancouver home. Of particular note are four internationally recognised chamber ensembles offering a diverse repertoire, a vibrant, polished sound, and emotively rich, musically exacting performances. They are the **Vancouver Chamber Choir** (604 738 6822, www.vancouverchamberchoir.com), **Phoenix Chamber Choir** (604 986 7520, www.phoenixchamberchoir.bc.ca), baroque specialists **Vancouver Cantata Singers** (604 730 8856, www.vancouvercantata singers.com) and the youthful 12-voice **Musica Intima** (604 731 6618, www. musicaintima.org). All of these groups have sung with an international roster of artists and ensembles, from Steven Isserlis to Chanticleer, and have participated in radio broadcasts and major choral symposia and competitions worldwide. Musica Intima's

conductorless, musically inventive concerts in particular epitomise Vancouver's fresh approach to classical music making.

The larger, semi-professional men's choir, **Chor Leoni** (604 999 6153, www. chorleoni.org), and women's choir, **Elektra** (604 833 1255, www.elektra.ca), perform less challenging, more populist fare.

Vancouver's largest singing group, the 160-voice **Bach Choir** (www.vancouver bachchoir.com) stages a stentorian sing-along *Messiah* in the 2,900-seat Orpheum Theatre each Christmas season; at the other end of the size and volume spectrum, the men's and women's **Scholae of Christ Church Cathedral** (690 Burrard Street, at Georgia Street, Downtown, 604 682 3848, www.cathedral.vancouver.bc.ca) alternate weekly to present a capella candlelight compline service each Sunday at 9.30pm. Smells and bells, and delicate eight- to ten-voice polyphony provide a meditative close to the weekend.

(604 215 0406, www.pacificbaroqueorchestra.com). In particular, the annual summertime Vancouver Early Music Festival draws national and international performers and consistent critical acclaim.

Vancouver New Music
604 633 0861/www.newmusic.org.
Vancouver New Music is one of Canada's major presenters of cutting-edge sonic art and electro-acoustic music. Regular season concerts, plus a yearly New Music Festival, showcase the likes of Pan Sonic, Laurie Anderson and Philip Glass, together with newly commissioned Canadian works ranging from multimedia sound installations to modern opera.

Vancouver Recital Society
604 602 0363/www.vanrecital.com.
The most significant force in Vancouver's classical music scene, the Vancouver Recital Society (RCS) presents established and emerging talents in concerts year-round. Artistic Director Leila Getz has a reputation for identifying rising luminaries before they become stars elsewhere: Vancouverites were treated to the voice of Cecilia Bartoli in 1992, when the diva had yet to perform in New York.

Performing groups

Vancouver Opera
604 683 0222/www.vancouveropera.ca.
Solid talent, resplendent costumes and the only people in town to bring you your dose of Puccini:

that's the Vancouver Opera. Modern classics, such as Robert Lepage's production of *Erwartung* and *Bluebeard's Castle*, occasionally hit the boards – but the typical fare here is traditional opera, traditionally staged. Seasons usually consist of four or five performances a month, starting in November and running into May.

Vancouver Symphony Orchestra
604 876 3434/www.vancouversymphony.ca.
Affable Music Director Bramwell Tovey's hard-working symphony presents 140 accessible concerts each season (Sept-June), with everything from flamenco dancers to Broadway show tunes spicing up the Bach and Beethoven. Free Symphony in the Park concerts at Stanley Park let you picnic while you listen to the VSO.

Venues

Short of larger theatres, Vancouver's principal venues tend to serve double duty, playing host to all kinds of musical performance and often theatre, as well. The Queen Elizabeth Theatre, for example, is home to the Vancouver Opera and Ballet British Columbia (*see p171*), but you are just as likely to find Brian Wilson playing there, or a theatrical event. On the plus side, you're quite likely to find a major name playing in a more intimate venue than would be the case elsewhere.

Stadiums/theatres

Phone or check the local press for ticket prices and opening times for the following.

Chan Centre for the Performing Arts

6265 Crescent Road, between East Mall & Main Mall, University of British Columbia (604 822 2697/www. chancentre.com). Bus 4, 17, 99. **Open** *Box office* noon-5pm Mon-Sat; noon-intermission performance days. **Admission** $10-$77. **Credit** AmEx, DC, MC, V.
The cylindrical, zinc-panelled exterior of the Chan Centre is striking, but it's the sonorous interior of the Chan Shun Concert Hall that has thrilled Vancouver audiences since it first opened in 1997. The Chan has impeccably clear acoustics that make the 20-minute trek through the traffic to the far west side of Vancouver well worth the effort. It's by far the best place in town for a discerning ear to listen to classical music.

General Motors Place

800 Griffiths Way, between Expo Boulevard & Pacific Boulevard, Downtown (604 899 7889/www. generalmotorsplace.com). Bus 22, 50, N8/SkyTrain Stadium. **Credit** AmEx, DC, MC, V. **Map** p249 K4.
If you really must see the likes of Coldplay or Gwen Stefani, this will see the place to do it. While popular opinion states that the 21,000-seat arena (built in 1995) betters its brethren in terms of sound and comfort, it's still more ideally suited for sporting events.

Orpheum

600 Smithe Street, at Seymour Street, Downtown (604 665 3050/www.city.vancouver.bc.ca/theatres). All city-centre buses. **No credit cards.** **Map** p249 K4.
Once the largest theatre on North America's Pacific Coast, this is an incredible venue for a live rock show. While unassuming from the exterior, inside its vaulted ceiling, ornate chandelier and gilded decor often rival stage performers for the audience's attention. The Orpheum is the permanent home of the Vancouver Symphony Orchestra but the room's acoustics lend themselves well to any style of music, though a lack of resonance means it's not great for soloists and smaller choirs. For these lower-volume performances, try to sit centre balcony, just behind the dress circle, for the best sound. *Photo p159.*

Queen Elizabeth Theatre

600 Hamilton Street, at W Georgia Street, Downtown (604 665 3050/www.city.vancouver. bc.ca/theatres). All city-centre buses/SkyTrain Stadium. **No credit cards.** **Map** p249 L4.
Built in 1959 by the City of Vancouver, the 2,900-person capacity Queen E is the home of Vancouver Opera and Ballet British Columbia (*see p171*). Its somewhat uneven acoustics are compensated for by a good sound system, but rock shows struggle to create any real atmosphere. However, the theatre is gradually being redeveloped, which will result in improvements to acoustics and sightlines.

Bars & clubs

The majority of the city's venues are located in the downtown core or downtown East Side. With the possible exceptions of the Cobalt, the Railway Club and the Yale, venues in Vancouver don't tend to have 'regular' patrons. The ambiance is largely dictated by the bands that are playing and the crowd they draw. The music scene is in a constant state of flux and venues have a nasty habit of changing formats (or simply closing) on a whim. It's highly advisable to consult local listings before venturing out.

Cobalt

917 Main Street, at Prior Street, East Vancouver (604 764 7865/www.thecobalt.net). Bus 3, 8, 19, N8, N19/SkyTrain Main Street-Science World. **Open** 5pm-1am daily. **Admission** free-$15. **No credit cards. Map** p249 N4.
The Cobalt's call for bands explicitly reads: 'Heavy shit preferred'. Managed by local legend Wendy Thirteen, the venue can accommodate 200 concert-goers and is the destination of choice if you prefer your music punishing and filed under punk, metal or hardcore. The decor is suitably decrepit and the drinks are undeniably cheap. Regular events include Scaryoke, experimental Fake Jazz Wednesdays and an alternative comedy night.

The fab **Commodore Ballroom**. *See p162.*

Railway Club.

Commodore Ballroom

868 Granville Street, between Robson & Smithe Streets, Downtown (604 739 7469/www.hob.com/ venues/concerts/commodore). All city-centre buses. **Open** phone for details. **Admission** $10-$50. **Credit** AmEx, DC, MC, V. **Map** p249 K4.

Located in the heart of downtown, the Commodore is the music scene's crown jewel. Having recently celebrated its 75th birthday, the 900-capacity venue has a renowned history and has staged early career shows by seminal bands such as Talking Heads, the Clash and Nirvana. As such, its closure for two years in the '90s marked the darkest hour for live music in the city. After a $3.5m makeover, it was relaunched in 1999, although the redevelopment robbed the art deco room of some of its charm. Nevertheless, it remains the principal destination for all varieties of high-calibre touring acts and rightfully so. The room's sound system is excellent and its layout offers an abundance of vantage points. Limited table seating with food service can be pre-booked. *Photo p161.*

Hoko Sushi Karaoke Bar

362 Powell Street, between Gore & Dunlevy Avenues, East Vancouver (604 685 4656/www.myspace.com/ hokos). Bus 4, 7, 10, 16, 20, N20. **Open** 6pm-2am daily. **Admission** free-$10. **Credit** DC, MC, V. **Map** p249 N3.

After traipsing through one of worst areas of town, you'll find yourself in Vancouver's most hospitable venue. The 100-seat hideaway regularly welcomes local indie bands to its miniscule corner stage. While the sushi and sound quality is average at best, the cover charge is cheap, the ambience is unique and you can even croon karaoke between acts.

The Media Club

695 Cambie Street, at W Georgia Street, Downtown (604 608 2871/www.themediaclub.ca). Bus 15, N15/ SkyTrain Stadium. **Open** check website for details. **Admission** free-$20. **Credit** MC, V. **Map** p249 L4.

A variety of promoters keep the Media Club teeming with an eclectic array of bands, including some well-regarded touring acts, every night of the week. One of the city's better small venues (a capacity of 150), the room boasts a simple design and friendly staff but is not without its failings. An undersized sound system and barely-raised stage don't always befit the calibre of entertainment. The poor acoustics and sightlines sometimes result in an easily distracted audience whose nattering then threatens to drown out the performers.

Pat's Pub & Brewhouse

403 E Hastings Street, at Dunlevy Avenue, East Vancouver (604 255 4301/www.patspub.ca). Bus 3, 10, 16, 20, N20, N35. **Open** 11am-midnight Mon-Thur; 11am-1am Fri, Sat; 11am-11pm Sun. **Admission** free-$15. **No credit cards**.

Despite being pretty much devoid of ambience or any of the other traits commonly found in a quality venue, tiny Pat's Pub occasionally serves up some of the city's most influential showcases of local talent. On the right night, every hipster in Vancouver will be present and accounted for.

Plaza Club

881 Granville Street, between Robson & Smithe Streets, Downtown (604 646 0064/www.plaza club.net). All city-centre buses/SkyTrain Granville. **Open** 9pm-3am daily. **Admission** $4-$30. **Credit** DC, MC, V. **Map** p249 K3.

Arts & Entertainment

Relatively new to live music, the 500-capacity Plaza has quickly become a prime destination for touring bands. Hype-laden indie acts can be found here several nights a week and the club also hosts a weekly showcase for local bands. A little too much of the venue's floor space is dedicated to an awkwardly situated central bar but an expansive balcony affords additional seating. Adorned in neon and chrome (and saddled with high beverage prices), the club doesn't boast much character but it consistently delivers the goods in terms of live music. *See also p165.*

Pub 340

340 Cambie Street, at W Hastings Street, Downtown (604 602 0644). Bus 4, 7, 10, 16, 20, N20, N35/ SkyTrain Stadium. **Open** 9am-midnight Mon-Wed; 9am-3am Thur, Fri; 11am-3am Sat; 11am-midnight Sun. **Admission** free-$8. **Credit** AmEx, DC, MC, V. **Map** p249 L3.

An unambitious, lower-rung venue, Pub 340 rarely receives any attention from influential promoters. So, more often than not, the 110-capacity room is host to local high-volume rock and punk acts recognisable to few other than their friends and family. However, to its credit, the bar does have friendly staff and a variety of food and drink specials.

Railway Club

579 Dunsmuir Street, at Seymour Street, Downtown (604 681 1625/www.therailwayclub.com). All city-centre buses. **Open** noon-2am Mon-Thur; noon-3am Fri; 2pm-3am Sat; 4pm-midnight Sun. **Admission** free-$12. **Credit** AmEx, DC, MC, V. **Map** p249 L3.

Simply put, the Railway Club is the best small venue in the city. Its capacity listing of 175 will reduce many a regular to knowing laughter. On a busy night (and there are many), the upstairs hangout is crammed wall-to-wall with sweaty patrons. Featuring three rooms, two miniature railroads and a kitchen that's open late, the club has been in operation since the 1930s and is steeped in local lore. Amicable employees lend the venue a neighbourhood pub ambience. Always eager to champion roots, folk and solo artists, the club also regularly opens its stage to both touring and local indie acts. A drunken sing-along is held on the first Monday of every month.

Red Room on Richards

398 Richards Street, between W Cordova & W Hastings Streets, Downtown (604 687 5007/ www.redroomonrichards.com). All city-centre buses/ SkyTrain Waterfront. **Open** 9pm-2am Mon-Thur, Sun; 9pm-3am Fri, Sat. **Admission** $10-$30. **Credit** AmEx, DC, MC, V. **Map** p249 L3.

The Red Room suffers from being promoters' third choice when it comes to venues of its size (400-capacity). As the staff aren't accustomed to hosting performances and live music fans aren't overly familiar with the venue, shows here tend to lack atmosphere. However, the room's functional layout and excellent sound quality ensure that it will continue to be used on a part-time basis for housing some prominent touring acts.

Richard's On Richards

1036 Richards Street, between Nelson & Helmcken Streets, Yaletown (604 687 6794/ www.richardsonrichards.com). Bus 20, all city-centre buses, then 5min walk. **Open** phone for details. **Admission** $12-$35. **Credit** DC, MC, V. **Map** p249 K4.

Having recently received a reprieve from the wrecking ball, Richard's will continue to serve as Vancouver's preeminent mid-sized venue (400-capacity) for another few years yet. Formerly a reluctant host to infrequent (and ungodly early) live shows, the club has since changed its focus and developed into one of the busiest venues in the city. Commonly cited by local musicians as their favourite room to play, Richard's regularly welcomes premier touring acts from every musical genre. The sound quality is always near perfect and the room's horseshoe design and balcony allow for an intimate atmosphere to be created regardless of the crowd size.

Royal Unicorn Cabaret

147 E Pender Street, between Main & Columbia Streets, Chinatown (604 961 5122). Bus 3, 8, 19, 22, N8, N19. **Open** phone for details. **Admission** $5-$15. **No credit cards. Map** p249 M4.

After establishing itself as a home for hipster club nights, this 205-capacity Chinatown club has recently begun hosting local rock and indie shows. It is still finding its form in this new capacity, but the promising venue boasts an excellent stage and sound system. With a selection of committed promoters already backing it, this could easily become a key fixture on the live music scene.

Yale

1300 Granville Street, at Drake Street, Downtown (604 681 9253/www.theyale.ca). Bus 4, 6, 7, 8, 10, 16, 17, 50, N17. **Open** 11.30am-2am Mon-Thur, Sun; 11.30am-3am Fri, Sat. **Admission** free-$30. **Credit** AmEx, DC, MC, V. **Map** p248 J4.

This 300-capacity bar pledges, 'If they're legends, they've played the Yale.' It's possible that the term 'legends' is being used rather liberally but it remains the only room in the city committed to booking blues artists on a regular basis. With live music every night, it's often the sole recourse for fans of traditional R&B.

Jazz

In Vancouver's cosy jazz world, a sprinkling of performance venues throughout the city support an intimate scene that's heavily influenced by the free jazz of late-era John Coltrane. Free jazz and improv bigwigs usually perform here to small houses of enthusiasts, and Vancouver plays low-key host to many of the same talents that sell out Amsterdam's Icebreaker and the Knitting Factory in New York. Local names to watch for include Coat Cooke and the NOW Orchestra, Francois Houle,

Arts & Entertainment

Unpretentious jazz joint **1067** is a real find (if you can find it).

John Korsrud, Peggy Lee and Dylan van der Schyff. Along more traditional lines, Oliver Gannon, Brad Turner and Sharon Minemoto are all standouts. Each summer, the **Coastal Jazz and Blues Society** (604 872 5200, www.coastaljazz.ca) puts on a two-week jazz festival featuring a bit of everything, from mainstream to free jazz.

For details on purchasing concert tickets, see p158. Detailed information on the local jazz scene, including links and listings, can be found at www.vancouverjazz.com.

1067

1067 Granville Street, at Helmcken Street, Downtown (www.myspace.com/1067granville). All city-centre buses. **Open** check website for show times. **Admission** $6. **No credit cards**. **Map** p248 J4.

If you can find it, the cavern-like space at 1067 (off the westward alley behind Granville Street) is a beatnik throwback that provides long, sometimes smoky evenings of everything from electro-acoustic honk-and-squeak to dazzlingly adept bebop.

The Cellar

3611 W Broadway, between Dunbar & Alma Streets, West Side (604 738 1959/www.cellarjazz. com). Bus 9, 17, 99, N9, N17. **Open** 6pm-midnight Mon, Wed; 6.30pm-midnight Tue; 7pm-midnight Thur-Sat. **Admission** free-$20. **Credit** AmEx, DC, MC, V. **Map** p251 B6.

More traditional jazz notes – by some of the city's best, including Brad Turner and Seamus Blake –

are heard at the Cellar, a restaurant and jazz club with sets six nights weekly at 8.30pm and 10pm.

Lime

1130 Commercial Drive, between William & Napier Streets, East Vancouver (604 215 1130/ www.rime.ca). Bus 20, N20. **Open** 5pm-1am Mon-Sat; 5pm-midnight Sun. **Admission** $5-$10. **Credit** AmEx, DC, MC, V.

This small restaurant (formerly Rime) is the most talked-about new venue in Vancouver, serving up live music almost every afternoon and evening, along with delicious Japanese cuisine; its programming includes some of the best improv and free jazz around.

O'Doul's Restaurant & Bar

1300 Robson Street, at Jervis Street, West End (604 661 1400/www.odoulsrestaurant.com). Bus 5, N6. **Open** 6.30am-1am Mon-Fri; 7am-1am Sat; 7am-midnight Sun. **Admission** free-$10. **Credit** AmEx, DC, MC, V. **Map** p248 J2.

Fabulous food and accomplished cool jazz on Vancouver's downtown shopping street. Sharon Minemoto's smooth, understated trio features here every Monday at 8pm.

Rossini's Kits Beach

1525 Yew Street, at Cornwall Avenue, West Side (604 737 8080/www.rossinis.bc.ca). Bus 2, 22, N22. **Open** 11am-2am daily. **Admission** free-$25. **Credit** AmEx, DC, MC, V. **Map** p251 F5.

You'll have to cut through the haze generated by the smouldering glances of amorous patrons at this fortysomething pick-up spot, but the reward is consistently good mainstream jazz.

Nightclubs

It's an underground and cyber world out there and no one seems to know it more than DJs and club kids. The best dance happenings don't take place in clubs and they're not promoted in mainstream media – you have to be 'on the list' to find out about them. But the most exciting roving-venue dub/jungle/grime dance producers on the planet might just be the city's Lighta! Sound crew – and most of their events are posted at www.myspace.com/lightasound. All the same, Vancouver's dance club scene is well worth a look; this is where house heavyweights Luke McKeehan and Tyler Stadius earned their international reputations and some of the city's top talents take weekly residencies. Vancouver also regularly attracts touring DJs; the most popular take over the Commodore Ballroom or pack out the Plaza. For comprehensive club happenings, log onto Clubvibes (www.clubvibes.com) or ClubZone (www.clubzone.com), or check out the Georgia Straight, Vancouver's free entertainment weekly.

Dance clubs along Granville Street, Vancouver's 'Entertainment District', draw a weekend crowd of flashy rowdies. Looking for good-looking company? Cruise Caprice Night Club (965 Granville Street, 604 681 2114), Tonic (919 Granville Street, 604 699 0469), Bar None (1222 Hamilton Street, 604 689 7000) and Au Bar (674 Seymour Street, 604 648 2227). Meanwhile, for their commitment to progressive music, courteous and unpretentious staff, and cool clientele, herewith, six choice clubs for your boogie-down pleasure.

Atlantis

1320 Richards Street, between Drake & Pacific Streets, Yaletown (604 662 7707/www.atlantis club.net). Bus 4, 7, 10, 16, 17, 50, N9, N10, N17. **Open** 9pm-2am Mon-Thur; 9.30pm-2am Fri, Sat. **Admission** $8-$14. **No credit cards**. DC, MC, V. **Map** p248 J5.
This colossus of a club boasts a $1.5-million light system, VIP area and eight bars (one for each drink!). The lavish visuals alone are worth the trip: the dancefloor is embedded with lights and surrounded by video screens featuring sultry imagery.

Fabric

66 Water Street, at Abbott Street, Gastown (604 683 6695/www.fabricvancouver.com/www.clubzone.com). Bus 4, 7, 8, 50, N20. **Open** 9pm-2am Thur; 9pm-3am Fri, Sat. **Admission** $10-$15. *Special events* $25-$50. **No credit cards**. **Map** p249 M3.
Audiophiles will appreciate the sound system in this two-room Gastown institution (the former Sonar), where some of the city's finest spinners play different flavours nightly and host international guests on an almost weekly basis. A fave venue for break-dance crews, the floor often gives way to headspinners circled by cheering b-boys and girls.

Lotus Sound Lounge

Lotus Hotel, 455 Abbott Street, at W Pender Street, Downtown (604 685 7777/www.lotussoundlounge. com). Bus 10, 16, 20, N20, N35. **Open** 9pm-3am Wed-Sat. **Admission** $5-$12. **Credit** DC, MC, V. **Map** p249 M3.
On Fridays, this subterranean club fills with young creatives sweating the week's worries away in a dark but friendly environment. Lotus is known for progressive house and techno, but Wednesday's indie dance-rock night with DJs Robin Banks, Snailrider and Morgan Muffler might be the club's biggest night. A bonus: should you get bored, you can always check out Lick (*see p157*), a womyn-friendly scene, and Honey, all chandeliers and red velvet (and mod music on Fridays) – both residing in the same hotel.

The Modern

7 Alexander Street, at Carrall Street, Gastown (604 647 0121/www.dhmbars.ca). Bus 50. **Open** 9pm-2am Thur; 10pm-3am Fri, Sat. **Admission** $5-$15. **Credit** AmEx, DC, MC, V. **Map** p249 M3.
One of Vancouver's newest dance clubs is a stunning update of the classic discotheque, with '80s-inspired neon lines and countless mirrors. Baby Grand Fridays lays on the funk, rare grooves, soul and hip hop, while This Is Not Detroit Saturdays features the talents of Jay Tripwire and DJ Timeline – two top house talents no doubt lured here by the ultra-swank sound system. Oh, and, dress to impress; strict dress code in effect.

Plaza Club

881 Granville Street, between Robson & Smithe Streets, Downtown (604 646 0064/www.plazaclub. net). All city-centre buses. **Open** 9pm-3am daily. **Admission** $4-$30. **Credit** DC, MC, V. **Map** p249 K3.
This upscale (read: dress code in effect) dance club drops everything from hip hop, R&B, top 40, dance techno and house music in an 8,000sq ft (740sq m) space complete with an oval bar and elevated DJ booth. The second level is more intimate, complete with leather armchairs and its own bar. DJs J-Swing and Flipout take the decks Wednesday for an electric trip through Brit pop, hip hop and current dancefloor hits. *See also p162.*

Shine

364 Water Street, at Richards Street, Gastown (604 408 4321/www.shinenightclub.com). Bus 4, 7, 8, 50, N20. **Open** 10pm-2am Mon-Thur, Sun; 10pm-3am Fri, Sat. **Admission** $5-$12. **Credit** AmEx, DC, MC, V. **Map** p249 L3.
Another venue that offers nightly genre specials (the pinnacle of which is Saturday's Big Sexy Funk), Shine attracts plenty of talented DJs. The vibe is more flirt party to great music than globally-conscious club action. This sleek, double room sounds fresh (think soul through breaks) and looks great, populated by a young, happy crowd. Nice staff, good drink prices.

Arts & Entertainment

Performing Arts

Vancouver in the cultural vanguard.

Theatre

'Vancouver is now the place to be,' says Ken Cameron, artistic director of the Magnetic North Theatre Festival, an annual showcase of English-Canadian theatre based in Ottawa (but held in a different city every other year; 2008 brings it to Vancouver). 'The spotlight shines on a different scene in Canada every decade and now it's Vancouver. There's some great site-specific work and there's a real avant-garde.'

Nevertheless, there's a lingering feeling in Vancouver that the performing arts is engaged in a losing battle with the natural beauty surrounding the city. How can theatre compete with the thrill of night skiing on the slopes on the North Shore mountains or distract an audience entranced by driftwood bumping along a dope-hazed nudist beach? In two ways, it turns out: lock yourself in a black box to create raw excitement, or step outside to create trippy environmental work.

The **Electric Company** (*see p167*), **Boca del Lupo** (*see p167*) and the **Only Animal** (www.theonlyanimal.com) have been especially successful in the site-specific arena. These companies are also part of an 11-company co-operative known as **Progress Lab**, which produced the phenomenally successful **HIVE** 'theatre installation' in 2006 and will create a second edition in June 2008 as part of the **Magnetic North Theatre Festival** in Vancouver (*see p167* **The buzz**). Olympic cash will also tempt Vancouver's best theatre-makers as 2010 approaches – and hopefully they'll make off with some loot without their work getting watered down.

The major employers in Vancouver – the Arts Club, the Playhouse and Bard on the Beach – thankfully retain the city's senior talent and offer up breaks to emerging artists. Collectively, they create a half-dozen of the best shows in any given season but many would say that hefty marketing, corporate sponsorship and the weight of their history help maintain their position.

Commercial theatre has had somewhat of a rough ride in Vancouver, as the number of touring productions (which usually land at the Queen Elizabeth Theatre) have dropped off in recent years. The short history of the former Livent venue, now known as the **Centre in Vancouver for the Performing Arts** (*see p168*), offers a crude case study in the realities facing extended-run commercial theatre in a city large enough to support it but too culturally fragmented to create a critical-mass audience.

In the national or international context, there are still no mid-sized theatre companies in Vancouver, although **Touchstone Theatre** (*see p168*), a well-established producer of 'essential Canadian plays' comes close. There are half a dozen companies that should be at this level but their efforts have been stymied by a lack of provincial and federal funding. The result is that the action is disproportionately happening at small theatre level – companies that produce plays in venues of 100 to 250 seats. One of those is a local gem known as the **Vancouver East Cultural Centre** (*see p170*), just off the vibrant Commercial Drive. The 'Cultch' hosts a savvy programme of national and international touring companies and local companies, as well as dance and music events.

In 1997, five small, established companies formed the **See Seven** subscription series. It has become the best deal in town for well-crafted contemporary work. The founders – Felix Culpa, Pi Theatre, Ruby Slippers, Rumble Productions and Theatre Conspiracy – form the foundation of a sharply curated line-up, along with Touchstone, Solo Collective and emerging bright lights like Horseshoes & Handgrenades. Visit www.seeseven.bc.ca for the current line-up.

FESTIVALS

Vancouver's theatre scene is augmented by three important festivals: the popular **Bard on the Beach Shakespeare Festival** (*see p138*) occupies two large tents in Vanier Park through the summer months; the **Vancouver International Fringe Festival** (*see p141*) offers nearly a hundred shows in a couple of weeks at the beginning of September; and the **PuSh International Performing Arts Festival** (*see p141*), which has expanded theatrical horizons in the city enormously in the past five years, bringing a mid-winter spark to the scene with a smart collection of international, national and local shows in January.

(side tab) Arts & Entertainment

TICKETS AND INFORMATION

Most performances are at 8pm Tuesday to Saturday, with 2pm matinees on Saturday and/or Sunday and (at the Playhouse and Arts Club) on Wednesdays. Tuesday evening is often a half-price or pay-what-you-can performance. Many shows can be seen for $12 and tickets in Vancouver tend to max out at about $70.

Individual box office information is provided here by venue but most companies sell some tickets through **Ticketmaster** (Pacific Centre Lottery, 701 W Georgia Street, Downtown, 604 280 3311, www.ticketmaster.ca) or **TicketsTonight** (booth in the Touristinfo Centre near Canada Place, Plaza Level, 200 Burrard Street, 604 684 2787, www.tickets tonight.ca, closed Mon & Sun), which also offers half-price tickets to many theatre productions (and other entertainment events).

Reviews and previews appear regularly in print and online in the daily *Vancouver Sun* and the *Province*, as well as the *Globe & Mail* and the weekly *Georgia Straight*, *WestEnder* and *Vancouver Courier*. UBC theatre prof and *Province* critic Jerry Wasserman posts valuable upcoming notes and a review archive at www.vancouverplays.com.

Companies

Boca del Lupo
604 684 2622/www.bocadellupo.com.
Boca del Lupo's brilliantly inventive free shows in Stanley Park old growth (some scenes are, literally, up in the trees) or under the Burrard Street Bridge are family favourites every summer.

Electric Company Theatre
604 253 4222/www.electriccompanytheatre.com.
The marvellous inventions of Jonathon Young, Kim Collier, David Hudgins and playwright Kevin Kerr (who, collectively, create most of the shows) are rightly popular with Vancouverites. They make a leap to the big stage in 2009 with an Arts Club commission for the Stanley Theatre, inspired by the vaudeville-era building itself.

Leaky Heaven Circus
604 488 0003/www.leakyheaven.com.
Stephen Hill combined commedia and circus arts to create a hit crazy Christmas show for kids, before moving on to a wicked cabaret version of *Solome and Blink*, a collection of pieces of one minute or less, seemingly inspired by the Malcolm Gladwell book.

Neworld Theatre
604 602 0007/www.neworldtheatre.com.
Neworld's adaptations, from Persian folk tales to James Fagan Tait's retrofit of *Crime and Punishment*, and the hilariously scathing satire *The Adventures of Ali & Ali and the Axes of Evil*, have brought the company national attention and due respect at home.

The buzz

In a former funeral home that shares a block with one of the busiest prostitute strolls in the city's Downtown Eastside, 11 independent companies created **HIVE**, the theatrical sensation of 2006. Essentially, it was a big party bent on stretching the conceptual limits of theatre. The coalition, known as Progress Lab, applied Dogme-like obstructions on the works – performances of no more than ten minutes for an audience of ten or fewer people and a budget of not more than $3,000. **Neworld Theatre** (*see left*) created a play in the embalming room; **Theatre Conspiracy** (*see p168*) produced a three-way peep show in the reception area; and **Felix Culpa** (www.felixculpa. bc.ca) enacted the fall of Troy with toy dolls. Other players included **Electric Company** and **Leaky Heaven Circus** (for both, *see left*), as well as **Theatre Replacement** (*see p168*).

Georgia Straight theatre critic Colin Thomas called his trip to HIVE 'the most exciting night Vancouver theatre has seen in decades.' With a hefty grant from an Olympic-related funding pool, Progress Lab is planning a second ten-day edition of HIVE (though it may be titled something else) to be held in a suitably unusual venue during the **Magnetic North Theatre Festival** (4-14 June 2008).
● *Tap into www.buzzbuzzbuzz.ca or www.magneticnorthfestival.ca for details.*

Pi Theatre
604 872 1861/www.pitheatre.com.
Formed as Pink Ink in 1984, the company became Pi in 1999 under artistic director Del Surjik. Expect polished English-language versions of Québécois plays and international works, such as Mark Ravenhill's *Shopping and Fucking*.

Playhouse Theatre Company
600 block of Hamilton Street, at Dunsmuir Street, Downtown (604 873 3311/www.vancouver playhouse.com). Bus 17/SkyTrain Stadium. **Open** 9.30am-8pm Mon-Fri; noon-4pm Sat. **Tickets** $33-$63; $20 rush tickets 15mins before showtime. **Credit** AmEx, DC, MC, V. **Map** p249 L4.
For 42 years, the Playhouse produced a balanced programme of classics, recent hits from the world stage and Canadian plays – the traditional mandate of the nation's regional theatres. In its prime, the Playhouse had a 12-show season; but that has now shrunk to five productions. Still, Playhouse

shows are usually well-directed and well designed, with casts featuring the finest national and local talent. Robert Lepage's *The Far Side of the Moon* and *The Anderson Project* were hosted by the Playhouse recently. The productions are staged in a downtown theatre also named the Playhouse, although the 700-seat venue is a city-owned property also used for concerts and dance events. After the 2010 games, the Playhouse will move to a new production centre in False Creek South, site of the Olympic Village. The facility will house a brand new 240-seat second stage and a bar.

Ruby Slippers Theatre
604 602 0585/www.rubyslippers.ca.
Diane Brown produces and directs smart, stylish productions of dark Canadian comedies such as Claudia Dey's *Trout Stanley* and presents choice picks of up-and-coming national acts.

Rumble Productions
604 662 3395/www.rumble.org.
Billed as Vancouver's 'all-terrain theatre vehicle', this baby's an energy-efficient hybrid with power to burn. Guiding light Norman Armour moved on to the PuSh Festival (*see p141*), but Craig Hall recently picked up the ball to devise Tremors, a spring showcase/party for emerging companies from across the country.

Theatre Conspiracy
604 878 8668/www.conspiracy.ca.
Artistic producer Richard Wolfe often produces the Canadian premiere of such critically lauded world stage work as *Closer*, *A Skull in Connemara* and *Stupidity (La Estupidez)*. Conspiracy also creates original work – the dystopian thriller *Omniscience*, for example – and high-octane cabarets.

Théâtre la Seizième
604 736 2616/www.seizieme.ca.
Théâtre la Seizième produces highly regarded French-language theatre for both adults and children. The 100-seat theatre in the French Cultural Centre is also used by independents.

Theatre Replacement
604 780 4084/www.theatrereplacement.org.
Perhaps the strongest new voice to emerge on the Vancouver scene in the past five years. Creators James Long and Maiko Bae Yamamoto join forces with top local collaborators to make elemental stage works that push the boundaries of genre. A collection of short pieces in the 2007 hit *Bioboxes* placed a single audience member in a theatre 'box' worn on the shoulders of a single actor.

Touchstone Theatre
604 709 9973/www.touchstonetheatre.com.
A cornerstone of the scene for 30 years, Touchstone produces 'essential Canadian plays' such as Kevin Kerr's *Unity (1918)*, which won the Governor General's award (the nation's top play award) in 2002. Well-produced, high-quality shows.

Theatre for young audiences

As well as the **Carousel Theatre** (*see below*), the **Green Thumb Theatre** (604 254 4055, www.greenthumb.bc.ca), **Axis Theatre** (604 669 0631, www.axistheatre.com) and **Théâtre la Seizième** (*see above*) all create world-class shows for children, focusing most of their attention on school tours, but all present shows in theatres from time to time. The Axis mime-and-mask show, *The Number 14*, which turns up regularly at the Arts Club, is a must-see for all ages.

Carousel Theatre
604 685 6217/www.carouseltheatre.ca.
Carousel Theatre produces full-length plays, with high production values, focusing on recent adaptations of classics like *Silverwing*, *The Odyssey* and *Seussical (the Musical)*. The company regularly packs the Waterfront Theatre (Festival House, 1412 Cartwright Street, 604 685 1731, www.gicultural society.org) on Granville Island.

Venues

Arts Club Theatre
1585 Johnston Street, Granville Island (box office 604 687 1644/office 604 687 5315/www.artsclub. com). Bus 50. **Open** 10am-showtime; noon-5pm Sun. **Tickets** $33-$46; $30-$42 reductions. **Credit** AmEx, DC, MC, V. **Map** p250 B2.
The Arts Club operates three separate venues, programming its own productions at the popular Stanley Industrial Alliance Stage (*see p169*), the Granville Island Stage (*see p169*) and the Revue Stage, which is also home to the Vancouver TheatreSports League (*see p170*).

Centre in Vancouver for the Performing Arts
777 Homer Street, between Robson & W Georgia Streets, Downtown (604 602 0616/www.centrein vancouver.com). Bus 17. **Open** Box office 2hrs before showtime. **Tickets** $30-$70. **Credit** AmEx, DC, MC, V. **Map** p249 K3.
So much trouble in so few years. Designed by Moshe Safdie, this 1,850-seat, $27-million venue opened as the Ford Theatre in 1995, as part of Garth Drabinsky's chain for Livent musicals. It closed in 1998 as Livent's financial troubles had Drabinsky spending more time with lawyers than artists. The Ford remained dark until a quartet of Hong Kong-born, Denver-based doctors, the Law bothers, bought the theatre for the firesale price of $7 million. Dennis Law's idea was to wow Vancouver's Asian audiences, as well as regular theatregoers, by creating 'action musicals': spectaculars steeped in (mainly) Chinese tradition, with dance, music and martial arts all to be illuminated by the Centre's state-of-the-art technology. The plan met with limited success and now it's mainly a roadhouse for

The **Granville Island Stage** is just one of the venues the **Arts Club Theatre** calls home.

touring productions such as *Stomp* or headline musical acts from Laurie Anderson and David Byrne to John Legend and Joshua Redman.

Firehall Arts Centre

280 E Cordova Street, at Gore Avenue, East Vancouver (604 689 0926/www.firehallartscentre.ca). Bus 4, 7. **Open** 9.30am-5pm Mon-Fri & 1hr before show. **Tickets** $20-$28; $16-$24 reductions. **Credit** AmEx, DC, MC, V. **Map** p249 N3.

Built in 1906, this ex-firehall was transformed into a lively theatre in 1982. The centre's programme leans towards work that's relevant to its Downtown Eastside location – from the breakthrough Canadian play *The Ecstacy of Rita Joe* by George Ryga to works by contemporary First Nations playwrights such as Drew Hayden Taylor or a hit production of *Urinetown*. The Firehall's a favourite venue for smaller professional companies as well.

Granville Island Stage

For listings, see p168 Arts Club Theatre.

The Arts Club was originally a loose collection of like-minded artists running a converted downtown gospel hall in the 1960s and '70s. Director Bill Millerd deftly moved it to touristy Granville Island in 1979 and then boosted prestige further with the conversion of the beautiful 1930s vintage Stanley Theatre in 1998. Today the Arts Club is Vancouver's unrivalled theatre machine. However, quality is still erratic, lurching from exquisitely designed and acted showpieces to under-rehearsed clunkers. One writer to look out for is Morris Panych (*7 Stories*, *Vigil*).

The ten to 12 shows each year range from Disney's *Beauty and the Beast* to *The Glass Menagerie* to a regional hit like David Lindsay-Abaire's *The Rabbit Hole*. The Stage boasts the Arts Club Backstage Lounge, one of the city's best waterfront outdoor patios, featuring a solid lineup of live music in the evenings, beer specials and pub food.

Pacific Theatre

1440 W 12th Avenue, between Granville & Hemlock Streets, West Side (604 731 5518/www.pacific theatre.org). Bus 9, 10. **Open** noon-7pm Tue-Sat & 1hr before show; noon-5pm wks with no shows. **Tickets** $17-$28; $8-$21 reductions. **Credit** DC, MC, V. **Map** p251 H7.

Pacific Theatre, a 125-seat alley configuration in the basement of Holy Trinity Anglican Church, pro-grammes work focused on ethical and spiritual issues by emerging locals, as well as literary greats like CS Lewis and Athol Fugard.

Queen Elizabeth Theatre

For listings, see p161.

Home to Ballet BC and Vancouver Opera, as well as touring theatre productions and occasional rock shows, the QET has a wide proscenium stage in the modern civic style of the late 1950s.

Stanley Industrial Alliance Stage

2750 Granville Street, at W 12th Avenue, West Side (www.artsclub.com). Bus 10. **Open** (show days only) 4.30-8.15pm Tue-Fri; noon-8.15pm Wed, Sat; noon-5pm Sun. **Tickets** $43-$67; $33-$49 reductions. **Credit** AmEx, DC, MC, V. **Map** p251 H7.

Arts & Entertainment

This theatre on the West Side occupies a beautifully renovated art deco cinema and is one of the Arts Club Theatre's (*see p168*) three venues.

Vancouver East Cultural Centre

1895 Venables Street, at Victoria Drive, East Vancouver (604 251 1363/www.vecc.bc.ca). Bus 20. **Open** 10am-5pm Mon-Fri & 1hr before show. **Tickets** $15-$30. **Credit** AmEx, DC, MC, V.

No venue in the city has the committed audience that the 'Cultch' has cultivated. The former Unitarian church, built in 1909, has been a 250-seat theatre, dance and music venue since 1973. The place was saved from financial ruin in the '90s and now Heather Redfern programmes an ambitious collection of touring shows and top-of-the-line independent work. Renovations, which will see the opening of a new 100-seat studio in 2008, continue until 2010.

Comedy

Due to a severe lack of appropriate clubs, almost all comedy in Vancouver takes place in restaurants and bars. Stand-up and improv dominate the scene but a growing sketch presence and overlapping burlesque and spoken-word scenes are making themselves felt. The free weekly *Georgia Straight* is the only publication that regularly covers comedy acts – however, for up-to-the-minute comedy listings, your best bet is to visit www.comedycouch.com.

Global ComedyFest

604 685 0881/www.comedyfest.com. Venues: River Rock Casino (8811 River Road, Richmond), Yuk Yuk's (see p171) & other downtown clubs. **Dates** mid Sept.

Vancouver's comedy festival has undergone massive revisions in recent years, with venues and acts getting progressively larger – big names like Stephen Wright, Scott Thompson, Mike Milmot and the rising stars of the US talk-show circuit are inspiring worries that local talent is getting nudged out.

Lafflines

26 4th Street, at Columbia Street, New Westminster (604 525 2262/www.lafflines.com). SkyTrain Columbia. **Shows** phone for times. **Tickets** $10-$15. **Credit** AmEx, DC, MC, V.

An appropriately energetic architectural design announces the **Scotiabank Dance Centre**.

A quick SkyTrain ride gets you to this popular suburban room featuring Grade A locals such as Roman Danylo and rising stars from the North American circuit. Thursday shows are sporadic, so call ahead.

Laugh Gallery

Lime, 1130 Commercial Drive, at William Street, East Vancouver (604 215 1130/thelaughgallery. blogspot.com). Bus 20. **Shows** 9.30pm Wed. **Tickets** $5. **Credit** AmEx, DC, MC, V.

Hosted by stand-up comic Graham Clark, this show is the antithesis to a standard comedy club: you'll hear no lame musings on how men and women are different. Clark gives away crazy prizes between the highly varied but always semi-alternative acts.

Vancouver TheatreSports League

Arts Club Theatre's New Revue Stage, 1601 Johnston Street, Granville Island (604 738 7013/ www.vtsl.com). Bus 50. **Shows** 7.30pm Wed; 7.30pm, 9.15 pm Thur; 8pm, 10pm & 11.45pm Fri, Sat. **Tickets** $10.50-$16.50. **Credit** AmEx, DC, MC, V. **Map** p250 B2.

TheatreSports' shows do boffo box office. It has something for all tastes from *The Improvised Works of Bill Shakespeare* (where a little literacy goes a long way) to the Friday and Saturday Extreme Improv nights (where literacy would only hamper your experience). The 8pm shows are two-for-one on Wednesdays.

Yuk Yuk's

Century Plaza Hotel, 1015 Burrard Street, at Nelson Street, Downtown (604 696 9857/www.yukyuks. com). Bus 2, 22. **Shows** 8.30pm Tue-Thur; 8pm & 10.30pm Fri, Sat. **Tickets** $5-$18. **Credit** AmEx, DC, MC, V. **Map** p248 J4.

High-profile comics including Mike Wilmot and Emo Philips make Yuk Yuk's their Vancouver stop, cementing its position as the town's top (and only) comedy venue. There's a corporate feel about the place – it's part of Mark Breslin's chain – but even shows early in the week approach capacity. Dinner packages also available.

Dance

Organisations in Vancouver's dance scene are not as well-heeled as they'd like to be, but check out the weekly listings in the *Georgia Straight* and you'll always find some independent experiment on the move. The Dance Centre, established in 1986, is home base for the community, offering education, performance space and workshops. You can't miss its glass headquarters, the Arthur Erickson-designed **Scotiabank Dance Centre** (677 Davie Street, 604 606 6400, www. thedancecentre.ca). The nexus of local dance creation, the building plays host to hundreds of companies that use their six studios (including favourites The Holy Body Tattoo).

November 2009 will see the next **Dance in Vancouver** festival, a biennial at the Dance Centre promoting local talent. Check out the website for the latest on its ongoing programmes, including the informal Discover Dance! noon sessions, one Thursday every month excluding December, from September to May. The Dance Centre's website will link you to the city's numerous festivals, including **Vancouver International Dance Festival** (604 662 7441, www.vidf.ca) in March, and **Dancing on the Edge** (604 689 0926, www.dancingontheedge.org) in early July.

Ballet British Columbia (604 732 5003, www.balletbc.com) provides the Vancouver's mandatory end-of-year *Nutcracker* ritual, and five other productions that run from September through April. It's led by talented director and choreographer John Alleyne. Tickets are available through Ticketmaster (*see p167*).

If you think you've got moves of your own, the **Harbour Dance Centre** (3rd Floor, 927 Granville Street, 604 684 9542, www. harbourdance.com) provides classes seven days a week in every style and for all levels.

Sport & Fitness

The lure of the great outdoors.

Vancouverites are obsessive when it comes to keeping fit, and who could blame them in such a fine natural playground? Within sweat-free reach, there are the mountains for hiking, biking and skiing, the Pacific Ocean for sailing, windsurfing and kayaking, and a vibrant city designed to be run, walked or bladed.

The average local trains for a minimum of three hours a week, but you'll find that's on the conservative side for many hardy Vancouverites, who'll be out there whatever the weather. As a visitor, it's easy to feel their energy for the great outdoors and even easier to join in the action. Rental equipment is widely available and the city paths are well mapped for cycling, blading or just plain walking around the waterfront. More organised runs (the Sun Run and Marathon; for both, see p138) are so scenic you're oblivious to the pain – well, almost. Forget lolling about on a beach: here locals de-stress with a game of volleyball after work (the posts are already set up and you can rent the nets; see p173) or dip into one of the city's outdoor swimming pools (see p180).

With six-packs and the body beautiful ubiquitous in Vancouver, only the weather holds this city back from having the élan of California or Hawaii. Remember, you will need to add taxes to most prices in BC, and for rentals – and some sports activities – you need a credit or debit card as a deposit, along with photo ID (passport/driver's licence).

Spectator sports

Most of Vancouver's home teams are pretty average, if we're honest, although that doesn't stop the locals passionately rooting for them. The notable exception is its hockey team, the Canucks, which usually offers a high-octane performance (with the all-important and highly entertaining sin bin for naughty players). The Canucks have also been contenders for the holy grail of their sport: the Stanley Cup. Don't expect to see any pro basketball in the city: the Vancouver Grizzlies relocated to Memphis a few years back, though UBC has a team.

For tickets, go through **Ticketmaster** (604 280 4400, www.ticketmaster.ca) or **Coast to Coast Tickets** (toll-free 866 800 2828, www.coasttocoasttickets.com), although some venues sell them at the door.

Baseball

Vancouver Canadians

Nat Bailey Stadium, 4601 Ontario Street, at 33rd Avenue, West Side (604 872 5232/www.canadians baseball.com). Bus 3, 15. **Open** 1pm afternoon game; 7pm evening game (phone to check game days). **Rates** $8-$12.50. **Credit** AmEx, DC, MC, V.
The Vancouver Canadians are the city's team in the Single-A Northwest League – against seven other groups – playing out of the dinky ballpark at Nat Bailey Stadium. Regular season is from June to September. At around the 7th inning stretch (out of nine), spectators go through the ritual of standing and stretching to music.

Football

BC Lions

BC Place Stadium, 777 Pacific Boulevard, between Griffiths Way & Terry Fox Way, Downtown (604 589 7627/www.bclions.com). Bus 15/SkyTrain Stadium. **Open** kick-off: 7.30pm June-Aug; 7pm Sept-Nov. **Rates** $27-$70. **Credit** AmEx, DC, MC, V. **Map** p249 L4.
Of course, we're not talking British footie – or real American Football for that matter. BC Lions is Vancouver's team in the Canadian Football League, with various differences to the game played in the US. The Lions have won four of the national competitions, the Grey Cup, as recently as 2000. The season runs from June until October.

Horse racing

Hastings Park

2901 E Hastings Street, at Renfrew Street, East Vancouver (604 254 1631/toll-free 800 677 7702/ www.hastingsracecourse.com). Bus 4, 10, 16, 44. Free shuttle bus every 30mins from SkyTrain Renfrew on race days only (see website for schedule & stops). **Open** 9am-11pm daily (until 3am on nights when it broadcasts live racing from Hong Kong). **Admission** free; $2 minimum bet. **No credit cards.**
This is no Epsom Derby, but it has to be one of the prettiest racecourses in the world. It's free, with thoroughbreds flat-racing on Saturdays and Sundays from April until November (and Friday afternoons from June to September), with the first gallop at 1.25pm until between 5pm and 6pm depending on the number of races on a given day (usually between eight and ten). Not everyone is here for the live geegees, however; Hastings Park

also televises races from across North America and around the world, and it's common for people to come here and not venture out to the track at all.

Ice hockey

Vancouver Canucks

GM Place, 800 Griffiths Way, at Pacific Boulevard, Downtown (604 899 7469/7444/www.canucks.com). SkyTrain Stadium. **Open** Face-off usually 7pm. **Rates** from $49.25. **Credit** AmEx, DC, MC, V. **Map** p249 L4.

Remember to call it just plain 'hockey'. The local team are thrilling to watch, with a hard and fast puck over the three time periods. The atmosphere's great in the 18,422-seat stadium but it's generally a lot more polite and less frenzied than a similar crowd playing elsewhere. The NHL season runs from September until April, and tickets tend to go quickly.

Soccer

Whitecaps Football Club

Swangard Stadium, at Kingsway & Boundary Road, Burnaby (604 669 9283/www.whitecapsfc.com). SkyTrain Patterson. **Open** kick-off usually 7pm. **Rates** $16-$35. **Credit** AmEx, DC, MC, V.

Previously known as the 86ers, the Whitecaps play soccer (football to the rest of the world) in retro jerseys in the USL A-League championship. The women's team is also worth catching.

Active sports & fitness

Beach volleyball

Posts are put up on beaches between Locarno/ Spanish Banks and Kitsilano on the Westside, and downtown at English Bay in the summer. Turn up with a ball and a volleyball net (lifeguard stations will loan them with ID deposit) – it works on a first come, first served basis. Many Vancouverites unwind with a game and a barbecue after work, so expect to wait. There is a league, so some courts will be in use on set nights. Try www.vancouver volleyball.com for drop-ins.

Boating

Bonnie Lee Boat Rentals

1676 Duranleau Street, Granville Island (604 290 7441/http://bonnielee.com/rentals.htm). Bus 50/ Aquabus Granville Island. **Open** Apr-Sept 10am-7pm daily. **Rates** $55-$60/hr (plus gas, taxes & insurance; 4hr minimum); $500 credit card deposit required. **Credit** AmEx, DC, MC, V. **Map** p250 A2.

To speed off in a rented Campion 565, you'll need to be over 21, show a valid driver's license and have some previous boating experience. They'll give you dockside instruction and a map detailing where the rocks are. Seats six; adult and child lifejackets provided. Fishing charters and tackle also available.

Kayakers. *See p177.*

Free wheeling

Vancouver is a cycling-friendly city, due to the temperate climate, the efforts of some bike-obsessed city officials, and a culture that tends to value the environment. In the last decade, the network of bike routes has grown substantially, and the transit system has woken up to its obligation to carry bikes on many buses and trains.

For most casual city visitors, bicycles are for exploring Stanley Park (see p66). The Seawall in summer throngs with cyclists and bladers, who are now blessedly separated from the pedestrian traffic (look for lane markings on the path; wheels get the inside track and generally overtake on the left). If you plan to spend a day in the park, a bicycle is a very attractive travel option. There are many rental shops nearby, and several more throughout the downtown core offering a wide selection, including tandem bikes, chariots for toddlers, and often inline skates.

Of course, in Vancouver most people have wide-tyred mountain bikes, even though they never need them. Put it down to the sort of steroidal cultural predisposition that gives the city so many unnecessary SUVs. Mind you, if you really want to use a mountain bike for its intended purpose, you are in the right place. The North Shore mountains are renowned for their extensive network of bike trails. But for most of us, cycling remains a mainly urban pursuit. The regional transportation authority TransLink (www.translink.bc.ca) publishes a route map available at most bike stores, and its website provides details of bike access rules on buses, the Seabus, and SkyTrain.

Preferred destinations? The Seawall connects Stanley Park in an almost unbroken manner to a waterfront ride all the way to West Point Grey's Pacific Spirit Park, where there are lovely, mostly level forest trails. If you don't want to go that far, the route from the park along English Bay and around False Creek is a pleasant way to double the length of a trip around the park. If you ride around to Granville Island, the charming Aquabus passenger ferry will take you and your bike back to the foot of Hornby Street downtown for a 50-cent premium on the $2.50 fare. If you like the sound of a guided cycle tour, try City By Cycle (see p61 **Tickets to ride**).

Cambie Bridge has a wide bike-friendly eastern sidewalk – Granville and Burrard bridges are a little narrow for the comfort of many cyclists. A ride out to the centre of Lions Gate Bridge (see p81) is a detour that is certainly worth considering.

For a cyclist in Vancouver, it's not so much a matter of where, as where not. In that regard, respect pedestrians and hikers who choose a bike-free place to walk – and avoid somnambulistic drivers on their cell phones.

The following neighbouring shops on Denman and Georgia Streets offer basic daily rentals between $20 and $25 and weekly rentals between $75 and $100. Many downtown bike shops also rent blades.

Bayshore Bike Rental

745 Denman Street, between Robson Street & Alberni Street, West End (604 688 2453/ www.bayshorebikerentals.ca). Bus 5. **Open** 9am-dusk daily. **Rates** $5.60/hour; $15.80/ 4 hours; $21.80/8 hours. **Credit** DC, MC, V.

Bikes 'n' Blades

718 Denman Street, at Alberni Street, West End (604 602 9899). Bus 5. **Open** *May-Sept* 9am-9pm daily. *Oct-Apr* 10am-4pm daily. Closed during bad weather. **Rates** $4.75/hour; $15/half day. **No credit cards**.

Spokes Bicycle Rentals

1798 W Georgia Street, at Denman Street, West End (604 688 5141/www.vancouver bikerental.com). Bus 5. **Open** 9am-dusk daily. **Rates** $5.66-$12.27/hour; $16.99- $36.80/half day. **Credit** AmEx, DC, MC, V.

Stanley Park Cycle Rentals

768 Denman Street, at Robson Street, West End (604 688 0087/www.stanleypark cycle.com). Bus 5. **Open** *May-Sept* 8am-9pm daily. *Oct-Apr* 10am-5pm daily. **Rates** $4.75/hour; $15/half day. **Credit** DC, MC, V.

Cooper Boating

1620 Duranleau Street, Granville Island (604 687 4110/toll-free 888 999 6419/www.cooperboating. com). Bus 50/Aquabus Granville Island. **Open** *June-Aug* 8am-6pm daily. *Sept-May* 9am-5pm daily. **Rates** $1,500-$12,500/5 days in high season (phone for seasonal discounts). **Credit** AmEx, DC, MC, V. **Map** p250 A2.

For longer charters and bigger boats, Cooper is a good stop. If you're not confident about sailing, you can also rent a skipper (from $350 a day).

Mac Sailing

Jericho Sailing Centre Association, 1300 Discovery Street, West Point Grey (604 224 7245/www.jsca. bc.ca/www.macsailing.com). Bus 4. **Open** *May, Sept* noon-5pm daily. *June-Aug* 9am-6pm daily. **Rates** *Sailboats* $30-$50/hr. **Credit** DC, MC, V.

Lessons for kids and adults, and yacht rentals. Wetsuits and life jackets also available for hire.

Camping

Porteau Cove Provincial Park

40km/25 miles north of Vancouver on Highway 99 (604 986 9371). 16 walk-in campsites available (some ocean-fronted), 5mins from the car park; 44 vehicle-accessible sites. **Rates** walk-in $10/party/night; vehicle $22/party/night. **Credit** (May-Oct only) DC, MC, V.

This is a popular weekend camping spot for locals. To guarantee a camping space for any campsite within BC, it's best to call the Discover Camping Reservation Service (604 689 9025). Most campsite reservations can be made up to three months in advance and no later than two days before your arrival date (www.discovercamping.ca).

Cycling

For information on cycling in the city, *see p229*; for mountain biking, *see p177*. For bike rental and the Seawall, *see p174* **Free wheeling**.

Fishing

Depending on the time of year and where you are in British Columbia, salmon is generally the catch of choice. There are five main types (sockeye, coho, chinook, pink and chum). A non-resident licence for freshwater fishing costs around $20 a day ($36 for eight); saltwater is $7.42 a day ($32.86 for five). It is governed by the **Recreational Fishing** (Pacific Region) department; for current licence information call 604 666 0566 (8.30am-4.30pm) or visit www.pac.dfo-mpo.gc.ca, where you'll find the whole gamut of recreational fishing regulations, seasons, and area openings and closures, including those caused by red tides and paralytic shellfish poisoning. While you will see the odd fishermen on Jericho pier and Sunset Beach, people normally take to boats

or go further up the coastline (Howe Sound is popular). Fishing licences are sold at tackle stores throughout the city.

Golf

Carved out of a rainforest, Vancouver's courses have such arresting views that they might just put you off your swing. See www.vancouverparks.ca for information on courses in or near the city. Most offer lessons and equipment to hire.

Gleneagles Golf Course

6190 Marine Drive, at Orchill Road, West Vancouver (604 921 7353). Bus 250, 257. **Open** dawn-dusk daily. **Rates** $20/9 holes. **Credit** AmEx, DC, MC, V.

Obviously named by a homesick Scot, the Gleneagles course is one of the oldest in the city and worth the trip out to West Vancouver for the backdrop of mountains and the ocean out in front.

Stanley Park Pitch & Putt

Lagoon Drive, Stanley Park, near Beach Avenue entrance (604 681 8847/www.vancouverparks.ca). Bus 6. **Open** *Nov-Feb* 9am-dusk daily. *Mar-Oct* 7.30am-dusk. **Rates** $11.75/18 holes; $3.25/putting green. **Credit** DC, MC, V.

Leave your woods behind for this popular spot in Stanley Park. It's free of anything approaching the word 'hazard' and the 18 holes are a maximum of 100 yards. Just turn up (there's no advance booking), and it's first come, first served (warning: weekends are very busy). Hungry? Try the Fish House restaurant (*see p101*).

University Golf Club

5185 University Boulevard, between Blanca Street & Acadia Road, University of British Columbia (604 224 7799/www.universitygolf.com). Bus 4, 17. **Open** dawn-dusk daily. **Rates** $45-$70/18 holes; $20-$40/18 holes twilight rate; $6/60 balls driving range. **Credit** AmEx, DC, MC, V.

An 18-hole course in the heart of the Pacific Spirit Regional Park (*see p176*) yet barely 15 minutes by car or bus from downtown, the University Golf Club is a great public course and driving range, and has been a city institution since 1929. It's good for all levels of play and lessons are available.

Gyms

Vancouverites take image seriously and train hard for it. Whether you're in for an intense spinning class or a chill-out yoga session, there will always be plenty of eye candy to distract you. On the 'Wet Coast', gyms are essential – but if it's sunny you'll find them deserted.

Sweat Co

736 Richards Street, at W Georgia Street, Downtown (604 683 7938/www.sweatcostudios.com). All city-centre buses. **Open** 8am-8pm Mon-Thur; 8am-7pm

Fri; 8am-2pm Sat. **Rates** $7.75/weights & cardio machines; $14.75/cardio class. **Credit** AmEx, DC, MC, V. **Map** p249 K3.

Well-equipped Sweat Co is a good choice for those who like their gyms small and intimate. Choose anything from body rolling to Gyrokinesis, and spot local celebrities – and others on location in Vancouver for filming – working out.

YWCA

535 Hornby Street, between Dunsmuir & W Pender Streets, Downtown (604 895 5777/www.ywcavan. org). All city-centre buses. **Open** 6am-10pm Mon-Fri; 8am-5.30pm Sat, Sun. **Rates** $16/day. **Credit** AmEx, DC, MC, V. **Map** p249 K3.

A day's membership will give you access to the Y's state-of-the-art facilities in a central location.

Hiking

Pacific Spirit Regional Park

W 16th Avenue, between Camosun Street & SW Marine Drive, University of British Columbia (Metro Vancouver parks office 604 224 5739/www. gvrd.bc.ca/parks/PacificSpirit.htm). Bus 25. **Open** daylight hrs; phone to confirm. **Admission** free.

Part of the University Endowment Lands, this park is far less touristy than its Stanley Park cousin. Enormous trees tower over 48km (30 miles) of trails crisscrossing one another. Maps are posted at the various entrances to the park. Bikers, riders and hikers all use different trails. *See also p76.*

Ice-skating

Ice-skating is huge in Vancouver. Outdoors in the winter you can always skate at the top of **Grouse Mountain** (*see p84*), and plans are afoot to reopen the outdoor rink below street level in Robson Square, potentially by winter 2008. For indoor skating, head to the rink at the **West End Community Centre**.

West End Community Centre

870 Denman Street, at Barclay Street, West End (604 257 8333/www.westendcc.vancouver.ca). Bus 5. **Open** Oct-Apr 9am-10pm Mon-Thur; 9am-9pm Fri; 9am-5pm Sat; 10am-5pm Sun. Closed May-Sept. **Rates** $4.85/hr; $2.45 skate rental. **Credit** DC, MC, V. **Map** p248 H2.

Indoor ice-skating facilities at accessible prices throughout the winter months.

In-line skating

Vancouverites swap their winter skates for in-line skates in the summer– there's a vibrant skating culture here. Undoubtedly the most stunning route is around the beautiful Seawall, through Stanley Park (some parts of which are still inaccessible due to the 2006 storms, but alternative routes are in place) and on to

Yaletown, False Creek, past Science World and on to Granville Island. The rule is to go in an anticlockwise direction around the park, and there are pictures of bladers and bikers on one side of the path to separate them from the walkers on the other. Nice theory, though it doesn't always work, so you need to keep your wits about you. The etiquette is generally to pass on the left and before you do, shout out 'on your left' so they know you're coming. You'll see people down to their Speedos, as well as those dressed up in the full body armour (helmet, knee, elbow and wrist pads) – a good idea if you're a beginner.

Speed freaks and experts might find the Seawall a frustrating ride what with all the walkers, strollers and bikers, so either head early or late to avoid the dawdlers, or for a real challenge check out the North Shore's Lower Seymour Conservation Reserve (formerly the Seymour Demonstration Forest) for the **Seymour Valley Trail**, which is 10km (six miles) long (604 990 0483, www.gvrd.bc.ca, bus 228 from Lonsdale Quay or bus 210 from downtown, open dawn-dusk daily).

Bayshore Rentals

745 Denman Street, between Robson & Alberni Streets, West End (604 688 2453/www.bayshore bikerentals.ca). Bus 5. **Open** May-Sept 9am-7pm; closes earlier in off-peak months. **Rates** *In-line skates* (incl helmet) $5/hr; $14.50/4hrs; $19.50/8hrs. *Protective pads* $1.50/day. **Credit** AmEx, DC, MC, V. **Map** p248 H2.

Rental of in-line skates (as well as mountain bikes, kids' bikes and baby joggers) close to Stanley Park.

Jogging & running

There are countless routes to enjoy in the city: the Seawall around Stanley Park and beyond (*see above* In-line skating); **Pacific Spirit Park** (*see above* Hiking); and the **Grouse Grind** (*see p82* **High jinx**) for something a hell of a lot more challenging.

Sun Run

604 689 9441/www.sunrun.com.

Usually held on the third Sunday of April, this long-established 10km (six-mile) run – Canada's largest road race – starting on Georgia Street Downtown seems like it involves the whole city. Most participants (and there are about 54,000) are named in time order in the *Vancouver Sun* newspaper, the main sponsor, which also has four months of training schedules to get you in the mood. *See also p138.*

Vancouver Marathon

604 872 2928/www.vanmarathon.ca.

Staged on the first Sunday of May, the marathon is run on scenic routes across the city. *See also p138.*

Arts & Entertainment

In-line skaters.

Kayaking

Ecomarine Ocean Kayak Centre

Jericho Sailing Centre *1300 Discovery Street, West Point Grey (604 222 3565). Bus 4.* **Open** *May-Sept daily; phone for details.* **Map** p250 A2.
Granville Island *next to the boatyard (604 689 7575). Bus 50/Aquabus Granville Island.* **Open** *daily; phone for details.* **Map** p250 A2.
English Bay Bath House *Denman & Davie Streets, West End (604 685 2925). Bus 6.* **Open** *June-Sept daily; phone for details.* **Map** p248 G2.
All *www.ecomarine.com.* **Rates** $34/2hrs single kayak; $46/2hrs double kayak. $69 lessons/3hrs. Tue 2 kayaks for price of 1. **Credit** DC, MC, V.
Ecomarine offers kayak rentals at its three easily reached access points. Instruction available.

Mountain biking

Once the snow's over, the local mountains test your mettle on the bike. It's easy to see why it's a legal requirement to wear a helmet if you're biking, so swallow your vanity and put one on. There are routes in **Pacific Spirit Park** (*see p176*), **Lower Seymour Conservation**
Reserve (*see p83*) and **Cypress Provincial Park** (*see below*). Skinny tyres are really not recommended on any of these routes.

Cypress Provincial Park

Cypress Provincial Park, Exit 8 off Highway 1, West Vancouver (604 926 5612/www.cypressmountain. com). Cypress Mountain Shuttle Bus at Lonsdale Quay ($17 return; phone 604 419 7669 for details). **Open** *due to reopen end summer 2008; check website for details.* **Rates** *lift $32; bikes $39-$79; full armour set (helmet & pads) $20.* **Credit** AmEx, DC, MC, V.
Cypress Mountain is the largest on the North Shore. That leaves plenty of room on its flanks for a mountain bike park and some serious trails. Although closed due to construction for the 2010 Winter Olympics, Cypress is set to open again by the end of summer 2008. Check the website for details.

Rock climbing

Vancouver has a good reputation for rock climbing. For the real thing, nothing beats the **Chief** in Squamish (www.stawamuschief park.ca) – the largest granite outcrop in the world – about 45 minutes north of Vancouver along the Sea-to-Sky Highway.

Powder play

Once summer's over, Vancouverites eagerly look north and anticipate the first dusting of snow on the local mountains. The three areas within easy reach – Cypress, Grouse (*pictured*) and Seymour – each offer enough for a day's snow fun within a mere half an hour of downtown. All three provide terrain for skiing, boarding and snowshoeing, and on Cypress, cross-country skiing. Thanks to great floodlights, the runs are open until around 10pm seven days a week during the main season. Many people zoom up after work and have a season pass for a specific night. The mountains are not on a par with **Whistler** (*see p215*) but what they lack in long and fulfilling runs, they make up in stupendous vistas – some of the sea, some of the city.

Generally, the three mountains are a great place to learn to ski, with plenty of blue and green runs. Snowshoeing is also gaining popularity. It takes next to no time to pick up the technique (you basically walk) and the treks are well marked. There's less of the hassle factor of skiing/boarding too – strap on the snowshoes (they're high-tech these days, no tennis rackets on your feet) and off you go. And don't forget the snowtubing parks for the kids.

If you're around in the third weekend in October, check out the **Vancouver Snow Show** at BC Place (www.vancouversnowshow.com; *see p141*) for a few bargains.

Cypress Mountain

Cypress Provincial Park, Exit 8 off Highway 1, West Vancouver (604 926 5612/snow & shuttle 604 419 7669/www.cypressmountain.com). Shuttle bus from Lonsdale Quay SeaBus. **Open** phone or see website for details. **Rates** *Shuttle* $18 round-trip. *Tickets* $53-$57/day downhill adult; $18/day cross-country; $10/day snowshoeing; $15/2hrs snow park. Lessons $84.80 drop-in lesson incl lift ticket; $122.38 with lift ticket & equipment rental; $83.74/hr private lessons. Rentals Downhill equipment $47 (skis, boots & poles, or snowboard & boots); clothing rentals $30; cross-country equipment (skis & poles) $21; snowshoeing equipment $21. **Credit** AmEx, DC, MC, V.

With Cypress comes a view of the Lions (two landmark Vancouver peaks) from the Sky chair, or of Mount Baker, Bowen Island and the city from the Panorama run. The peak is set to host the snowboarding and freestyle skiing competitions of the 2010 Olympics (*see p22* **Games on!**), so it's undergone a makeover with a new high-speed quad chair (Lions Express) up the east face of Black Mountain and another nine new ski trails, opening up almost another half of the mountain to gravity freaks. There are quite a few black diamond runs (the most difficult) on the slope but they are short-lived.

Grouse Mountain

6400 Nancy Greene Way, North Vancouver (604 984 0661/snow report 604 986 6262/www.grousemountain.com). Bus 232, 236. **Open** 9am-10pm daily. **Rates** *Lift tickets* $47/day downhill adult. *Downhill lessons* $40/hr drop-ins. *Rental* 1-day ski/snowboard package $39 (jacket & trousers $25); snowshoes $15. **Credit** AmEx, DC, MC, V. Grouse's attractions include a 300ft half-pipe for snowboarders, snowshoe trails, a mountain top ice rink, and the Observatory restaurant for fine dining with a fabulous view of the city. Head up via the Skyride cable car (*see p82* **High jinx**).

Cliffhanger Vancouver

670 Industrial Avenue, East Vancouver (604 874 2400/www.cliffhangerclimbing.com). Bus 3, then 10mins walk. **Open** 11am-11pm Mon-Thur; noon-9.30pm Fri-Sun. **Rates** $15-$17/day. **Credit** DC, MC, V. **Map** p252 O6.
Excellent indoor climbing gym with walls for all levels (including children; *see p142*).

Scuba diving

It's a little known fact that Vancouver is a world leader in the creation of artificial reefs (formed from old ships that have been especially scuppered to provide a suitable habitat for reef-forming organisms), and plenty of divers head this way to see the results off **Vancouver Island** (the *Saskatchewan* and *Cape Breton* near Nanaimo; see www.artificialreef.bc.ca for details).

Closer to Vancouver, smaller ships sunk as training wrecks by the Artificial Reef Society of BC can be found at **Porteau Cove Park** (www.env.gov.bc.ca/bcparks) on the Sea-to-Sky highway, and the area is better suited to people not experienced with West Coast currents. It is a diver-friendly park with showers and changing rooms. Also on the

Mount Seymour

*1700 Mount Seymour Road, North Vancouver
(604 986 2261/www.mountseymour.com).
Shuttle bus from Lonsdale Quay SeaBus.*
Open *9.30am-10pm Mon-Fri; 8.30am-10pm
Sat, Sun. Closed Apr-Dec, exact dates
depending on snow. Snowtube park 10am-
4pm Mon-Thur, Sun; 10am-8pm Fri, Sat.*
Rates *Lift tickets $39.50 adult. Lessons
$39/hr drop-ins; $66 incl lift ticket;
$92 with lift ticket & equipment rental.*
Credit *AmEx, DC, MC, V.*
There's a $4 shuttle service seven days
a week (24-hour snow report 604 718 7771).
Some people use the 10km (six-mile) network
of snowshoe trails for cross-country skiing,
but note that you can't rent skis here.

divers' radar are the stunning **Howe Sound**
and **Indian Arm**, which are both magnets for
underwater enthusiasts. Both can get crowded
in the tourist season. **Whytecliff Park** in
West Vancouver (bus 250) offers a classic dive
called 'the Cut', with a wall that goes down
hundreds of feet and the spot is home to some
200 species of marine life. As a general rule,
all divers must watch for the currents.

Diving Locker

*2745 W 4th Avenue, between Macdonald & Stephens
Streets, West Side (604 736 2681/www.divinglocker.
ca). Bus 2, 4, 7, 22, 44.* **Open** *10am-6pm Mon-Fri;*
10am-5.30pm Sat; 10am-4pm Sun. **Rates** $100/day
for full set of diving gear. **Credit** AmEx, DC, MC, V.
Extensive range of diving equipment available to
buy or hire, plus courses.

Skateboarding

Skaters are celebrated in Vancouver, with the
city council providing well-respected spaces
for tricks and general practice.

Vancouver Skate Plaza

*Under the Georgia Viaduct, at Union & Quebec
Streets & Expo Boulevard, Downtown. Bus 22/
SkyTrain Main Street-Science World.* **Map** p249 L4.

Arts & Entertainment

Strike a pose

Yoga aficionados can forget stuffy studios – there's nothing like a bit of omming in the sand with a vista of verdant mountains and a cooling ocean breeze. Head to Kitsilano, Jericho or Sunset beaches in the summer and you are likely to spot some downward-dogging and sun salutations supervised by teachers holding sporadic drop-in classes.

Such is the popularity of yoga here that, even if you are in the most contorted of poses, fellow beach aficionados hardly give you a second look. Drop-ins usually last an hour to an hour-and-a-half, are held after work (most start at 6pm to catch the last of the rays) and payment is by donation (usually around $8). For a taste of outdoor yoga but in a more formal arrangement, check out the outdoor yoga for all levels at the **Showboat**, right by Kitsilano Beach Pool (6-7.40pm Tue, Thur, 9-10.40am Sat, drop-ins $10); visit www.vancouveryoga. com for more information.

If yoga in 90-degree heat is more your bag, then try one of the **Bikram's Yoga College of India**'s three locations (2893 Cambie Street, West Side, 604 876 9642; 2681 W Broadway, Kitsilano, 604 742 3830; 1650 Alberni Street, West End, 604 662 7722); for all, see www.bikramyoga vancouver.com. Two drop-in classes cost $20. It's demanding but addictive and each studio offers classes throughout the day. Be sure to leave yourself a bit of time afterwards to cool down. For a more earth-mothery yoga venue, try a session at the friendly **Prana Yoga & Zen Centre** (1083 Cambie Street, 604 682 2121, www. pranayoga.com, $17/drop-in class).

Many people hang out in yoga gear all day long in Vancouver, and the ultra-urban **Lululemon Athletica** sports clothing store (its most central shops are on Robson Street and on W 4th Avenue; see p125) is a local brand synonymous with yoga. It's also a great place to hear of courses from staff who practise what they sell.

With its ramps, rails and steps, it's no wonder skate-boarders are dubbing this recently opened street-style park the best this side of LA.

Skiing

For information about skiing in the Vancouver area, see p178 **Powder play**.

Swimming pools

Vancouver's outdoor pools are ideal when the weather is fine. Otherwise, try the **Vancouver Aquatic Centre** (see p142).

Kitsilano Pool

2305 Cornwall Avenue, at Yew Street, West Side (604 731 0011/www.city.vancouver.bc.ca/parks/ rec/pools). Bus 2, 22, 44. **Open** *Mid May-mid June noon-8.45pm daily. Mid June-early Sept 7am-8.45pm daily. Sept 7am-7.15pm daily.* **Rates** $4.85; $2.85-$3.65 reductions. **Credit** AmEx, DC, MC, V. **Map** p251 F5.
A saltwater pool (Canada's largest), divided in half between a play area and a swimming area (with swimmers all going in an anti-clockwise direction; the lifeguards will set you right if you try swimming against the flow). It's a popular place for families to hang out and the views are spectacular.

Second Beach Pool

Stanley Park Drive, West End (604 257 8371/ www.city.vancouver.bc.ca/parks/rec/pools). Bus 6. **Open** *Mid May-mid June noon-8.45pm daily. Mid June-late July 10am-8.45pm daily. Late July-early Sept 7am-8.45pm daily. Sept 11.30am-7pm daily.* **Rates** $4.85; $2.85-$3.65 reductions. **Credit** AmEx, DC, MC, V. **Map** p248 F1.
This freshwater pool has plenty of lanes and slides in a great location.

Tennis

The city is home to some 180 free courts, in varying conditions. The 15 popular Stanley Park free courts are well kept, and other good ones include Kitsilano Beach Park and Queen Elizabeth Park. The rules for these courts are: from the moment you turn up to wait for a court, the players have no more than 30 minutes left. If queuing does not appeal, head for the courts at **Jericho Beach Park** (by the **Jericho Youth Hostel**; see p53), which are far less crowded. Other good courts are available in **Stanley Park**, costing $5 per 30 minutes in summer (they are free until 3pm during the week; you pay between 3pm and dusk and should call 604 605 8224 to pre-book).

Windsurfing

Windsure Windsurfing

Jericho Sailing Centre Association, 1300 Discovery Street, West Side (604 224 0615/www.windsure. com). Bus 4. **Open** *Apr-Oct 9am-8pm daily.* **Rates** *Windsurf hire $17.70/hr (incl wetsuit & lifejacket). Lessons $49/2hr intro group lesson.* **Credit** AmEx, DC, MC, V.
As well as windsurfing, Windsure offers introductions to kiteboarding ($139/2hrs) and stand-up paddle surfing ($49/hr) and skimboarding ($49/2hrs).

Trips Out of Town

Features

Maps

Fisherman's Wharf. *See p196.*

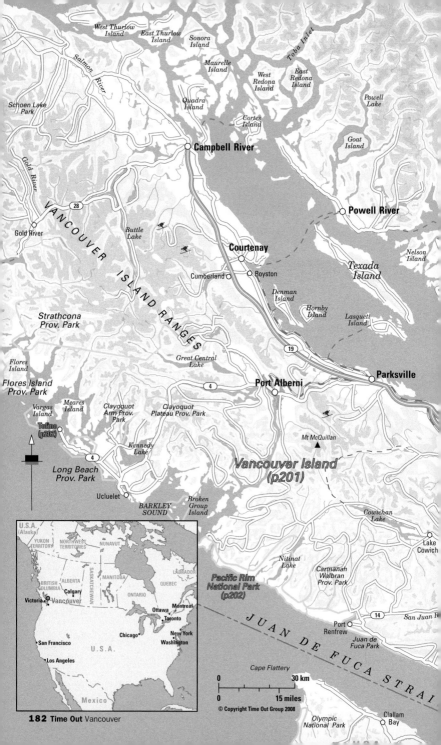

Trips Out of Town

Clendinning
Prov. Park

Tinniswood

Pemberton
Ice Cap

Pemberton   Nairn Falls

Callaghan
Lake P. Park

Whistler
(p215)   Blackcomb
(p215)

Whistler Ski Resort

Squamish River

Tantalus
P. Park

Brackendale
(p215)

Squamish
(p213)

Britannia
Beach
(p213)

99

Elaho River

Squamish River

Stein River

LILLOOET RANGE

Lillooet
Lake

Duffey
Lake

Stein Valley
Prov. Park

Skihist Mtn
2944m

Mehatl Creek
Prov. Park

Nahatlatch River

Garibaldi
Prov. Park

Golden
Ears
Prov. Park

Harrison
Lake

Sechelt

Gibsons

Horseshoe Bay
Bowen Island
(p187)

West Vancouver

VANCOUVER

New Westminster

See pp246-247

Richmond (p189)
Steveston (p189)

Ladner   Delta

Tsawwassen

Lions
Bay

Mt Seymour
Park

Indian
Arm
Park

North   Vancouver

Burnaby   Port Moody

Coquitlam

Haney

Pinecone
Burke
Prov. Park

Pitt
Lake

Stave
Lake

Harrison
Hot Springs
(p191)

Chilliwack

Cultus
Lake

Nanaimo

Valdes
Island

Ladysmith

Chemainus

Duncan

Salt Spring
Island

Galiano
Island

Mayne
Island

Gulf Islands
(p204)

Saturna
Island

Pender
Island

STRAIT OF GEORGIA

Surrey

Langley
Fort Langley
(p191)

White
Rock

Aldergrove

Blaine

Mission

7

Abbotsford   See p207

1

5

Orcas
Island

Lummi
Island

Bellingham

Lake
Whatcom

Mt Baker
3285m

USA

Salish
Bay

9

20

Sidney

Butchart
Gardens

VICTORIA (p194)

See p195

Sooke
(p197)

17

1

San Juan
Island

Lopez
Island

Whidbey
Island

20

Oak Harbour

Dungeness

Camano

Salish
Bay

5   530

Sedro Wooley

Arlington

Time Out Vancouver **183**

Getting Started

The road from here.

British Columbia is nearly four times the size of Great Britain. It's 1,300 kilometres (800 miles) long (north-south), and 700 kilometres (435 miles) wide. Vancouver is nestled in the south-west corner. More than three quarters of BC's four million population live either in the Metro Vancouver region or on Vancouver Island – so there's an awful lot of wilderness left over to explore in the hinterlands.

Those characteristics that make BC so attractive – the coast, dotted with bare, rocky outcrops; the mountain ranges, thick forests and glacier-fed rivers and lakes – have protected much of the province from development. But don't worry: 20,000 tourism-related businesses exist to help you make the most of it.

There are two trips that almost all visitors to Vancouver make: the mountain resort of Whistler (see p212) is just 120 kilometres (75 miles) north of the city and **Victoria**, BC's provincial capital, is a couple of hours away by ferry, or 30 minutes by float plane (see p185).

When they want to get away for the weekend, locals flock to the Gulf Islands, of which there are dozens. In summer, the **Okanagan** (see p206) is another popular retreat about five hours drive to the east. With some planning, you can try sea kayaking with whales, ski off-piste, watch grizzly bears, or ranch in cowboy country.

But even if you only have time to get a flavour, there is enough on the city's doorstep to serve as a microcosm for the rest of BC. You can hike in Manning Park; bathe in the hot springs at Harrison; visit Bowen Island, just a 20-minute ferry ride from West Vancouver, or take a flight in a seaplane. And an afternoon is all you need to get up close and personal with the killer whales that make their home in the southern gulf waters.

TOURIST INFORMATION

The Tourism Vancouver Tourist Info Centre at the Plaza level, 200 Burrard Street (near Canada Place) has a free reservation and information service and offers some discounts. Despite the name, it covers all of British Columbia. It's open 8.30am-5pm Mon-Sat (604 683 2000, www.tourismvancouver.com).

TELEPHONE CODES

When calling long distance from Vancouver, you will need to dial 1 before the area code. That includes numbers beginning 604 that aren't in the local Vancouver area.

GETTING AROUND

British Columbia has relatively few major highways. The basic choice is east–west or north–south. From Vancouver you can take Highway 99 north to Horseshoe Bay and Whistler, or south to the ferry terminal at Tsawwassen and the United States (Seattle is a 225-kilometre/140-mile drive; factor in at least another 30 minutes at the border, or up to two hours in busy periods). Or you can take Route 1, the Trans-Canada Highway, which runs east by way of the Fraser Valley and Kamloops, through the Rockies to Calgary, and all the way to Newfoundland (7,821 kilometres; 4,860 miles).

Pacific Coach Lines (604 662 8074, toll free 1-800 661 1725, www.pacificcoach.com) runs a cheap daily shuttle service to Vancouver Island, as does **Greyhound** (toll free 1-800 661 8747, www.greyhound.ca). Greyhound also runs a bus to Whistler and to Seattle. **TransLink** (604 953 3333, www.translink.bc.ca) operates bus routes to the ferry terminals at Horseshoe Bay and Tsawwassen, and a good cheap public transport system throughout the Lower Mainland.

BC Ferries (toll free 1-888 223 3779, www. bcferries.com) connects the mainland with the larger Gulf Islands. Book in advance for peak holiday periods and check in at least 30 minutes prior to departure time. Tsawwassen, an hour south of Vancouver, is the best port for Victoria; Horseshoe Bay is a quicker route to Nanaimo and the north of Vancouver Island. Seaplanes flying out of Coal Harbour are an option and are an experience in their own right (see p185 **Plane sailing**). **Helijet** (604 270 1484, toll free 1-800 665 4354, www.helijet.com) also provides a Vancouver–Victoria service, at $219 one way.

British Columbia is not well served by rail, and to catch a train down the west coast to San Francisco, you will first need to get to Seattle – **Amtrak** (toll free 1 800 872 7245) runs one train daily ($37 one-way) and three buses ($28).

Although transport between large urban centres is relatively straightforward, to really explore British Columbia you will need to rent a car – a small four door can be as cheap as $30 a day, plus taxes. Gas prices are high by North American standards, but are still a fraction of those in the UK. (For car rental services, see p229.) In the winter months, driving conditions in the north can be treacherous, but snow is rarely a problem on the Lower Mainland.

Plane sailing

Unless you happen to live in one of the apartments overlooking Coal Harbour – in which case you're likely to begrudge the regular gnat-like drone – the sight of a seaplane coming in over Stanley Park, gracefully banking round and down in front of Grouse Mountain before coasting to a stop on the calm waters of the Burrard Inlet is a Vancouver image you'll cherish. And the residents have little to complain about. Float planes have been built and harboured on this spot since 1915, long before any of the apartment blocks went up (and 16 years before Vancouver had its own airport).

In aviation's infancy the float plane (a plane with pontoons rigged under the fuselage) was considered the safest option for a flight over any body of water, but by 1927, when Charles Linbergh circumnavigated the globe in a landplane, the writing was on the wall for the less aerodynamic model. Yet BC's cluster of remote coastal communities have kept the seaplane busy in this part of the world, and **Harbour Air** (604 274 1277, www.harbour-air.com; *pictured*) – which operates a frequent weekday commuter run between Vancouver and Victoria, Vancouver and Nanaimo, and Vancouver and the Gulf Islands – is the largest all-seaplane airline in the world.

Flying low over the city and across Howe Sound, the planes offer the chance to see the lie of the land in all its glory. Though the engine noise is louder than you might expect, there's something truly mesmerising about this bird's eye view. And what's not to get excited about taking off and landing on water?

Harbour Air maintain single pilot DeHavilland float planes which went out of production in the mid 1960s, but which remain the most successful seaplanes ever built. The Beaver seats six passengers, the Otter up to 14. **West Coast Air** (604 606 6888, www.westcoastair.com) runs a similar daily service between Vancouver and Victoria, also with the DeHavilland Beaver and a slightly larger Twin Otter aircraft. Both companies offer boarding at Coal Harbour (the terminal is at 1075 W Waterfront Road, two blocks west of Canada Place) or at Vancouver Airport (South Terminal) and fly to Inner Harbour, Victoria for $120 one-way. Both also offer a range of enticing tours and private charters to the Sunshine Coast, coastal mountains and glaciers, and the Gulf Islands at $100-$300 per person, depending on the size of your party.

Clean water. It's the most basic human necessity. Yet one third of all poverty related deaths are caused by drinking dirty water. Saying *I'm in* means you're part of a growing movement that's fighting the injustice of poverty. Your £8 a month can help bring safe water to some of the world's poorest people. We can do this. We *can* end poverty. Are you in?

shouldn't everyone get clean water? I don't think that's too much to ask for

Let's end poverty together.
Text 'WATER' and your name to 87099 to give £8 a month.

Standard text rates apply. Registered charity No.202918

oxfam.org.uk

I'm in

Oxfam

Sarite Morales, Greenwich

Excursions

Adventures galore.

Day Trips

Bowen Island

A mini-paradise of mountains, rainforest and lakes, the 52-square-kilometre (20-square-mile) Bowen Island is just nine kilometres (5.5 miles) across the water from West Vancouver and 20 minutes by ferry. A tourist magnet since the early 1900s, Bowen still has the peace and tranquility of a different age. Nearly half the island is forest, with abundant trails for walking, biking and horseback riding. Though the ferry takes cars, most visitors prefer to leave their vehicle at Horseshoe Bay (be sure to leave enough time to find a parking spot). Bus 257 will take you from downtown right to the terminal in approximately 40 minutes.

A great day trip might include stocking up on picnic supplies at the **Ruddy Potato**, hiking through Crippen Park woods to Killarney Lake and then back to Snug Cove for a sup of local-brewed beer at **Doc Morgan's Inn & Pub** before dinner at **Blue Eyed Mary's**.

Day-trippers can rent bicycles from a seasonal operation located next to the ferry terminal if they want to add more distance to their itinerary, including a visit to **Artisan Square** (www.artisansquare.com). Featuring a dozen galleries and studios for weaving, pottery, jewellery, yoga and dance, a handful of shops and two cafés, this little village reflects the creative flare of Bowen Island's substantial artistic community.

Ruddy Potato
996 Dorman Road (604 947 0098/www.ruddypotato. com). **Open** 9am-7.30pm Mon-Thur, Sat; 9am-8.30pm Fri; 9am-6.30pm Sun. **Credit** DC, MC, V.

Where to stay & eat

Many come to Bowen Island just to stroll along the boardwalk and have dinner in pretty Snug Cove. The aforementioned Blue Eyed Mary's offers the finest dining on the island, from chef Carol Wallace, formally of Vancouver's acclaimed Bishop's. **Tuscany Wood Oven Pizza** has a patio but it's classier inside, where smoked wild salmon pizza and southern Italian dishes are expertly prepared. **Bowen**

Island Pub serves good burgers in addition to the usual pub fare and features live music on Saturday nights.

There are no hotel, motel or camping operations on Bowen, but plenty of B&Bs and some cabins to rent. Check www.bowen-island-bc.com/directory/accommodations.html for listings, and note that in the summer, many places insist on a two-night minimum stay.

Blue Eyed Mary's
433 Trunk Road (604 947 2583). **Open** 5-10pm Thur-Sun. **Main courses** $18-$31. **Credit** DC, MC, V.

Bowen Island Pub
479 Bowen Trunk Road (604 947 2782/www. bowenpub.com). **Open** noon-midnight Mon-Thur, Sun; noon-1am Fri, Sat. **Main courses** $8-$15. **Credit** DC, MC, V.

Tuscany Wood Oven Pizza & Mediterranean Cuisine
451 Bowen Trunk Road (604 947 0550/www. tuscanypizza.com). **Open** *June-early Sept* 5-9.30pm daily. *Sept-May* 5-9.30pm Wed-Sun. **Main courses** $14-$22. **Credit** DC, MC, V.

Union Steamship Company Marina
(604 947 0707/www.steamship-marina.bc.ca). **Rates** (2 night min stay May-Oct) $130-$250. **Open** *Restaurant* 11am-10pm Mon-Thur, Sun; 11am-midnight Sat, Sun. Closed Jan, Feb. **Main courses** $15-$30. **Credit** AmEx, DC, MC, V.

Tourist information

Take the first right after leaving the ferry for the **Visitors Info Centre** (432 Cardena Road, 604 947 9024, www.bowenisland.org) and pick up a *Bowen Island Guide*, which lists accommodation, restaurants, cafés, kayak rentals, ferry and water taxi information, and a brochure, *Things to See or Do on Bowen.*

Getting there

Ferries run hourly from Horseshoe Bay (the journey from downtown via Highway 99 north over Lions Gate Bridge takes 15 minutes). The crossing takes 20 minutes. Pre-book during peak periods.

BC Ferries
Horseshoe Bay (toll free 1-888 223 3779/www. bcferries.com). Bus 250, 257. **Rates** *to Bowen Island* $7.20/passenger; $3.60 5-11s; free under-5s; $20.55/ passenger vehicle. **Credit** AmEx, DC, MC, V.

Steveston.

Trips Out of Town

Richmond

The city of Richmond lies on the south side of the airport, a 20-minute drive from downtown Vancouver. It's an island city situated in the mouth of the Fraser River with a population of upwards of 185,000 – approximately 60 per cent of whom are Asian, predominantly Chinese. With reasonable real estate prices and great restaurants, it's not hard to see why the city has grown so fast. Unfortunately it also stands to be the local sacrifice to global warming – most of it sits just one metre above sea level. Though it's laid out on a grid, Richmond is infuriatingly difficult to navigate, its flat landscape and strip mall architecture offering few useful landmarks. The arrival of the SkyTrain's Canada Line will make for a far less arduous trip – the main reason to visit being the best Chinese food in North America (*see p190* **China town**) and visit the summer Night Market.

Loud, crowded, and buzzing with fairground energy, the insanely popular **Richmond Night Market** is the largest in North America, with attendance climbing to over a million visitors during its run. From May through September, on Friday, Saturday and Sunday evenings, four hundred stalls sell every trinket, fashion accessory and flashing bit of electronica imaginable. The food selection is staggering, with everything from dim sum and chow mein to satays and grilled meats. More exotic fare includes deep-fried fermented stinky tofu, Korean fried mochi cakes with brown sugar fillings, Japanese yakitori balls, and Malaysian rotis. For dessert, sweet bubble teas, dragon's beard candy (thin strands of pulled sugar wrapped around chopped peanuts), and cakes with red bean fillings should satisfy anyone with a sweet tooth.

A victim of its own success, the Night Market was evicted from its usual location after the 2007 season. Check local papers or **Tourism Richmond** (604 271 8280, www.tourism richmond.com) for details of its new home.

Steveston

Strolling past the brick storefronts and boardwalk bistros, it's easy to presume that Steveston was assembled just for tourists. In fact, the 100-year-old fishing village is very much a working town, home to the largest fishing fleet in Canada – more than 600 vessels. That's not to say they don't take kindly to visitors: in summer, Steveston's shops and restaurants are packed, and the fishing boats line up at the pier to sell fresh fish straight out of the net. You can go whale-watching from here, though if you're heading out to Vancouver

Island it has better options. And if you're around on Canada Day (1 July) the annual Salmon Festival is a popular family day out.

But it's more than just fish and kitsch. Like much of the greater Vancouver area, Steveston's heritage is diverse and at times controversial. A substantial population of Japanese immigrants settled here at the turn of the 20th century, but their stay was marred first by a devastating fire, then by forced internment during World War II. For a peek at Steveston's Japanese roots, head to the **Murakami Visitor Centre**, part of the **Britannia Heritage Shipyard**, on the southern end of Railway Avenue. The complex consists of ten buildings, four of them restored: canneries and boatyards dating back as far as 1885. These are the finest surviving examples on the BC coast of a way of life essential to the development of the province. You may also find volunteers restoring old wooden boats using traditional craft methods. **Murakami House** was built on stilts over the marsh, and features artifacts from the Murakami family, two parents and ten children, who lived there from the early 1930s to 1942 (when Japanese immigrants were interned).

Other immigrant groups, including British, Europeans and most recently Chinese, found a happier life in town, and their influence is seen in the storefronts on Moncton Street, Steveston's main thoroughfare. The latter group also made their mark with an entry point to a Buddhist temple (just east of town on Steveston Highway), which was constructed in the 1970s and houses an impressive Chinese classical garden.

Steveston is proud of its fishing history. Though all but one of its 15 working canneries are now gone, the **Gulf of Georgia Cannery** remains in operation, offering tours and a lively account of the town's signature profession. For another taste of small town history, head back to Moncton Street for the unmistakably small town **Steveston Museum and Post Office** – and post a letter home as you soak up the local culture. Just up the road from the cannery is Garry Point Park (entrance at the corner of 7th Avenue and Moncton Street), an open field abutting rocky beaches that give the locals some respite from the summer heat. At the eastern end is a small Japanese garden, and a fisherman's monument – a 15-foot sculpture of a needle used to mend fishing nets. The park also serves as entry point to a five-kilometre (three-mile) seafront dyke trail, popular with walkers and bikers alike.

Back in town, there are a surprising diversity of dining options, including Greek, Indian, Japanese and even Mexican. But fish and chips is the signature dish in Steveston, with a half-dozen restaurants offering it.

Trips Out of Town

China town

Given Vancouver's location along the Pacific Rim, it's not surprising that it has been a magnet for Chinese immigrants. But rather than Chinatown, the epicentre of Chinese Canadian life exists south of the city, in the neighbouring city of **Richmond**.

Why Richmond? Factors include good feng shui (Richmond sits like a dragon's pearl on the Fraser River delta), having the word 'Rich' in the name, close proximity to the airport, and reasonable real estate prices. Whatever the reason, more than half of Richmond's residents are now of Chinese descent.

Successive waves of arrivals from Hong Kong, mainland China and Taiwan have each left their culinary mark. The relative wealth of the immigrants has raised the level of culinary sophistication to exacting standards. Outside of China and Hong Kong, Vancouver and Richmond probably has the finest Chinese food in the world.

Cantonese cuisine, with its emphasis on clean flavours and fresh ingredients, is the dominant culinary style. Dim sum lunches are favoured for variety and family friendliness. **Fisherman's Terrace Seafood Restaurant** (Aberdeen Centre, 4151 Hazelbridge Way, Unit 3580, 604 303 9739) is a wood panelled light-filled room with an imaginative and comprehensive menu. Steamed pork neck meat with spicy XO sauce (a mix of chilies and dried seafood) and the pan-fried egg tofu are highlights. At the other end of decor scale, the Mao-meets-Versailles interior at **Shiang Garden** (4540 No. 3 Road, 604 273 8858) provides the perfect backdrop for lusty and generous dim sum. The famous baked BBQ pork buns are pillow-soft and sweetly glazed.

For the Chinese, a special dinner usually means seafood. At **Sea Harbour Restaurant** (3711 No. 3 Road, 604 232 0816) local Dungeness crab is braised in an intoxicating sauce of kobocha pumpkin, garlic, and fermented black beans. Alaskan king crab season (early spring) is a real highlight in Vancouver's culinary calendar and **Sun Sui Wah Seafood Restaurant** (4940 No. 3 Road, Unit 102, 604 273 8208, www. sunsuiwah.com) is justifiably famous for its crab festival. The legs are steamed with chopped garlic to enhance the natural succulent sweetness and the shell is stuffed with fried rice.

Northern Chinese cuisine, in particular Shanghai cooking, has always been popular. Steamed soup buns, or *xiao long bao* are a must-order. Served with slivered ginger and dark vinegar, each little dumpling is a molten burst of pork broth. **Shanghai River Restaurant** (7831 Westminster Highway, Unit 110, 604 233 8885) serves the Asian Burberry Set in a beautifully modern room with a focus on clean refined flavours. Along with the soup buns, sample the cold poached drunken chicken and the amazingly flaky daikon pastries. At **Chen's Shanghai Kitchen** (8095 Park Road, 604 304 8288), soup buns are rustically large, the spicy peanut dan dan noodles are richly satisfying, and the black sesame pastries provide the perfect sweet finish. **Northern Delicacy** (Aberdeen Centre, 4151 Hazelbridge Way, Unit 2788, 604 233 7050, www.northern-delicacy.com) specialities include a delicate tea-smoked duck, cold chicken with glass noodles and peanut sauce, and shredded pork in a spicy garlicky 'fish flavoured sauce'.

Taiwanese style eateries mix Northern robustness with Cantonese refinement. Forward interior design and service staff at ease with English makes for a relaxed dining experience. Starkly modern **Vogue Chinese Restaurant** (3779 Sexsmith Road, Unit 1118, 604 244 8885) is famous for its three cups chicken, a satisfying stew with soy, sesame oil, and rice wine. At **Dinesty Chinese Restaurant** (8111 Ackroyd Road, Unit 160, 604 303 7772), watch the glass-walled busy kitchen preparing items from the noodles and dumpling-focused menu. The house-made kimchee is refreshing and bright.

For the indecisive, a food court can provide authentic alternatives for the adventurous eater. On the third floor of Aberdeen Center (4151 Hazelbridge Way), **Shanghai Shanghai** has handmade dumplings, braised meatballs and one of the best sweet and sour soups around. Line up with the locals for luscious cream puffs from **Beard Papa**. Evoking a scruffy Chinese train station, the second floor food court at the **Richmond Public Market** (8260 Westminster Highway) is a culinary surprise: Xian Cuisine Food Stall's wide ranging menu includes hand pulled noodles, fresh breads, and the best lamb noodles this side of Beijing. Eat up!

One of the best is **Pajo's**, which operates from a floating platform, just a stone's throw from the arriving fishing fleet. The fish (your choice of cod, halibut, or the local fave, salmon) is coated in a light, almost tempura-style crispy batter, and the chips are just crisp enough. For a more traditional option, try **Dave's Fish and Chips**, in the centre of town, where the batter is thick, the cod is light and flaky, and the beer selection is generous (Pajo's isn't licenced). Back on the water, the **Charthouse** offers solid sit-down fare, with an emphasis on local seafood and lovely views of the wharf.

When you've had your fill of fried seafood, take a walk along the well kept riverside trails to Garry Point Park or take the kids to the well-equipped playground and waterpark in the centre of town (4011 Moncton Street).

Britannia Heritage Shipyard
5180 Westwater Drive, at Railway Avenue (604 718 8050). **Open** *May-Sept* 10am-6pm Tue-Sun. *Oct-Apr* 10am-4pm Sat; noon-4pm Sun. **Admission** free.

Gulf of Georgia Cannery
12138 4th Avenue, at W Chatham Street (604 664 9009/www.pc.gc.ca/gulfofgeorgiacannery). **Open** 10am-5pm most days (phone or check website to be sure). **Admission** $7.15; $3.45-$5.90 reductions; $17.80 family; free under-6s. **Credit** AmEx, DC, MC, V.

Steveston Museum & Post Office
3811 Moncton Street, at 1st Avenue (604 271 6868). **Open** 9.30am-1pm, 1.30-5pm Mon-Sat. **Admission** free.

Where to eat & drink

Charthouse
3866 Bayview Street, at 2nd Avenue (604 271 7000). **Open** 11am-10pm daily. **Main courses** $7-$40. **Credit** DC, MC, V.

Dave's Fish & Chips
3460 Moncton Street, between 2nd & 3rd Avenues (604 271 7555). **Open** 11am-8pm daily. **Main courses** $7-$15. **Credit** DC, MC, V.

Pajo's on the Wharf
Floating platform, at Bayview Street & 3rd Avenue (604 272 1588/www.pajos.com). **Open** *16 May-15 Sept* 11am-8pm daily (weather permitting). *16 Sept-15 May* phone ahead for hours. **Main courses** $4-$12. **No credit cards.**

Tourist information

Steveston Visitor Kiosk
Moncton Street & 3rd Avenue (Tourism Richmond 604 271 8280/www.steveston.bc.ca). **Open** *21 May-30 June, Labour Day-30 Sept* 10am-6pm Fri-Sun. *1 July-Labour Day* 10am-6pm daily.

Getting there

Steveston is 25 minutes from downtown. Take Highway 99 south (down Oak Street), then turn left on to the Steveston Highway to No. 1 Road and follow that south to Steveston. Alternatively, take the 491 bus from Burrard Station (rush hour Mon-Fri only), or the 98 B-Line from Burrard Station to Richmond Centre and transfer to 401, 402, 407 or 410.

The Fraser Valley

It's an hour's drive east along the Trans-Canada Highway (Route 1) before the city landscape gives way to the farming flatlands of the Lower Mainland, and another hour until the road weaves into the Cascade Mountains beside Hope. From here, the road forks eastward to Manning Park or north along the canyon walls of the Fraser River. Either choice makes for a terrific day trip, with any number of destinations along the way. If you have time for a longer trip, Manning Park is en route to the Okanagan Valley, and the northern route affords a roundabout journey to Whistler, popularly known as the Circle Trip.

Fort Langley

One of the BC's earliest European settlements, **Fort Langley National Historic Site** (*see p144*) is a reconstructed Hudson's Bay Company trading post where costumed interpreters give visitors a feel for pioneer life. The surrounding village, not to be confused with fast-sprawling Langley town, is charming and has galleries, bookstores and quality coffee houses. Langley's pastoral countryside is an equal delight, for its horses, hot-air balloon rides and even the odd winery. If you have kids, the trip is easily combined with a visit to the **Greater Vancouver Zoo** (*see p144*).

Harrison Hot Springs

Only 90 minutes from Vancouver, **Harrison Hot Springs** has been a favourite getaway for city folk ever since prospectors first discovered its mineral hot springs in the 1850s. Harrison quickly became British Columbia's first resort, and today the Harrison Hot Springs Resort & Spa – and its famous Copper Dining Room – attracts a loyal family crowd. In addition to fishing and boating on its 64-kilometre (40-mile) lake, Harrison offers hiking, cycling, camping and an amazing sand sculpture competition, held annually during the second week of September. At nearby **Harrison Mills**, sights include the 1906 Kilby General Store and Rowena's on the River, a refurbished

Trips Out of Town

heritage home turned elegant B&B. Rowena's River's Edge Restaurant is a great pit stop, especially when combined with a round of golf at the adjoining Sandpiper Golf Club. Garden enthusiasts should include a visit to David Minter Gardens; it's a stunning showcase of 22 themed gardens spread over 11 hectares (27 acres) with two restaurants on site.

Beyond Hope

Nearer to Hope are two detours: **Bridal Falls** where water tumbles down 122 metres (400 feet) on the face of Mount Cheam, and the **Othello Quintette Tunnels**. Built between 1911 and 1916 as the last leg of the Kettle Valley Railway, they are a Herculean feat of engineering.

By and large, **Hope** itself is a pretty, pass-through community, though its two dozen or so chainsaw carvings encourage a few photo opportunities, and there's always the Rambo tour (the movie *First Blood* was filmed here in 1982 and they're still talking about it). Outdoor adventurers will likely want to head to **Manning Park** for activities that range from easy-to-hike interpretive trails (some of which are wheelchair accessible), to fishing, canoeing and skiing. **The Okanagan Valley** is another couple of hours' drive from here.

River rafters, however, will head north past Hell's Gate towards **Lytton**. This is where the Thompson River converges with the Fraser (BC's longest), and you can raft both (try Kumsheen Raft Adventures, 250 455 2296, www. kumsheen.com). The spring snow melt creates furious whitewater in the tall, narrow canyons.

For many folks though, driving through the canyon to **Hell's Gate** is reward enough; this is where the Fraser River surges some 200 million gallons of water through a 35 metre (110 foot) gorge. That's the volume of Niagara Falls, doubled! The Hell's Gate Airtram takes visitors on a gentle 150m (500ft) descent from the highway, into the gorge, where it hovers over the gushing water before continuing to the patio and restaurant on the other side.

If you've time, drive on to **Lillooet**, an historic community that marks Mile 0 of the Cariboo Trail which, in the 1800s, took miners north to the goldfields. It's also where Highway 99 turns west for an achingly beautiful drive towards Pemberton and 'the back door' into Whistler. Just be sure your vehicle has good brakes; the mountain inclines are very steep and it's not a drive to be done in winter.

Hell's Gate Airtram

43111 Trans Canada Highway, Boston Bar (604 867 9277/www.hellsgateairtram.com). **Open** *Apr-Oct* 10am-4pm daily. **Admission** $16; $10-$13 reductions; free under-5s. **Credit** DC, MC, V.

Minter Gardens

52892 Bunker Road, Rosedale (604 794 7191/www. mintergardens.com). **Open** *Apr, Oct* 10am-5pm daily. *May, Sept* 9am-5.30pm daily. *June* 9am-6pm daily. *July, Aug* 9am-7pm daily. **Admission** $15; $6-$12.50 reductions; free under-5s. **Credit** DC, MC, V.

Where to stay, eat & drink

The usual suspects are scattered through the Fraser Valley but there are some good restaurants in Langley Village and Harrison. The eateries at Minter Gardens and Hell's Gate are surprisingly good.

Harrison Hot Springs Resort & Spa

100 Esplanade Avenue (604 796 2244/www. harrisonresort.com). **Open** 7am-9pm daily. **Main courses** $5-$35 (patio fare to fine dining). **Rates** $129-$250 doubles. **Credit** AmEx, DC, MC, V.

Lakeview Restaurant

150 Esplanade, Harrison Hot Springs (604 796 9888). **Open** *May-Sept* 8.45am-6pm daily. *Oct-Apr* 8.45am-7pm daily. **Main courses** $11-$20; fish & chips $10-$17. **Credit** DC, MC, V.

River's Edge Restaurant

Rowena's Inn on the River, 14282 Morris Valley Road, Harrison Mills (toll free 1-800 661 5108/ www.rowenasinn.com). **Open** 8am-9pm daily. **Main courses** $7-15 lunch; $19-$29 dinner. **Rates** $175-$250 doubles. **Credit** DC, MC, V.

Tourist Information

Lytton Visitor Centre

400 Fraser Street, Lytton (250 455 2523/ www.lytton.ca). **Open** 9am-5pm Mon-Sat.

Getting there

By car take the Trans-Canada Highway 1 east out of Vancouver and just keep going. As you near Hope, there are signs for Harrison, Minter Gardens and other detours. Fill up at Hope, and continue heading East on Highway 3 to Manning Park or take the Trans-Canada north through the Fraser Canyon.

Expeditions

Few places in the world offer the diverse nature of British Columbia: the following are some choice, once-in-a-lifetime BC experiences.

Backcountry huts

Amid the mighty ranges of British Columbia's Rocky and Selkirk Mountains is a series of self-service backcountry huts operated by the **Alpine Club of Canada** (403 678 3200, www.alpineclubofcanada.ca).

Sea kayaking.

Bill Putnam Hut in the Selkirks is renowned for its access to epic powder skiing. Surrounded by towering, Gothic-looking peaks, the two-storey lodge is more like a wilderness palace than a hut and comes complete with a wood-fired sauna – a luxury on crisp winter nights. A helicopter ferries groups of up to 20 people from Golden, BC. Most days start with expeditions up majestic peaks and end with a long ski down to the hut. Nicknamed Fairy Meadow, this hut sees near capacity year-round, so book early.

For summer hiking, **Elizabeth Parker Hut**, in Yoho National Park, is surrounded by trails through cathedral-like rainforest of cedar and hemlock. Visitors arrive here for a chance to spot wolf, cougar, deer, elk, moose, mountain sheep, and bears. You'll also find streams of salmon and trout. This hut can be used as a base for a trip to the **Abbot Pass Hut**, an all-stone cabin at almost 3,000 metres (10,000 feet).

Reservations are required at all huts, most of which range from $22 to $36 per person, per night. In winter high-season Bill Putnam Hut costs $725 per person, per week, including helicopter; book a year in advance.

Fishing

If fishing is your passion, a stay at a remote floating lodge can transform the catch of the day into a metaphor for how all of nature is interconnected. Framed by mountains and accessible by boat or float plane only, **Blackfish Lodge** (206 789 1224, www. blackfishlodge.com), on the north-east coast of Vancouver Island, is a place of seclusion and contemplation, and is home to some of the choicest salmon, trout, steelhead and halibut fishing on the continent. Freshwater spots are located about a half-hour boat ride from the lodge and require moderate hikes. Once there, though, you're rewarded with enchanting scenery and great fishing.

Rates for the lodge (capacity: six) range from $550 (April or October) to $700 (July, August) per person per night, including food, drink (beer, soft drinks, and wine), and guide fees, and do not include air transport to the lodge.

Sea kayaking

In the northern wilderness of BC, grizzlies are found in larger, more accessible numbers than perhaps anywhere else on earth. **Coast Mountain Expeditions** (250 285 2823, www.coastmountainexpeditions.com) runs an expedition that begins at Quadra Island (near Campbell River on Vancouver Island) with sea kayaking practice and the first night at a lodge. Three days of kayaking and camping brings you to PapKnach River camp, home of the First Nations Xwemahlkwu people. Up to 50 bears gather within ten kilometres (six miles) of the camp in the peak autumn season, when salmon return to the river, and viewing takes place both from platforms and your kayak. After two days getting to know grizzlies and the local culture – accommodation is in simple bunkhouses and all meals are taken with the First Nations people, learning about their customs and traditions – a boat will pick you up for the return journey. Paddling averages five hours per day in single or double kayaks, for a maximum of ten fit participants. Cost for the week is $1,525.

(For kayak rentals and lessons along English Bay and False Creek in Vancouver, *see p177*.)

Trips Out of Town

Victoria & Vancouver Island

Whales, Victoriana and islands to explore.

It wouldn't be unreasonable to think that Vancouver, the biggest city in British Columbia, would be its capital. Nor to expect it to be sited on Vancouver Island. But no. Vancouver sits firmly on the edge of the continental mainland, while Victoria, the provincial capital, lies south-west across the Strait of Georgia on Vancouver Island. The island stretches 454 kilometres (282 miles) along the western coast of BC, with Victoria tucked away in its far south-eastern corner. With a population of 750,000 in an area the size of England, Vancouver Island has plenty to offer long- and short-stay travellers.

Victoria & around

British Columbia's provincial capital, Victoria, has the look and feel of Vancouver's maiden aunt: old-fashioned and decorous, with a somewhat faded charm. Things were not always this way. Located on the southern tip of Vancouver Island, Victoria was prized by the British for its natural harbour, clement weather and fertile hinterland, and it prospered during the 1850s and '60s – the gold rush years – when it became both an essential staging post and an administrative centre. In 1866 it was the obvious capital for the province; the Parliament Buildings were completed in 1897.

By the 1920s the city's lustre began to fade as Vancouver began to eclipse it in importance, but Victoria was undaunted. The town cultivated its British heritage, preserving the architecture that was demolished or allowed to fall into disrepair and disrepute in Vancouver.

A century on, British visitors may find the 'olde England' accoutrements twee and chintzy, and the city isn't about to shake its retirement community atmosphere, but at least it stands in sharp relief to the sprawling strip malls that dominate the North American urban landscape. A contained, walkable town that makes the most of its waterfront, Victoria is a congenial spot to recharge your batteries before venturing into the wilds of Vancouver Island.

Victoria's delightful **Inner Harbour**.

Sightseeing

Attracting a seemingly unstoppable flood of tourists, Victoria has devised more attractions than many cities twice its size. Admittedly, you won't want to spend much more than an hour in the Art Gallery, Craigdarroch Castle, Crystal Gardens, the Maritime Museum, Miniature World, the Pacific Undersea Gardens, the Royal London Wax Museum, the Victoria Butterfly Museum or the Bug Zoo, but at least most of them are priced accordingly.

Victoria's appeal stems not from these cultural institutions, but rather from its ambience and environment. Its heart is centred on the Inner Harbour and the Old Town – a compact area easy to cover on foot (*see p197* **Echoes of the past**). Horse-drawn carriage tours and open-topped buses will expand your horizons to take in the borough south of downtown towards Ogden Point, a man-made breakwater with views across the Juan de Fuca Strait.

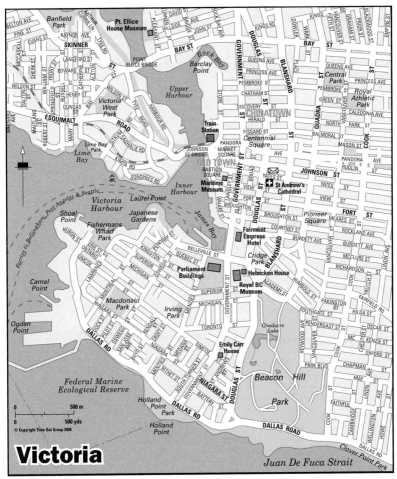

Victoria

Juan De Fuca Strait

The Inner Harbour is dominated by two Francis Rattenbury buildings: the **Parliament Buildings** at 501 Belleville Street (250 387 3046) and the **Fairmont Empress Hotel** at 721 Government Street (250 384 8111, www.fairmont. com/empress). Rattenbury was just 25 years old when he won the commission to design the provincial legislature in 1893. An Englishman from Leeds, he had recently arrived in Victoria; it is thought that the pen name under which he entered the competition helped his cause: 'A BC Architect'. The Parliament Buildings are grand, with six turrets facing the harbour and a rotunda at the centre. Free guided tours are available (every 20 minutes in summer; hourly in winter)

but it's best seen at night, when more than 3,000 light bulbs give it a fairyland glow – a tradition which dates from its opening in 1897, when the lights were a Diamond Jubilee tribute to Queen Victoria. The grand seven-storey Empress, commissioned by the Canadian Pacific Railway, is more imposing even than the Parliament Buildings from which it takes its turrets.

Despite his success, Rattenbury was ostracised in British Columbia after he divorced his wife and married the twice-divorced Alma Pakenham, 30 years his junior. In an affair that scandalised and fascinated the nation, he was clubbed to death by Alma's lover, 17-year-old chauffeur George Stoner. Alma was acquitted

Trips Out of Town

but stabbed herself through the heart after Stoner was sentenced to hang. Stoner later had his sentence commuted to life imprisonment.

Between the Empress and the Parliament Buildings, but off to the side on the corner of Belleville and Government, the **Royal BC Museum** is the city's cultural jewel. The collection goes back to the 19th century, but the current building was opened in 1968, with a new foyer added in 1996.

In the south-east corner of the complex, Heritage Court encompasses Thunderbird Park, a cedar longhouse and carving shed alongside a thicket of totem poles; and Helmcken House, a log cabin dating back to 1852. A few blocks further south is the **Emily Carr House**, which takes fashions forward to the early 1870s.

Strolling north up Government Street into the Old Town, take a peek in at **Rogers' Chocolates** (913 Government Street) for the original art nouveau interior and delicious aroma – speaking of which, **EA Morris** at number 1116 is a splendidly tangy tobacconist.

Munro's Books at 1108 Government Street is a relatively new tenant for the 1909 Royal Bank. It's handsomely designed and makes an impressive setting for this fine bookstore. The warehouses on Wharf Street are also well preserved, many dating from the 1860s.

Bastion Square is the site of the original Fort Vancouver, and a successful example of civic regeneration. Hard to believe now, with its sidewalk cafés and gas lamps, but for 50 years this was a car park. **The Maritime Museum** on the east side of the square has all manner of seafaring paraphernalia, though again, it's the building itself – BC's Supreme Court for most of its lifetime – which is more impressive. It's another Rattenbury design, from 1889. **Market Square**, north of Bastion, is also a recovered public space that maximises access to restored many 19th century storefronts and restaurants.

Chinatown, a block north on Fisgard Street, has also been restored, although you won't find the opium dens, brothels and gambling joints which earned it the nickname 'Forbidden Town' in the 1880s. **Fan Tan Alley**, between Fisgard and Pandora Streets, is said to be the narrowest street in the whole of North America.

Victoria Harbour Ferries (453 Head Street, 250 708 0201, www.victoriaharbourferry.com) runs small boats on a daily schedule (every 12-15 minutes in summer) to half a dozen stops along the Inner Harbour. Tickets are $4 for a short harbour hop ($2 for under-12s) and $20 ($10-$18 reductions) for the 45-minute Harbour Tour or 55-minute Gorge Cruise.

Fisherman's Wharf – west of the US customs office on Belleville Street, and a stop on the Harbour Ferry route – is a pretty marina filled with houseboats and yachts. You can buy fresh fish here, or sign up for whalewatching excursions with the legendary Captain Ron (*see p202* **Spout and about**).

Emily Carr House

207 Government Street (250 383 5843/www.emily carr.com). **Open** *May, Sept* 11am-4pm Tue-Sat. *June-Aug* 11am-4pm daily. **Admission** $5; $3.50 6-18s; free under-6s; $15 family. **Credit** DC, MC, V.
The birthplace of the artist and writer has been painstakingly restored to the way it would have looked in 1871. Note that the paintings here are reproductions, for the real thing head to the Art Gallery of Greater Victoria, at 1040 Moss Street (250 384 4101, www.aggv.bc.ca); *see also p33 and p60.*

Maritime Museum of British Columbia

28 Bastion Square (250 385 4222/www.mmbc. bc.ca). **Open** *16 Sept-14 June* 9.30am-4.30pm daily. *15 June-15 Sept* 9.30am-5pm daily. **Admission** $8; $3-$5 reductions. **Credit** AmEx, DC, MC, V.

Royal BC Museum

675 Belleville Street (250 356 7226/www.royalbc museum.bc.ca). **Open** *Museum* 9am-5pm daily. *IMAX* 10am-8pm daily. **Admission** *Museum* $14; $9 reductions; free under-5s. *Museum & IMAX film* $22.50; $17.75-$19 reductions; $5 under-5s. **Credit** AmEx, DC, MC, V.
The Royal BC, with its three permanent galleries, is one of the finest museums in Canada. The First Peoples Gallery has an array of Kwakwaka'wakw ceremonial masks (a *son et lumière* exhibit provides some keys to deciphering the iconography); carvings, models, a longhouse, and some extraordinary early 20th-century footage of native ceremonies.

In the Modern History Gallery you can board a partial replica of George Vancouver's HMS *Discovery* from the 1790s, join the gold rush, or explore the streets of turn of the century Victoria. If you have children, the Natural History Gallery is a must-see, with its artfully rendered dioramas of BC ecologies, interactive climate-change models and – the museum's undisputed prize – a life-size woolly mammoth.

Butchart Gardens

Butchart Gardens, 21 kilometres (14 miles) north of Victoria on Highway 17, is the city's most marketed attraction. Begun in 1904 by the wife of RP Butchart, a local cement pioneer, the gardens fill 20 hectares (50 acres) of the former limestone quarry. An organised tour mecca, the gardens get crowded in summer; if you can, get here first thing or late in the day. Summer evenings see classical concerts and fireworks displays on the lawns. The best areas are the Japanese garden – though this is a pale imitation of the real thing – and the bog garden, a quieter wooded area. High tea is available, and a fairly snooty affair it is too.

Walk Echoes of the past

HERALD ST
Train Station
FISGARD STREET
Centennial Square
PANDORA AVE
MARKET SQUARE
City Hall
JOHNSON ST BRIDGE
OLD TOWN
JOHNSON ST
WADDINGTON ALLEY
YATES ST
Start
Finish
BASTION SQUARE
Maritime Museum
VIEW STREET
St Andrew's Cathedral
FORT STREET
WHARF STREET
BROUGHTON ST
250 m
250 yds
© Copyright Time Out Group 2000

Start: Bastion Square, at Wharf Street.
Finish: Trounce Alley, at Government Street.

Victoria may seem genteel to a fault, but a stroll through Old Town reveals another side to the capital's character. At the foot of Bastion Square, look out over the harbour; during the 1920s US Prohibition this was known as 'Rum Row' as smugglers loaded boats with booze for midnight meetings south of the border.

Next, stand in front of the Maritime Museum of British Columbia at 28 Bastion Square. Built as a courthouse in 1889, formerly it was the site of the jail where public hangings occurred in the 1860s. Unclaimed victims were buried behind the jail; their remains are now embedded in the foundations of the museum.

Turn left onto Langley Street in order to reach Chancery Court, where lawyer Harry Pooley had his office. In the 1930s cult leader Brother XII put a curse on Pooley who was prosecuting him for embezzlement. Pooley won the case and died of old age, Brother XII skipped town.

Continue along Langley to Yates Street. Cross at the crosswalk, turn left and stop at the Leiser Building (524 Yates Street). Once a grocery warehouse owned by German-born Simon Leiser, it was ransacked in May 1915 after a German submarine torpedoed the passenger liner *Lusitania*.

Beside the Leiser Building, turn right into Waddington Alley, Victoria's last street paved with wooden blocks. Stop at 525 Johnson Street. The Salvation Army's building on the corner was the site of the California Saloon in the 1890s, where cigar-smoking Little Annie Roonie, a transvestite who loved to don the uniforms of tipsy sailors, played the piano.

Cross Johnson Street and continue along Store Street, just left of Market Square. Enter Market Square, if it's open. Once part of the red light district, the block used to be home to numerous saloons and hotels. Here in 1898 prostitute Belle Adams famously slashed the throat of her two-timing boyfriend, Charlie Kincaid, with his own straight razor.

Stay on Store Street, cross Pandora Avenue, walk to the left of Swan's Hotel (506 Pandora Ave). Across the street in the 1870s the Chinese bone house containing 1000 boxes of bones destined for China burned to the ground.

Turn right onto Fisgard Street and then continue your way through Chinatown until you reach Fan Tan Alley (next to 545 Fisgard). Once famous for gambling and opium dens, it's now an enclave of boutiques.

Continue up Fisgard to the Gate of Harmonious Interest. Cross Government Street and walk diagonally to the right across the open plaza, past the 'Bright Pearl' sculpture, toward Centennial Square. Walk through City Hall's arched colonnade, cross Pandora Avenue and continue along Broad Street to Johnson Street. Cross Johnson and stand in front of the Duck Block (1318 Broad Street), which is the second building on the right. Until 1905 it was home to Stella Carroll's high-end brothel.

Continue along Broad Street, cross Yates Street and then, after walking part-way down the block, turn right into Trounce Alley, a 19th-century shopping concourse. At Government Street look left across the street to the archway entrance to Bastion Square. On the left through the arch is the Garrick's Head (69 Bastion Square), one of the city's oldest saloons, and where spectators of the public hangings used to go to quench their thirst.

● *John Adams runs regular walking tours of Victoria. See www.discoverthepast.com.*

The best guides to enjoying London life

(but don't just take our word for it)

'More than 700 places where you can eat out for less than £20 a head... a mass of useful information in a geuinely pocket–sized guide'

Mail on Sunday

'Armed with a tube map and this guide there is no excuse to find yourself in a duff bar again'

Evening Standard

'I'm always asked how up to date with shopp and services in a city as London. This guide the answer'

Red Magazine

'Get the inside track on the capital's neighbourhoods'

Independent on Sunday

'A treasure trove of treats that lists the best the capital has to offer'

The People

Rated
'Best Restaurant Gui

Sunday Times

Available at all good bookshops and imeout.com/shop from £6.99

100% Indepen

Butchart Gardens

800 Benvenuto Avenue, Brentwood Bay (toll free 1-866 652 4422/www.butchartgardens.com).
Open 9am-dusk daily (later on fireworks evenings).
Admission $16-$26; $3-$13 reductions.
Credit AmEx, DC, MC, V.

Sooke

About 34 kilometres (21 miles) west of Victoria along Highway 14, the small forestry, fishing and farming centre of **Sooke** has made it onto the international tourist map by way of the **Sooke Harbour House** (1528 Whiffen Spit Road, 250 642 3421, www.sookeharbourhouse. com, set multi-course menu $75, tasting menu $120, doubles $250-$640). Luxurious waterfront accommodation is superseded only by the quality of the restaurant. Once you are rested and sated, the 3,512 acres of the East Sooke Regional Park (www.crd.bc.ca/parks/eastsooke) and its 50 kilometres (31 miles) of trails offer everything from seaside strolls to major treks. Wildlife is in abundance – sea otters, mink sea lions (Sept-May) are common, and late summer witnesses the annual congregation of hundreds of turkey vultures making ready to migrate.

Fisherman's Wharf. *See p196.*

Where to stay

Though it is crowded with hotels and B&Bs, Victoria in the summer months is even more crowded with visitors. Finding a decent room at an affordable price can be a challenge and you'd be crazy to come without making a reservation. If you do find yourself without a room go to the **Tourism Victoria Visitor Info Centre** (*see p201*), or call their reservation hotline on 1-800 663 3883. Off-season rates plummet and there's usually a deal for the asking. Check www. tourismvictoria.com for up-to-date listings or www.bestbnbvictoria.com for the best B&Bs.

There's no getting away from the **Fairmont Empress Hotel** (721 Government Street, 250 384 8111, toll free 1-800 441 1414, www.fairmont. com/empress, doubles $179-$449), the number one landmark of Victoria's inner harbour.

If you're after more up-to-date elegance, the **English Inn & Resort** (429 Lampson Street, 250 388 4353, toll free 1-866 388 4353, www. englishinnresort.com, suites $109-$399) is a luxurious option. A few minutes by water taxi from the inner harbour, its classy rooms provide a tranquil respite from the tourist throng.

For contemporary surroundings on the Inner Harbour, try **Laurel Point Inn** (680 Montreal Street, toll free 1-800 663 7667, 250 386 8721, www.laurelpoint.com, doubles $70-$204). Spacious rooms all have water views, and there's an indoor pool and Japanese garden.

Bed and breakfasts don't come more swish than **Andersen House** (301 Kingston Street, 250 388 4565, www.andersenhouse.com, doubles $145-$275), where rooms are large and beautifully turned out, with soaker tubs or jacuzzis, CD players and free Wi-Fi.

Off the waterfront, **Swans Suite Hotel** (506 Pandora Avenue, toll free 1-800 668 7926, 250 361 3310, www.swanshotel.com, suites $119-$359), in an 1880s grain store, offers high-ceilinged lofts with full kitchens.

Isabella's Guest Suites (537 Johnson Street, 250 812 9216, www.isabellasbb.com, suites $150-$195) are two self-contained stylish units in the heart of the Old Town with high ceilings, hardwood floors and claw foot tubs. Breakfast is provided at the downstairs bakery.

A 20-minute walk from the Inner Harbour, the cheap and cheerful **Surf Motel** (290 Dallas Road, 250 386 3305, www.surfmotel.net, doubles $95-$170) offers perhaps the best views in town – of the ocean and distant US mountains. There is also a simple three-bedroom bungalow.

Hostelling International Victoria (516 Yates Street, 250 385 4511, toll free 1-888 883 0099, www.hihostels.ca, dorm beds $18-$24.75) is the most central hostel, just a few blocks from the Inner Harbour.

Trips Out of Town

Where to eat & drink

As you might expect of a city that gets crammed with tourists, there are plenty of bad places to eat, many in the 'Olde English' pub grub style. If you want to avoid being left with no other choice during high season, make reservations.

For breakfast, **John's Place** (723 Pandora Avenue, 250 389 0711, www.johnsplace.ca, main courses $6-$21) is popular for traditional big-portioned American-style diner fare in a bustling place. An altogether different vibe can be found at **Mo:Lé** (554 Pandora Avenue, 250 385 6653, www.molerestaurant.ca, main courses $7-$19), where locals come for plates laden with artful takes on traditional brunch fare. For healthy food with pizzazz go to **Rebar** (50 Bastion Square, 250 361 9223, www.rebar modernfood.com, main courses $7-$14), where a few fish options fill out a vegetarian menu supported by a made-to-order juice bar.

Much is made of high tea in Victoria, but if you're going to do it, go the whole hog and reserve at the **Fairmont Empress Hotel** (721 Government Street, 250 384 8111, toll free 1-800 441 1414, www.fairmont.com/empress, afternoon tea from $39-$60) where finger sandwiches and scones have been a fact of life for almost a century. (Note: no ripped jeans, short shorts or jogging pants.) The hotel's unapologetically colonial Bengal Lounge provides an alternative trip down upper crust memory lane – as well as a decent cocktail and reasonably priced curry buffet (you must be 19 or over).

For something a little more casual, head to **Red Fish Blue Fish** (1006 Wharf Street, 250 298 6877, www.redfish-bluefish.com, main courses $5-$17) where former employees of Vancouver's Go Fish (*see p109*) have set up their own operation, serving out of a recycled shipping container. Excellent fish and chips and grilled fish are all guaranteed sustainable.

Canada's oldest brewpub, **Spinnakers Gastro Brewpub** (308 Catherine Street, 250 386 2739, www.spinnakers.com, main courses $10-$21), serves upscale pub food using local produce and free range meat.

Reliably good French country cooking can be had at **Brasserie L'École** (1715 Government Street, 250 475 6260, www.lecole.ca, main courses $19-$21). Fancy Italian? Try **Zambri's** (911 Yates Street, 250 360 1171) for a trattoria-style lunch of own-made sausages or gutsy pasta, or come back for a more upscale dinner.

Resources

Hospitals

Victoria General Hospital
1 Hospital Way (250 727 4212/emergency 250 727 4181).

Internet

James Bay Coffee and Books
143 Menzies Street (250 386 4700). **Open** 7.30am-10pm daily. **Rates** $6/hr. **Credit** DC, MC, V.

Relive those genteel bygone days at the **Fairmont Empress Hotel**. *See p199.*

Stain Internet Café

609 Yates Street (250 382 3352). **Open** 10am-2am daily. **Rates** $3.50/hr. **Credit** AmEx, DC, MC, V.

Police

In an emergency, dial **911**.

Victoria Police Department

850 Caledonia Avenue (250 995 7654).

Post office

Main Post Office

706 Yates Street, between Douglas & Blanshard Streets (250 953 1352). **Open** 8am-5pm Mon-Fri. **Credit** AmEx, DC, MC, V.

Tourist information

Tourism Victoria Visitor Info Centre

812 Wharf Street (250 953 2033/www.tourism victoria.com). **Open** *1 Sept-15 June* 9am-5pm daily. *16 June-31 Aug* 8.30am-7.30pm daily.

Getting there

By air

Air Canada (toll free 1-888 247 2262, www. aircanada.com) and **West Jet** (toll free 1-888 937 8538, www.westjet.com) operate many daily flights between Vancouver International Airport and Victoria International Airport. Prices start at around $109. For seaplanes, *see p85* **Plane sailing**.

By ferry

BC Ferries (*see p227*) runs from Tsawwassen, about an hour south of Vancouver, into Swartz Bay, just 20 minutes from downtown Victoria by Highway 17. From Swartz Bay Ferry Terminal or the nearby Victoria International Airport, downtown Victoria is 26km (16 miles) by route 17 (the Patricia Bay Highway). The number 70 bus connects Victoria with Swartz Bay. (To access Tofino and the north of the island, the faster ferry route is from Horseshoe Bay on Vancouver's North Shore to Nanaimo.)

In summer, another option is the four-hour boat crossing combined with whale-watching tour run by **Prince of Whales** out of Vancouver Harbour (see *p202* **Spout and about**).

By car

There is only one main artery running south-north: Route 1 (the Trans-Canada Highway) continues in Victoria and hugs the east coast passing through pretty Cowichan Bay, Duncan ('the city of totems'), Chemainus (with its 33 life-sized murals) and Ladysmith (the birthplace of Pamela Anderson) before turning into Highway 19 at Nanaimo, 113km (70 miles) from Victoria.

From Nanaimo you can take either Highway 19 or the old, scenic Highway 19A to Campbell River – the halfway point up the island, 231km (144 miles) from Victoria, 220km (137 miles) from Port Hardy on the farthest tip. Campbell River is also the exit for Highway 28 into the Strathcona Provincial Park.

By rail

The Malahat (toll free 1-888 842 7245, www. viarail.ca) is a pleasant and cheap alternative to car or bus. One train runs each way, daily, from Victoria to Courtney (and the ski possibilities of Mount Washington) by way of Nanaimo. The hop-on hop-off Victoria–Nanaimo round trip costs as little as $30. Check the website for schedule and fare alternatives.

Vancouver Island

Vancouver Island is going places. In September 2005 seismologists detected the island had slipped three millimetres towards Japan in the course of just a few days. Comparable tectonic slips occur every 14 months, and are a possible trigger for the long-awaited megathrust earthquake, the 'big one' due to visit this coastline in the next two hundred years. Looking on the bright side, forest, rock, brush, wetland, lakes and rivers cover 96 per cent of the island. If and when the big one hits, it will likely take it in its stride.

There are plenty of ways to explore this wilderness. Kayaking, canoeing, whale watching, fishing, yachting and diving tour companies are ubiquitous (this is considered one of the best diving areas in the world for its exceptional visibility, rich marine life and a number of artificial reefs). The west coast provides BC's best surfing and storm watching, at **Tofino**. On land, cycling, skiing, hiking and climbing are all readily available in season. Black-tailed deer, elk and black bears are relatively plentiful in the north of the island. Bird watching is another common pursuit, especially during the migration period. More than 1,000 limestone caves have been explored and recorded. The forests include the world's largest yellow cedar and towering spruce, conifers, arbutus trees and Garry oaks. Then there's **Della Falls**. At 440 metres (1,445 feet), these are nearly eight times as high as Niagara Falls – but to get there requires a 34-kilometre (21-mile) boat trip up Great Central Lake, followed by a seven hour, 16-kilometre (10-mile) trek through Strathcona Park (for guided trips, try Ark Resort, 250 723 2657, www.arkresort.com). For more island adventures, *see p204*.

Trips Out of Town

Tofino & Pacific Rim National Park

Although it was named as early as 1792 after a Spanish explorer, Don de Vincent **Tofino**, it's only since Highway 4 was extended out to land's end in the early 1970s that this Clayoquot village on the western shore of Vancouver Island opened up to the world.

The Pacific Ocean here is tumultuous and the weather fierce – the tourism industry has even capitalised by charging peak prices for storm watching from December to February, when the coast is buffeted by ten to fifteen storms a month

and waves up to six metres (20 feet) high. Japan is the nearest port of call, some 7,456 kilometres (4,633 miles) due west. Long Beach is a jagged 11-kilometre (seven-mile) stretch of white sandy beach framed by rocky outcrops, sitka spruce, dense rainforest and the MacKenzie Range. It's the best spot in Canada for windsurfers and surfers; you can rent boards and wetsuits from Tofino town and Ucluelet 40 kilometres (25 miles) south. Numerous well-marked trails provide hiking at all levels of difficulty – the 800-metre (2,625-foot) Bog Trail is wheelchair accessible. The Wickaninnish Centre on Wickaninnish Bay (250 726 4701) has

Spout and about

Playing Ahab is one of BC's most popular tourist activities. Not that you'll see a great white, but there are plentiful orcas, and you might see Pacific grays. More than 20,000 tour the west coast of Vancouver Island en route for the Bering Straits in March and April, 40 to 50 stay in the area through the summer. Seals, dolphins, otters and sea lions are fairly common.

The quality of your whale-watching depends on how far you're prepared to go. Lower mainland tours can't compete with the sea kayak experiences you'll find on the northeast coast of Vancouver Island, with orcas in abundance and improved chances of seeing humpbacks (*see p203*) or the convoys of gray whales which pass by Tofino and Ucluelet on the west. You can sign up for tours in Granville Island, Vancouver, but the nearest whale boats actually leave from Steveston, the fishing village 25 minutes south of downtown. From there, the expedition lasts between three and five hours.

Victoria offers greater choice of boats and shorter journey times: there are three pods of orcas (about 100 animals) resident year round in the Juan de Fuca Strait. In addition, between May and October up to 30 smaller pods of transient orcas pass through this area. The orcas range about 100 miles a day, but tour operators routinely guarantee sightings – which means that if the pods are too far away for comfort, or if the weather conditions aren't conducive, they won't go out. (Cancellations are by no means uncommon.) If the forecast is for wind and rain, come back another day. Boats are not allowed to run motors within 100 metres of the whales, but contact is often much closer

than that, as an experienced captain will let the craft drift into the orcas' route.

When choosing a tour, the deciding factor has to be the type of craft. In Victoria, the market-leader is **Prince of Whales**, operating a fleet of open-air zodiac boats (1 888 383 4884, www.princeofwhales.com, rates $85 three hour tour; $69 under-12s). The zodiacs offer plenty of splash, but limited room to move and they don't all have toilet facilities. Covered boats are more comfortable, but less of a thrill – and higher passenger numbers cut down your access to the skipper. (In the summer season Prince of Whales runs a covered boat out of Vancouver Harbour to Victoria, a four-hour whale-watching trip tailored with several add-ons.) We recommend **SeaKing Adventures** (Fisherman's Wharf, Pier 4, 250 381 4173, www.seaking.ca). Captain Ron has been running whale tours for over ten years and fished these waters for 25 years before that. His motorboat offers seating for parties no larger than 12. Chances are you'll see a harbour seal before you even leave Fisherman's Wharf. In high season expect to pay about $80 plus tax; $55 under-16s.

information, films, observation decks with telescopes and a café, mid March to mid October.

The town itself is small, but there are some worthwhile shops and attractions in the vicinity: the **Tofino Botanical Garden** (1084 Pacific Rim Highway, 250 725 1220, www.tbgf.org) cuts a marked contrast with the Butchart's Victoriana – here you'll find the children's garden, the First Nations garden, and the hippie garden. It's open daily from 9am to dusk, admission is $10, with under-12s free. The **Eagle Aerie Gallery** (350 Campbell Street, at 2nd Avenue, 250 725 3235) is the best known of more than 20 art galleries. And the **Raincoast Interpretive Centre** (451 Main Street, 250 725 2560, www.tofinores.com) is a mine of information about the local ecosystem.

Tofino is a great spot to watch whales – from late February to May you can see pods of Pacific gray whales migrating without even leaving the beach. Up to 50 grays are resident throughout summer. Increasing numbers of humpbacks are also being spotted on the west coast – expect to pay $60 for a three hour whale-watching voyage. All the local tour operators also offer bear-watching, and most are more than happy to do a tour to the geothermal springs, where natural pools are supplied by a hot waterfall.

Where to stay

The **Wickaninnish Inn** (Osprey Lane, Chesterman Beach, 250 725 3100, toll free 1-800 333 4604, www.wickinn.com, doubles $220-$440) is top spot here for its superb location on a promontory. The rooms – all with views – have double soaker tubs next to picture windows.

The **Long Beach Lodge Resort** (1441 Pacific Rim Highway, 250 725 2442, toll free 1-877 844 7873, www.longbeachlodgeresort.com, doubles $169-$349) is another high-end treat, with similar amenities to the Wickaninnish Inn, plus a lodge room and 12 two-bedroom cottages.

A good mid-price option is the **Middle Beach Lodge** (Mackenzie Beach Road, 250 725 2900, toll free 1-866 725 2900, www.middlebeach.com, doubles $110-$230), with rooms in the oceanfront lodge or self-contained beach cabins.

You can camp for $21 to $46 at **Bella Pacifica Campground** (250 725 3400, www.bellapacifica.com) two miles south of Tofino near Mackenzie Beach. Or check out the accommodation section of www.tofino time.com for a range of houses to rent and B&Bs.

Where to eat

The **Pointe** at the Wickaninnish Inn (Osprey Lane, Chesterman Beach, 250 725 3100, www.wickinn.com, main courses $14-$48) is the destination restaurant in the area, so reserve

ahead for dinner. The signature Wickaninnish potlach is a delectable dish of local seafood, the perfect accompaniment to watching the Pacific roll in through the panoramic windows.

The vibe at **Shelter** (601 Campbell Street, 250 725 3353, www.shelterrestaurant.com, main courses $16-$36) is a more relaxed affair. Its cosy, contemporary interior includes an open fire and an open kitchen. Portions in the restaurant are hearty; the lounge offers a simpler menu including rice bowls and burgers.

SoBo (311 Neill Street, 250 725 2341, www.sobo.ca, main courses $20-$30) is the cult upstart that started life as a catering truck serving 'killer' fish tacos and Asian-inspired salads. Food remains simple and bold.

If you fancy a bona fide hippie experience, head to the **Common Loaf Bakery** (180 1st Street, 250 725 3915, main courses $4-$8) for pizza, soups, and curries. And it's licenced.

Tourist information

The **Tofino Visitor Info Centre** (Pacific Rim Highway, 250 725 3414, www.tofinobc.org) is eight kilometres (five miles) out of town and open 10am-4pm; phone for winter hours. www.longbeachmaps.com and www.tofinotime.com have good listings, maps and advice.

The rustic luxury of the **Wickaninnish Inn**.

Trips Out of Town

Getting there

For travel via Victoria and the southern end of Vancouver Island, *see p201* **Getting there**.

By car

To reach Tofino from Vancouver, take **BC Ferries** (*see p227*) from Horseshoe Bay to Nanaimo, drive north on Highway 19. Take exit 60, about 30km (19 miles) north of Nanaimo, onto Highway 4 for a scenic but twisty 180km (112-mile) drive by way of Port Alberni. Cathedral Grove, just past Cameron Lake, is a worthwhile stop: a strip of old growth forest where 800-year-old Douglas firs tower 70 metres (230 feet).

By bus

Tofino Bus (toll free 1-866 986 3466, www.tofino bus.com) runs a direct express service from Victoria to Tofino and Ucluelet daily, picking up from Hostelling International, 516 Yates Street at 8.15am, and Ocean Backpackers Inn, 791 Pandora Avenue, 15 minutes later in summer (departures are from the bus depot, 700 Douglas Street, in winter). The trip takes five hours and costs $64.29 one-way/$128.58 return.

The Southern Gulf Islands

Idyllic in landscape and rustic in character, the Southern Gulf Islands are a favourite getaway for urbanites seeking quiet, pastoral havens. While some 300 islands sprinkle British Columbia's southern coastline, the majority are picturesque rock formations or wilderness reserves visited only by boaters. The larger islands, however, support substantial communities – artists, city escapees and folks who live to the beat of a different drummer. Getting there via BC Ferries (toll free 1-888 223 3779, www.bcferries.com) is half the fun.

Salt Spring Island

www.saltspringtoday.com.
The largest of the Gulf Islands (pop.10,000), **Salt Spring** is where west coast temperate rainforest meets English countryside. Sheep graze on grassy hills, deer meander freely, and gardens are filled with shasta daisies and other wild flowers. **Ganges** is 'island central' and home to numerous shops, galleries and restaurants, including the award-winning **House Piccolo** (108 Hereford Avenue, 250 537 1844, www.housepiccolo.com, main courses $26-$37) and the more casual, local hangout **Moby's Marine Pub** (124 Upper Ganges Road, 250 537 5559, main courses $7-$13). More than 150 inns and B&Bs make staying longer easy. **Hastings House** (160 Upper Ganges Road, toll free 1-800 661 9255, 250 537 2362, www.hastingshouse.com, doubles $295-$910) is the hot spot for the well heeled traveller, but you need to book at least six months ahead. At the other end of the scale, **Ruckle Provincial Park** (Beaver Point Road, 250 539 2115, campsite $14) is the in-place for campers and hikers. While on Salt Spring, be sure to take the self-guided art studio tour, following a trail of potters, weavers, glass blowers and painters, and try to include Ganges's Saturday market.

Galiano Island

www.galianoisland.com.
Galiano is the second largest island, yet has only 1,000 residents, and although it's the shortest ferry ride from Vancouver, it has managed to retain a distinctly hippie ambience. It's also regarded as the prettiest of the Gulf Islands, with log-strewn beaches, windswept coastlines, parks, views and abundant wildlife, including more than 130 species of bird and many rare and protected plants. Most commercial activity is located in and around Sturdies Bay where the ferries dock, where you'll also find one of the island's nicest inns, **Galiano Inn & Madrona Del Mar Spa** (134 Madrona Drive, 250 539 3388, toll free 1-877 530 3939, www.galianoinn.com, doubles $179-$399). Head north and the landscape of this long, skinny island gives way to lush forests and magnificent parks: two of note are **Montague Harbour** and **Dionisio Point**.

Mayne Island

www.mayneislandchamber.ca.
Mayne Island's compact size makes it an ideal day trip. If you're a cyclist, **Mayne** is also the easiest island to manoeuvre around. There are a few tough climbs but you're rewarded with plenty of beaches, bays and vistas to explore, among them Campbell Bay for its swimming and sculpted sandstone cliffs, Horton Bay for its quaint boat harbour and Piggott Bay for its wide, sandy beach. The hub of the community is Miner's Bay. Here's where to find **Springwater Lodge** (C-27 Miners Bay, 250 539 5521, www.spring waterlodge.com, main courses $7-$15, doubles $40-$95), one of BC's oldest watering holes, plus an 1896 gaol (now a museum) and a good stop for groceries, liquor and kayak rentals (www.maynekayak.com). An unexpected delight is the Japanese Memorial Garden at Dinner Bay, minutes away from the island's

Spa partners

If time and travels permit, a spa break is pure vacation indulgence. So why not indulge?

URBAN GETAWAYS

The Aerie and Brentwood Bay Lodge & Spa are newsmakers in terms of travel destinations, and both are within a 30-minute drive of Victoria. The **Aerie Resort & Spa** (108 Malahat, 250 743 7115, toll free 1-800 518 1933, www.aerie.bc.ca, rates $160-$195/90-minute treatment, $350-$600 two-night package) is perched atop Malahat Mountain, with views of the coastal peaks and valleys. The eight-room, oceanfront **Brentwood Bay Lodge & Spa** (849 Verdier Avenue, 250 544 2079, toll free 1-888 544 2079, www.brentwoodbaylodge.com, rates $175-$185/80-minute treatment, $438-$1,418 two-night package) is one of Canada's few members of Small Luxury Hotels of the World.

ISLAND RETREATS

Parksville's **Tigh-Na-Mara Seaside Spa Resort** (1155 Resort Drive, 250 248 2072, www.tigh-na-mara.com, rates $165-$195/90-minute treatment, $238-$578 2-night package) balances the concept of adult retreat with family togetherness and includes the two-storey Grotto Spa, a large mineral pool set in an oasis of ferns, rocks and waterfalls. **Kingfisher Oceanside Resort & Spa** (4330 Island Highway South, 250 338 1323, toll free 1-800 663 7929, www.kingfisher spa.com, rates $110-$150/90-minute treatment, $381-$399 two night package) in Courtenay is a popular getaway for city folk and visitors alike. Its 22 treatment rooms, steam cave, sauna, hot tub and outdoor heated pool absorb everyone with ease.

THE WESTERLY WILDS

Ancient Cedars Spa at the famed Wickanninish Inn (*see page 203*, rates $150-$175/90-minute treatment, $555-$842 two-night package) is geared to well-heeled spa goers with a wide range of quality services, featuring windows overlooking the crest of ocean-splashed rocks. The ultimate west coast spa experience must be at the **Healing Grounds Spa & Wellness Centre**

Aerie Resort & Spa.

at Clayoquot Wilderness Resort (888 333 5405 www.wildr etreat.com, rates $200-$225/90-minute treatment; $4,750-$5,500 three-day package). A 20-minute boat ride from Tofino, this indoor-outdoor spa offers fern-shaded massage decks alongside intimately appointed treatment rooms. The outdoor, waterfall-fed pool and steamy cedar hot tubs are an added bonus.

choicest inn, **Oceanwood Country Inn & Restaurant** (630 Dinner Bay Road, 250 539 5074, www.oceanwood.com, set four-course menu $55, doubles $139-$299).

Sailing on...

As the transfer point for inter-island ferries, Mayne is a good base for island-hopping, particularly if you're heading to Pender (www.penderislandchamber.com) or Saturna (www.saturnatourism.com). From Vancouver, however, ferry schedules make it difficult to do these islands justice as a day trip. Stay over, and you'll discover **Pender Island** to be a thriving community of 2,000 residents with diverse B&Bs and sophisticated spots like **Poets Cove Resort & Spa** (9801 Spalding Road, South Pender Island, toll free 1-888 512 7638, www.poetscove.com, doubles $169-$249). Pender's sheltered anchorages and accessible beaches make it a boater's paradise. Add to this areas such as Mount Norman and Mount Menzies, both part of the Gulf Islands National Park Reserve, as well as Brookes Point, and you begin to see why Pender Island deserves more than a passing visit. **Saturna Island** is somewhat different, and its 400 homesteaders, while friendly, tend to relish their isolation.

Trips Out of Town

The Okanagan

BC's wine and fruit country.

The most populated area of British Columbia outside the Lower Mainland, the **Okanagan** is just a five-hour drive or 60-minute flight from Vancouver, yet it basks in a much milder, predominantly semi-arid climate, making it a desirable spot for retirees and the summer vacation crowd. In recent years the wine industry has put this picturesque lake region on the tourism map. Following Highway 97 for 234 kilometres (145 miles) – from Salmon Arm in the north to Osoyoos in the south – you can visit more than 50 wineries, many with Vintner Quality Alliance (VQA) certification. Varietals range from a regional signature pinot blanc and other European-style whites, made with grapes grown mainly in the cooler north, to pinot noir, merlot, cabernet sauvignon and other reds from fruit nurtured in the dips and slopes of the central and southern mountains. World-famous ice wines are made from grapes picked mid-winter at precisely minus eight degrees Celsius.

Reliably hot and rainless in the summer, the region attracts families for swimming, boating, fishing and other sports on five almost contiguous lakes and several rivers. Factor in 28 golf courses and innumerable hiking and biking trails, and you have a multifaceted, laid-back recreational paradise. In winter, with cold but largely dry, sunny weather, full-facility ski resorts at Vernon (Silver Star, www.skisilverstar. com) and Big White (Big White, www.bigwhite. com) cater to mostly local ski enthusiasts, and boast cheaper deals than Whistler.

THE LAY OF THE LAND

Highway 97 runs the length of the Okanagan, with roads to wineries, recreational and wilderness sites branching out along the way. For wine seekers, the region can be divided into north, central and south – each with clusters of wineries and subtly different products. The highest concentrations are near Kelowna, Penticton, and south of Oliver. Major resorts are located in and around Kelowna and Penticton. Smaller hotels, motels, B&Bs and camping sites can be found the length of the region. Similarly, culinary, cultural and recreational attractions are scattered throughout.

TOURS

Though you can fly directly from Vancouver into Kelowna or Penticton, you will need to hire a car to get around. If driving is likely to cramp your winery style, customised small group tours are available. Discover Okanagan Tours (toll free 1-800 797 6335, www.discover okanagantours.com) offers a variety of different tours at reasonable prices. The Great Estates of the Okanagan tour (250 433 0451, toll free 1-877 433 0451, www.greatestatesokanagan.com) was set up in 2007 by five of the big wineries and offers both a set day trip with lunch and dinner, or personalized and multi-day trips.

Sightseeing

Kelowna (pop. 150,000) straddles the 144-kilometre (89-mile) long Lake Okanagan at mid girth. A bit of a sprawl, the city is sited on the east bank, then meanders over on to what's called Westbank. A dozen wineries are found on both sides of the lake, including Mission Hill, Quails' Gate and Cedar Creek.

Calona Vineyards, the granddaddy of Okanagan wineries, turns out award-winning VQA varietals, as well as beers and spirits. Its downtown winery, open daily year-round, showcases BC wine industry history and the mechanics of big-time beverage production.

For similar insight into the fruit growing industry, visit the Kelowna Land & Orchard Co, in the city's northeast. Covered wagons take visitors on hour-long tours of the 50-hectare - working orchard. There's a petting farm, store, restaurant and fine cidery.

Downtown Kelowna boasts an attractive lake front, and a burgeoning cultural district (www.kelownasculturaldistrict.com) with a new arts centre for visitors and galleries, theatres, shops and restaurants. The Laurel Packinghouse is a former fruit-packing facility that now houses the Wine Museum & VQA Wine Shop and the delightful little Orchard Museum that charts the region's development using a real apple tree and a 15-metre (49-foot) model railway. Nearby are the Okanagan Heritage Museum (470 Queensway Avenue, 250 763 2417, www.kelownamuseum.ca) and Okanagan Military Museum (1424 Ellis Street, 250 763 9292, www.okmilmuseum.ca).

The city's early history is encapsulated at the Father Pandosy Mission (3685 Benvoulin Road, 250 860 8369), a reconstructed mission site run by the Central Okanagan Heritage Society. For serious walkers and cyclists, the Mission Creek

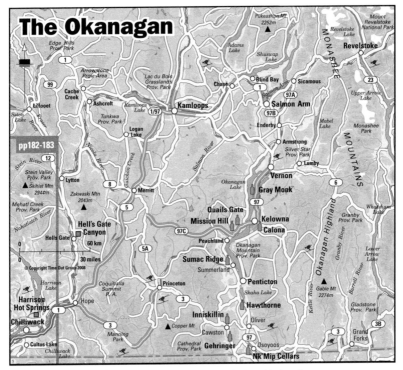

The Okanagan

Greenway (www.greenway.kelowna.bc.ca) begins on Lakeshore Road and wends 16.5 kilometres (10 miles) eastward.

In 2003 a fire ravaged the Kelowna region, destroying 12 of 18 trestles along the former Kettle Valley Railway route, a national historic site. They're being rebuilt and the 18-kilometre (11-mile) Myra Canyon cycling and hiking route (www.trailsbc.ca) is open with bypasses.

In and around Kelowna you'll see images of a Loch-Ness-like monster that is known as the Ogopogo. The creature reputedly mainly lurks on the east side of Okanagan Lake, while residing in a cave near Peachland.

Highway 97 runs north through **Vernon**, with historic O'Keefe Ranch (www.okeefe ranch.ca) nearby, and **Armstrong**, with several artisan cheese-makers. At Highway 97's extremity (connecting with Highway 1) are **Salmon Arm** and **Sicamous**, both on Shuswap Lake, and renowned for their hot-season house boating.

Heading south on 97 from Kelowna, you pass through Westbank, Peachland and Summerland and into **Penticton**. Historically

an agricultural hub and watersports mecca, the city of 40,000 has of late acquired a glossier patina thanks to the burgeoning wine industry.

More than a dozen smallish wineries perch along the lovely **Naramata Bench**, lined with orchards and vineyards, to the northeast of the city. The 16-kilometre (ten-mile) Naramata Road, one of BC's best short drives, follows the bench to the lakeside village of Naramata.

Penticton attractions include the permanently moored stern-wheeler SS *Sicamous* (1099 W Lakeshore Drive, 250 492 0403, www.ss sicamous.com) and the Kettle Valley Steam Railway, which offers two-hour trips from Summerland on a ten-kilometre (six-mile) stretch of track built between 1910 and 1915.

Sandy beaches bless both ends of the city. On Okanagan Lake in the north there's water-skiing, wind-surfing and boat rentals. Skaha Lake in the south (slightly warmer, some say) offers water slides and barbecue firepits. A mid-city channel that connects the lakes is reserved for rubber-tube floating. Tubes can be rented.

Golf is huge in the Okanagan. The most prestigious course in the Penticton region is

Trips Out of Town

It's a vine life

Wineries are so numerous and so varied that choosing standouts is foolish. The following list therefore spans regions, varietals, eateries and access. Many are open year-round, but the hours change, so check ahead. All offer wine tastings, sometimes with a modest charge; many provide tours. Some also have excellent restaurants and accommodation. All make reputable wines.

Getting to **Gray Monk Estate Winery** from Highway 97 north of Kelowna requires a little map work. But the lake setting and crisp, fruity wines enjoyed in the patio restaurant with a sophisticated meal make the travel and effort worthwhile.

Mission Hill Winery (*pictured*), whose monastery-like complex with bell tower rises from a hill west of Kelowna, is a worthy destination. While the signature wine is a Bordeaux-inspired Oculus, Mission Hill makes many varietals. The alfresco Terrace restaurant is one of the region's best.

Nearby **Quails' Gate Estate Winery** maintains a stellar reputation not just for its many wines, but also its historic log house and well-regarded Old Vines restaurant, which is open year-round.

Sumac Ridge Estate Winery is a major producer with an enviable reputation for its many award-winning wines, appealing wine room, and year-round Cellar Door Bistro restaurant. It's on 97 near Summerland.

Along the Naramata Road, a dozen or so well-signposted wineries are young, playful, and turning out commendable wines. They include producers of an increasingly popular rosé and the aromatic Noble blend, Joie (2825 Naramata Road, 250 496 0093,

www.joie.ca); Elephant Island Winery (2730 Aikins Loop, 250 496 5522, www.elephantislandwine.com), a crafter of alternate fruit-based wines; and the Red Rooster Winery (891 Naramata Road, 250 492 2424, www.redroosterwinery.com).

Blasted Church, in the same region, gets its controversial name from the dynamiting of a place of worship in 1929. The tasting room is nicely sited with views over the lake; the wines (and art labels) are worthy of close attention.

South of Oliver on the Black Sage Road, the relatively new adobe-style **Burrowing Owl Estate Winery** has taken its place among the finest producers. The unparalleled setting includes a good restaurant and lovely new guest house.

Serious wine-seekers will set aside time for the major wineries located on the southern stretch of 97. For variety and price, a good bet is **Gehringer Brothers Estate Winery**, which makes more than 20 wines, including a signature ice wine. Another biggie known for its ice wines is **Inniskillin Okanagan Vineyards**.

Head south to Osoyoos, and you'll find **Nk'Mip Cellars**, recently emerged to dramatic effect from a dry, sage-covered landscape overlooking Osoyoos Lake. Built by the Nk'Mip Indian Band in co-operation with Vincor International, both builders and vintners appear to be doing everything right, including an excellent restaurant and plush accommodation.

There are wine festivals in every season, but the biggest is the Fall Wine Festival. It takes place over ten days at the beginning of October.

the 18-hole Penticton Golf and Country Club. Kelowna boasts five courses of similar championship status, including Predator Ridge, Gallagher's Canyon, Harvest, and the Quail and the Bear. Other courses are located as far north as Vernon and south in Osoyoos. Many are also resorts and spas. Hiking and mountain biking over the mountains are increasingly popular.

From Penticton, Highway 97 continues to the southern region where the Okanagan embraces the northern end of the Sonoran desert (which begins in Mexico). Protectors of this unique and endangered desert environment have been struggling to save at least some of it

from ever-encroaching vineyards, which have become so numerous that the town of **Oliver** calls itself the 'wine capital of Canada'.

North of Oliver, near the village of Okanagan Falls and Vaseaux Lake (a pristine wildlife reserve), nestle mostly smaller wineries, some with enviable reputations. From Oliver south on 97 stretches the Golden Mile, with big operations like Tinhorn Creek, Gehringer Brothers and Inniskillin. To the east of 97, from just outside Oliver, the Black Sage Road winds along hills said to grow the best red grapes anywhere. Here wineries range from the boutique-like Black Hills to the destination estate called Burrowing Owl.

Blasted Church

378 Parsons Road, Okanagan Falls (250 497 1125/www.blastedchurch.com). **Open** *May-Oct* 10am-5pm daily. *Nov-Apr* Sat only; phone for times. **Credit** AmEx, DC, MC, V.

Burrowing Owl Estate Winery

100 Burrowing Owl Place, off Black Sage Road, Oliver (toll free 1-877 498 0620/www. burrowingowlwine.ca). **Open** 10am-5pm daily. **Credit** DC, MC, V.

Gehringer Brothers Estate Winery

Highway 97, at Road 8, between Osoyoos & Oliver (250 498 3537/toll free 1-800 784 6304). **Open** *June-mid Oct* 10am-5pm daily. *Mid Oct-May* 10am-5pm Mon-Fri. **Credit** AmEx, DC, MC, V.

Gray Monk Estate Winery

1055 Camp Road, Okanagan Centre (250 766 3168/1-800 663 4205/www.graymonk. com). **Open** *Apr-June, Sep, Oct* 10am-5pm daily. *July, Aug* 9am-9pm daily. *Nov-Mar* 11am-5pm Mon-Sat. *Tours* see website, or phone for schedule. **Credit** AmEx, DC, MC, V.

Inniskillin Okanagan Vineyards

Road II, C5, Oliver (250 498 6663/toll free 1-800 498 6211/www.inniskillin.com). **Open** *Nov-Apr* 10am-5pm daily. *May-Oct* 10am-6pm daily. **Credit** DC, MC, V.

Mission Hill Winery

1730 Mission Hill Road, Westbank (250 768 6448/www.missionhillwinery.com). **Open** *May-Sept* 10am-6pm daily. *Oct-Apr* 10am-5pm daily. **Credit** AmEx, DC, MC, V.

Nk'Mip Cellars

1400 Rancher Creek Road, Osoyoos (250 495 2985/www.nkmipcellars.com). **Open** 9am-5pm daily. *Tours* phone for schedule. **Credit** DC, MC, V.

Quails' Gate Estate Winery

3303 Boucherie Road, Kelowna (250 769 4451/toll free 1-800 420 9463/www. quailsgate.com). **Open** 9am-6pm daily. *Tours* phone for schedule. **Rates** *Tours* $5. **Credit** DC, MC, V.

Sumac Ridge Estate Winery

17403 Highway 97N, Summerland (250 494 0451/www.sumacridge.com). **Open** *Tours* May-Oct 10am-3pm daily. Nov-Apr phone to reserve. **Rates** *Tour & tasting* $5; *tutored tasting with specialist* $10. **Credit** AmEx, DC, MC, V.

Near the town of **Osoyoos** nestles Nk'Mip Cellars, operated by the Osoyoos Indian Band. The large complex ncludes a winery, restaurant, deluxe accommodations, and the Nk'Mip Desert & Heritage Centre, devoted to regional history and ecology with self-guided trails over 20 hectares (50 acres), a reconstructed traditional village and an adopt-a-rattlesnake programme. For those who prefer their wildlife one step removed, the Desert Centre (250 495 2470, www.desert.org), located on 97 north of Osoyoos, offers guided interpretive tours along an elevatedboardwalk.

In BC, Highway 3 travels west through the **Similkameen Valley**, an extension of the

Okanagan with ranching, fruit-growing and increasingly, grape-growing. In summer and autumn fruit sellers populate **Keremeos**, dubbed 'the fruit stand capital of Canada'. From here the 3 becomes the twisty Hope-Princeton before rejoining the 1 at Hope. Osoyoos to Vancouver is 396 kilometres (246 miles), about the same as the distance between Kelowna and Vancouver via the Coquihalla Highway.

Calona Vineyards

1125 Richter Street, Kelowna (250 762 9144/ www.calonavineyards.ca). **Open** 9am-6pm daily. **Admission** *Tastings* $3-$4; *no tours.* **Credit** AmEx, DC, MC, V.

Kelowna Land & Orchard Co
*3002 Dunster Road, Kelowna (250 763 1091/toll
free 1-888 246 4472/www.k-l-o.com).* **Open** (Apr-Oct)
Tours 11am and 1pm daily. *Restaurant* 11am-3pm
daily. **Main courses** $14. **Admission** $6.50; $3
reductions; free under-12s. **Credit** DC, MC, V.

Kettle Valley Steam Railway
*Prairie Valley Station, 18404 Bathville Road,
Summerland (250 494 8422/www.kettlevalleyrail.
org).* **Open** May-Oct; phone for details. **Tickets** $19;
$11-$18 reductions; $65 family. **Credit** DC, MC, V.

Laurel Packinghouse
*1304 Ellis Street, Kelowna (250 763 4761/
www.kelownamuseum.ca).* **Open** *Wine Museum
& VQA Shop* 10am-6pm Mon-Fri; 10am-5pm Sat;
11am-5pm Sun. *Orchard Museum* 10am-5pm Mon-
Fri; 10am-4pm Sat. **Admission** by donation.
Credit DC, MC, V.

Nk'Mip Desert Cultural Centre
*1000 Rancher Creek Road, Osoyoos (250 495 7901/
toll free 1-888 495 8555/www.nkmipdesert.com).*
Open *May-Oct* 9.30am-4.30pm daily. *Nov-Apr*
9.30am-4.30pm Mon-Sat. **Admission** $12; $8-$11
reductions; $36 family. **Credit** DC, MC, V.

Penticton Golf & Country Club
*Comox Street, off Eckhardt Avenue, Penticton
(250 492 8727/www.pentictongolf.ca).* **Open** phone
for tee times. **Rates** $46-$55. **Credit** DC, MC, V.

Nk'Mip Desert Cultural Centre.

Where to stay

Okanagan accommodation is plentiful and
varied. Mid-range resorts are numerous and
there are many very basic roadside motels.
Wineries are waking up to the fact that if they
provide good rooms and a great restaurant,
they'll sell more wine (*see p208* **It's a vine
life**). More accommodation is listed on the
tourism information websites, *see p211.*

The newest and most upscale resort near
Kelowna is the **Cove Lakeside Resort**,
offering luxury suites, pools, a spa and the
Bonfire restaurant, overseen by two of BC's top
chefs. Also on Okanagan Lake is the mid-size,
historic and luxurious **Hotel Eldorado**. The
original inn was built in 1926, today it boasts
luxury suites and a fancy spa. The nearby
contemporary **Manteo Resort Waterfront
Hotel** provides a gorgeous waterfront setting.

A modestly priced option in Kelowna's city
centre is the **Royal Anne Hotel**, with a
fitness centre and Irish pub on site.
Penticton's elegantly restored **Naramata
Heritage Inn & Spa** offers packages with
wine tours and spa treatments. For something
completely different, head from Penticton south
to **God's Mountain Estate** near Summerland,
a delightful if slightly eccentric inn perched on
a ledge above Skaha Lake. It comes complete
with glassed-in temperature-controlled private
balconies, swimming pool and hot tub.

Cove Lakeside Resort
*The Cove Lakeside Resort, 4205 Gellatly Road,
Westbank, Kelowna (toll free 1 877 762 2683/
www.covelakeside.com).* **Rates** $145-$300 one-
bedroom suite. **Credit** AmEx, DC, MC, V.

God's Mountain Estate
*4898 Lakeside/Eastside Road (at the white gazebo),
Penticton (250 490 4800/www.godsmountain.com).*
Rates $139-$199 double. **Credit** DC, MC, V.

Hotel Eldorado
*500 Cook Road (on the lake) Kelowna (250 763 7500/
toll free 1-866 608 7500/www.eldoradokelowna.com).*
Rates $109-$299 double. **Credit** AmEx, DC, MC, V.

Manteo Resort
*3762 Lakeshore Road, Kelowna (250 860 1031/
www.manteo.com).* **Rates** $160-$295 double.
Credit AmEx, DC, MC, V.

Naramata Heritage Inn & Spa
*3625 1st Street, Naramata (250 496 6808/toll free
1-866 617 1188/www.naramatainn.com).* **Rates**
$116-$289 double. **Credit** AmEx, DC, MC, V.

Royal Anne Hotel
*348 Bernard Avenue, Kelowna (250 763 2277/
toll free 1-888 811 3400/www.royalannehotel.com).*
Rates $79-$189 double. **Credit** AmEx, DC, MC, V.

Where to eat & drink

Okanagan wine makers have long out-
performed their culinary equivalents, but
the restaurateurs have started to catch up.
The major centres now have good restaurants
serving fresh regional produce and a
commendable range of Okanagan (and
other) wines. Some larger wineries now
also run restaurants – usually with patios
and some are open all through the year
(*see p208* **It's a vine life**).

In Kelowna, **Bouchons** is a classic
French bistro with an 800-bottle wine cellar.
Fresco Restaurant serves adventurous
contemporary cuisine and is considered
to be the best in town.

Penticton's **Theo's** is often hailed as
one of BC's best Greek restaurants. The
Naramata Heritage Inn's **Cobblestone
Wine Bar & Restaurant** is also good –
delivering locally inspired fare, including some
inventive pizzas, at both lunch and dinner.

In Oliver, the **Toasted Oak Wine Bar** in
the VQA complex focuses on fine BC and local
fare, while in Osoyoos, casual dining **Wildfire
Grill** includes a pleasing courtyard patio.

Bouchons

*1180 Sunset Drive, Kelowna (250 763 6595/
www.bouchonsbistro.com).* **Open** 5.30pm-midnight
daily. **Main courses** $20-$33. **Set meal** $37.
Credit DC, MC, V.

Cobblestone Wine Bar
& Restaurant

*Naramata Inn, 3625 1st Street, Naramata (250
496 6808/www.naramatainn.com).* **Open** *Feb,
Mar* 11am-9pm Fri-Sun. *Apr-Oct* 11am-9pm daily.
Reservations advised. **Main courses** $10-$30.
Credit AmEx, DC, MC, V.

Fresco Restaurant & Lounge

*1560 Water Street, Kelowna (250 868 8805/www.
frescorestaurant.net).* **Open** *May-Oct* 5.30pm-late
Tue-Sun. *Nov, Dec, Feb-Apr* 5.30pm-late Tue-Sat.
Main courses $22-$37. **Credit** AmEx, DC, MC, V.

Theo's

*687 Main Street, Penticton (250 492 4019/www.
eatsquid.com).* **Open** 11am-10pm Mon-Thur; 11am-
11pm Sat; 4-10pm Sun. **Main courses** *lunch* $6-$14;
dinner $14-$28. **Credit** DC, MC, V.

Toasted Oak Wine Bar & Grill

*34881 97th Street, Oliver (250 498 4867/www.
winecountry-canada.com).* **Open** noon-9pm daily.
Main courses *Lunch* $10-$12. *Dinner* $15-$25.
Credit DC, MC, V.

Wildfire Grill

8526 Main Street, Osoyoos (250 495 2215). **Open**
11am-3pm, 5-9pm Mon-Sat. **Main courses** *lunch*
$7-$13; *dinner* $13-$21. **Credit** DC, MC, V.

Resources

Hospitals

Kelowna General Hospital

*2268 Pandosy Street, between Royal & Christelton
Avenues (250 862 4000).*

Post office

Canada Post

*571 Bernard Avenue, Kelowna (250 868 8480/
www.canadapost.ca).* **Open** 8.30am-5.30pm Mon-Fri.
Credit DC, MC, V.

Tourist information

Penticton & Wine Country
Chamber of Commerce

*553 Railway Street, between Chase & Eckhardt
Avenues (250 492 4103/toll free 1-800 663 5052/
www.penticton.org).* **Open** 9am-5pm Mon-Fri.

Tourism Kelowna
Visitor Info Centre

*544 Harvey Avenue, at Ellis Street (250 861 1515/
www.tourismkelowna.com).* **Open** *Jun-Aug* 8am-7pm
daily. *Sept-May* 9am-5pm Mon-Fri; 10am-3pm Sat.

Wine Country Welcome Centre

*34881 97th Street, Oliver (250 498 4867/toll free
1-888 880 9463/www.winecountry-canada.com).*
Open *Wine store & gift shop* 11am-7pm Mon-Thur;
10am-8pm Fri, Sat; 10am-6pm Sun.
The complex includes the Toasted Oak Wine Bar
& Grill (*see above*) as well as a wine store.

Getting there

By air

Both Kelowna (www.kelownaairport.com) and
Penticton (www.cyyf.org) airports are served by
regional carriers; Kelowna also has direct flights
on major airlines. Both have cars hire.

By car

The principal route from Vancouver to the
Okanagan is via highways 1 (the Trans-Canada)
and 5 (the Coquihalla) to Kelowna – which is
almost a 400km (250-mile) drive. From Calgary,
Alberta, Kelowna it's 600km (375 miles); from
Edmonton it's almost 900km (560 miles). Or
you could always drive highways 1 and 3
(the Hope–Princeton) from Vancouver to
Osoyoos (400km/250 miles).

By bus

Greyhound serves all the major centres in the
Okanagan (www.greyhound.ca).

Trips Out of Town

Whistler

Coast along to a mountain getaway.

Just one of the many glorious views along the **Sea-to-Sky Highway**.

Vancouver's co-host for the 2010 Winter Olympics (*see p22* **Games on!**), the resort of **Whistler** is a purpose-built ski town 120km (75 miles) to the north. Rated one of the top ski and snowboarding resorts in the world, Whistler is establishing itself as a summer destination too, with some of the best mountain biking terrain in North America, as well as hiking, canoeing and white water rafting.

Whistler's rapid development continues to accelerate in the run up to the Olympics, and comes at some cost – the village doesn't feel quite "lived in", and the rest of BC tends to view it with some cynicism. There is a core community here, and they're probably more actively concerned with the environment than their neighbours further south in the lower mainland, but such swift commercial development is hard to overlook in these surroundings. Of course if you want to escape into the wilderness, then by all means bypass Whistler and pitch your tent deep in the Garibaldi Provincial Park. But if, on the other hand, you want to savour BC's mountains, lakes and forests, don't object to letting a gondola take the strain, and fancy sampling some of the best dining in the country while you're at it – all within a stunning two-hour drive (or train ride; *see p221* **On the tracks**) of Vancouver – then you need look no further.

Sea-to-Sky Highway

Unless you are staying in Whistler Creekside (a couple of miles from the main village) you won't need a car in Whistler, especially in winter, when the focus is squarely on the Whistler-Blackcomb slopes and free shuttle buses constantly circle the perimeter of the village. (There is free parking on the edge of the Lower Village, but overnight parking is at a premium and hotels take advantage of this, adding $12-$20 a night to your bill.)

However, in the summer months a car opens up several worthwhile destinations en route. Route 99, the Sea-to-Sky Highway, affords spectacular viewpoints over Vancouver, Howe Sound, and the Coast Mountain range. Britain's *Guardian* newspaper rated it among the world's five best road trips. Exit Vancouver by way of W Georgia Street, through Stanley Park and over the Lions Gate Bridge.

In the run up to the Olympics, Highway 99 is getting a $600-million upgrade which will supposedly knock an hour off the journey time. While the engineers blast their way through the mountains, current journeys may be disrupted.

Fifty kilometres (31 miles) from Vancouver, **Britannia Beach** (population of 300) is a hippiefied outpost skirting the **BC Museum of Mining** (you can't miss the monster truck standing sentinel beside the highway as it edges Howe Sound). The copper mine dates back to 1905, and is now a National Heritage Site. It's an extensive facility – in 1929 the Britannia mines were the largest copper producer in the British Commonwealth, and the mill remains an impressive sight. There are several side attractions – panning for gold, environmental education displays – but the museum's highlight is an electric train ride through one of the old tunnels. Guides point out fossils, minerals and the hostile working conditions the miners used to face, and will demonstrate drills of different vintages. The potty wagon is also on hand for inspection. The museum is a good example of a community

rehabilitating a toxic industrial relic, and further improvements are planned. The site is also a favourite with moviemakers: among its 50-plus screen credits are *We're No Angels*, *This Boy's Life*, and *Insomnia*.

Britannia Beach also offers an art gallery and shop featuring local Salish paintings, carvings and jewellery and a couple of decent, unpretentious food joints. The Mountain Woman Take Out, in a converted bus, does good fish and chips, poutine (chips, cheese and gravy) and burgers at rock bottom prices.

Twelve kilometres (seven miles) further up the road, **Squamish** marks the halfway point to Whistler. From the road, this is a typical North American pitstop: gas, burgers, and more of the same. Explore a little deeper and this First Nations municipality affords enough activities to boast it's 'the outdoor capital of Canada'. Rock climbers and windsurfers flock here to tackle the Stawamus Chief – a 652 metre (2,139 foot) granite outcrop with more than 200 climbing routes – and to pit themselves against the strong winds that gust across Howe Sound. 'Squamish' means 'Mother of the winds'.

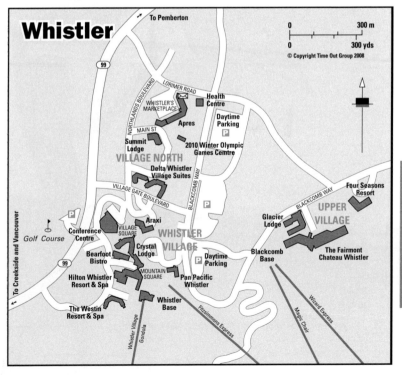

Trips Out of Town

Airline flights are one of the biggest producers of the global warming gas CO_2. But with **The CarbonNeutral Company** you can make your travel a little greener.

Go to **www.carbonneutral.com** to calculate your flight emissions then 'neutralise' them through international projects which save exactly the same amount of carbon dioxide.

Contact us at **shop@carbonneutral.com** or call into the office on **0870 199 99 88** for more details.

CarbonNeutral®flights

If you're looking for food or a place to stay in Squamish, your best bet is the Howe Sound Inn & Brewing Company (37801 Cleveland Avenue, 604 892 2603, toll free 1-800 919 2537, www.howesound.com, main courses $9-$15, doubles $99-$109), a microbrewery with 20 simply furnished but attractively priced rooms and the best dining in town.

In this vicinity you'll also find the **West Coast Railway Heritage Park** (39645 Government Road, Squamish, 604 898 9336, www.wcra.org), with more than 65 pieces of rolling stock, pretty **Shannon Falls**, and **Alice Lake**, a popular campsite and picnicking spot 13 kilometres (eight miles) north of Squamish (www.alicelakepark.com). **Brackendale** is a must-see if you're here between November and February, when thousands of bald eagles feast on the carcasses of salmon in the Squamish river after the spawning season (*see p141*). There's a viewing platform along Government Road.

BC Museum of Mining

Highway 99, Britannia Beach (toll free 1-800 896 4044/www.bcmuseumofmining.org). **Open** *May-Thanksgiving* 9am-4.30pm daily. *Thanksgiving-Apr* 9am-4.30pm Mon-Fri. **Closed** Dec, Jan. **Admission** *May-Thanksgiving* $17; $12-$14 reductions; free under-5s. *Thanksgiving-Apr* $7.50. **Credit** DC, MC, V.

Whistler Village

A large bronze plaque on the floor of Whistler's shoebox of a museum tells the story of the resort's development. In the 1960s, an IOC representative surveyed the area and proclaimed it 'one of the best sites in North America to meet all criteria for an Olympic bid'. Roads and lifts were subsequently built, and in February 1966, **Whistler** – until then known as London Mountain, with a local population of 25 people – commenced operation. Three failed bids to host the winter games were a source of much frustration, losing to Sapporo in 1972, Innsbruck in 1976 and Lake Placid in 1980. It will have taken 44 years when Whistler finally achieves its goal and hosts the 2010 Winter Olympics.

Plans to develop a town centre began in the late 1970s on a site that was then the community garbage dump but which today commands some of the highest prices in Canadian real estate. According to the Canada Mortgage and Housing Corporation, the average price of a Whistler home is over a million dollars, making it the most expensive municipality in the country. If you're after a $20 million mansion, come and get it. But if you need rental accommodation in line with

your salary, you're likely to be out of luck, or in for a long wait – currently three years.

Little help is available to the thousands of seasonal workers from Australia and the UK, who fly here each November in search of work and a place to live for the season. The problem isn't expected to ease until after 2010 when the facility built for Olympic athletes will be handed down and converted into staff housing.

Nevertheless, Whistler/Blackcomb remains an irresistible magnet for snow hounds. For one thing, it is North America's best bet in the category of longest ski season, generally from late November stretching into June. And if at the end of the season you're still dying for snow, the Blackcomb Glacier is open through the summer with various specialised ski and snowboard camps. In fact, the latest visitor numbers show that summer outstrips winter in popularity by almost a half a million people. A newly developed mountain bike park is the principal draw, but Whistler's fresh water lakes, parks for picnicking, bear watching, camping and hiking are increasingly appealing to travellers on a more modest budget.

Occasionally, visiting foreigners are under the impression that they have landed smack in the middle of the Rockies – the Rocky Mountain Range is further to the east, running through Banff, Alberta – when, actually, Whistler and Blackcomb are part of the much more climatically temperate Coast Mountain Range. The area is considered part of British Columbia's rainforest. The average winter alpine temperature rarely dips below minus five degrees centigrade (23 degrees Farenheit). Compare that to Sunshine Village in Banff at minus 12 degress centigrade (ten degrees Farenheit), and you're looking at one layer of clothing less at least. The 'rainforest' aspect can make for worrisomely wet village weather but more often than not the prodigious precipitation means powder in the alpine. Whistler's average snowfall is a towering nine metres (30 feet).

Navigating the village can be a challenge. Bear in mind that the Upper Village (at the foot of Blackcomb) is a five-minute walk from the more developed Lower Village. (Whistler Creekside is a quieter, self-sufficient resort with its own gondola, but it's five minutes' drive from the dining options of the Lower Village.) Most stores and restaurants face inward along a zigzag pedestrian mall of identikit faux-alpine architecture that some locals describe as the 'Disneyland of the North'. Parking is scarce and the no-car zone means that taxis can't always deliver to the doorstep of the restaurant you've booked. Luckily, what will never be lost to you are the mountains in front: Whistler to your right; Blackcomb to your left.

Trips Out of Town

Acres of powder and incredible views are just two of the reasons to ski at **Whistler**.

Skiing

Whistler's greatest feature is its offer of two distinct, fully operating mountains sitting side-by-side. Growing tired of the resort's terrain is almost unfeasible. There is simply too much ground – 2,800 hectares (7,000 acres), 200 trails, 38 lifts combined – to think that you can cover it in a week's stay. The resort's latest toy makes it all the more appetizing: the Peak-to-Peak Gondola is scheduled to open in December 2008. It will be the longest free-span lift in the world, with a total length of 4.4km (2.7 miles) – more than three times the length of the Golden Gate Bridge. Standing 415 metres (1,360 feet) at its highest point, it will also be the highest detachable lift in the world. The journey will take 11 minutes, and cars will leave approximately every 50 seconds carrying up to 28 passengers apiece. The ski bum's favourite epithet seems certain to apply: Epic!

Blackcomb vs Whistler

In general, boarders prefer Blackcomb. It's the newer of the two developments, the result of which is a better-designed fall line – a good fall line means fewer flat patches to traverse. Traversing is anathema to boarders, who have to unbuckle from their boards and then trudge across the flats. By contrast, Whistler's infamous nickname is 'Traverseler'; wide flat patches are not uncommon.

That said, on days of massive, fresh snowfall, powder addicts of both ski and board persuasion invariably head to Whistler, where the opportunity to scoop lap after lap of untouched high alpine powder is greater. And pay attention here because this is the top, big secret among locals: Harmony Chair and Peak Chair on Whistler are the fastest, most direct lines to the good stuff on a powder day. Sure, Blackcomb's bowls of Ruby, Diamond, Garnet and Sapphire offer some of the best, steep, avalanche-controlled powder in the world, but here's the deal: they take two chairlifts to get to. You don't have time for this. 'Whistler for freshies. Blackcomb for leftovers.' Remember this old chestnut and you're on the right track.

Note: when you're in line at the Peak chair on Whistler, look to your right at the long cliff band known as the Waterfalls, and further along, the famous rocky outcropping known as Air Jordan. This is live coverage of one of the sport's most dangerous attractions: skiers and boarders lined up like lemmings to throw themselves off cliffs from life-threatening heights. They're insane but it's fun to watch. Oh, and if you're a beginner and it's a powder day, the locals have this to say, with all due respect, of course: 'Take a lesson or go shopping.' Beginners hate powder. It's like death by quicksand.

Whistler Mountain's other big plus is the sun factor. The sun crests Whistler before illuminating Blackcomb. A Fresh Tracks ticket (extra $16.78; $12.20 reductions; free under-7s) allows you to load early at 7.30am to watch the sun rise while eating scrambled eggs and bacon in the Roundhouse at the top of Whistler. With the exception of Seventh Heaven, most of Blackcomb doesn't see sun until 11am.

Not that this should deter you from Blackcomb. Seventh Heaven is the Shangri La of mountain vistas. Frequently, when village weather is socked-in with fog and rain the chairlift ascent through the clouds is like a new day. You're literally lifted through a ceiling of cloud into an ear-popping altitude of blue sky and airplane-like views. Likewise, the intermediate skier should not miss a chance to cruise and conquer Blackcomb's glacier. The glacier is inbounds, patrolled, and avalanche controlled, yet the short hike in makes it feel like serious, backcountry terrain. The word 'glacier' even sounds black diamond-ish, when in reality Blackcomb's glacier is just a giant mellow marshmallow.

Also on Blackcomb, treat yourself to the resort's best lunch at **Crystal Hut**, with its wood-burning oven, roasted salmon and chicken, and decadent dessert waffles. But arrive before noon. The Crystal Hut is the cutest log cabin, and packs out early. In fact, wherever lunch is concerned, it's best to arrive early or late, avoiding the madness of noon to two o'clock. Don't bother skiing to the base for lunch, either. Lift traffic is at its worst at the bottom. As mountain employees say: 'Go high and stay high.'

Beginners

For the Very First Time Beginner, there's really no better experience than on Whistler Mountain. Ski school meets at mid-station, which means you get to take the gondola like a normal person, elbow to elbow with the gnarliest of experts. You've travelled to the big leagues, after all. Who wants to be ostracised at the bottom on Blackcomb's bunny hill beside the pavement? Ski instructors also warn that Blackcomb's many narrow roads are a hazard to first time beginners, whose newly-learned stopping skills may not fully eradicate all disappearances over the edge.

For the more experienced beginner (those able to do solo green runs), either mountain is a great choice. You'll find long, cruisey trails from every lift, running from top to bottom (with the exception of the two T-bars on Blackcomb, which are designated intermediate). A team of 80 friendly red-jacketed 'Mountain Hosts' patrol the slopes to answer your questions and provide directions, and to police the orderly, wait-your-turn etiquette

of lift lines for which Whistler/Blackcomb has become the shining antidote to the chaos of European resort 'queuing'.

Children

Whistler is a great place for children to learn to ski and snowboard. Programmes start for three-year-olds and continue up to 18. If your children are tiny and just beginning, then the bunny hill at the base of Blackcomb is probably the best (they won't have to negotiate the Gondola as well as all the equipment which, even at three, they are expected to carry themselves). Small groups start off making pizza slices (snow plough), learn to stop, and sing their ABCs while standing on the magic carpet. If they get too tired, or upset, they can play inside the adjoining nursery. Fives and up will prefer Whistler, where they travel half way up the mountain for lessons. (Tip: kit your child out with their skis, boots, helmet etc the night before they start – it can be really overwhelming for them otherwise.)

Groups are organised first by age (three and four; five and six; seven-12; 13-18) and then by ability; snowboarding lessons are only available for six years and up. Choose between

Blackcomb.

High rollers

If you're looking for powder without the crowds and lift queues, you might want to consider these alternatives.

Callaghan Lodge (604 938 0616, toll free 1-877 938 0616, www.callaghan country.com) 20 kilometres (12 miles) north of Whistler, offers ski-touring, snow-shoeing and cross-country skiing in unadulterated backcounty terrain. This is pure wilderness. The lodge is a three-storey Whistler-style cabin with eight private rooms. It sleeps 18 people, that's it. Packages are available for one to six days. Prices include all meals and non-alcoholic beverages. A standard room starts at $349.

Whistler Heli-Skiing (604 932 4105, www.whistlerheliskiing.com), in operation since 1981, offers single-day trips from Whistler Village for the intermediate, advanced and expert powderhound. A typical day consists of three runs with anywhere from 1,370 to 2,300 vertical metres (4,500-7,500 vertical feet) at a cost per person of $730. The Whistler Heli-Skiing Store is located in the Crystal Lodge (4154 Village Green). The day ends at Buffalo Bill's with a recap of the day (including video footage). All guides are trained in avalanche safety, first aid, mountaineering, and rope handling.

Powder Mountain Catskiing (604 932 0169, www.powdercatskiing.com) delivers the same vertical and powder but at prices cheaper than heli-skiing. Bombardier snowcats transport passengers high into the untracked lines of Tricouni Mountain, 20 kilometres (12 miles) south of Whistler. Departures are from the Gone Bakery in Whistler Village. Prices includes lunch and is $479 plus GST, per day, per person.

three and five day adventure camps, where your child stays with the same instructor all week, or book individual days. Lunch and snacks are included.

Whistler Kids

Toll free 1-800 766 0449/www.whistlerblackcomb.com. Prices for lesson, lift and rentals range from $136-$159 (increasing with age) per day. If you're travelling off-season check the dates for 40% off 'Whistler Days'. Day care is available for babies and toddlers aged three-48 months at $101 per day. Advance booking is recommended.

Lift prices

Ticket pricing fluctuates throughout the season from early pre-Christmas pricing to spring. Best to check online at www.whistlerblackcomb. com/tickets/winter for latest pricing.

Summer activities

Whistler now attracts more visitors in the summer months than during the ski season – in fact this area has been pulling Vancouverites north for some backwoods adventure since the 1920s, when the trip involved ferry, rail and horse travel (and you still got change from $5).

The mountains are still the main attraction, and the Whistler Village Gondola remains the quickest way to climb to 1,830 metres (6,000 feet) (a single ride costs $30; $24 reductions; $12 seven-12s; free under-sevens). You can snack at the Roundhouse Lodge and choose between a dozen mountain top trails, ranging from an easy 30-minute stroll to a 21 kilometre (13 mile) trek back to the village via Singing Pass. Even in August there is still snow on the peaks; you are advised to stick to the prescribed trails. More adventurous souls can try glacier walking, mountaineering, rap jumping (a twist on abseiling that in essence involves walking – or running – down from Whistler peak face first) or horseback and ATV tours.

There are more hiking and cycle trails down in the valley, along with such gentle pursuits as golf, horseback riding, fishing, canoeing and kayaking on Alta Lake and/or Green Lake. You probably don't want to swim here: Alta Lake is fed by glacier waters, so the average summer temperature hovers around 16 degrees centigrade (61 degrees Fahrenheit). If you really feel the need for a dip, there is an indoor municipal pool. At the base of Blackcomb in the Upper Village a kids' adventure zone includes a bungee trampoline, a 315 metre (1,033 feet) luge, a maze, a climbing wall, a human gyroscope, pony rides, and even a flying trapeze – open to all-comers, early June to October.

Several local tour operators also offer white water rafting. The rafting itself is a fun day out – with tremendous scenery to enjoy on the calmer stretches – but be aware that it takes two hours each way to reach the rapids on the Elaho river.

See www.tourismwhistler.com for links and information on local tour operators and hotels.

BEAR ESSENTIALS
It is by no means uncommon to see bears in Whistler. These are black bear, not grizzly. If you keep your distance, the bear will likely do the same. If it's a close encounter, back off

slowly, facing the animal, speaking in a normal voice. If you're face-to-face, waving a large stick and screaming is in order – as is climbing the nearest tree (although the bear may follow you up). In an effort to minimise serious human/bear contact (usually necessitating killing the beast) various measures have been implemented involving electric fences and closing areas to humans. If you are planning to do some independent hiking or camping, it would be an idea to read up on guidelines regarding the storing and cooking of food – www.bearsmart.com is a good place to start. Although organised bear walks are available, sightings are not guaranteed. The tour takes you through their typical habitat – both woodland and alpine meadow – pointing out food sources and old hibernation dwellings. It's a pleasant walk and you'll learn a lot, but you're just as likely to spot a bear in the parking lot.

Mountain biking

Despite the body armour mountain bikers wear (crash helmets, gloves, goggles, elbow and knee pads are absolutely *de rigueur*), and despite the vertiginous trails and jumps they throw themselves down, the sport itself is relatively easy to pick up. As in any other kind of cycling, you regulate your speed with the brake. Unlike conventional cycling though, you'll rarely be

troubled to pedal; gravity does the work for you. The trick of it is to steer with your eyes. Look down at the ground and that's probably where you'll end up. Instead, keep your eyes fixed on the route ahead – spotting the best line on corners and through obstacles natural and man-made – and your bike will automatically follow. That's the theory anyway.

What Hawaii is to surfboarders, Whistler has become to 'free riders'. The sport was more or less invented on Vancouver's North Shore, but Whistler has the chairlifts. When your bike weighs about 20 kg (50 lbs) that makes a big difference. There are now more than 200 kilometres (124 miles) of lift-serviced bike trails on Whistler/Blackcomb catering to all levels of expertise and attracting 100,000 visitors a year.

Whistler Mountain Bike Park

(604 932 3434/toll free 1-800 766 0449 /www. whistlerbike.com). **Open** *May, Oct* 10am-5pm daily. *Jun-Sept* 10am-8pm daily. **Rates** $47/day; $41/day 13-17s; $25 10-12s. Bike & armour rental approx $120/day. **Credit** AmEx, DC, MC, V.

Zip trekking

A kids' playground ride scaled up for adults, zip trekking involves harnessing yourself to a high tension steel cable and a pulley, then launching from one of five tree-top platforms which crisscross Fitzsimmons Creek in the

Mountain biking and kayaking: get out and explore **Whistler** by land or water in summer.

Zip trekking.

valley between Whistler and Blackcomb mountains (the Bear Tour). A new addition, the Eagle Tour, involves the same mechanics, but with longer, potentially faster lines. Depending on your weight, you could reach speeds of up to 80 kilometres per hour (45 miles per hour). Part thrill ride, part bird's-eye-view nature trail, the zip trek lasts 2.5 to 3 hours. Minimum weight: 31 kilograms (70 pounds).

Ziptrek Ecotours

Carleton Lodge, Whistler Village (604 935 0001/ toll free 1-866 935 0001/www.ziptrek.com). **Open** year round; phone for reservations. **Rates** $98; $78 reductions. **Credit** AmEx, DC, MC, V.

Shopping

The 'village stroll' is seemingly designed to get visitors from A to B by way of as many store-fronts as possible. If you're in the market for ski-wear, fleeces and woolly jumpers, you'll be in hog heaven. Roots, Gap, and Spirit of the North rub shoulders with countless lesser-known brands. There are two supermarkets in the Lower Village, one in the Marketplace, and the other at the Village Square. You will have to go next door to the liquor store to buy alcohol, and show valid ID. Cuban cigars, on the other hand, are available in abundance, reminding visiting Americans what they're missing. There is a farmers' market every Sunday in the Upper Village from mid June to early October, 11am-4pm (www.whistlerfarmersmarket.org).

Where to stay

Most tourists will arrive in Whistler on a package deal, although the new low-cost flights from Europe to Vancouver are bringing in increasing numbers of independent travellers. Budget rooms are at a premium all year round and virtually unknown in the ski season. A central reservation system (1-888 403 4727, UK toll free 0800 731 5983, www.whistler blackcomb.com) is in place for all properties in the Whistler area. Prices fluctuate wildly. We have quoted for the cheapest rooms in low and high season.

At the top end, the **Fairmont Chateau Whistler** (4599 Chateau Boulevard, 604 938 8000, www.fairmont.com/whistler, doubles $159-$389) is the granddaddy on the block, an imposing manse-like structure in the quieter Upper Village at the foot of Blackcomb. The cavernous lobby is a sightseeing attraction in itself, and the suites for Gold level guests are also huge. There are three restaurants, an indoor/outdoor pool with hot tubs, a sauna and eucalyptus steam rooms (swimming outside as the snow falls is a real treat here).

On the tracks

Even more spectacular than the Sea-to-Sky Highway, nothing beats the **Whistler Mountaineer** (*see p224*) when it comes to sheer unadulterated scenery. From spring to fall, this refurbished classic Canadian train departs daily from North Vancouver, offering a variety of day trips (round-trip by train; train and bus; train and seaplane) – if you want more than an hour in Whistler, there are overnight packages available, or just buy one-way.

The track winds slowly through the refined neighbourhoods of the city of West Vancouver, then hugs the side of Howe Sound until it reaches the mountains and the Cheakamus Canyon. It slows down as it traverses the pinnacle of Brandywine Falls so everyone can look down at the rush of water cascading beneath.

Stumping up the extra cash for the Glacier Dome car is highly recommended – apart from the more upscale snacks and service, the extra roof windows are needed for the full sea-to-sky experience. Onboard staff proffer a reasonably unintrusive commentary of facts and anecdotes about the terrain. If it gets too much, for some fresh air and a more rustic experience, make sure to spend some time in the heritage observation car.

The Chateau has been usurped in the luxury stakes by the nearby **Four Seasons Resort Whistler** (4591 Blackcomb Way, 604 935 3400, www.fourseasons.com/whistler, doubles $245-$545), completed in 2004, and with an altogether more contemporary feel. An intimate lobby reflects the hotel's boutique attitude (no conventions here), local art is prominently displayed and the rooms all feature wonderful walk-in slate showers, soaker tubs and a range of L'Occitane products. Ski store facilities are at the base of Blackcomb.

The **Pan Pacific Whistler Mountainside** (4320 Sundial Crescent, 604 905 2999, www. whistler.panpacific.com, $119-$389 studio suite; *photo p222*), in the Lower Village, has the prime location: you can practically step out of your room on to the lifts for either mountain and the pool deck overlooks the lower ski slopes. Rooms are all suites, with picture windows and full kitchen facilities.

If you are looking for more independent accommodation, there are apartments, condos and houses in every price range. On the edge

Trips Out of Town

Dig the view at the **Pan Pacific**. *See p221.*

gondola, **First Tracks Lodge** (2202 Gondola Way, toll free 1-866 385 0614, www.firsttracks lodge.com, suites $209-$800) offers plush suites with kitchens good enough that you won't need to eat out every night anyway.

Where to eat

There is no shortage of places to eat – and eat well – in Whistler. Compared to Vancouver, however, it is expensive. With a great location on the Village Square and a reputation to match, **Araxi** (4222 Village Square, 604 932 4540, www.araxi.com, main courses $30-$40; *photo p224*) is the place to see and be seen. A large, vibrant room includes an excellent seafood bar at the front and a patio (heated in winter) to people-watch in style. The menu draws deep from local produce and results in smart, unfussy plates.

The Four Seasons' **Fifty Two 80 Bistro** (4591 Blackcomb Way, 604 966 5280, www. fourseasons.com/whistler, main courses $15-$40), named after Whistler peak's vertical mile, has been tempting people to the Upper Village for its elegant surroundings, inventive use of regional produce and some exclusively held BC wines. Summer brings a more casual (and affordable) weekly seafood barbecue out on the patio.

For equally elegant dining with a twist, try the **Bearfoot Bistro** (4121 Village Green, 604 932 3433, www.bearfootbistro.com, set meal $45, tasting menu $98), for its elaborate multi-course tasting menus created by the extraordinary and youthful talent of executive chef Melissa Craig. Its hospitality and grand theatrics – champagne bottles are regularly sabred open – makes the Bearfoot a thoroughly unique experience. More affordable and lighter options are available in the oyster bar.

The **Rimrock Café** (2117 Whistler Road, 604 932 5565/www.rimrockwhistler.com, main courses $30-$48), is an unpretentious log cabin specialising in fish and game. But for an upscale meal in more modern surroundings head for **Après** (4338 Main Street, 604 935 0200, www.apresrestaurant.com, main courses $35-$68, tasting menu $85), where the boldly creative dishes are served in a coolly contemporary atmosphere.

You don't have to break the bank to find good food however. **Ciao-Thyme Bistro** (4573 Chateau Boulevard, 604 932 9795, www.ciaothymebistro.com, main courses $10-$16) serves breakfast and lunch, then morphs seamlessly into Fitzsimmons Pub for dinner (main courses $19-$26). Under either name this Upper Village eatery ticks all the right boxes: fresh ingredients simply

of town in Village North, the **Valhalla** (4375 Northlands Boulevard, toll free 1-877 887 5422, www.whistlerblackcomb.com, suites $190-$449) offers spacious accommodation for those on a moderate budget. Two-bedroom condos, with sofabeds in the living room and full kitchen facilities are comfortable and well-appointed. Cheaper still, **Glacier Lodge** (4573 Chateau Boulevard, 604 938 3455, toll free 1-866 580 6644, www.glacier-lodge.com, suites $99-$329) in the Upper Village is basic, but handily situated. **Le Chamois** (4557 Blackcomb Way, 604 932 4113, www. wildflowerlodge.com/lechamois.html, suites $125-$260) is a good mid-range choice in the Upper Village, although cooking facilities in some suites are confined to a microwave and toaster-oven. For groups and families, the **Villas Snowberry** (Upper Village, toll free 1-877 887 5422, www.whistlerblackcomb.com, suites $213-$602) in the Upper Village offer smart and commodious two- and three-bedroom townhouses.

Ski-in, ski-out rooms are also available on both mountains: check the www.whistler blackcomb. com website for details.

Whistler Creekside has its own gondola and amenities, but it's five minutes' drive to the village dining options. At the base of the

Trips Out of Town

Bro-Speak
Lessons in the local lingo

Amped *adjective* – stirred emotionally, aroused, as in: 'Dude, I'm amped. It dumped all night.'

Blower *noun* – snow prized for its fine, arid texture and float-away lightness, as in: 'Dude, it's blower. I'm totally amped.'

Chowder *verb* – to humiliate oneself through human error, as in: 'Dude, I totally chowdered that line.'

Dump *noun* – copious snowfall. **Dumped, dumping** *verb* – past and present tense of copious snowfall or snow falling during a storm, as in: 'Dude, it's dumping. I'm stoked.'

Eating It *adverbial phrase* – meaning spectacular fall or crash. **To eat** *verb*, past tense **ate**, as in: 'Dude, he ate it.'

Epic *noun* or *adjective* – referring to a series of great (most likely personal) achievements worthy of lengthy alcohol-induced narration, as in: 'Dude, it was epic,' etc and so forth.

Gorby *noun* (pl. Gorbies) – derogative reference to novice skier, esp. tourist, derived from G (geek) O (on) R (rental) B (boards).

Poacher *noun* – morally impaired individual involved in the crime of butting ahead in the lift queue.

Shredding the Gnar *adjectival phrase* – circa 1999. Current usage is ironic, implying the successful execution of a sick line by a Gorby, as in: 'Dude, look! He's shredding the gnar! No wait! He's eating it!'

Sick *adjective* – exceptionally good or unusual; marvellous, superb.

yet precisely prepared and at surprisingly reasonable prices from the Chateau Whistler's former executive chef.

In the Lower Village the regular queue outside **Caramba! Restaurante** (4314 Main Street, 604 938 1879, www.caramba-restaurante.com, main courses $13-$27) speaks volumes. A wide range of pastas (all available in half portions), pizzas and spit-roasted meats with mashed potatoes hit the spot after a day on the slopes. Or, for an alpine experience from a different continent, make your way to **Bavaria Restaurant** (4369 Main Street, 604 932 7518, www.bavaria-restaurant.com, main courses $27-$40) in the Village North. The menu fairly sags with hearty schnitzel and *spaetzle*, but the real fun is to be had with the fondues – choose from meat or cheese and finish off with the yummy chocolate.

For lighter fare, there are cafés around every corner and plenty of faster food-type options. **Ingrid's Village Café** (4305 Skiers Approach, 604 932 7000) dispenses a great selection of veggie burgers, sandwiches and soups, while **Splitz Grill** (4369 Main Street, 604 938 9300) proffers the best meat burgers with endless trimmings to hungry hordes. For casual fare that's full of flavour, but light on the wallet, **Elements in the Summit Lodge** (4359 Main Street, 604 932 5569) delivers a variety of tapas, perfect for sharing – and they muster a mean breakfast too.

Nightlife

Nightclubbing with the in-crowd for the 19- to 26-year-olds (be sure to bring some form of valid photo ID or risk being arrested, jailed

Trips Out of Town

Araxi. *See p222*.

and fined) rotates around a cluster of options, with individual nights' offerings best checked out in the local press.

Otherwise there's not much to choose between **Tommy Africa's** (4216 Gateway Drive, 604 932 6090, www.tommyafricas.com, admission free-$28), the **Savage Beagle** (4222 Village Square, 604 938 3337, admission free-$15), **Buffalo Bill's** (4122 Village Green, 604 932 6613, www.buffalobills.ca, admission free-$20), **Garfinkel's Whistler** (1-4308 Main Street, 604 932 2323, www.garfswhistler.com, admission free-$12) or **Moe Joe's** (4115 Golfer's Approach, 604 935 1152, www.moejoes.com, admission free-$15).

Saturday is best spent wherever you can get in (read: a good night for a house party). Clubs don't start rocking until late, so on nights out, **Merlin's** (Blackcomb Daylodge, Upper Village, 604 938 7700), at the base of Blackcomb, is a good place to start the evening with the cheapest beer and burgers in town, and a stack of nachos almost as tall as the peak.

For the slightly older crowd the **Dubh Linn Gate** (Pan Pacific, 4320 Sundial Crescent, toll free 1-800 387 3311, www.dubhlinngate.com) serves up live Celtic music and cover tunes (Van Morrison, Beatles) in a pub setting.

For the even older, higher financed and mellow crowd, **The Mallard Lounge** (4599 Chateau Boulevard, 604 938 8000) at the Fairmont Chateau is all about sofas and fireplaces and scotch on the rocks, and usually someone crooning at the grand piano.

Tourist information

The Tourism Whistler Activity & Information Centre
4010 Whistler Way (604 938 2769/toll free 1 877 991 9988/www.tourismwhistler.com). **Open** 10am-6pm daily.

Getting there

By bus

Perimeter (604 266 5386, toll free 1 877 317 7788, www.perimeterbus.com) runs an express bus service from Vancouver airport to Whistler. There are nine departures daily during ski season, seven in summer. Some services also stop at downtown Vancouver hotels. Tickets are $67 each way, plus GST. Reservations are required. Journey times range from 2 hours and 15 minutes to 2 hours and 45 minutes.

Greyhound (toll free 1-800 661 8747, www.greyhound.ca) runs eight buses a day from Pacific Central Station, 1150 Station Street, Vancouver for $18.80 plus GST. Average journey time is 2 hours and 20 minutes.

By rail

The **Whistler Mountaineer** (604 606 7245, www.whistlermountaineer.com; *see p221* **On the tracks**) offers a daily service (Apr-mid Oct) departing the platform at Philip Avenue and W 1st Street, North Vancouver at 8.30am. Downtown pick-ups and a light meal are included in the price, $110 one-way, $199 round-trip – or $185 one-way in the Glacier Dome viewing carriage. Reservations are required.

Directory

Features

Directory

Getting Around

By air

Vancouver International Airport

604 207 7077/www.yvr.ca.
The airport is situated on Sea Island, 10km (6 miles) south of downtown. The largest airport on the west coast of Canada, it's a major hub for both international and domestic flights. Besides flights to Canadian cities, and a host of smaller destinations within British Columbia, Vancouver International Airport is particularly convenient for flights to and from the west coast of the USA. Anyone flying from Vancouver to the US should note that American customs and immigration checks must be gone through before you board the plane. Allow at least an hour for these.

There are three terminals at Vancouver International Airport: the International Terminal (arrivals are on Level 2, departures are on Level 3); the Domestic Terminal (arrivals are on Level 2, departures are on Level 3); and the South Terminal. The South Terminal is on the Fraser River and provides access to seaplane facilities, helicopter operations and an array of small plane airlines that serve destinations in and around Vancouver, Vancouver Island, the Gulf Islands, as well as mainland British Columbia.

Every year, more than 15 million passengers pass through Vancouver International Airport, making it Canada's second busiest. To improve airport facilities in time for the 2010 Olympics and to meet growing demands for air travel, the Airport Authority has embarked on a $1 billion development plan. An Airport Improvement Fee ($5 for passengers travelling to a destination within British Columbia or the Yukon, and $15 for all other destinations), is now included in all airline tickets to help fund this development.

There are several means of getting to and from Vancouver International Airport. The quickest and most convenient is by taxi. More than 400 licensed taxis serve the airport on a 24/7 basis, charging between $25 and $30 (inclusive of taxes) for a trip to or from downtown.

The airport bus service, or Airporter (604 946 8866, www.yvrairporter.com) as it is known, runs every 20 minutes from 9am to 9.30pm, calling at major hotels in downtown, the Canada Place Cruise Ship Terminal and the bus depot/train station. Adult fares are $13.50 one-way, $21 return; children $6.25 single or $12.50 return; seniors $10.50 or $21; families $27 or $42 return.

For those not in a hurry, or on a budget, Vancouver city buses offer the best alternative to the Airporter and taxi services. Buses arrive and depart from the Airport Station Bus Terminal, which is located near the Delta Hotel. A connecting service (Route 424) then transfers passengers to and from the Ground Level of the Domestic Terminal. Fares must be paid in exact change when boarding the bus. The standard fare is currently $3.75, or $2.50 after 6pm weekdays and all day weekends. Tickets can also be purchased at the 7-11 store, which can be found on the lower level of the Domestic Terminal. Popular routes include the 98 B Line and Route 496 to downtown Vancouver, Route 620 to BC Ferries at Tsawwassen, and Route C 92 which provides a connecting service to the Airport's South Terminal.

A rapid transit rail link between Richmond, Vancouver International Airport and downtown is due for completion in 2009. Although its primary role will to be ease commuter traffic, the rail link will also be of benefit to air passengers. Check www.canadaline.ca for current information about opening dates.

For information about car rentals, *see p229* **Car Hire**.

Airlines

Air Canada Toll free *1-888 247 2262/www.aircanada.com*
Air Canada Jazz Toll free *1-888 247 2262/www.flyjazz.com*
Air France *Toll free 1-800 667 2747/www.airfrance.com*
American Airlines *Toll free 1-800 433 7300/www.aa.com*
British Airways *Toll free 1-800 247 9297/www.britishairways.com*
Cathay Pacific *Toll free 1-800 268 6868/604 606 8888/www.cathaypacific.com*
China Airlines *Toll free 1-800 227 5118/604 682 6028/www.china-airlines.com*

Japan Airlines *Toll free 1-800 525 3663/www.jal.com*
Lufthansa Airlines *Toll free 1-800 563 5954/604 303 3086/www.lufthansa.com*
Northwest Airlines *Toll free 1-800 225 2525/www.nwa.com*
Singapore Airlines *Toll free 1-800 663 3046/604 689 1223/www.singaporeair.com*
United Airlines *Toll free 1-800 241 6522/www.united.com*
Westjet Airlines *Toll free 1-800 538 5696/www.westjet.com*

By bus

The bus station is located in Pacific Central Station at 1150 Station Street, off Main Street, on the corner of Terminal Avenue. **Greyhound Canada** (toll free 1-800 661 8747, www.greyhound.ca) operates services across Canada and also links Vancouver with Seattle, as well as other cities in the USA.

Pacific Coach Lines (toll free 1-800 661 1725, www.pacificcoach.com) run buses to Victoria, on Vancouver Island, throughout the day. The schedule varies according to the season. Tickets include the ferry crossing. Adult $37.50, children $19.75, seniors $25.

Quick Coach Lines (604 940 4428, www.quickcoach.com) offers a daily shuttle service between Vancouver and Seattle, stopping at Sea-Tac airport and Bellingham Airport along the way. Adult tickets cost $46.55 one-way, $82.65 return ($38-$45/$67-$81 reductions); $22/$40 5-12s.

By rail

VIA Rail (1-888 842 7245, www.viarail.ca) operates from Pacific Central Station. Its flagship service, *The Canadian*, departs Vancouver three times a week (Tue, Fri, Sun), bound for Toronto. The journey takes three days and calls at Jasper, Edmonton, Saskatoon, Winnipeg and Toronto. At Jasper passengers can connect with 'The Skeena', a VIA train that runs north-west through the Rocky Mountains to Prince Rupert on the coast of British Columbia. 'The Skeena' stops for the night in Prince George, (accommodation isn't included in the ticket), and takes one day to reach Prince Rupert.

Amtrak (toll free 1-800 872 7245, www.amtrak.com), America's major rail carrier also runs four trains a day from Pacific Central Station to Seattle. The journeys take between 3-4hrs and depart at 5.30am, 8am, noon and 5pm. Ticket prices vary. From Seattle, connections can be made for most other US destinations. **Rocky Mountaineer Vacations** (1-877 460 3200, 604 606 7245, www.rocky mountaineer.com) specialises in luxury rail journeys through the Canadian Rockies. Trains depart from Rocky Mountaineer Station (1755 Cottrell Street) and stop at Whistler, Kamloops, Banff, Jasper and Calgary. High season runs from mid April to mid October, but December packages are also available.

By ferry

BC Ferries' (1-888 223 3779, www.bcferries.com) routes range from Prince Rupert, on the northwest coast of British Columbia to Victoria, on the southern tip of Vancouver Island. In between lie the Queen Charlotte Islands, the Gulf Islands and the 'sunshine' coastal towns of Vancouver Island and mainland British Columbia. The company runs 36 vessels and has 47 ports of call. BC Ferries operates two main routes in and out of greater Vancouver. Tsawwassen, about an hour's

drive south of downtown, is the terminal for ferries to and from Swartz Bay, which in turn is a 30-minute drive from Victoria. Horseshoe Bay, less than half-an-hour's drive north-west of downtown, is the terminal for ferries to and from Nanaimo. The crossings take between one and two hours. There is usually one crossing every one or two hours, with special sailings on holiday weekends – check the website for updates and details.

The most convenient way for foot passengers to use the ferry service is to book a ticket with one of the bus lines that connect with BC Ferries. Buses depart from Pacific Central Station on a regular basis.

If you are driving to Tsawwassen or Horseshoe Bay be aware that, unless you reserve in advance, during busy periods you may have to watch one or two ferries sail away before you get to board.

By cruise ship

The Vancouver-Alaska cruise route is one of the most popular in the world. Large, luxurious liners arrive and depart from the Port of Vancouver's Canada Place and Ballantyne terminals. The Canada Place terminal is located in the city centre (999 Canada Place); the Ballantyne terminal is just east of Canada Place (655 Centennial Road) near the Port's container terminals. If arriving by cruise ship, be aware that queues for taxis are often long. If you're traveling light, bear in mind that Canada Place is an easy stroll from the downtown core.

More than 30 ships call at Vancouver. Details of the cruise lines, their vessels, schedules and fares can be found on the Port of Vancouver's website (www.portvancouver.com).

Passengers requiring long-term car parking facilities should contact Cruisepark

(1-800 665 0050, www.cruise park.com) or Citipark (604 684 2251, www.canadaplace parking.ca) for details about long-stay deals.

Public transport

Vancouver has a varied, efficient and well-integrated public transport network. This is currently operated by the Greater Vancouver Transportation Authority (TransLink), though the authority is under threat from the governing BC Liberal party.

City buses offer the most effective and comprehensive means of getting around the city. During the daytime there is at least one bus every ten minutes on most routes, and the NightBus service operates at 30-minute intervals, seven days a week, until 3am. Travelling by bus during rush hour should be avoided. Note that you will need the exact fare when making your journey by bus (*see p228*).

The **SkyTrain** is an iconic symbol of Vancouver, but it does not cover enough of the city to be a stand-alone mode of transport. The addition of the Canada line in 2009 will go some way to addressing this problem. However, used in conjunction with the bus service it is a fast, fun and uncrowded way of getting around. Services on the SkyTrain run between 5am-1am Mon-Fri; 6am-1am Saturday; 7am-midnight Sun. The average wait for a train is approximately four minutes, but the frequency of the service can range from two to eight minutes depending on the time of day. *See p228* for details and fares.

The **SeaBus** links the downtown Waterfront Station with Lonsdale Quay in North Vancouver. Sailings in both directions occur at 15-30 minute intervals depending

Directory

on the time of day. The service runs from 6am to midnight Mon-Sat; and from 8am to 11pm Sun. The crossing takes around 12 minutes. The SeaBus service connects with the SkyTrain and buses at Waterfront Station.

If you begin your journey by bus and plan on making a connection, ask the driver for a transfer. Tickets for SkyTrain and SeaBus are available from stations and terminals. Ticket machines accept $5 and $10 bills, as well as coins.

TransLink information

For an in-depth guide to public transport in Vancouver visit www.translink.bc.ca or call the information line on 604 953 3333. The *Transportation Services Guide For Greater Vancouver* is a map of bus, SkyTrain and SeaBus routes. It's available from bookstores, convenience stores and tourist information offices. SkyTrain and SeaBus are wheelchair accessible, but not all city buses provide this service. If you know the bus route you'd like to take contact TransLink for accessibility details.

Fares & tickets

Vancouver is divided into three zones for the purpose of ticketing. The Yellow Zone (Zone 1) covers downtown; the Red Zone (Zone 2) covers the suburbs, and the Green Zone (Zone 3) covers the city's metropolitan districts. Although the majority of visitors will spend most of their time in downtown it should be noted that North Vancouver and Vancouver International Airport are in the Red Zone.

If you will only be making one or two trips a day on public transport a cash fare is your best option. A Zone One journey will cost $2.50 adult, $1.75 reductions; a Zone 1-2 journey will cost $3.75 adult, $2.50 reductions; and a Zone 1-3 journey will cost $5 adult, $3.50 reductions. After 6.30pm an All Zone ticket is $2.50 adult, $1.75 reductions. Cash tickets are only valid for 90 minutes, but this is an ample amount of time for any journey you are likely to make on the TransLink system.

If your day is likely to involve using a lot of public transport, your best option is a DayPass. It's valid all day and covers all three zones for $9 for an adult ($7 reductions).

An alternative to a DayPass is a book of ten FareSaver Tickets. A book of Zone 1 tickets costs $19; a book of tickets for Zones 1-2 costs $28.50, and for Zones 1-3 it's $38. Visitors should note that these tickets can only be used up to 6.30pm and, as with cash fares, each ticket a maximum validity of 90 minutes.

If you are staying in Vancouver for a month, consider buying a Monthly FareCard. They cost $73 for travel in Zone 1; $99 for travel in Zones 1-2, and $136 for travel in Zones 1-3. If you are entitled to a concessionary fare an All Zone Monthly FareCard costs just $42.

DayPasses, FareSaver Tickets and Monthly FareCards are available from SkyTrain stations, SeaBus terminals and any shop displaying the FareDealer sign.

As a tourist you will be entitled to the concessionary fares if you are a senior citizen or a child between the ages of 3-13. If your children are around the age of 13 it would be best to have some photo ID handy as proof of age. Children under the age of 3 travel free.

SkyTrain

Vancouver's **SkyTrain** (604 953 3333, www.translink. bc.ca), is the longest automated light rapid transit system in the world. It covers 49km (30 miles) and stops at 33 stations across the Greater Vancouver area. The system comprises two lines: the Millennium Line runs from Waterfront Station through downtown and out towards the suburbs before looping back East Vancouver; the Expo Line follows the same branches off into the suburbs. The soon to be completed Canada Line will connect downtown with the airport and Richmond.

Fares & tickets

You do not need the exact fare to purchase a ticket but, be sure to ask for a transfer if you are making a connection. The longest journey on the SkyTrain system takes approximately 40 minutes, but all TransLink cash tickets are valid

for 90 minutes so you should have no problem completing your journey within the allotted time.

SkyTrain fares vary according to age, the zones you travel in, and the time of day you are travelling. If you plan on using the SkyTrain regularly a book of ten FareSaver tickets, or a DayPass, might be your best option. FareSaver tickets also serve as transfers.

Fares for the SkyTrain range from $2.50 for a single journey in Zone 1 to $38 for a book of ten FareSaver tickets that allow travel across all three zones. A DayPass valid for all zones is $9. Children four years and younger travel free, and there are reductions for older children, students and seniors.

Taxis

All taxi firms in British Columbia are regulated by the Passenger Transportation Board (250 953 3777). In the Lower Mainland, the meter starts at $2.75 (inclusive of taxes) and the cost for each successive kilometre is $1.60. Many of Vancouver's taxi operators have switched to hybrid vehicles, resulting in a severe depletion of the number of larger cars available – if there are more than four in your party, you may need to book two cars.

If you think you may have left any belongings in a taxi call the firm directly. Taxis can be hailed in the street or ordered on these numbers:
Black Top & Checker Cabs *604 731 1111.*
Maclure's Cabs *604 683 6666.*
Vancouver Taxi *604 871 1111.*
Yellow Taxi 604 *681 1111.*

Driving

Vancouverites love to complain about congestion, but save for the main commuter arteries at rush hour (the Lions Gate Bridge, Highway 99 towards the Oak St Bridge) you are unlikely to encounter anything that visitors from London, New York, LA or Paris would consider even a minor hold up. This city is eminently traversable by car – but you probably won't need one until you explore the North Shore or venture further into the interior of British Columbia.

The city speed limit is 50 km/h (31mph) unless otherwise specified. In school zones it drops to 30km/h. On the bridges, it rises to 60 km/h. On freeways the limit ranges between 80 and 110 km/h.

Driving regulations are similar to those in Britain and the United States, with the obvious proviso that you drive on the right-hand side of the road. Seat-belts are mandatory. You are obliged to yield to public buses. Keep your eyes out for overhead traffic lights and stop at stop signs. You may turn right on a red light once pedestrians have crossed and it is safe to do so.

When turning left at intersections, vehicles are expected to cross in front of their opposite number. Pay attention to overhead signs with restrictions on turns at certain times of day.

Pedestrians have right of way at crosswalks and intersections, and outside of the main thoroughfares drivers will generally stop if a pedestrian is even approaching the curb at an intersection.

Car hire

To rent a car in BC you will have to be 21 years of age (some companies require drivers to be over 25) and be in possession of a driving licence and a credit card. All the major companies have offices in downtown Vancouver and at the airport; in Victoria; and many have representatives in Whistler. In high season, reserve ahead. Prices start at about $30 a day. Check whether your travel insurance covers driving before taking out additional coverage.

Hire companies

Alamo *1132 W Georgia Street, at Thurlow Street (604 684 1401/ www.alamo.ca).*
Avis *757 Hornby Street, at W Georgia Street, Downtown (604 606 2869/www.avis.ca).*
Budget *416 W Georgia Street, at Homer Street (694 668 7090/ www.budget.com).*
Enterprise *585 Smithe Street, at Seymour Street (604 688 5500/ www.enterprise.com).*
Hertz *1128 Seymour Street, at Helmcken Street (604 606 4711/ www.hertz.ca).*
National *1130 W Georgia Street, at Thurlow Street (604 609 7150/ www.nationalcar.ca).*
Thrifty *413 Seymour Street, at W Hastings Street (604 606 1666/ www.thrifty.com).*

Breakdown services

Unless your home automobile association has a reciprocal arrangement with the Canadian Automobile Association (CAA; 604 268 5600, 604 293 2222 for road service) you will need a towing service. In Vancouver, Busters tow trucks are ubiquitous as they're contracted by the city to impound illegally parked vehicles (call 604 685 7246 if your parked car has vanished). But the company also offers an emergency road service (604 685 8181, www.busters towing.com). Alternatives include Mundie's (604 526 9677), Canuck Towing (604 254 0501) and Drake Towing (604 251 3344).

Parking

Most downtown streets are metered and enforced by parking wardens between 8am-6pm daily. Expect to pay $2 for 60 minutes – but note that even some metered streets have parking restrictions in the rush hour period. On non-metered streets, park only in the direction of the traffic, and not within six metres (20 feet) of a stop sign or within five metres (16 feet) of a fire hydrant. Park illegally and you will be towed (*see*

above). Car parks are common throughout the city. Most ticket machines take credit cards or change. You can pay between $8 and $20 for all-day parking in the downtown area.

Cycling

Vancouver is an ideal city for cyclists, with cycle routes alongside the Seawall around the downtown peninsula, Stanley Park and False Creek (*see p174* **Free wheeling**.). TransLink publishes a route map which is available from most bike stores.

It is illegal to ride a bike without a helmet, a law which also applies to child passengers. Buses on the North Shore and increasingly elsewhere are equipped to take bikes on racks mounted on the front of the bus. This excellent service is free; TransLink's website (www.translink.bc.ca) has further details.

The North Shore, a boat trip away across Burrard Inlet, and Whistler 120 kilometres (72 miles) to the north are both renowned for their mountain bike trails. Victoria, Vancouver Island and the Okanagan Valley are also popular cycling holiday destinations. (For more information on mountain biking, *see p177*.)

Walking

There can't be many cities with such spectacular nature walks in their midst. Stanley Park and the Seawall are obvious places to start, but the walk from Kitsilano Beach all the way out to Wreck Beach at the University of British Columbia is also scenic, if long (approximately 10 kilometres or 6 miles). The Pacific Spirit Regional Park (also known as the Endowment Lands) east of UBC is a wilder alternative to Stanley Park, and there are many good hikes within easy reach on the North Shore.

Directory

Resources A-Z

Addresses

Despite the city's grid-like street patterns, the logic of postal addresses is complicated by the peculiar shape of the downtown peninsula. Street numbers climb 100 per block as you head south from Canada Place pier or west from Carrall Street (in downtown) or Ontario Street (the West Side). East of Main Street the street numbers climb again and take on the prefix East. It sounds confusing but once you've cracked the code you can pinpoint any address without the cross-street. Note that suite numbers sometimes precede the street number.

Age restrictions

Buying/drinking alcohol 19; driving 16; sex (hetero/homosexual) 14; smoking 19.

Attitude & etiquette

Vancouver is easygoing in most things. When it comes to attire, business suits are the exception, not the rule; even formal occasions are casual by European standards. Some Victoria establishments have a standard dress code, but these are rare on the mainland. Courtesy is very much the norm.

Business

Business etiquette is similar to North American standards, where politeness and manners are valued but there is a lack of deeply entrenched customs and rituals. In general, shaking hands and showing up on time is sufficient; presenting gifts is not required. However, given Vancouver's location on the Pacific Rim, business with

Japanese and other Asian nationals is becoming more common. The astute business person will be sensitive to cultural expectations.

Conventions & conferences

Vancouver Convention & Exhibition Centre *999 Canada Place, Downtown (604 689 8232/www.vcec.ca). All city-centre buses.*
BC Place Stadium *777 Pacific Boulevard, between Griffiths Way & Terry Fox Way (604 669 2300/www.bcplacestadium.com). Bus 15/SkyTrain Stadium.*

Couriers & shippers

For shipping, *see p136.*
Purolator Courier
1090 W Pender Street, between Burrard Street & Thurlow Street, Downtown (1 888 744 7123 or 604 257 2425/www.purolator.com). All city-centre buses. **Open** 9am-6pm Mon-Fri. **Credit** AmEx, MC, V.

Office services

For photocopying, *see p136.*
Able Translations *1000-355 Burrard Street, between W Hastings Street & W Cordova Street, Downtown (604 646 4888/www.able translations.com). All city-centre buses.*
Hunt Personnel *760-789 W Pender Street, at Howe Street, Downtown (604 688 2555/www.hunt.ca). All city-centre buses.* 8.30am-5pm Mon-Fri.

Consumer

For advice on your rights as a consumer, contact the Business Practices and Consumer Protection Authority of British Columbia (1-888 564 9963, www.bpcpa.ca). Note that in BC shops are not obliged to refund your money unless goods are faulty.

Customs

While all the usual checks will be made at Canadian ports of entry the thoroughness of the checks will vary according to

your nationality, where you have come from, and your general demeanour. If you are arriving from a country with known links to the drug trade, illicit trafficking of immigrants, or ties to Islamic terrorism you should expect closer scrutiny.

Do not attempt to enter Canada carrying firearms or weapons of any description. Drugs, other than prescribed drugs with documentation, should never be brought into the country. Other things to avoid passing through customs with are cultural antiquities, endangered species, meat, fruit and any form of plant material. You're allowed to enter Canada with 200 cigarettes, 50 cigars, 1.5 litres of wine, 1.14 litres of liquor or 24 cans of beer without having to pay tax. For more regarding Canada Customs and Immigration call 1-204 983 3500 outside Canada; 1-800 461 9999 inside Canada, or visit www.ccra-adrc.gc.ca/visitors or www.cbsa-asfc.gc.ca.

British citizens returning to the UK can bring back £145 worth of duty-free goods, and any amount of money under £10,000, as long as they can prove it is theirs. For more details of UK Customs and Excise visit www.hmce.gov.uk.

American citizens can return home from Canada with US$800 worth of duty-free goods. For further details about US Customs visit www.customs.ustreas.gov.

Disabled

Vancouver prides itself on its accessibility for people with disabilities. The airport exceeds national and provincial standards for people with hearing, visual or mobility impairments, airport rental car agencies can provide vehicles with hand controls and there are wheelchair-accessible taxis (call 604 871 1111 to book). All buses servicing the airport are also wheelchair accessible; within the city, most have ramps or are lift-equipped. Check with TransLink (www. translink.bc.ca) for details. The SkyTrain and SeaBus are also accessible. Wheelchair-accessible vans can be rented from Freedom Rentals (604 952 4499, www.wheelchairvan rentals.com) at around $150/ day plus tax (cheaper rates for longer term rentals). If you are driving and have a disabled parking permit, it is valid in Vancouver. On BC Ferries, ask for parking near the elevators when purchasing tickets; deck areas and washrooms are all accessible. Pacific Coach Lines (604 662 7575, www.pacific coach.com) offers accessible services between Vancouver and Victoria – book at least 48 hours to guarantee accessible service. Greyhound Canada (toll free 1-800 661 8747, www.greyhound.ca) has lift-equipped services; book at least 48 hours in advance, more for long-haul trips. If you want to ski, Whistler's Adaptive Ski Program (toll free 1-800 766 0049, www. whistlerblackcomb.com) offers lessons and equipment at all levels of special need. The Canadian government runs its own website (www. accesstotravel.gc.ca) with details of national and local travel access. For more information contact the British Columbia Paraplegic Association (604 324 3611, www.bcpara.org).

Drugs

In keeping with many west coast cities Vancouver does have a laid-back vibe and an active drug culture. However, Canada's police and judicial authorities take a very stern line with drug offences, so you would be wise to avoid narcotics while in the country.

Electricity

Canada operates a 110-volt, 60 cycle electric power supply. Plugs and sockets are two-pronged, so if you are visiting from anywhere except the US you will need a plug adaptor in order to be able to use your electrical appliances from home. Adaptors can be bought from most department stores.

Embassies & consulates

Australian Consulate General *1225-888 Dunsmuir Street, at Hornby Street, Downtown (604 684 1177/www.australiantrade.ca). All city-centre buses.* **Open** 9am-noon, 1-5pm Mon-Fri.

British Consulate General *800-1111 Melville Street, at Thurlow Street, Downtown (604 683 4421). All city-centre buses.* **Open** 8.30am-4.30pm Mon-Fri.

Consulate General of the People's Republic of China *3380 Granville Street, at W 16th Avenue, West Side (604 734 7492/ http://vancouver.china-consulate. org/eng/). Bus 10, 98.* **Open** Visas 9am-1pm Mon-Fri. All other enquiries 9am-noon, 2-5.30pm Mon-Fri.

Consulate General of France *1100-1130 W Pender Street, at Thurlow Street, Downtown (604 681 4345/www.consulfrance-vancouver. org). All city-centre buses.* **Open** Visas 9.30am-noon Mon-Fri. Citizens 9am-1pm Mon-Fri or by appointment.

German Consulate General *Suite 704, World Trade Centre, 999 Canada Place, at Hornby Street, Downtown (604 684 8377/www. vancouver.diplo.de). All city-centre buses.* **Open** 9am-noon Mon-Fri.

Consulate General of India *201-325 Howe Street, at W Cordova Street, Downtown (604 662 8811/ www.cgivancouver.com). All city-centre buses.* **Open** phone for hours.

Consulate of the Republic of Ireland *10th Floor, 100 W Pender Street, at Abbott Street, Downtown (604 683 9233). All city-centre buses.* **Open** phone for hours.

Consulate General of Japan *800-1177 W Hastings Street, at Bute Street, Downtown (604 684 5868/www.vancouver.ca.emb-japan.go.jp). All city-centre buses.* **Open** 9am-noon, 1-5pm Mon-Fri.

New Zealand Consulate General *1200-888 Dunsmuir Street, at Hornby Street, Downtown*

(604 684 7388). All city-centre buses. **Open** 9am-5pm Mon-Fri.

Consulate General of the Republic of Singapore *1820-999 W Hastings Street, at Burrard Street, Downtown (604 669 5115/www.mfa.gov.sg/vancouver). All city-centre buses.* **Open** 8.30am-12.30pm, 1.30-5pm Mon-Fri.

South African Honorary Consul *1700-1075 W Georgia Street, at Burrard Street, Downtown (604 688 1301). All city-centre buses.* **Open** 8am-5.15pm Mon-Fri.

United States Consulate General *1075 W Pender Street, at Thurlow Street, Downtown (604 685 4311/http://vancouver.usconsulate. gov). All city-centre buses.* **Open** phone for hours and appointments.

Emergencies

In the event of an emergency that requires police, medical assistance or firefighters, phone **911**. This service is free from all telephones.

Gay & lesbian

Look out for the free biweekly gay paper, *Xtra West*, in stores and cafés. **The Centre** (1170 Bute Street, 604 684 6869, www.lgtbcentrevancouver. com) is a valuable community service resource. (For HIV/ AIDS services, *see below*.)

Health

Vancouver is renowned (or at least, likes to think it is) for being a 'healthy city' – vaccinations are generally not required for visitors to Canada, there is a large natural food culture in the city, and the local tap water is perfectly fine for drinking. To be safe and to avoid hassles at customs, prescription medication should be brought complete with documentation.

Walk-in clinics are abundant and doctors in British Columbia will not turn away those in need of medical attention, regardless of whether they appear unable to pay. The Pine Free Community Health Youth

Directory

Clinic (1985 W 4th Avenue, at Pine Street, 604 736 2391) provides general medical care and birth control. The clinic serves youth 24 years of age and under, as well as uninsured people of any age – though hours for the latter group are restricted to weekday mornings and all day Wednesdays.

Accident & emergency

If you are in a situation that requires an instant response from any of the emergency services dial 911. It's free from any telephone.

If you develop a non life-threatening medical problem during your stay in Vancouver the Care Point Medical Centre (711 W Pender Street, 604 687 4858, www.carepoint.ca) or the Khatsahlano Medical Clinic (920 Seymour Street, at Nelson Street, 604 731 9187, www.khatsclinic.ca) should be able to assist you on a walk-in basis.

The hospitals listed below all have 24 hour emergency departments.

St Paul's Hospital
1081 Burrard Street, at Helmcken Street, Downtown (604 682 2344). Bus 2, 22, 44, 98.
UBC Hospital & Urgent Care Centre *2211 Wesbrook Mall, between University Boulevard & W 16th Avenue, West Side (604 822 7121). Bus 4, 17, 25, 41, 49, 99.*
Vancouver General Hospital *855 W 12th Avenue, at Oak Street, West Side (604 875 6111). Bus 17, 99.*

Complementary medicine

See p133.

Contraception & abortion

Options for Sexual Health
Women's Clinic, BC Women's Hospital, 4500 Oak Street, West Side (604 731 4252/www.options forsexual health.org). Open phone for appointment.

Everywoman's Health Centre
210-2525 Commercial Drive, East Vancouver (604 322 6692/ www.everywomanshealthcentre.ca). **Open** phone for appointment.

Dentists

British Columbia Dental Association *Referrals 604 736 7202/www.bcdental. org.*

Doctors

Stein Medical Clinic *Bentall 5 Lobby, 188-550 Burrard Street, at W Pender Street, Downtown (604 688 5924/www.steinmedical.com).* **Open** 8.30am-5.30pm Mon-Fri. No appointment necessary.

Hospitals

See above **Accident & emergency.**

Opticians

See p133.

Pharmacies

See p133.

STDs, HIV & AIDS

Aids Vancouver
1107 Seymour Street, at Helmcken Street, Downtown (604 893 2201/ www.aidsvancouver. org). Bus 4, 6, 7, 10, 16, 17, 50, 98. **Open** 9am-4.30pm Mon-Fri.

Downtown Community Health Clinic
569 Powell Street, at Princess Avenue, East Side (604 255 3151). Bus 4, 7. **Open** phone for hours and appointment.

Helplines

Alcoholics Anonymous *604 434 3933 (24 hrs)/www.vancouveraa.ca.*
Crisis Intervention & Suicide Prevention Centre of British Columbia *604 872 3311 (24 hr distress line)/www.crisiscentre.bc.ca.*
Narcotics Anonymous
604 873 1018/www.bcrscna.bc.ca/.
Vancouver Rape Crisis Line
604 872 8212.

ID

You need to be 19 to legally purchase alcohol and tobacco in British Columbia. You will be expected to provide two

pieces of ID if you are buying alcohol and your age is at all in question or if you appear under the age of 25. If you're out clubbing, it's a good idea to have ID to hand as they are likely to screen everyone at the door, regardless of age. When driving you must always carry picture ID.

Insurance

Canada does not provide health or medical services free to visitors, so make sure you have travel insurance in place before you arrive, and carry your documents with you.

Internet

Most Vancouver hotels provide internet access – though the form that access takes varies a good deal, and so does the price. Acess in coffee shops is increasingly available and all public libraries offer free Wi-Fi (*see p233* **Libraries**). Visit http://vancouver.wifimug.org for a directory of coffee shops offering free Wi-Fi access.
Internet Coffee *1104 Davie Street, at Thurlow Street, Downtown (604 682 6668). Bus 6.* **Open** 9am-1.30pm. **Rates** $4/hr. **Credit** MC, V.

Left luggage

CDS Baggage offers storage in the domestic and international arrivals terminal (604 303 4500, level 2, pre-security). Rates range from $3.50 to $7 per item per 24 hours. Open 5am-11pm. CDS also has a storage facility downtown at Canada Place, but the office only opens from 8am-4pm on cruise ship days (604 303 4500). Most hotels will hold your luggage for you when you check-out.

Legal help

If you have any legal problems during your stay in Vancouver contact your insurers or your national consulate (*see p231* **Embassies & consulates**).

Libraries

The Vancouver Public Library (350 W Georgia Street, 604 331 3603, www.vpl.ca) is in the heart of downtown. The VPL is the third largest public library system in Canada and has 20 branches across the city. Opening times are 10am-9pm Mon-Thur; 10am-6pm Fri-Sat; noon-5pm Sun. All branches now offer free wireless internet, available from opening until 5 minutes before closing.

Lost property

Airport

If all or any of your luggage has been lost in transit inform your airline straight away. If you have lost or misplaced property in the airport contact the Customer Service Counter on 604 276 6104. It's open 9am-5.30pm daily and can be found on Level 3 of the International Departures Terminal.

Public transport

If you lose property on Vancouver's public transport system contact TransLink on 604 682 7887. The lost property office is open 8.30am-5pm and can be found at the Stadium SkyTrain Station, 590 Beatty Street.

Taxis

If you lose anything in a cab call the taxi company directly (*see p228*).

Media

Daily newspapers

Vancouver's media is in some need of a good shake-up. The two local newspapers, the broadsheet *Vancouver Sun* and tabloid *The Province*, are both owned by right-leaning media conglomerate CanWest, which publishes a number of other dailies across Western Canada, the *Victoria Times Colonist* and the *National Post*, and also owns the cable television company Global TV. (The daily freesheet *24 Hours* draws on content and copy from the *Sun Media* tabloid chain.)

An online newspaper, *www.thetyee.ca* is a lively union-backed corrective to this near monopoly, largely staffed by ex-CanWest writers.

Canada's other national daily, the *Globe and Mail*, is perhaps your best bet for serious, relatively unpartisan news coverage, and makes some efforts to extend its reach and widen its scope in British Columbia with a daily BC news section.

For newspaper junkies who can't do without their hometown fix, the *New York Times* and European titles are fairly easy to get hold of in the downtown area. Try Chapters bookstore at 788 Robson Street (*see p123*).

Magazines & weekly newspapers

The *Georgia Straight* is the dominant alternative weekly in town. It celebrated its 40th anniversary in 2007, and is showing signs of its advancing years. It has become more complacent, baggy, and in dire need of a redesign. Nevertheless, its market position is entrenched, and for many consumers of art and entertainment it's the only (or at least, the most important) game in town. Happily, it's also free. You can hardly miss the distribution boxes on any downtown artery.

Rival weekly the *WestEnder* does a fair job of filling in the gaps. 2007 saw a redesign, and improved editorial content. Another local magazine, the *Vancouver Courier* is Canada's largest distributed community paper, with four different weekly editions: east and west editions are distributed on Wednesdays, city-wide and downtown editions are distributed on Fridays.

The city's glossy monthly, *Vancouver Magazine*, tends to reflect the twin local obsessions: food and real estate. The magazine also publishes two annual special interest issues: the *Eating & Drinking Guide*, a handy (but not always accurate) guide to the city's restaurants, bars and food shops, and *Guestlife Vancouver*, a hotel room magazine covering must-sees for visitors to the city.

Television & radio

Canadian radio and television stations rely heavily on American programming. Where cable television is available, the local and national stations (CBC, CTV, Global, City TV, and Channel M) are drowned out by the many American channels.

The *Vancouver Sun* and the *Province* newspapers carry comprehensive television schedules. The weekly *TV Guide* magazine is sold at most grocery and drugstores. Canadian radio content requirements, intended to provide more air-time for home-grown artists, actually result in the few Canadian formulaic pop/rock giants that have broken onto the world market being nauseatingly overplayed. The local stations that have evaded this curse are CBC One's news and more station (690 AM), CBC Two's 'Classics. And Beyond' (105.7 AM), Co-op Radio (102.7 FM), and the eclectic university station, CiTR (101.9 FM). The rest are as follows:

Rock & Top 40

94.5 FM The Beat Hip hop and R&B.
96.9 FM Jack Contemporary and classic rock.
101.1 CFMI Classic rock.

Directory

Soft rock & other 'adult favourites'
650 AM CISL Oldies.
93.7 JR FM New country.
95.3 FM Crave Pop.

Talk & news
980 CKNW News talk.
1130 CKWX All news.
1410 CFUN All talk.

Money

There are 100 cents in each Canadian dollar. The one cent piece is a copper colour; the five cent piece (nickel), ten cent piece (dime) and twenty-five cent piece (quarter) are all silver and feature a beaver, bluenose schooner and caribou respectively. The one dollar piece (loonie) is a gold colour and the two dollar (toonie) is a two-tone silver and gold colour.

Notes (called bills in Canada), come in denominations of $5 (blue), $10 (purple), $20 (green), $50 (pink) and $100 (brown). It's wise to avoid $50 and $100 bills due to counterfeit concerns. The Bank of Canada changed the design of its $5, $10, and $20 bills recently, but the old-style notes are still legal tender.

Banks & ATMs

Most banks will have an ABM (automatic bank machine) as they are referred to in Canada, and bank operated machines can be found along most streets in downtown Vancouver. Bars, clubs and shops operate private machines, but you will be charged $1-$2 for the convenience of using them. Canadian ABMs are part of the Cirrus, Interac or Plus networks, so visitors should have no problem getting access to their home accounts through these machines. If in doubt check with your bank before travelling. It is also advisable to find out what charges your bank will make for accessing your account from abroad.

All the banks listed below are downtown branches (there are others throughout the city) and can be found on a stretch of West Georgia Street that runs from Burrard Street to Granville Street.

CIBC *1036 W Georgia Street, at Burrard Street (604 665 1472/www.cibc.com).* **Open** 9.30am-4pm Mon-Wed; 9.30am-5pm Thur-Fri.
Royal Bank of Canada *1025 W Georgia Street, at Burrard Street (604 665 6991/www.royal bank.ca).* **Open** 9am-5pm Mon-Fri.
Scotiabank *650 W Georgia Street, at Seymour Street (604 668 2094/www.scotia bank.com).* **Open** 9.30am-4pm Mon-Thur; 9.30am-5pm Fri.
TD Canada Trust *700 W Georgia Street, at Howe Street (604 654 3665/www.tdcanada trust.com).* **Open** 8am-6pm Mon-Wed, 8am-8pm Thur-Fri, 8am-4pm Sat.

Bureaux de change
Vancouver Bullion & Currency Exchange *120-800 W Pender Street, at Howe Street, Downtown (604 685 1008/www.vbce.ca).* **Open** 9am-5pm Mon-Fri.
Other locations throughout the city.

Credit cards

Most businesses in Vancouver take Visa, MasterCard and American Express. Some take Diners Club. Some smaller restaurants are cash only – check before you order. These cards all have toll-free numbers available around the clock if your credit card should be lost or stolen:
American Express 1-800 668 2639.
Diners Club 1-800 363 3333.
MasterCard 1-800 307 7309.
Visa 1-800 847 2911.

Tax

When shopping in British Columbia, remember that marked prices do not include sales tax. The Goods and Services Tax is five per cent and levied by the federal government on almost everything. The Provincial Sales Tax is seven per cent and is applied to almost everything except some groceries and children's clothes. Accommodation is taxed at ten per cent, as is the taxman's favourite, alcohol.

Natural hazards

Close proximity to the San Andreas fault line means earthquakes are Vancouver's most feared natural hazard. Bears and cougars have been spotted on the North Shore, but pose more of a nuisance than a threat. Just keep your distance.

Opening hours

Shops generally open from 10am onwards and close around 5pm. Some, depending on the type of business, may stay open till 9pm or later.

Travel advice

For up to date information for travelling to a specific country – including the latest news on safety and security, health issues, local laws and customs – contact your home country government's department of foreign affairs. Most have websites packed with useful statistics, advice and background information for would-be travellers.

Australia
www.smartraveller.gov.au

Canada
www.voyage.gc.ca

New Zealand
www.safetravel.govt.nz

Republic of Ireland
http://foreignaffairs.gov.ie

UK
www.fco.gov.uk/travel

USA
http://travel.state.gov

The pharmacy chain Shoppers Drug Mart is open 24/7. Banks generally open at 9am and close at 5pm Monday to Friday although some branches may open Saturday and close Monday. Post offices usually open between 9am and 5pm Monday to Saturday.

Police

If you need assistance in an emergency, dial 911 free from any telephone. If it's not an emergency ring the police at 604 717 3321. Vancouver Police Department headquarters is at 2120 Cambie Street. See also www.vancouver.ca/police.

Postal services

Posting a standard letter or postcard within Canada costs 52 cents, so long as it weighs 30 grams or less. To the US the cost is 93 cents. If you want to send a letter or card anywhere else it will cost $1.55 up to 30 grams, and $2.20 between 30 and 50 grams.

Post offices

Vancouver's main post office in is at 349 W Georgia Street (1-800 267 1177, www. canadapost.ca) is open 8am-5.30pm on weekdays. If you only need stamps, avoid the queues and try a corner shop or pharmacy instead. Some drugstores and department stores also contain post office counters (for instance, in the basement of the Hudson's Bay Company department store, 674 Granville Street, at W Georgia Street, Downtown (*see p121*).

Poste restante/ general delivery

If you need to receive mail while in Vancouver, but do not have a permanent address, it is possible to have it delivered to any post office with a postal code, indicating

'GD' for General Delivery. You will be required to show at least one form of photo ID before the post office can hand over your mail.

Religion

Anglican
St Paul's Anglican Church
1130 Jervis Street, at Pendrell Street, Downtown (604 685 6832/www. stpaulsanglican.bc.ca). Bus 6.

Baptist
First Baptist Church
969 Burrard Street, at Nelson Street, Downtown (604 683 8441/www. firstbc.org). All city-centre buses.

Buddhist
Universal Buddhist Temple
525 E 49th Street, at St. George Street, East Vancouver (604 325 6912). Bus 3, 8.

Catholic
Holy Rosary Cathedral *646 Richards Street, at Dunsmuir Street, Downtown (604 682 6774/http:// hrc.rcav.org). All city-centre buses.*

Islamic
Vancouver Mosque
655 W 8th Avenue, at Heather Street, West Side (604 803 7344/ www.islamicinfocenter.org). Bus 15, 17.

Jewish
Temple Sholom *7190 Oak Street, at W 56th Avenue, West Side (604 266 7190/www.templesholom.ca). Bus 17.*

Lutheran
Christ Lutheran Church
375 W 10th Avenue, at Yukon Street, West Side (604 874 2212). Bus 15.

United Church of Canada
St Andrew's Wesley Church
1022 Nelson Street, at Burrard Street, Downtown (604 683 4574/ www.standrewswesleychurch.bc.ca. All city-centre buses.

Safety & security

It is important to stress that Vancouver is a safe city. Violent crime is rare, particularly in the tourist areas, but this does not mean you can be complacent about your safety or the security of your belongings.

Burying your head in a street map tends to identify you as the stranger in town, so it's best not to do it. If you really are having difficulty orientating yourself why not pop into a café or a shop and ask directions.

Try not to carry too much cash on your person. It's also a good idea to make a note of the relevant lost/stolen credit card telephone numbers so that you can cancel any cards the moment you notice they are missing.

Women travelling on their own should apply all the usual safety procedures, especially at night. Avoid alleyways, don't take shortcuts across parking lots and keep an eye on your drink when in bars and clubs. Also, if you've been out for the night, get a registered cab back to where you're staying; public transport can sometimes leave you with a long walk at the end of your journey.

The worst crime area is East Hastings Street, especially the section between Carrall Street and Main Street. Even though it's a relatively small, self contained area, visitors should note that it backs on to Gastown and Chinatown respectively, so be aware which direction you are going in when exploring these popular tourist areas.

Smoking

All indoor spaces in Vancouver were decreed smoke-free by law in 2000. If you want to light up, you're out on the street – not a great prospect in the rainy season. Smoking on restaurant and bar patios was also banned in January 2008.

Study

Despite the abundance of English as a Second Language 'colleges' and other institutions offering higher learning (including the Vancouver

Directory

Community College, Kwantlen University College, British Columbia Institute of Technology, and Langara College), the Vancouver area is home to only two accredited universities. Note that foreign nationals wishing to study in Canada require a study permit and, depending on their country of origin, also a temporary visa. Applications should be made through local Canadian embassies or high consulates.

Simon Fraser University

8888 University Drive, Burnaby (604 291 3111/www.sfu.ca). Bus 135.
Simon Fraser University (SFU) comprises three campuses: the main (designed by acclaimed local architect Arthur Erickson) sits 20km (12.5 miles) east of downtown in the suburb of Burnaby, with additional satellites in Surrey and in downtown's Harbour Centre. It has managed to maintain a strong reputation in terms of its progressive approach to learning and strong liberal arts department and takes around 25,000 students.

University of British Columbia

2329 West Mall, West Side (604 822 2211/www.ubc.ca). Bus 4, 9, 17, 25, 41, 44, 49, 84, 99.
The third largest university in Canada, UBC is well known for its excellent academic standards and its breathtaking setting. In addition to its wide cultural diversity, the campus includes the Museum of Anthropology, the Pacific Spirit Regional Park, the botanical gardens, UBC Farm, and Wreck Beach (also known as Vancouver's only nude beach). Bursting at the seams with some 43,000 students, the campus continues to expand, with new academic and residential buildings and sports arenas set to house the 2010 Olympics popping up fast.

Telephones

Dialling & codes

Vancouver and much of the Lower Mainland (including Whistler) share the area codes 604 and 778. (Vancouver Island's code is 250). Although Vancouver businesses often place the prefixes in brackets

or drop it altogether, you must dial the code no matter where you are calling from. Even though they share the same area code, calls between Whistler and Vancouver are long distance, so you must add '1' before '604'. Toll free (freephone) numbers begin with the codes: 1-800, 1-855, 1-866, 1-877 and 1-888.

Canada shares the same international dialling code as the US (1); dialling from one to the other is the same as calling long-distance within the US. To call Canada from the UK, dial 001 then the number. To call overseas from North America, dial 011, the country code, then the number (in some cases dropping the initial zero). The country code for the UK is 44, for Australia 61, New Zealand 64, Republic of Ireland 353 and South Africa 27. If you're making a number of long distance calls, a dial-in phone card is the cheapest option, making international calls the cost of a local call. Convenience stores sell $5, $10 or $20 cards.

Mobile phones

As in the US, Canada's mobile phone (cellphone) network operates on 1900 megaHerz. This means that, depending on their billing plan, US travellers should be able to use their usual handset (but should check their tariffs for costs). Tri-band phones will work throughout most of North America; quad-bands tend to give some additional coverage but there is still the odd area with no coverage at all. If you have a dual-band phone or your tri- or quad-band phone might not work, contact your service provider to find out if it has a way around the problem. You could buy a pay-as-you-go phone from around $125 from one of the ubiquitous local carriers (Bell, Fido, Rogers or Telus).

Alternatively you could rent a phone via your hotel or from a private company such as Hello, Anywhere (toll free 1-888 729 4355, www.hello anywhere.com, credit card deposit required), who will deliver a phone to your hotel from about $40 a week, or Cita (*see p125*).

Operator services

Dial 0 from any phone to speak to an operator (free from payphones). Dial 00 for the international operator. For directory enquiries, dial 411 from any phone; this service costs 75 cents.

Public phones

If you can find one, payphones cost 25 cents per local call, and require change. Most hotels offer free local calls rom your room, so check before embarking on a hunt for a public payphone.

Time

Vancouver is located in the Pacific Time Zone and is eight hours behind Greenwich Mean Time. Daylight Saving Time runs from 2am on the first Sunday in April to 2am on the first Sunday in November.

Tipping

Tipping is de *rigueur* in Canada. Everyone from cab drivers to hairdressers to bellhops expects to receive one. Tips average 15-20 per cent depending on the type and quality of service you have received. If a restaurant adds a service charge to the bill you are under no obligation to leave an additional tip.

Toilets

They used to say finding a public toilet in Vancouver is about as easy as finding a stand of old growth forest in downtown. As of 2008 the city has improved its game somewhat. There are half a dozen free automated public toilets in the downtown area, including Richards near Davie; Robson west of Richards; Homer south of Dunsmuir; Davie west of Thurlow and Nelson west of Granville. There are underground conveniences located at Hastings and Hamilton (Victory Square), and Hastings and Main. Note that toilets in cafés and coffee shops are often locked and reserved for customers only.

Tourist Information

Vancouver Tourist Info Centre

Plaza Level, Waterfront Centre, 200 Burrard Street, at Canada Place (604 683 2000). **Open** 8.30am-6pm daily. Other tourist information centres can be found at the Canada Place Cruise Ship Terminal; the Ballantyne Cruise Ship Terminal, and Vancouver International Airport. If you are driving up to Vancouver from the US there is a Tourist Information Centre at the Peace Arch Border Crossing, Highway 99, Surrey, BC.

Visas & immigration

Citizens of the UK, the US, Australia, New Zealand and Ireland do not require visas to visit Canada. Citizens of other countries can get up-to-date information regarding visa regulations at www.cic.gc.ca/english/visit/visas.asp.

The US administration's proposal to bring in passport controls between Canada and the US is a cause of great concern to British Columbia. Since January 2007, Canadian citizens entering the US have required a valid passport and a return date; the same is not yet true for Americans crossing into Canada.

Weights & measures

Canada uses the metric system of weights and measures.

1 centimetre = 0.394 inches
1 metre = 3.28 feet
1 square metre = 1.196 square yards
1 kilometre = 0.62 miles
1 kilogramme = 2.2 pounds
1 litre = 1.76 UK pints, 2.113 US pints

When to go

Climate

In contrast to most of the rest of Canada, Vancouver enjoys a temperate climate not unlike that of the UK. Owing to the ameliorating effect of the surrounding sea, winters are never that cold and summers are rarely oppressively hot. Vancouver's close proximity to Grouse Mountain (20 minutes from downtown) makes it an ideal base from which to enjoy winter sports. Whistler is only 100km (60 miles) further north. For those who enjoy the sunshine, the summer months will give you ample opportunity to get a tan on one of the many beaches that line the Vancouver shoreline. The only climatic drawback to the city is the rainfall, particularly in the winter months. From October through February the average monthly rainfall ranges from 115mm/4.5 inches to 167mm/6.5 inches and it's been known to rain for 29 days without respite.

Public holidays

New Year's Day 1 Jan
(if it falls on Sun, then the holiday is the following Mon)
Good Friday Mar/Apr
Easter Monday Mar/Apr
Victoria Day 3rd Mon in May
Canada Day 1 July
BC Day 1st Mon in Aug
Labour Day 1st Mon in Sept
Thanksgiving 2nd Mon in Oct
Remembrance Day 11 Nov
Christmas Day 25 Dec
Boxing Day 26 Dec

Average temperatures

Month	High (°C/°F)	Low (°C/°F)
January	5/42	2/36
February	7/44	4/40
March	10/50	6/43
April	14/58	9/48
May	18/65	12/54
June	21/69	15/59
July	23/74	17/63
August	18/65	16/29
September	23/73	12/54
October	20/68	8/46
November	14/57	4/39
December	7/44	3/37

Women

Vancouver is generally a safe city and is no less so for women travelling alone who exercise common sense. Avoid the notorious Downtown Eastside, particularly at night.

For a list of helplines *see p232*. For links to organisations dealing with women's health visit www.womenshealthcollective.ca, and www.womenspace.ca for information and links to organisations dealing with equality issues.

Directory

Further Reference

Books

Fiction

Emily Carr *Klee Wyck; The Book of Small; The House of All Sorts* In the last decade of her life, painter Emily Carr took to writing. Some critics rate her literary work higher than her art.
Wayson Choy *The Jade Peony; All That Matters* Vancouver-born Choy's 1995 novel *The Jade Peony* is set in Chinatown in the Depression years. *All That Matters* continues in the '40s – which is also the setting for Choy's memoirs, *Paper Shadows*.
Douglas Coupland *Generation X; Life After God; Microserfs; Girlfriend in a Coma; Hey Nostradamus!; J-Pod* North Vancouver born (and still resident), the Gen X writer and art phenomenon revisits his hometown regularly in his fiction (*see p35*).
William Gibson *Neuromancer; Mona Lisa Overdrive; All Tomorrow's Parties; Spook Country* The science fiction writer who coined 'cyberspace' is a long-term Vancouver resident.
Pauline Johnson *Legends of Vancouver* Born in 1861, Johnson was half English, half Mohawk. A poet and performer, she is known best for this collection of Squamish myths, published in 1911 (*see p69*).
Nancy Lee *Dead Girls* This 2002 debut is an evocative, provocative collection of stories in response to the murders of at least 27 Downtown Eastside women by Robert Pickton.
Malcolm Lowry *Under the Volcano* English-born but a restless traveller, Lowry finished his masterpiece while living in a squatter's shack in Dollarton, BC in the early 1940s.
Alice Munro *Runaway; Lives of Girls and Women; Hateship, Friendship, Courtship, Loveship, Marriage* The acclaimed short-story writer divides her time between Ontario and British Columbia – though Vancouver only gets the occasional look-in in her work.
Timothy Taylor *Stanley Park; Story House* Taylor's 2003 debut novel is based on two of Vancouver's passions: its park and its restaurants.
Various *The Vancouver Stories* Published by Raincoast Books in 2005, this is a collection of tales set in the city, by a variety of authors.

Non-fiction

John Atkin & Michael Kluckner *Vancouver Walks: Discovering City Heritage* Twenty-eight city strolls with historical commentary. Michael Kluckner is a painter and historian,

and combined these attributes in the book *Vanishing British Columbia*.
Lance Berelowitz *Dream City: Vancouver and the Global Imagination* An eloquent and fascinating account of Vancouver's urban development.
Jack Christie *50 Best Day Trips from Vancouver; Inside Out British Columbia; The Whistler Outdoors Guide* Christie is the 'outdoors' columnist for the *Georgia Straight*.
Douglas Coupland *City of Glass* As you'd expect from the prolific novelist and conceptual artist, this 2000 guide to Vancouver is full of odd, illuminating perceptions.
Mike Gasher *Hollywood North* A thoughtful analysis of the history of cinema in 'Brollywood'.
Paul Grant & Laurie Dixon *The Stanley Park Companion* Stunning photographs and lively text characterise this park guide, which is long on history and commentary.
John Mackie & Sarah Reeder *Vancouver: The Unknown City* A lively, eccentric guide to the city with fascinating anecdotes and titbits.
Various *The Greater Vancouver Book* Nearly 900 large-format pages of the city's history and anthropology.
Various *Vancouver Cooks* Choice recipes from BC's top chefs.
Rex Weyler *Greenpeace* Authoritative account of the birth of the ecology movement in Vancouver.

Film

The Corporation (Mark Achbar, Jennifer Abbott, Joel Bakan, 2003) Vancouver filmmakers Achbar and Abbott teamed up with UBC law professor Joel Bakan for this polemic about the psychotic inclinations vested in the corporate stranglehold.
Everything's Gone Green (Paul Fox, 2006) With a script by Douglas Coupland, this does for Vancouver what *Manhattan* does for New York.
The Grey Fox (Philip Borsos, 1982) Probably BC's best home-grown film, this was Borsos' fiction feature debut. It's the true story of Bill Miner (Richard Farnsworth), a train robber who comes to Canada to continue his trade in the early 20th century, after spending 33 years in jail.
Kissed (Lynne Stopkewich, 1996) Maple Ridge girl Molly Parker stars in this chilly story of necrophilia.
Ladies and Gentlemen, the Fabulous Stains (Lou Adler, 1981) A cult classic, this punk rock saga stars a young Diane Lane, Ray Winstone and Laura Dern. Shot in and around Vancouver, the setting is indeterminate in the film. Jonathan Demme co-wrote the script.

McCabe and Mrs Miller (Robert Altman, 1971) Set in the fictional town of Presbyterian Church and shot near West Van, this seminal western evokes BC in the Gold Rush era.
My American Cousin (Sandy Wilson, 1985) Sweet autobiographical film about a 12-year-old BC girl's infatuation with her American cousin.
The Sweet Hereafter (Atom Egoyan, 1997) Victoria-raised Egoyan's most successful film was shot in Merrit and Spence's Bridge in northern British Columbia.
That Cold Day in the Park (Robert Altman, 1969) Altman's first feature is set in Vancouver – though it could have been anywhere. He shot it in Tatlow Park, on the West Side.

Music

The Be Good Tanyas *Blue Horse* (2000) Rustic blues and roots from BC trio Frazey Ford, Trish Klein and Sam Parton (plus Jolie Holland).
Geoff Berner *Light Enough to Travel* A passionate indictment of the city's grimmer elements from the cult songwriter/accordionist.
Black Mountain *Black Mountain* (2004) Stephen McBean (also of Jerk With a Bomb and Pink Mountaintops) fronts this foreboding masterpiece that evokes the city's overcast gloom.
Destroyer *Thief* (2000) Songwriter Dan Bejar's unabashedly literary attempt to romanticise Vancouver.
Diana Krall *The Girl in the Other Room* (2004) The most personal album to date from the Nanaimo-born jazz singer.
Sarah McLachlan *Surfacing* (1997) Although she was born in Nova Scotia, the Grammy-winner has made her home (and her studio) in Vancouver since the late '80s.
The New Pornographers *Mass Romantic* (2000) AC Newman's indie outfit are something of a local super-group; contributions from vocalist Neko Case and Dan Bejar of Destroyer.
P:ano *The Den* (2003) A grand orchestral pop affair conducted by wunderkind Nick Krgovich.
Various *Vancouver Complication* (1979/2005) Reissued snapshot of Vancouver's punk scene, including DOA, the Pointed Sticks and U-J3RK5.

Websites

www.discovervancouver.com.
www.hellobc.com.
www.katkam.ca.
www.thetyee.ca
www.tourismvancouver.com
www.tourism-bc.com.
www.vancouver2010.com

Index

Note: page numbers in
bold indicate section(s)
giving key information
on a topic; *italics*
indicate photographs.

Advertisers' Index

Please refer to the relevant pages for contact details

Major sight or landmark	▢
Hospital or college	▢
Railway station	▢
Park	▢
River	▢
Highway	▬
Main road	▬
Main road tunnel	⌐ ⌐
Pedestrian road	▬
Airport	✈
Church	✚
Subway station	⬤
Area name	WEST SIDE

Maps

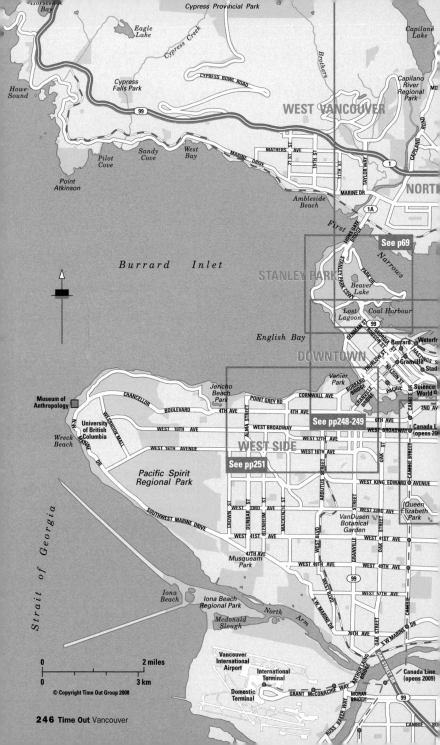

Cypress Provincial Park

Eagle
Lake

*Capilano
Lake*

*Howe
Sound*

CYPRESS BOWL ROAD

Cypress Creek

Brothers

*Cypress
Falls Park*

WEST VANCOUVER

Capilano
River
Regional
Park

99

*Pilot
Cove*

*Sandy
Cove*

*West
Bay*

MARINE DRIVE

MATHERS   AVE

21ST ST

15TH

11TH

TAYLOR WAY

CAPILANO ROAD

1

NORTH

*Point
Atkinson*

MARINE DR

*Ambleside
Beach*

1A

Burrard   Inlet

First

Narrows

See p69

STANLEY PARK

PARK DR

STANLEY PARK CSWY

*Beaver
Lake*

*Lost
Lagoon*

Coal Harbour

99

English Bay

DENMAN ST

GEORGIA

ROBSON ST

Burrard

Waterfr

THURLOW ST

NELSON ST

HASTINGS ST

DOWNTOWN

Granville

Stad

*Vanier
Park*

BURRARD BRIDGE

GRANVILLE BRIDGE

PACIFIC

CAMBIE BR

Science
World

*Museum of
Anthropology*

CHANCELLOR

BOULEVARD

*Jericho
Beach
Park*

POINT GREY RD

CORNWALL AVE

4TH AVE

2ND AV

4TH   AVE

ALMA STREET

See pp248-249

6TH   AVE

Canada L
(opens 20

WEST BROADWAY

*University
of British
Columbia*

WESBROOK MALL

WEST 10TH   AVE

WEST BROADWAY

CAMBIE STREET

*Wreck
Beach*

N.W. MARINE DR

WEST 16TH   AVENUE

WEST SIDE

WEST 12TH AVE

WEST 16TH AVE

See pp251

ARBUTUS ST

OAK ST

*Pacific Spirit
Regional Park*

WEST KING EDWARD   AVENUE

*Queen
Elizabeth
Park*

Strait   of   Georgia

SOUTHWEST MARINE DRIVE

CROWN ST

DUNBAR ST

3RD

GLENHOLME ST

MACKENZIE ST

WEST 33RD   AVE

GRANVILLE

OAK   STREET

*VanDusen
Botanical
Garden*

WEST 41ST   AVE

WEST 41ST   AVE

47TH AVE

*Musqueam
Park*

WEST BLVD

WEST 49TH   AVE

WEST 49TH   AVE

*Iona
Beach*

*Iona Beach
Regional Park*

North

*McDonald
Slough*

Arm

WEST 57TH   AVE

99

CAMBIE

70TH   AVE

S.W. MARINE DR

OAK STREET

S W MARINE DR

0   2 miles

0   3 km

© Copyright Time Out Group 2008

*Vancouver
International
Airport*

International
Terminal

GRANT McCONACHIE WAY

ARTHUR LAING BRIDGE

OAK STREET

MORAY
BRIDGE

*Canada Line
(opens 2009)*

99

Domestic
Terminal

RUSS BAKER WAY

CAMBIE   RD

Greater Vancouver

Grouse Mountain Skyride

Grouse Mountain Ski Area

Lynn Headwaters Regional Park

Lynn Creek

Rice Lake

Indian Arm Provincial Park

Seymour Skiing & Hiking Area

Mount Seymour Provincial Park

Seymour River

Mount Seymour Rd

Indian Arm

ROYAL BLVD

HIGHLAND BLVD

Mosquito Creek

WEST QUEENS RD

EAST 29TH ST

LYNN VALLEY ROAD

MOUNTAIN HWY

LYNN VALLEY ROAD

ARBORLYNN DR

BERKLEY RD

Deep Cove

DEEP COVE

Belcarra Regional Park

Bedwell Bay

BELCARRA

VANCOUVER

MARINE DR

WEST 13TH ST

LONSDALE AVENUE

EAST GRAND BLVD

E 11TH ST

EAST KEITH RD

MOUNT

SEYMOUR PARKWAY

Belcarra Regional Pa

3RD ST

COTTON RD

MAIN ST

DOLLARTON HWY

Burrard Inlet

Vancouver Harbour

See p253

Second Narrows Bridge

Second Narrows

Burrard Inlet

BARNET ROAD

POWELL ST

WALL ST

McGILL ST

DUNDAS ST

ETON STREET

Confederation Park

HASTINGS STREET

Kensington Park

INLET DRIVE

Burnaby Mountain Park

BURNABY MOUNTAIN PARKWAY

HASTINGS STREET

PRIOR ST

VENABLES ST

COMMERCIAL DRIVE

BOUNDARY ROAD

GILMORE AVENUE

WILLINGDON AVENUE

CURTIS STREET

HOLDOM AVENUE

SPERLING AVENUE

Pacific Central Station

VCC-Clark

BLACK DRIVE

VICTORIA DRIVE

NANAIMO STREET

1ST AVE

Rupert Park

RUPERT STREET

LOUGHEED HWY

Brentwood Town Centre

Gilmore

Holdom

DOUGLAS ROAD

Sperling

BURNABY

EAST BROADWAY

Broadway

Commercial Dr

Renfrew

GRANDVIEW

Rupert

GRANDVIEW HWY

7

Lake City

Production Way

EAST 12TH AVE

Trout Lake

RENFREW STREET

RUPERT STREET

CANADA WAY

WINSTON ST

John Hendry Park

22ND AVE

SPROTT ST

WINSTON ST

Nanaimo

E 29TH AVE

Burnaby Lake Park

CANADA WAY

Burnaby Lake

Burnaby Lake Regional Park

EAST VANCOUVER

FRASER STREET

KNIGHT STREET

See p252

RUPERT ST

JOYCE ST

Joyce

WILLINGDON AVE

EAST 33RD AVE

Deer Lake Park

Deer Lake

Robert Burnaby Park

EAST 41ST AVE

VICTORIA DR

EAST 41ST AVE

Memorial Park South

GRANGE ST

OAKLAND ST

BURRIS ST

EAST 49TH AVE

EAST 49TH AVE

Central Park

Patterson

Metrotown

KINGSWAY

IMPERIAL ST

CANADA WAY

NEW WESTMINSTER

EAST 57TH AVE

FRASER STREET

KNIGHT STREET

ARGYLE ST

54TH AVE

KERR ST

CHAMPLAIN CR

Patterson

IMPERIAL STREET

Royal Oak

ROYAL OAK AVENUE

GILLEY AVE

EDMONDS STREET

KINGSWAY

10TH AVENUE

6TH ST

8TH AVE

7TH AVE

SOUTHEAST MARINE DRIVE

KENT AVENUE

Everett Crowley Park

BOUNDARY ROAD

PATTERSON AVE

RUMBLE STREET

Byrne Creek Ravine Park

Edmond

CANADA WAY

10TH AVENUE

QUEENS AVE

ROYAL AVE

North Arm

KNIGHT ST BRIDGE

MARINE DRIVE

SOUTHRIDGE DR

20TH STREET

BRIDGEPORT ROAD

KNIGHT ST ROAD

NO. 6 ROAD

RICHMOND

MARINE WAY

BYRNE ROAD

22nd St

New Westminster

QUEENSBOROUGH BRIDGE

91

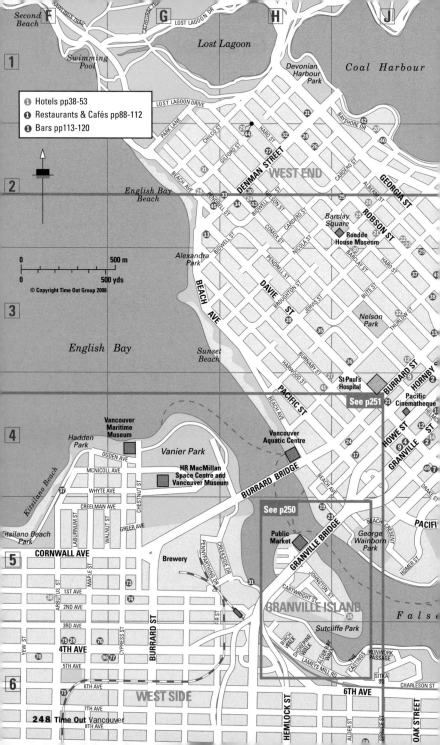

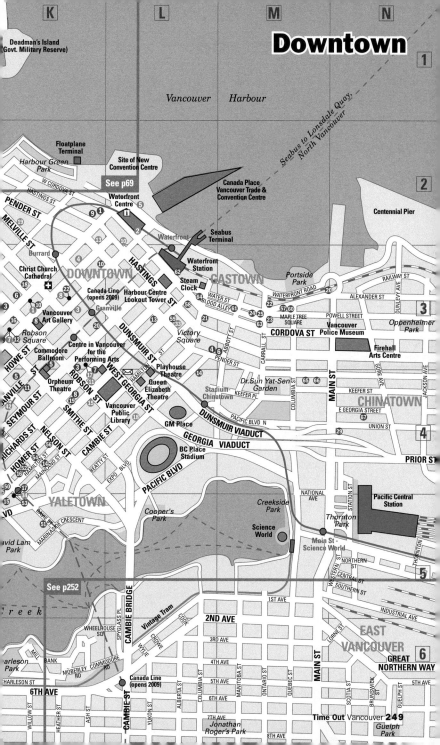

Downtown

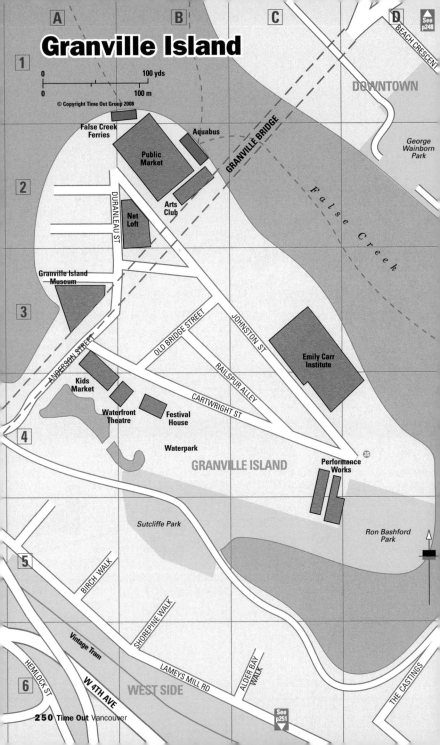

Granville Island

A B C D

See p248

1

0   100 yds
0   100 m

© Copyright Time Out Group 2008

BEACH CRESCENT

DOWNTOWN

GRANVILLE BRIDGE

George
Wainborn
Park

2

False Creek
Ferries

Aquabus

Public
Market

Arts
Club

Net
Loft

DURANLEAU ST

False Creek

3

Granville Island
Museum

ANDERSON STREET

OLD BRIDGE STREET

JOHNSTON ST

RAILSPUR ALLEY

Emily Carr
Institute

4

Kids
Market

Waterfront
Theatre

Festival
House

CARTWRIGHT ST

Waterpark

GRANVILLE ISLAND

35

Performance
Works

Ron Bashford
Park

5

Sutcliffe Park

BIRCH WALK

SHOREPINE WALK

ALDER BAY WALK

THE CASTINGS

6

HEMLOCK ST

Vintage Tram

W 4TH AVE

LAMEYS MILL RD

WEST SIDE

See
p251

West Side

0   500 m
0   500 yds

© Copyright Time Out Group 2008

To UBC Museum of Anthropology ↓

Hotels pp38-53
Restaurants & Cafés pp88-112
Bars pp113-120

See pp250

See pp248-249

North Shore

W | X | Y | Z

1

2

3

4

5

6

0 ___ 1 mile
0 ___ 1 km
© Copyright Time Out Group 2008

Grouse Mountain Skyride

Grouse Mountain Ski Area

Capilano Lake

Grouse Grind Trail

Mosquito Creek

NANCY GREENE WAY

Capilano River Regional Park

MONTROYAL BLVD

EYREMOUNT DR

SOUTHBOROUGH DR

STEVENS DR

Capilano Golf and Country Club

HIGHLAND BLVD

Mosquito

DELBROOK AVE

LONSDALE AVENUE

OSBORNE RD

CREEK RD

EYREMOUNT DR

Capilano River

Suspension Bridge

EDGEMONT

RIDGEWOOD

CAPILANO ROAD

DR

BLVD

QUEENS RD

29TH ST

ROSS

Hollyburn Country Club

Capilano View Cemetery

BURLEY DR

TAYLOR WAY

LEWOOD AVE

11TH ST

WEST VANCOUVER

Capilano River

FELL AVE

LARSON RD

WESTVIEW DR

23RD ST

23RD ST

MARINE DRIVE

NORTH VANCOUVER

18TH ST

18TH ST

AVENUE

AVENUE

AVENUE

15 TH ST

PEMBERTON AVE

MARINE DRIVE

13TH ST

13TH ST

mbleside Park

LIONS GATE BRIDGE

WELCH ST

3RD ST

CHESTERFIELD

LONSDALE

ST GEORGES

3RD ST

First Narrows

PARK DR

Lonsdale Market

ESPLANADE

Seabus to Waterfront Station, Vancouver

STANLEY PARK CAUSEWAY

Beaver Lake

Burrard   Inlet

tanley Park

LAGOON DR

Lost Lagoon

Coal Harbour

❶ Hotels pp38-53
❶ Restaurants & Cafés pp88-112
❶ Bars pp113-120

Vancouver Harbour

Time Out Vancouver **253**

Street Index

Downtown transport

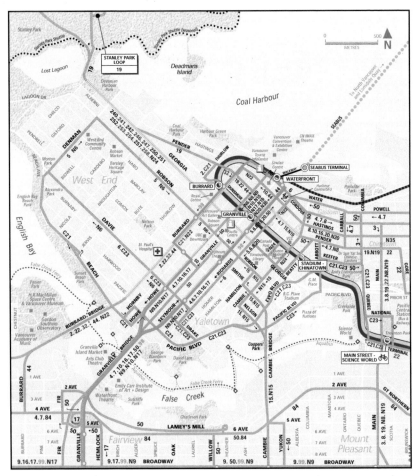

Note: The new SkyTrain line, the **Canada Line**, is due for completion in 2009. It will run from Waterfront Station, through downtown, then south along Cambie Street before the line splits, terminating at Vancouver International Airport and Richmond. See the maps on pp246-252 for station locations. For updates, visit www.translink.bc.ca or www.canadaline.ca.